Reckonings

Reckonings

Contemporary Short Fiction by Native American Women

EDITED BY

HERTHA D. SWEET WONG

LAUREN STUART MULLER

JANA SEQUOYA MAGDALENO

OXFORD

UNIVERSITY PRESS

2008

OXFORD
UNIVERSITY PRESS

Oxford University Press, Inc., publishes works that further
Oxford University's objective of excellence
in research, scholarship, and education.

Oxford   New York
Auckland   Cape Town   Dar es Salaam   Hong Kong   Karachi
Kuala Lumpur   Madrid   Melbourne   Mexico City   Nairobi
New Delhi   Shanghai   Taipei   Toronto

With offices in
Argentina   Austria   Brazil   Chile   Czech Republic   France   Greece
Guatemala   Hungary   Italy   Japan   Poland   Portugal   Singapore
South Korea   Switzerland   Thailand   Turkey   Ukraine   Vietnam

Published by Oxford University Press, Inc.
198 Madison Avenue, New York, New York 10016

www.oup.com

Oxford is a registered trademark of Oxford University Press

Library of Congress Cataloging-in-Publication Data
Reckonings : contemporary short fiction by native American women / edited
by Hertha D. Sweet Wong, Lauren Stuart Muller, Jana Sequoya Magdaleno.
    p.   cm.
ISBN 978-0-19-510924-5; 978-0-19-510925-2 (pbk.)
1. American fiction—Indian authors. 2. American fiction—Women authors.
3. American fiction—20th century. 4. Indians of North America—Fiction.
5. Short stories, American. I. Wong, Hertha Dawn.
II. Muller, Lauren. III. Magdaleno, Jana Sequoya.
PS508.I5R36 2008
813'.01089287—dc22   2007024147

Printed in the United States of America
on acid-free paper

All royalties earned from *Reckonings* will be donated to the InterTribal Friendship House (IFH), a nonprofit organization and the oldest American Indian community center in the United States. Established in 1955 in Oakland, California, in response to the needs of American Indians relocated from their tribal lands as part of the Federal Relocation Program, IFH has been dedicated to improving the lives of Native people in the San Francisco Bay Area for more than five decades. A center of Indian activism in the 1960s and 1970s, IFH continues to support artistic and cultural activities and to serve as a home away from home for today's Bay Area Native American community.

Credits

The editors and publisher thank the following who have kindly given permission for the use of copyrighted material:

Paula Gunn Allen

"Burned Alive in the Blues." Copyright © 2002 by Paula Gunn Allen. Reprinted with permission of Paula Gunn Allen.

"Deer Woman." Copyright © 1991 by Paula Gunn Allen. From *Talking Leaves: Contemporary Native American Short Stories: An Anthology*, edited by Craig Lesley, published by Dell Publishing, New York. Reprinted with permission of Paula Gunn Allen.

Kimberly M. Blaeser

"Like Some Old Story." Copyright © 2002 by Kimberly M. Blaeser. Reprinted with permission of Kimberly M. Blaeser.

"Growing Things." Copyright © 1996 by Kimberly M. Blaeser. From *Blue Dawn, Red Earth: New Native American Storytellers*, edited by Clifford E. Trafzer, published by Anchor Books, New York. Reprinted with permission of Kimberly M. Blaeser.

Beth E. Brant

"Swimming Upstream" and "Turtle Gal." Copyright © 1991 by Beth E. Brant. From *Food and Spirits: Stories* by Beth E. Brant, Firebrand Books, New York. Reprinted with permission of Firebrand Books, Milford, Conn.

Anita Endrezze

"Grandfather Sun Falls in Love with a Moon-Faced Woman." Copyright © 2000 by Anita Endrezze. From *Throwing Fire at the Sun, Water at the Moon* by Anita Endrezze, published by the University of Arizona Press. Reprinted with permission of the University of Arizona Press.

"The Humming of Stars and Bees and Waves." Copyright © 1998 by Anita Endrezze. From *The Humming of Stars and Bees and Waves: Poems and Short Stories* by Anita Endrezze, published by Making Waves, Guildford, U.K. The story appeared

Contents

Introduction

*Stories create us. We create ourselves with
stories. Stories that our parents tell us,
that our grandparents tell us, or that our
great-grandparents told us, stories that
reverberate through the web.*

Joy Harjo, interview with Angels Carabi
in *The Spiral of Memory*

The stories we hear and tell, those we inherit and those we generate, all shape who
we are and who we might become. The stories in this collection will delight, con-
found, excite, and disturb you, fool you repeatedly, then coax you on. Grappling
with Native American histories and contemporary realities, these stories docu-
ment intergenerational suffering and celebrate survival. The protagonists, though
inevitably wounded, do not fear struggle. Whether tracking a panther in hurricane
country or escaping pursuers across an icy glacier, swimming upstream through
grief or diving into the mysterious depths of a lake, their journeys traverse the
depths of memory and the expanses of the heart. When Paula Gunn Allen's character Joseph Joe riffs about the blues in the San Francisco Bay Area, we remember
the Relocation Act of the 1950s that, with promises of employment and housing,
displaced Native people from homelands to urban centers. When Patricia Riley's
Eddie T. surreptitiously teaches her granddaughter the old Tsalgi (Cherokee) ways
in order not to offend her Christian daughter-in-law, we remember the missionary
boarding school officials who stole Native children and force-fed them English,
Christianity, and European American epistemologies so that when they returned
home, they were strangers to their own families. When Louise Erdrich's mysterious Fleur Pillager, betrayed by the selfishly brutal actions of yet another white man,
is launched into radical trickster resistance, we remember the long trail of broken
treaties. As these stories show, the past is alive in the present, carried on by memory,
grit, and story.

What is it about these stories that is characteristic of Native American experiences?
A way of perceiving the natural world, feeling connected to the land, rather than
assuming dominion over it? Whether rejoicing or grieving, intuiting a small but mean-
ingful place in the web of life? Affirming a connection to a home/land, a first language,

a culture, a tribe, or a sovereign nation? Perhaps it is a journey that shows the struggle of those who live and breathe the daily experience of survival—of "those who were never meant to survive."[1] Like the women in traditional Tsalgi (Cherokee) deer dancer stories, the storyteller seduces readers into following her anywhere. Native stories are not "just stories," though. "They are all we have, to fight off illness and death," says Laguna Pueblo writer Leslie Marmon Silko. "We don't have anything if we don't have the stories."[2] Whether beading, dancing, listening, mourning, remembering, working, or celebrating, the women in the stories in this anthology are ferociously striving and, against all odds, loving as they "unglue the talking spirit from the pages."[3]

To tell a story is a great responsibility because words carry power. To receive a story is also a profound responsibility: the act binds the listener/reader to the teller and to the expansive web of storytelling. These stories are survival stories, reckonings with the brutal history of colonization and its ongoing consequences: they calculate indigenous positions, settle overdue accounts, note old debts, and demand an accounting. A reckoning requires a dive inward and a resurfacing with new insights and aspirations. In these stories, women and men reveal an understanding of life in its various modes of torment, loss, struggle, and compassion. These are the stories that "keep us from giving up in this land of nightmares, which is also the land of miracles."[4]

Attuned to the power of story, Anishinaabe writer Kimberly M. Blaeser has noted what is unique to Native and Native women writers:

> Many Indian authors have chosen purposefully to ignore standard rules and forms ill suited to Native storytelling. They strive to introduce different codes. Their works teach readers and critics new ways of reading and interacting with voices on the page. The work of Native women writers especially carries a new vision as it refuses to separate the literary and academic from the sacred and the daily, as it brings to the text the unpaginated experiences of contemporary tribal reality.[5]

As Blaeser articulates and as the stories in this collection demonstrate, contemporary writings by Native women continue a tradition of verbal art even as they generate new inventions and interventions. From "the sacred" to "the daily," entire cultural communities are kept dynamically alive as traditional stories are translated and transformed by contemporary writers. Like the oral narratives that precede and parallel them, contemporary written stories celebrate survival, resist erasure, transmit culture and history, and educate the community about how (or how not) to behave, while holding the audience spellbound. Even if read in isolation, the stories create community. The storytelling in this volume builds on foundations of both oral and textual traditions. Because of the persistent marketing of Indian stereotypes in the wider culture, as well as the ongoing assault of colonialism and its attendant forms of violence (both discursive and physical), most Native writers, male or female, find it necessary to write through and against established representations of American Indians in order to be seen or heard or read at all. In bringing "to the text, the unpaginated experiences of contemporary tribal reality," both unwriting and rewriting "Indian-ness" becomes a crucial function of contemporary Native women's storytelling.

To acknowledge the "new ways of reading" that Blaeser invokes, we use the term "short fiction," rather than "short story," within the title of this book. "Short story" suggests the particular European American literary tradition of a finely crafted fic-tion with a beginning, middle, and end, where the end dramatizes a resolution of the story's conflict. "Short fiction," although still academic, offers a more inclusive definition that may include retellings of oral narratives, story cycles, networks of short stories, anecdotes, conversations, and stories that may be, as Leslie Marmon Silko describes in a Pueblo context, organized around geographical sites rather than tem-poral development or, as Paula Gunn Allen explains, that are based neither on action nor on individual protagonists.[6] We do not, however, wish to suggest that contem-porary European American and Native American literatures are entirely separate spheres or to overgeneralize about the characteristics and forms of either realm. Such distinctions break down as soon as they are articulated, especially because the writ-ers included in this anthology are thoroughly contemporary women whose work is often transnational and transdisciplinary.

As Native women writers narrate personal, cultural, and historical experiences, they often adapt traditional story structures. Recurrent structural elements in the short fiction in this anthology include cyclical (rather than linear) narrative, layering of multiple perspectives, emphasis on the geographical over the temporal (place over time), translation of orality into text, blurring of Western temporal distinctions (the past and the present coexist), depiction of land as a character, and interweavings of myths and contemporary stories.

Just as stories flow from one generation to the next—and as, in many indigenous cultures, honored elders are first to speak—we present the stories in this volume by author, eldest to youngest. It might be helpful to identify four capacious, often overlapping themes that recur throughout the collection: *mythic cycles*—blendings of traditional and contemporary stories; *life cycles*—articulations of a full range of life stories, young to old, mundane to fantastic; *cycles of resistance*—stories of survival strategies and escape stories; and *healing cycles*—re/tellings of stories from indigenous perspectives that are linked to the natural and spiritual worlds and heal the wounds of history. The writings in this volume reconfigure both myth and history, highlighting story as profoundly regenerative.

MYTHIC CYCLES

Many of the writers retell traditional tribal stories in contemporary contexts or interweave mythic and contemporary narratives. For example, in the opening story, published here for the first time, Paula Gunn Allen retells a Diné (Navajo) story of Changing Woman, the personification of Earth's generative transformations, in a startlingly vivid, urban Indian voice. Told by a relocated Diné man and former roadie for a rock band, Allen's "Burned Alive in the Blues" recontextualizes the San Francisco of the 1960s, when "the fires of change and winds of revolution took our breaths away." In Allen's earlier story, "Deer Woman," "two strikingly beautiful young women" who may or may not be Deer Women—mythical figures known to appear in the form of irresistible beauties in order to lure men to the spirit world—seduce two young men at a stomp dance. Whether Linda and Junella are Tsalgi (Cherokee) Deer Women or not, the protagonists, and perhaps the readers, will never be the same. The transnational nature of these stories is evinced by the fact that Allen, a Laguna Pueblo/Lakota writer, retells Tsalgi stories.

Anita Endrezze's stories also blend the old and the new. "The Humming of Stars and Bees and Waves" recounts parallel stories of Yomumuli, Enchanted Bee, who created the world, and the elderly Rosa, who can no longer see clearly. The half-Yaqui woman "begs for a dream that would speak healing words" and finds that she must go on her own quest deep into some old caves to be instructed by the spider women on "seeing with her heart." In "Grandfather Sun Falls in Love with a Moon-Faced Woman," Endrezze tells a version of her grandfather Emiterio's story in the form of a Yaqui myth about the Sun and the Moon.

Likewise, Joy Harjo refashions two traditional Haudenosaunee (Iroquois) myths—Sky Woman and Star Husband stories—in "The Woman Who Fell from the Sky." Lila, the falling woman, "was neither a murderer nor a saint"; she was "the girl with skinned knees whose spirit knew how to climb to the stars." Lila survives attending boarding school, cleaning houses, working at Dairy Queen, and being beaten by her lover through dreams of flying away to marry one of the stars in the night sky. In "The Flood," a story of a sixteen-year-old girl's drinking, driving, and drowning, Harjo adapts the story of the Muscogee (Creek) watermonster, who "will do what he can to take us with him" to his watery lair. Or is it a story of the girl's coming-of-age as "the wife of the watermonster"? Offering a different register, Harjo's "the crow and the snake" is a kind of animal fable in which the perspectives of human, dog, and bird are equal. Through careful observation, the wise old crow discovers that the feared snake is only an illusion. Will the crow people believe him and return to their homeland?

LIFE CYCLES

As Carolyn Dunn and Carol Comfort note, "one common characteristic of Native women's stories...is that they follow the cycles of women's lives, focusing on birth, power, family and regeneration, as opposed to men's stories, which generally center upon themes of death and ritual rebirth through death."[7] The stories in this anthology cover the full range of life cycles—from young girls learning early life lessons to elderly women facing death. In Anna Lee Walters's "Apparitions," third-grader Wanda Horses accompanies her mother into the white town and learns about racism and sexism from a particularly despicable shoe salesman. After her mother dies, "burnt out from alcohol and welfare," nine-year-old Sue Linn in Beth E. Brant's "Turtle Gal" is left alone in their apartment. She is taken in by a kindly neighbor, a gay African American man, who hides her from Child Protective Services and "the penalties that lay in wait for little girls with no mother." On the other end of the age spectrum, the almost one-hundred-year-old Rosa Lopez in Walters's "Las Vegas, New Mexico, July 1969" spends a day trying to remember her long life (what was her first husband's name?) and comes to an illuminating revelation just before she dies. In Patricia Riley's "Wisteria," against the protests of her born-again Christian daughter-in-law, Eddie T. gives her granddaughter one last lesson about being Cherokee.

Several stories in this collection represent the cycle of women's lives on a diurnal scale, focusing on the wondrous minutiae of everyday life. In "Damping Down the Road," Patricia Riley depicts interactions of a family torn by opposing notions of Indianness. A survivor of Indian boarding school, Mama rejects everything Indian. Mama and daughter Ruby like perms, while Carnel and her dad prefer "good old Indian hair"; Mama battles the "red dirt," while Papa shapes it into tiny figures. For Mama, dirt is a mess; for Papa, dirt is home.

Like Riley's short fiction, Diane Glancy's stories focus on the everyday life of Christianized Cherokees. In "minimal indian," the born-again Renah is partial to skittering along her kitchen floor in "a holyghost dance." When her brother and his friend Crowbar come to visit, Renah sees another chance for them to be saved. All three are "a somewhat farming/backyard-hung-with-quilts/canning-jar-cellared-for-a-long-winter/vegetable-patched-in-summer/few-hogged/sort of folk" who never anticipate what awaits them. In another of Glancy's stories, "Stamp Dance," Mack, a little boy "who always wanted to go places," thinks about the role of the post office—a place linked to life (food stamps) and death (army registration). Just as the post office is associated with his father who left for Vietnam and was declared missing in action, "stamps were like angels that took things away." In the very short story "An American Proverb," Glancy presents the musings of a traumatized Vietnam veteran who, like Renah, ponders the relationship between God and humans.

Kimberly M. Blaeser and Beth H. Piatote share stories of the everyday as well. In Blaeser's "Growing Things," a woman named Spanish ponders seducing the tree doctor who comes to help cure her ailing oak tree but may or may not know any healing ways. The narrator of "Like Some Old Story" listens to neighborhood gossip and her grandpa's stories of hunting man-deer, who makes an appearance every forty years. In Piatote's conversational monologue, "Beading Lesson," an auntie teaches her niece the intricate patterns of beading. During the process, the younger woman learns about a lot more. Piatote's "Life-Size Indian" tells the story of Nathaniel Red Moon, a Persian Gulf veteran who tries to hook up with a white woman in a local bar. In Joy Harjo's new story, "The Reckoning," the first-person narrator, who is a single mother, artist, and university student, tells an all-too-familiar tale of falling in love, against her better judgment and the advice of sane friends, with a charismatic, handsome, political, and alcoholic Indian man.

CYCLES OF RESISTANCE

Because, as Paula Gunn Allen explains, Indian people "survive in the face of a brutal holocaust that seeks to wipe us out,"[8] it is not surprising that several stories dramatize resistance to imprisonment and lack of self-determination. Mental institutions, senior citizen homes, and boarding schools abound. Claire, in Janet Campbell Hale's long short story by that name, plans an elaborate escape from the senior citizen home in Oakland, California. As a child, her attempts to run away from boarding school were brutally unsuccessful, but now at seventy-nine and masquerading as a man, she breaks free to make the long journey home. Similarly, kept under guard "on the sixth floor of the whiteman hospital, in the mental ward," the elderly Mrs. Smith in Anna Lee Walters's story insists that she is Buffalo Wallow Woman, a woman saved by the buffalo people in long-ago stories. She, too, plans her escape, soliciting the young Indian night nurse to help set her free.

Like Buffalo Wallow Woman, the women in Reid Gómez's "electric gods" and "Touch. Touch. Touching." are declared insane, guilty of thinking like an Indian. The "crazy bitches" are given electric shock therapy to realign their minds. Electrodes penetrate the women's skulls like railroad spikes gouging the earth, performing, in a very personal and bodily way, the colonization of Native land and minds. All of these women, whether in homes for the aged, mental wards, or boarding schools, are seemingly rendered ghostlike, their true selves unseen by the white world. But the central characters in these stories resist invisibility by insisting on maintaining their Native ways of being and thinking.

Other struggles for individual and communal wholeness—to overcome alcoholism or self-doubt, for instance—are less tangible but just as real. In Beth E. Brant's "Swimming Upstream," Anna May mourns the drowning of her six-year-old son and struggles to resist a relapse into drinking. The protagonist of Misha Nogha's "Memekwesiw" battles to reconcile her Native and non-Native selves. Anna May finds her way by reconnecting to the natural world, while the narrator of Misha Nogha's psychological tale finds self-understanding through her bear dreams.

Two short chapters excerpted from novels and presented here as linked stories feature clever, tricksterlike narrative strategies of resisting oppression and certain death. Leslie Marmon Silko's "Mistaken Identity" and "Old Pancakes" (from *Almanac of the Dead*) tell the fanciful story of multiple "Geronimos" who keep the U.S. Cavalry on the move. "Of course the real man they called Geronimo, they never did catch," the story begins. In this narrative the Natives manipulate the white man's blindness for their own ends. Such a theme, of course, resonates with the many European American misperceptions of Natives in this anthology—Native people who are invisible to a dominant society that sees only its own prejudiced projections.

The second set of linked stories is Louise Erdrich's "Almost Soup" and "Lazy Stitch" (from *The Antelope Wife*). The only stories narrated by nonhumans (in this case, a dog), they present tragic-comic tales of survival. A trickster, mixed-breed descendant of Original Dog is saved from becoming "puppy soup" by little Cally. Almost Soup, as he is named, devotes himself to her ever after.

Two stories by Erdrich tell part of the multigenerational family saga of Ojibwe (Chippewa) and mixed-blood survival in North Dakota and Minnesota. In "Le Mooz," she presents the hilarious tricksterlike tale of the elderly Margaret Kashpaw and Nanapush. Bound to each other in loving misery, they embark on a final hunting journey. In "Summer 1913/*Miskomini-geezis*/Raspberry Sun," mixed-blood Pauline Puyat tells the story of the wild, strong, beautiful, twice-drowned Fleur Pillager, possible consort of Misshepeshu, the Ojibwe water monster. All of these stories highlight resistance and survival; all call for a reckoning.

HEALING CYCLES

Healing "the wounds of history" is a common theme in stories by Native women. With its focus on memory, community, and ritual, Linda Hogan's "Bush's Mourning Feast" exemplifies the communal nature of healing. A great-granddaughter remembers her great-grandmother's stories. She hears about the night that Bush, mourning the return of her granddaughter to her abusive mother, hosts a feast and giveaway. Over the frozen countryside, Bush's guests carry away everything that she owns— clothing, furniture, blankets—but "the most important thing they carried was Bush's sorrow." "Too large for a single person," the grief of personal (her granddaughter taken away by the court) and historic loss ("all the children lost to us, taken away") must be disassembled and shared to be endured.

In "Descent" the young protagonist, linked to ancient ways and subterranean waters, longs to "find an entrance to another world" and break free from the world of shopping malls and gas stations. After a violent hurricane and the mysterious murder of a protected panther, she must explain herself to her family. Last of the few Taiga (a fictional tribe in Florida) and a descendant of the Panther Clan, the protagonist finds herself enmeshed in a powerful story much older and bigger than she can comprehend.

Silko's "Storyteller" chronicles not only surviving the wounds of history but also rectifying them. Like the central character in "Descent," the unnamed protagonist in "Storyteller" knows the icy Alaskan land intimately. She uses that knowledge (and the ignorance and greed of the white people) to take revenge for the murder of her parents many years before. More important than her controversial action, though, is the story she must now tell about cultural and environmental loss, not just her own personal loss. "I will not change the story, not even to escape this place and go home," she tells her attorney. "The story must be told as it is." Silko's story is, in part, about the necessity of retelling history from indigenous perspectives. And like many stories in this collection, "Storyteller" demonstrates one of the ways Native women grapple with this responsibility.

Like many women of color, Native women are not generally inclined "to define themselves in gender-based terms and are often suspicious of 'mainstream' feminisms that reflect neither their sociopolitical concerns nor their historical positions within their own nations. With notable exceptions, instead of identifying as a (universal) woman, a Native woman is far more likely to define herself by tribal, national, or cultural affiliation."[9] For many Native women, reconnecting to a tribal history and culture entails reconstituting female power that may have been muted by colonization. Like the female characters represented in this anthology—those claiming victories over ordinary losses; those facing the extraordinary losses brought about by colonialism, racism, and homophobia on top of the mundane vagaries of everyday life; those struggling for clarity in mental institutions or postapocalypse futures; those searching for comfort by imagining the past or connecting to loved ones or creating community or celebrating their connection to the land—contemporary Native women must be multiply vigilant. As Natives, they must resist being relegated to the past as anthropological objects of study and refuse to perform Indian "authenticity"; as women, they must negotiate the gender roles within their particular cultures and assert their presence within the larger U.S. society.

Not surprisingly, contemporary Native American women writers are often astute theorists of story. Like storytellers of old, they combine creativity with critical interpretation and reinvention. All of the contributors to *Reckonings* have written and spoken eloquently about the power and purpose of story. In addition, most of the contributors have themselves published anthologies featuring Native American literature, women's literature, or short fiction.[10] Their long list of publications attests to the vitality, audacity, and abundance of work by Native women today, not only as writers but also as stewards of multiple literary landscapes. As editors, teachers, performers, reviewers, and writers, they establish, sustain, and broaden the scope of Native American literature and simultaneously promote artists from multiple backgrounds and communities.

HISTORICIZING ANTHOLOGIES OF CONTEMPORARY NATIVE AMERICAN LITERATURES

With its expansive inclusiveness, the genre of the anthology offers an appropriate vehicle for the community building and stewardship that characterize the work of the Native American women included in this book. Contributions by emerging writers can be found next to those of established writers, and the stories themselves cross and recross similar terrain. By design, this anthology offers a multiplicity of voices articulating a panoply of contemporary Native American perspectives and experiences. In this section, we briefly consider the history of contemporary anthologies of Native American literature by focusing, in particular, on the sociopolitical contexts in which they arise and their links to community building, political activism, and Native women's literary production.

Several events mark the era of Indian activism that assisted the Native writers whose work is included in this book to come into public voice and recognition. In 1968 the American Indian Movement (AIM), the Indian rights organization devoted to Native self-determination and Native nation sovereignty, was formed. In 1969 N. Scott Momaday was awarded the Pulitzer Prize for his novel *House Made of Dawn*, Vine Deloria Jr. published his Indian rights manifesto *Custer Died for Your Sins*, and American Indians occupied Alcatraz Island in the San Francisco Bay. By 1973 Indian activists had gathered at Wounded Knee, the site of the 1890 massacre of more than three hundred women, children, and elderly men by the U.S. Seventh Cavalry, in order to challenge the federally designated tribal government. When federal forces attacked this time, AIM members took up arms, fighting back in remembrance of Big Foot's unarmed band, slaughtered almost a hundred years earlier. The violent confrontation lasted more than two months. Out of such activism, Native women, many involved with AIM, founded Women of All Red Nations (WARN).[11] Although the Native resistance at Wounded Knee was controversial and divisive within American Indian communities and the federal invasion that followed a national horror, the event was a generative moment of contemporary Native political and literary articulations.[12]

The advent of "Red Power" resulted in a mini-explosion of anthologies of American Indian fiction and poetry.[13] To write a history of anthologies of Native American literatures, and their role in both reflecting and shaping Native American literature overall, is too large and complex an endeavor for this introduction, but we do wish to situate this anthology in relation to those that came before. Several basic organizing structures of anthologies of Native American literature recur; some of them overlap. *Survey* anthologies provide an introduction to and overview of the field of American Indian literature. Generally, they have a broad historical scope and include a variety of literary forms, such as poetry, nonfiction prose, fiction, translations of oral narratives, and chants (e.g., Turner, Sanders and Peek, Velie, Vizenor, and Witalec with Malinowski). *Genre-specific* anthologies offer a more in-depth sampling of one literary form and may intervene in ongoing debates about defining the parameters and forms of the genre (e.g., Rosen, Trafzer, Ortiz, Lesley). *Place-specific* anthologies emphasize Native connectedness to particular land bases/homelands, Native nations, or American regions (e.g., Blaeser, Hobson, Lerner, Sarris, Walters). Anthologies focused on *women's writings* (e.g., Allen, Brant, Dunn and Comfort, Erdrich and Tohe, Fife, Green, Harjo and Bird), like those focused on *gay and lesbian* Native writers (e.g., Roscoe) and like any anthology to some degree, serve the dual purpose of articulating and building a political and literary community.

Published in 1974, *The Man to Send Rain Clouds: Contemporary Stories by American Indians*, edited by Kenneth Rosen, is the first collection of contemporary stories by American Indians. Still in print today, it played a pivotal role in establishing Native

American short fiction not as ethnography or history but as finely crafted literature. Since 1974, the date that Paula Gunn Allen selects as the beginning of the second wave of Native literature (1974–1994),[14] writings by Native women writers have played a prominent role in many anthologies. As well as circulating literature from often-ignored perspectives, these anthologies have the express agenda of community formation and political intervention.[15] The 1980s saw the emergence of anthologies focusing specifically on Native women's writing as part of a larger movement, an outpouring of publications by women of color. Such multigenre collections as *The Third Woman: Minority Women Writers of the United States* (1980), *This Bridge Called My Back: Writings by Radical Women of Color* (1981), and *HomeGirls: A Black Feminist Anthology* (1983)[16] were joined in 1984 by Beth E. Brant's compilation of grassroots Indian women's writing, *A Gathering of Spirit: A Collection of North American Indian Women*, and Rayna Green's *That's What She Said*, featuring contemporary poetry and fiction by Native women. Four years later, these were followed by the first anthology devoted to work by gay and lesbian American Indians.[17] Other significant anthologies from the 1980s focused on genre and place and contemporary retellings of traditional myths and story cycles.[18]

The number of anthologies related in some way to Native American short fiction (and often to women's writing) more than doubled in the 1990s. Some sought to provide overviews of Native American literature and others to introduce new fiction or present a regionally specific literature,[19] but one of the most important events of the decade for readers of Native American literatures was not a book but an unprecedented assemblage of Native writers. In the summer of 1992, American Indians met in Oklahoma for the First North American Native Writers' Festival, "Returning the Gift," gathering "more Native writers together in one place than at any other time in history."[20] This event brought together aspiring, emergent, and accomplished Indian writers and resulted in the establishment of two Native-writer organizations: Native Writers' Circle of the Americas (NWCA) and Wordcraft Circle of Writers and Storytellers (WC).[21] Housed in the Native American Studies program at the University of Oklahoma, Native Writers' Circle of the Americas maintains records of Native writers' addresses, houses a collection of Native-authored literature, and awards three literature prizes annually. Wordcraft Circle mentors emerging Native American writers. Together they support a network of Native writers and continue to foster a spirit of cooperation, mentorship, and hope. In addition, the festival helped to clarify a set of possibilities for defining Native identities: "provable Native heritage, self-identification as a Native person, and affiliation with the tribal community." Some of the Festival's creative output was published two years later as *Returning the Gift: Poetry and Prose from the First North American Native Writers' Festival*, edited by Joseph Bruchac. Many of the writers in this anthology—Allen, Blaeser, Erdrich, Glancy, Harjo, and Hogan—have received awards from Wordcraft Circle of Native Writers and Storytellers and Native Writers' Circle of the Americas.

Particularly significant for the work of Native women writers is the 1997 anthology *Reinventing the Enemy's Language: Contemporary Native Women's Writings of North*

America, edited by Joy Harjo and Gloria Bird. With its focus on Native women, *Reinventing the Enemy's Language* picks up the earlier work of Allen, Brant, and Green from a decade before and continues the efforts of the First North American Native Writers' Festival in the attempt to include an extensive collection of Indian writers and to define precisely who is "authentically" Native and, as a consequence, what constitutes Native American literature. Notably, both *Returning the Gift* and *Reinventing the Enemy's Language* arose from Native gatherings and focus on "the collective voices of nations."[22]

In the twenty-first century, key anthologies include *Nothing but the Truth: An Anthology of Native American Literature* (2000), edited by John Purdy and James Ruppert, and *Sister Nations: Native American Women Writers on Community* (2002), edited by Heid E. Erdrich and Laura Tohe. The Purdy and Ruppert anthology extends Bruchac's comprehensive literature collection, and the Erdrich and Tohe book highlights Native women and their central, but varied, relations with community.

PARAMETERS OF THIS ANTHOLOGY

Even as we appreciate the vital role of anthologies in shaping Native American literature, we acknowledge their limitations. The selection process for any anthology exposes the problems of defining and categorizing American Indian identities and literatures, shaped as these are by the colonizer's language and law. These difficulties parallel the limitations of the anthology form that likewise tends to gloss over differences in the name of community. Choosing depth over breadth, we limit the writers in this anthology to a few within the United States, not Mexico, Latin America, or Canada (though Brant is claimed by both Canada and the United States).[23] There is simply such an abundance of creative short fiction by Native women in what is now the United States that no one volume can adequately represent it. Regrettably, there are many wonderful writers whose work is not represented here. We resisted the anthologizing tendency to present a single sample of a writer's work that carries the burden of representing her entire corpus. Rather than include a single story by many writers, then, we decided to offer two to three stories by fewer writers with the hope that readers will gain a deeper sense of the range and registers of each writer. The one exception to this is Janet Campbell Hale, from whose many stories we have selected a single, very long one. In addition to a few, well-loved, often-taught stories by well-known writers (such as Leslie Marmon Silko's "Storyteller," Louise Erdrich's "Summer 1913...," and Joy Harjo's "The Woman Who Fell from the Sky"), we have included several new works, by both established writers like Paula Gunn Allen and Joy Harjo and by more recently recognized writers like Beth H. Piatote and Reid Gómez.

In selecting the writers to include in this anthology and with respect for each tribe and nation's right to define its members or citizens, we chose not to require tribal enrollment, a decision that risks judgments of "inauthenticity" but ultimately

acknowledges the historical and legal erasures, the political articulations and defor-
mations, and the personal reformulations and recovery of American Indian identity
and citizenship. As Jana Sequoya Magdaleno has written, "The question of who
and how is an Indian is an ongoing contest of stories in North America—a contest
in many ways emblematic of global struggles to contain and control difference in
modern societies."[24] Contestation over whose stories are legitimated and whose are
discredited is an ongoing effect of colonial rupture and political erasure of American
Indian identity formations in the United States. Both tribal enrollment and refusal to
enroll have therefore been among the strategies to consolidate or to resist federally
sanctioned relationships to the dominant society. Particularly in the Southeastern
region of the country, a common response to early U.S. government policies that
"alternately sought to exterminate, eliminate, incarcerate and assimilate Native peoples and cultures was to obliterate evidence of Indian identity."[25] Lakota intellectual
Vine Deloria Jr.'s distinction between "tribal" and "ethnic" Native Americans is
helpful here. "Tribal" Natives have citizenship in two nations; "ethnic" Natives are
part of an internal U.S. diaspora.[26] Although many of our contributors are enrolled
members of tribal nations, tribal enrollment—which we see as only one of many
ways to define American Indian identity—is not among the requirements for inclusion in this anthology.

Reckonings, then, is a confluence, sometimes a collision, of voices and visions.
In this anthology you will find the intermingling, overlapping, interfacing, con-
tradicting voices of tribally enrolled, deculturated, disidentified, misidentified, and
self-identified contemporary Native women writers. Here women initiate the creative adaptations and cyclical transformations necessary to survival. In these stories
Native women call for a reckoning.

As with all worthwhile projects, there are many people to thank. First, we'd like
to thank the many gifted Native women writers whose work, though not included
in this short collection, enriches the field. We are grateful to the contributors who
were not only generous enough to share their stories but also patient enough to wait
for this volume to become manifest. Our deep gratitude goes also to Kathryn Koo,
our research associate and dear friend, who was the model of organization, clarity, and
grace. Once she took charge of obtaining permissions and organizing files, the clouds
lifted. A warm thank you goes to Andrea Dominguez, our research assistant, who read
everything with insight and clarity. Thanks also go to Yooujin Park for her timely
word-processing skills. A special thank you goes to Sita Wong, whose proofreading
skills were incredible. We are profoundly grateful to Michelle Raheja and Jon Peterson
for their incisive readings of and thoughtful recommendations for the introduction.
Thanks also are due to several editors at Oxford University Press: Elizabeth Maguire,
who commissioned this volume, as well as Susan Chang, Elissa Morris, and Shannon
McLachlan, whose support has been invaluable. We are thankful to Christine Dahlin
and Christina Gibson, of Oxford University Press, for their outstanding work on this
book. In addition, we gratefully acknowledge our families and friends, who kept us

going throughout it all. Finally, special thanks go to Hertha's daughters, Sita and Xian, who shared their mother and inspired us all.

Hertha D. Sweet Wong
Lauren Stuart Muller
Jana Sequoya Magdaleno

Berkeley, California

1. Audre Lorde, "Litany for Survival," *The Black Unicorn: Poems* (New York: W. W. Norton, 1978), pp. 31–32; repeated in Joy Harjo, "Anchorage," *She Had Some Horses* (New York: Thunder's Mouth Press, 1983), p. 15.

2. Leslie Marmon Silko, *Ceremony* (New York: Penguin, 1977).

3. Joy Harjo, "The Book of Myths," *In Mad Love and War* (Middletown, Conn.: Wesleyan University Press, 1990), p. 56.

4. Joy Harjo, "Reconciliation: A Prayer," *The Woman Who Fell from the Sky* (New York: W. W. Norton, 1996).

5. Kimberly Blaeser, "Like 'Reeds through the Ribs of a Basket': Native Women Weaving Stories," *Other Sisterhoods: Literary Theory and U.S. Women of Color*, edited by Sandra Kumamoto Stanley (Urbana: University of Illinois Press, 1998), p. 266.

6. See Leslie Marmon Silko, "Language and Literature from a Pueblo Indian Perspective," *Yellow Woman and a Beauty of the Spirit: Essays on Native American Life* (New York: Simon & Schuster, 1996), pp. 48–59; and Paula Gunn Allen, *The Sacred Hoop: Recovering the Feminine in American Indian Traditions* (Boston: Beacon Press, 1986). In Silko's "Old Pancakes" (included in this volume), for instance, the narrator says, "The story did not run in a line for the horizon, but circled and spiraled instead like the red-tailed hawk."

7. Carolyn Dunn and Carol Comfort, eds., *Through the Eye of the Deer: An Anthology of Native American Women Writers* (San Francisco: Aunt Lute Books, 1999), p. xiii.

8. Paula Gunn Allen, "Introduction," *Spider Woman's Granddaughters: Traditional Tales and Contemporary Writing by Native American Women* (Boston: Beacon Press, 1989), p. 2.

9. Hertha D. Sweet Wong, "First-Person Plural: Subjectivity and Community in Native American Women's Autobiography," *Women, Autobiography, Theory: A Reader*, edited by Sidonie Smith and Julia Watson (Madison: University of Wisconsin Press, 1998), p. 170.

10. Paula Gunn Allen, who compiled the first collection of short fiction specifically by Native American women, *Spider Woman's Granddaughters* (1989), also edited several others: *Grandmothers of the Light: A Medicine Woman's Sourcebook* (1991), *Voice of the Turtle: American Indian Literature, 1900–1970* (1994), *Song of the Turtle: American Indian Literature, 1974–1994* (1996), and *Hózhó, Walking in Beauty: Native American Stories of Inspiration, Humor, and Life* (2001). Beth E. Brant introduced and produced one of the first multigenre anthologies of writings by Native American women: *A Gathering of Spirit: A Collection of North American Indian Women* (1984). Diane Glancy coedited *Two Worlds Walking: Short Stories, Essays, and Poetry by Writers with Mixed Heritages* (1994) and *Visit Teepee Town: Native Writings after the Detours* (1999). Anna Lee Walters edited *Neon Pow-wow: New Native American Voices of the Southwest* (1993). Linda Hogan has coedited three books featuring writings by women: *The Stories We Hold Secret: Tales of Women's Spiritual Development* (1998), *Intimate Nature: The Bond between Women and Animals* (1998), and *The Sweet Breathing of Plants: Women Writing on the Green World* (2001). Patricia Riley compiled *Growing Up Native American: An Anthology* (1993). Louise Erdrich was selected as editor of *The Best American Short Stories 1993* (1993). Joy Harjo coedited *Re-inventing the Enemy's Language: Contemporary Native Women's Writings of North America* with Gloria Bird, and Kimberly M. Blaeser edited *Stories Migrating Home: A Collection of Anishnaabe Prose* (1998).

11. The precise date of WARN's founding is uncertain. Some say it was 1974; others, 1978.

12. Of course, American Indian activism and literary production began much earlier. Early literary forebears to contemporary Native American women writers include Pauline Johnson, Gertrude Simmons Bonnin (Zitkala-Sa), Mourning Dove, Ella Deloria, and Alice Callahan. European Americans concerned with justice for Native Americans founded the Indian Rights Association in 1882. In the early twentieth century, Gertrude Simmons Bonnin (Zitkala-Sa) (1876–1938) and Carlos Montezuma (~1866–1923) were both active in the Society of American Indians, a Native rights organization founded by Native intellectuals in 1911. The National Congress of American Indians (NCAI), formed in 1944 as a way to resist federal termination policies, is "the oldest and largest tribal government organization in the U.S." Its mission is "to inform the public and the federal government on tribal self-government, treaty rights, and a broad range of federal policy issues affecting tribal governments" (see http://www.ncai.org). Founded in 1970, the Native American Rights Fund (NARF) is "the oldest and largest nonprofit law firm dedicated to advertising and defending the rights of Indian tribes, organizations and individuals nationwide" (see http://www.narf.org).

13. As early as 1918, George W. Cronyn edited *The Path on the Rainbow: An Anthology of Songs and Chants from the Indians of North America* (New York: Boni and Liveright, 1918). In this collection of indigenous verbal art, Cronyn argues for its inclusion as aboriginal "American" poetry. (This was preceded by a 1917 "Indian" issue of *Poetry* magazine that argued much the same point.) In *The American Rhythm* (New York: Harcourt, 1923), Mary Austin, who had written the introduction to Cronyn's anthology a few years before, presents Native "poetry" as a model on which to develop the foundations of what would become imagism and American modernism. Both focus on translations of verbal art (excerpts of traditional myths and ceremonies), whereas the post–Wounded Knee anthologies tend to include more contemporary writers who often translate old stories into new contexts. See also Helen Carr's description of the rebirth of primitivism as an escape from modernity in *Inventing the Primitive: Politics, Gender and the Representation of Native American Literary Traditions, 1789–1936* (New York: New York University Press, 1996).

John Milton edited the first full collection of contemporary writings by Native Americans, *The Indian Speaks* (1969), and *American Indian II* (1971). Departing from earlier practices of presenting Indian literature as ethnography or the romantic American originary voice, these books announced the vibrant presence of late-twentieth-century Native authors. In 1972, Shirley Hill Witt and Stan Steiner's *The Way: An Anthology of American Indian Literature* and Natachee Scott Momaday's *American Indian Authors* presented oratory, narratives, and legends of the past alongside current literary and political writings, further countering the notion of the "Vanishing Indian" by making visible a wide array of Native American writers. Similarly, *Literature of the American Indian* (1973), edited by Thomas Edward Sanders and Walter W. Peek, and *The Portable North American Indian Reader* (1974), edited by Frederick W. Turner III, included "traditional" myths and tales, poetry and oratory, excerpts of personal narratives, and stories of exploration and captivity, as well as dominant images of Indians. Gloria Levitas, Frank Robert Vivelo, and Jacqueline Vivelo organized *American Indian Prose and Poetry: We Wait in the Darkness* (1973) ethnographically and historically. Although their commentary calls attention to differences among "socio-cultural systems" in order to portray the variety and complexity of American Indian literary expression, it also conveys an image of Natives as tragically doomed, as the subtitle "we wait in darkness" indicates.

14. Paula Gunn Allen, "Introduction," *Song of the Turtle: American Indian Literature 1974–1994* (New York: One World, Ballantine Books, 1996), p. 8.

15. See Cynthia G. Franklin's discussion of the political and literary functions of anthologies in *Writing Women's Communities: The Politics and Poetics of Contemporary Multi-Genre Anthologies* (Madison: University of Wisconsin Press, 1997).

16. Dexter Fisher, ed., *The Third Woman: Minority Women Writers of the United States* (Boston: Houghton Mifflin, 1980); Cherríe Moraga and Gloria Anzaldúa, eds., *This Bridge Called My Back: Writings by Radical Women of Color* (Watertown,

Mass.: Persephone Press, 1981); and Barbara Smith, ed., *Home Girls: A Black Feminist Anthology* (New York: KitchenTable–Women of Color Press, 1983).

17. Will Roscoe, *Living the Spirit: A Gay American Indian Anthology* (New York: St. Martin's Press, 1988).

18. Geary Hobson's important anthology, *The Remembered Earth* (1981), emphasizes land and place (Oklahoma) and the proliferation of creative writing throughout Native America. Simon Ortiz's 1983 *Earth Power Coming* features contemporary short fiction, followed six years later by Paula Gunn Allen's *Spider Woman's Granddaughters* (1989), in which she links traditional myths (story cycles) and their contemporary retellings and adaptations in short fiction by contemporary women.

19. Like *Literature of the American Indian*, edited by Sanders and Peek two decades before, several anthologies were designed to introduce readers to an overview of Native American literature. Alan R. Velie's *American Indian Literature* (1979, 1991) and Gerald Vizenor's *Native American Literature* (1995) are both geared toward classroom use.

Many anthologies, though, have focused on defining contemporary Native American short fiction: Craig Lesley's *Talking Leaves* (1991), Alan R. Velie's *The Lightning Within* (1991), Clifford E. Trafzer's *Earth Song, Sky Spirit* (1992), and Paula Gunn Allen's *Song of the Turtle: American Indian Literature 1974–1994* (1996).

A few, like Trafzer's *Blue Dawn, Red Earth* (1992) and Arlene B. Hirschfelder and Beverly R. Singer's *Rising Voices: Writing of Young Native Americans* (1992), aim specifically to introduce new Native voices.

Through the Eye of the Deer (1999), edited by Carolyn Dunn and Carol Comfort, follows the model of Paula Gunn Allen's *Spider Woman's Granddaughters* in its emphasis on the continuity of spirituality in Native women's stories and the creative contemporary retellings of oral narratives.

Several regionally specific anthologies were published in the nineties: Andrea Lerner's *Dancing on the Rim of the World* (1990) focuses on Native writers of the Northwest, Anna Lee Walters's *Neon Pow-wow* (1993) introduces many emergent Native writers from the Southwest, and Greg Sarris's *The Sounds of Rattles and Clappers* (1994) features contemporary Native Californian writers.

20. Joseph Bruchac, "Introduction," *Returning the Gift: Poetry and Prose from the First North American Native Writers' Festival* (Tucson: University of Arizona Press, 1994), p. xix.

21. You can check out Native Writers' Circle of the Americas (Project Director, Geary Hobson) at http://www.ou.edu/cas/nas/writers.html. As of the publication date of this book, service for Wordcraft Circle of Native Writers and Storytellers (National Director, Lee Francis, 1991– ca. 2003) at http://www.wordcraftcircle.org was "no longer active."

22. Joy Harjo, "Introduction," *Reinventing the Enemy's Language: Contemporary Native Women's Writings of North America*, edited by Joy Harjo and Gloria Bird (New York: W. W. Norton, 1997), p. 31.

23. Although we recognize the artificial and contingent nature of national boundaries and the importance of transnational indigenous alliances, our aim is to present a selection of short fiction by Native women within the United States.

24. Jana Sequoya Magdaleno, "How? (!) Is an Indian: A Contest of Stories, Round 2," *Postcolonial Theory and the U.S.*, edited by Amrit Singh and Peter Schmid (Jackson: University Press of Mississippi, 2000), pp. 279–280.

25. Ibid., p. 280.

26. Vine Deloria Jr. and Clifford Lytle, *The Nations Within: The Past and Future of American Indian Sovereignty* (New York: Pantheon Books, 1984), p. 245.

Paula Gunn Allen
(1939–)

"There is something about stories
that hooks humans into culture, that
makes human psyches and human
societies all but indistinguishable
from texts....The old ones'
recognition of the intrinsic identity
of text and human consciousness
informs the structures of the whole
of the oral tradition, and critical
theory in Indian Country consists of
the subtle junctures of story cycles."

Paula Gunn Allen, "Don't Fence
Me In" in *Off the Reservation:
Reflections on Boundary-Busting,
Border Crossing, Loose Canons*

Burned Alive in the Blues

Paula Gunn Allen

The thing to remember about life is it causes death. It's about fire, truth to tell. You know, you eat and breathe to get fuel to run the body, right? And a calorie is a way of measuring the burn, which is what happens. Your body, employing oxygen just like any merry blaze does, burns the stuff you eat and drink. Over time, the oxygenation process, which you gotta have to live, causes a build up of ashes, just like the Catholics say. It's those ashes that slowly make things break down. Now, of course, the new craze is anti-oxidant type supplements, to get a slower burn. Funny to think of carbon-based life forms as the type of cosmic dust that burns itself up. Well, it's ecologically sound, I'll give it that.

But, here's the thing: some lives burn up faster than others, and while the medicos can talk about what you eat and whether you work out and all that physical stuff, how many are talking about soul-burn? It seems to me that some people have too much oxygen, and that makes them burn bright and burn out quick. A flash that dazzles, and then the dark. Of course, the dark isn't. I mean, after the afterimage fades from your retinas, you can see that the stars are all over the sky. In time, you get just as dazzled by starlight as by lightning flash-burn. And maybe starlight-burn lasts longer.

Or maybe some people get so caught up in the winds of the times, especially when like now everything's changing faster and faster so that the energy moves faster and hotter, and it steals all the air out of their lungs. You know, like happens in a firestorm where anything not made of metal ignites. There was this one grass fire, out on the plains in the Midwest, and a couple of kids were on the wrong side of the blaze. They tried to run through the fire and the hot air stole the breath from them. They collapsed in the middle of the blaze. You could see them trying to scream, but the heat had taken all the oxygen so they had no breath. They were burning alive, see.

I think *chindi** does that to you, so you don't want to get caught in one. It seems to me that eras are like people in that way. Like some are firestorms so hot that everything ignites, everyone who tries to run through the flames has their breath

* According to Allen, *chindi* is the Diné word for dust devil or whirlwind.

stolen. They are burned alive. Maybe the past goes with them, up in flames. Maybe the firestorm is what makes a space for another round of life.

The sixties were like that, and the blazing lights of the time—Lenny Bruce, Janis Joplin, Jimi Hendrix, Jim Morrison, Bob Marley, on and on, we all know some of their names—were icons of a pattern that ran beyond them and through them. It burned them up and blew them away all in such a blaze we were all too dazzled to see the stars in their subtle and slow burn, eternally keeping time. When cold war met hot beat there was a humongous convection current formed. It was a whirlwind, a tornado, plucking bits of this and pieces of that and whirling them apart. It tore and smashed—in weird patterns, in minuscule spaces, in huge swathes. It was a time-changer, a social dust devil, a hot, hot wind.

Over the years since, I've spent a lot of time thinking about those times, the ineffable power, magic, ok? of them, the mysteriousness of their appearance and disappearance. Where did that power come from? Where did it go? A lot of us survived to testify, but no one knows what we bear witness to, and that's the fascination of it, and the power of those brief years that still holds us enthralled. You know what I think? I think it was all about the revolution of the blues.

You know, the blues live on love and hope like oxygen lives on life. And when you know the blues, you know that love is a fire that never goes out, and loneliness is as faithful as the stars. You realize that you, like fire, must have oxygen to live.

Thinking these morose thoughts, and worse, I'd made it down to my usual corner table at the Royal, corner of 4th and B Street in San Rafael. No getting around it, I was down for the count. I had been through another long night—another one of the thousands in the thirty years since I'd removed myself to the Bay Area. I had been a roadie back then, working mostly for Clark Kent and the Supermen, but I worked some of the big festivals, like Monterey during the Summer of Love, and for mega producers like Bill Graham. Those were heady times, but after all the years since, I was so over it, but never mind. It just kept keepin' on. You know, it's a lot like a bad acid trip. Flashbacks, nightmares, strange dreams when you aren't even asleep. You'd think it would quit, or it would at least get less surreal. But it doesn't. No matter how the climate and the social scene change—Starbucks instead of dingy coffee bars with mind-cooling jazz or opera non-stop, baskets of petunias and begonias dangling from light fixtures, instead of dingy black walls and unmopped asphalt linoleum, all the slick and way too chic places to hang: bistros, hot tubs, stratospheric rents, floors instead of cruddy bars and piss-stinking crash pads—you keep getting caught in the grotty glamour of those times before this time, the time before the world came smacking all hard-edged and plastic-cool into a focus you wish would blur softly away. Nothing ever changes, you know, but once we thought it did, it would. It might get polish over the sludge and slime, but it's still the same ol' filthy game. We don't believe in change now. Not anymore. Same ol', same ol', keeps keepin' on. Once we thought those were words of hip and cool and revolution. Now we know them for what they are: could get better, but it won't.

Like here in this coffee bar where I hang most mornings, which is called the Royal. I think that's a joke, a bit of ironic commentary, because the Royal where I sit is just up the street from the New George where the latest early twenty-first-century bands appear. Old Royal, New George, same game. So here we are. The same sequence on the cd player, the same morning faces lined up for lattes, decaf double caps with soy—you gotta wonder why they bother. Fake cognoscenti, made to almost seem real. I guess the question answers itself, put that way. Me, I drink the Colombian. Looking for Juan Valdez, looking for a reminder, a connection maybe, to better times, to home that's gone the way of everything else. Too bad they don't serve Folger's at the Royal. Old Juan must be way too downscale for San Rafael. Although looks like Señor Valdez, or his nephew, anyway, is behind the counter—all the counters in California—these days. I guess that's new. Unless it's older still: maybe the Royal will soon be rechristened El Real, and Main Street will revert to El Camino Real. Who knows?

Anyway, here I am, hanging in San Rafael, California, twenty miles north of anywhere. Wasn't Raphael the angel who blows his horn? Probably hot jazz, none of the acid rock, acid rain. You think about it, you see they go together. Like they came. The A-Train. Angel on blow. Miles and Coltrane. Bessie and Janis. Wailing frails, man. That's what they were, what we heard and about lost it, man. At the sound of a woman's voice, a hot, hot horn. In Janis's case, it wasn't an archangel blowing the changes in the wind: it was an Indian supernatural, Kokopelli, the humpbacked fluteplayer and lover extraordinaire, aaaiii! The original American blues player, consort of the Goddess Iyatiku, signaler of a new world. "As above, so below" the ancient old world mystics say, and as I see it, from above and all around and beneath this world the Old Ones bring the winds of change. All that the musicians, the poets, the politicians, the conspirators against change do is reflect it, blow around in it. *Chindi* here, god-wind elsewhere. Here the change, there the change, and here and there those who oppose it. Like the ghoul in human form, Janis's demon lover. Like the Shadow government. Like the assassins. They think killing the harbingers of the new will end the change. They don't know you can't kill the wind. Speaking of the undead, the thing that has me going this a.m. is seeing old man Skinwalker, Shapeshifter, doing his Frail Fence of Fancy thing. You gotta wonder what a skinwalker wants a fence for—a screen? Maybe he thinks you can build a fence that will wall off the changes. Like the Maginot Line, China's Great Wall, or the one that used to cross Berlin. His struttin' and stridin' "hey, look at me" act; he's still as creepy as way back then. Then was when he should have figured out what the Navajo people have known since the beginning: without a strong woman to lead, you ain't shit. But when you got a woman like that, and you don't know that it's her making YOU, not the other way around—well, at home and away, she's gonna dump you in the end. Which is why Janis dumped him and his "holding company." Big Brother? No way. More like Big Joke! Maybe he's a brother in the biblical sense: like Cain was Abel's.

Still, in the face of everything it is always just the same, his main act Joplin was a different thing altogether, and that's no joke, no more than the ones the clowns over at First Mesa or down at Zuni and the other Pueblos are joking. They just do the truth as their main act, and while a lot of people laugh, most get the point. If you look carefully while they're clowning, you'll see the wisdom of the earth is their act, cloaked in body-puns on whatever bullshit's come down among the community all that year. Pueblo clowns aren't like circus clowns, or not like circus clowns are now. Maybe like their forebears in medieval times back in Europe. Pueblo clowns have a role to play that's about the *Yei*, the Holy People, and how the people are supposed to walk in Beauty, and how we're not making it, exactly in what ways we're not making it, how we're making Beauty into Ugly, how Ugly is doing us because we've turned off the Beauty Road. Not the pretty as in, "let's pave some more streets and build some more concrete boundaries," but Beauty, like what is good, true, real. What makes our spirits sing. Alive, alive. Janis and some other notable and not-at-all-noted *bilagáana** at that time were doing that sacred clown thing. But not Big Brother. See, he's just Old Man Missionary in drag. But you can tell what he is because he thinks chicks are for back up, to make him and his holding company look good. He doesn't know that if women are the walls, they are the walls that shelter us and keep us free. Only Spam I Am didn't like being a joke. And he sure could never have been a clown. He was Big Brother, and to him that meant Heap Big Shit. He didn't know that some of us knew that his name was really the name of his boss: big brother. Like in Orwell, *1984*. Pueblo clowns are doing a spiritual job: letting us know how we look in a sacred view. Big Brother, now he wants to know what we're up to so he can use the information for himself. Big Brother and the Hold Onto Faded Glory Co. Some of us believe that Janis figured it out. Maybe during a heavy trip. Maybe during a long bus ride. Maybe in a drunken haze of screwing and despair. However she got to the facts of the matter, she got there, and she went home. She went straight. She thought she could go back to innocence and ignorance. As though she had ever been either. Not her. Somehow, I don't know how, she had learned Beauty Way or Nightway Chant,† the *Yei Bei Chi*.‡ Imagine, all the way over at the Texas-Louisiana Border. It's clear she did, though. How else did she know the Blues? How else did she feel wind blowing, long before so many had a clue? A true-blue Country-and-Western girl, smart, open, alive—not pretty: beautiful beyond sight, and beyond words. I dunno.

Maybe she knew because that's what time it was. I thought so at the time, when I headed west, following Changing Woman.** Maybe that's who she was following too. I don't imagine she knew about the monster slayers, and how Killer of Alien Mon-

---

* Diné term for "the white man."
† Diné healing ceremonies.
‡ *Yei Bei Chi* is the Diné phrase for holy beings.
** A Diné deity, Changing Woman (Estsánatlehi) is the personification of the earth in all its stages. Changing Woman is associated with growth and regeneration.

sters and his sidekick Child of Water* had long ago destroyed them all. But then again, it seems to me that they slipped back. Maybe through the cracks around the Grand Canyon or the Barrancas down south in Mexico. Maybe even through the caverns and tunnels in the Mohave and under L.A. Or maybe she did know, maybe I did too. Maybe that's what we were aiming for. The new war between the good gods and the old monsters. One thing I know is that you never know. The thing about knowing is once you've salted its tail it never lets go. And you can't either. Can't forget what you saw, what you heard, what you know. Can't remember and don't dare remember. You know you're dead if you do.

I'd heard Green Eggs and Spam was around, but hadn't run into him. It'd been years, and there wasn't much love lost between us to begin with. I suspected he'd come back to put an end to the spirit that still hung around the area, borne on breezes from the Marin County Coast, fine-sprayed on trees and grass and walls by the fog that piled over the hills and gathered the hollows to its soft, old woman tits. I think he knew she was still around, and it was up to him to put a lid on it, on her. But who was gonna forget "Me and Bobby McGee"? Who could forget "Buried Alive in the Blues"? Well, ok. Skinwalker could. But that's because he never heard them. Not really.

Then last night I decided to drop by one of the clubs where I hang, and there he was. Up on stage trying to rock and roll. Trying to look golden and sleek but looking sloppy and dingy, looking like an aging good ol' boy, belly hanging so heavy over his jeans you couldn't see his belt buckle. His band was composed of some younger dudes, trying to make up to the old dude, and several women who sang back-up. One or two did numbers with him, and I could see that they were hot for his attention. You know how it is—life's tough in the business for chicks, and one of the few ways to get a leg up was through a connection. He'd have been a haul, only he was him. From his point of view, the only thing that was gonna get hauled was his ashes, aaii! Not that they could see it. They were too young, couldn't remember what it'd been like in the years before, when the scene was young and shiny, full of rage and something that felt alive, like a wild horse, a herd of them, loping across the plains. It was that feeling that got me, I think. That and a kind of restlessness, wanting what was bright and modern, hip. Pulled me off the reservation like an iron bit's pulled by a magnet. I guess riding to the squaw dances† out in the mesas somewhere under the black sky and billion stars seemed tame. You know, the wind was always blowing dust, and it was either too hot or freezing. Winters, the cattle would be out there freezing, no way to get feed to them, and the sheep were sheep. Bad-smelling, stupid. Their wool not worth the labor of grazing them. It was like I could see the lights of L.A. from as far away as Greasewood, and the neons, the city streets, the lighted store windows, the parties I imagined when I sat out in the blazing sun with nothing to look at but miles of empty mesa land, infinities of July hot sky. There wasn't much

* Key figures in Diné myth.
† Informal social dances hosted and attended by Natives from various nations.

doing on the Rez,* only hauling water sixty, seventy miles, broken axles, trucks stuck deep in the mud, mutton stew and the women smelling like rancid mutton fat.

Guess I wasn't into that old-time religion—which for us is the Beauty Way. Me, I couldn't wait to head out to California, to where it was happening, in the fog upon L.A., or in the City where everything was at. It was the Summer of Love, and all those *bilagáana* were trying to go native, fringe and face paint, altered states and a kind of music the world had never heard. I bet it blew old Raff's mind far, far away. The way I grew up, listening to stories my uncles told about the big world, I'd never had a lot of use for life on the Rez. Life sounded so much more exciting off the Rez to a younger like me. One of my uncles had been in Korea, and him and his buddies would hang out sometimes, smoking and drinking Thunderbird, talking about the winters in Korea, the cold, the mud. They thought the Koreans looked like Navajos, used to call it The Old Country and laugh. They'd seen some times, and one of 'em had gotten taken prisoner. He'd somehow escaped, and walked across the country until he got to the coast. No one questioned him—*Diné*, Korean—who knew? He said he never talked, just kept his head down and walked. We know how to do that, walk from prison. It's in our blood, you might say.

Another uncle, a Big Clan uncle—that's the mother side—had been in the War, in the Pacific. He'd been one of the famous Navajo Code Talkers. Man, the stories they used to tell, laughing about how they'd fooled the Japs. They spoke Navajo, but it was a special one, something that had been an old way of talking to each other earlier, maybe at Redondo, Fort Sumner, or something. See, that way if anyone figured that some GIs were Indian, and even that they were Navajo and talked *Dinetah*, even so they'd have to know the slang version these guys knew.

My mother had a spread out by Greasewood, near the Joint Abuse area†—aaiii!— and it was always dry there. We had a drought that went on for decades, maybe since the People had been hauled off to the Colorado border in the nineteenth century and left to die. A lot did, but plenty survived. They walked home, singing a walking song. It goes sort of "I am alive. I am walking." Good song. Just because the human world around you wants you dead, you don't have to obey them.

My mother and my grandmother wanted me to go to college. The Council was making money available, and so was the BIA,‡ and since our side was in office over in Shiprock, I got funds to go to school. I went to Flagstaff, not too far from home, geographically. In other ways it was another world. But I wanted to go even farther.

---

* "Rez" is a slang term for reservation.

† Joint Abuse area is a pun on Joint Use Area, a site that was designated by the federal government as a "joint use area" for both Navajo (Diné) and Hopi nations, but which has been a source of serious conflict between the two peoples.

‡ "Council" refers to Tribal Council. BIA is the Bureau of Indian Affairs.

I was always singing that walking song. Then, one time someone in the dorm was playing some sides, some stuff like I'd never heard. It was the sound, maybe, or the wind. I think it was more like a dawn wind, and it was blowing out of the west. I just had to go. I figured I could walk there if I had to. One of my friends up at boarding school in Colorado where I went for a couple years had run away. The place was a dump, and they were giving us half-rotten meat, potatoes, maybe some canned green beans. Kids kept getting sick, and there wasn't a lot you could do about it. The superintendent was taking money the government sent for food, medicine, blankets and stuff, and pocketing it. We got fed on what little he had to spend, and forget our health. Fewer Navajos, fewer nits I imagine was their point of view. You know, like the old white general or whatever said when one of his officers questioned the order to kill the babies: "Nits breed lice," he said. And that's an order. Ten little, nine little, eight little Navajos. They wish! To some kids, it seemed like walking home, even over the mountains with the possibility of getting lost, falling down a ravine, freezing to death, getting attacked by bears—or worse—was better than staying put to die. One of the guys never made it home. They said he'd been attacked by wolves and killed. But then a lot of kids never graduated. They got sent home in boxes. Like Janis did, in the end. Maybe she decided that a powerful dose, over and out, was better than staying put in too muchness. She died, and the whole scene turned ugly. Maybe she knew it would.

Or maybe her dying started the downward spiral that sent the Summer of Love swirling down to summers of organized crime and drug wars. Or wars ON drugs, which is probably more of the same ol' thing. Maybe she got the idea of dying as a way out from old Lenny Bruce, the badmouth comic. Well, not a comic, not really. Like Janis he was a sacred clown. And at some level I think they both knew it. But sacred clowns in the scene are tragic figures. They gotta die so everyone else can boogie.

Back then, I used to wish I had learned sand painting and the old chantways. They were for healing, you know. The main one, Beautyway, the mother chant, was given to the *Diné* by two girls who got stolen by some monsters masquerading as handsome young hunks. They were both shapeshifters, skinwalkers. Not good, not where I come from. They hang out around cemeteries and battlefields. And, I guess, crack dens and bars. Maybe they even hang out in trendy hi-ho coffee bars. Who knows? Maybe she dropped by the same coffee bar in L.A. the night she died that Lenny had dropped in for a cup of joe the night, four years before that, he died.

Did you know that, to us, four is a sacred number? Four and seven. Hanta Virus strikes about every four years, and for sure there will be a big hit every seven. That's what the *hatali** say, and they know. The thing about rain is it comes pretty good every four and even better every seven years. And rain makes the pine trees have lots of babies. And mice eat pine nuts. And with so much food, they have lots and lots of

---

* *Hatali* is a Diné term for the shaman or chanter of a healing ceremony.

babies that survive and hang out in woodpiles and storerooms. Like the ones at the old armaments depot at Fort Wingate in Arizona, just a few miles from where the first victims of the killer virus died, around '93 or '94. Those traditionals also say that the Hanta Virus hit so hard because young people do dumb things, dangerous things. Like hanging out in graveyards with corpses. Like watching horror movies on TV. *The Amityville Horror. The Exorcist. Psycho. Nightmare on Elm Street. Tales from the Crypt!* See what the Singers mean? They say that these shows make us open to the Uglies. Stuff no good heart should get near. I never knew if they were right about it, but when you get to thinking about it, and what happens when a human with a good heart crosses Ugly Street, you gotta wonder. Hanta Virus is a relative of Ebola Virus; you know, the one that eats flesh. Like shapeshifters do, like the Undead.

Old Lenny died in his place up in the Hollywood Hills. You know, where the sign is that we see in movies and TV shows so we know where we are. What hardly anyone knows is that those hills are one of the old sacred places. You can still feel it, the power or whatever. The vortex, they call those places in the New Age press. We had names for them, you know, all the tribes did, and maybe vortex is as good a word as any. A vortex when it's caught its breath is a whirlwind. And where I come from we called those *chindi*, dust devils. They weren't nice. Sort of connected to skinwalkers and their kind, the undead kind. *Chindi* are the ones who died but didn't get over to the west. They get stuck, see, and they are caught between worlds. Sort of like a lost Navajo who can't live there and can't live here. Sort of like ladies who sing the blues, which is the color you turn when you freeze, when you don't get enough oxygen. Once I saw a guy with pneumonia. He had sort of olive skin, not too dark, and they were wheeling him into the emergency room where I was waiting for a friend. Man, that dude's skin was black from no air. But not the Hollywood Hills. Those spirits there are okay. Sad? Amused? Hard to know with those guys. You can feel them up there though. Mellow. I figure that Lenny got the news early. He died during the summer following the Summer of Love. Or that's what it was called up north here. Maybe the L.A. fog was ahead of the game, knew something it hadn't yet shared with its northern relative. He o.d.'d, or that's what they put out. Actually they don't know what he died of, there in his house in the hills.

One of his obituaries said he died of an overdose of police—or of police state, I'd say. He died because he knew, and the knowing ate at him, ate him alive. I think a lot of power minds wanted him and his kind dead. Evidently, he, like too many others known and unknown, obliged. He should have left the saltshaker on the table, aaiii! Maybe someday soon they'll have signs out everywhere saying "Surgeon General's Warning: Knowledge Kills." Or on salt cartons and saltshakers. You know, come to think of it, bet there were shapeshifters or that kind in some of the clubs he played. Some of those places, you're paying attention, give you some spine tingles. I wasn't ever much on traditional stuff, you know. But I saw some things, growing up, back staying on the Rez over the years, I think what the old men, the *hatali*, say about these things is true. Even in the cities, maybe especially in the cities, because no one cares about them. Most people don't think about a city at all, even when they live in it. Or if they do, they think depressing and angry things. That's what makes it bad, a city. Puts them far, far from Beautyway. It's not, you know, that living out there makes you noble or anything! Far from it. It's not that city people are more violent or more disconnected or stories suburban folk tell themselves about someplace they've never been are so off-the-wall, not really.

But out there away from cities and even large towns, there aren't so many people. Not so many ugly thoughts. That's the thing. Of course, the modern ways, the cynical, the ugly, the ratty, they all come out there too. The ugly—that's the other one, the one that's not Beautyway—is like smog, dirty, dying air. It's the real reason for all the pollution, or that's what the old timers say. Even the women, and if they say it, you know it's real. Dead and dying air, dead and dying water, dead and dying earth—Whoa! That's about living in a corpse. Which is what skinwalkers do. Which is why they like places where half-dead and the ones who prey on half-dead hang out. Bars, clubs, coffeehouses, crash pads, crank houses. Opium dens. Places Lenny used to play. Places like the Coffee Gallery in North Beach, near where he lived until he went down to L.A., places where Janis sang, before the Summer of Love and Monterey, the Hill King, as it's named in English.

That's where I met Janis. In The Coffee Gallery. On Grant just above Broadway, and Columbus, up from Vesuvio's and City Lights.* North Beach was where the San Francisco Rolling Renaissance, the Beat response to a brave new nuclear fission vision, got its initial push. North Beach was where the real new world burst into full flame. That's the neighborhood where Chinatown and Italian Town collide. Their energies leave a kind of no man's land strung with strip joints and cross-dressing shows. For decades, Carol Doda's big mamma boobs hung over Broadway, Mom gone mad. Playboy Club's around there, and a Greek place where wanna be Salomes dance the Dance of the Seven Veils two times a night and three on Saturday. No one here knows it, but the dancing girls in the Taverna are way too skinny. A real Arabian dancer is full-bodied, full-bellied. Like the Navajo women in R. C. Gorman paintings. There was a Purple Onion there. There was a Purple Onion everywhere. I used to hang out and groove on the poetry, the nuts that read it, the bongos that beat it, groove on the jazz, the blues, the smoky, alcohol-fumed fog-damp air. No one paid much attention to a Navajo cat—they thought I was Chinese or Samoan or something. They were too blasted or too stoned to notice much of anything, truth was. One night I was hanging in the front room, next to the bar, listening to the dice box slam down on the bar as dudes smashed dice for drinks. Every now and then the bartender would come around the bar and throw beer bottles into the barrel kept under the bar for bottles. He took delight in smashing them one by one, splinters all going into the barrel. His aim was good. Maybe he never got as drunk as we did.

---

* Vesuvio's is a well-known bar and City Lights is a well-known bookstore in North Beach (known as Little Italy), nestled on the northern tip of San Francisco's Chinatown. Both are associated with the Beat poets.

I had a pitcher and was sitting there looking stoic, thinking about chicks and the Rez, thinking maybe I oughta go home. I'd heard that they were having a sing for one of my relatives who had been really sick. But hitching all the way to Lukachukai seemed like an eternal trip. I knew a bunch of riding songs, "I am Turquoise Woman's Son" type songs, but they didn't go so well in eighteen-wheelers as on horseback. I was getting pretty blasted, and then there was this chick, she had a really cool grin, and she was leaning over peering down at me. Probably because Sunshine, who was waiting tables there for a while, had been stopping to rap with me between tables. I had the idea that the woman had come in to the Gallery because Sunshine worked there. They seemed to know each other, anyway.

Unlike Sunshine who was into the hippie and hooker look, this woman was wearing ripped jeans and some kind of scruffy shirt and of course a sweater. It was July and in those days summers in the City were as cold as winters out at Greasewood. She asked if she could have some of my pitcher, and I was happy to nod, albeit stoically. She sat down and grinned at me. She was high on being in the City she said. She'd hitched up here and it was her first time and it was cool. I could hear Texas in her voice, but I already knew she was from somewhere around home. The way she dressed, the way she drank. Reminded me of home. There was a quality about the look in her eyes. Something in the way she talked, just out there. She was quiet spoken, but I could tell she was cool. She was like some Navajo women, one of the ones who liked to party and to ride hell bent for leather across the Rez. She knew how to laugh, and what was funny, what was crap. She had a compact body, like a Pueblo woman. A lot of the women around Greasewood were built like that. All those Pueblo men, we used to say, always wanting kids with Navajo women, aaaiii! After we finished off the pitcher and I got another one, she stuck out her hand. "I'm Janis," she said.

"Ja-Nice?" I punned. "Like, Yah-nice?"

She gave a small grin. "Nope. J.A.N.I.S." She spelled it.

"Oh," I nodded. "Like the Greek god with faces going two ways." Putting her on.

She nodded. "Maybe that's it."

"I'm Joseph Joe," I said. "They call me Joe."

She picked up her glass and drained it before responding, "Hey, Joe-Joe," and grinned.

We sat and watched the action for a while, not talking. She was in constant motion, lifting her glass and putting it down, watching it make wet rings on the light wood table, plucking at the fringed holes in the thigh of her jeans, poking her finger into one particular hole and pulling it out repeatedly. She wasn't being seductive, and she didn't seem nervous. I decided she was shy, and probably jazzed on something more than beer. After a while she shrugged her shoulders and inhaled. "Drink up, why don't you," she said. "Let's blow this joint."

We split. Walking to my place in the cold fog, the air filled with whatever it was that filled it back in those liminal times. The whole country was in interstitial space, or if not the country, then parts of it. Like the Coast, and the North Atlantic seaboard. Mostly us, though, way out there in the Vortex. It was a cosmic tornado, a *chindi* that was the mother of all *chindi.*

We walked to my place in the Tenderloin, just off Powell. I had a room in a residence hotel. Not much, but what the hey. It wasn't home, but nothing off the Rez is. I had a record player, some 78s and 45s, and I set a stack on to play while we talked, or whatever. I had on some John Lee Hooker, some Coltrane, some Miles, a little Bessie Smith.

Janis told about how she only liked to sing the blues. "It's my LIFE, man," she said. She said she had been singing some country and some folk, but it wasn't really her scene. She got really into Bessie, I mean, like intent. When I put on a 33 album I had of Smith, she didn't talk, she hardly breathed. Just kept pullin' on the Coors I gave her, and stared at the black disc going round and round. Like in a trance, but more animated. Like, blown away. Then the record changed to some hard-core boogie and so did we. Whoo! What a night. She seemed to be having a great time. No shy retiring Southern Belle Janis, but a red-hot mama. Only thing she got pissed, then sad, because I just kept banging and banging. "Christ, Man," she finally exploded. "Why don't you get off, for godsakes!" So I got off her, but that wasn't what she meant, I guess. She started crying and hitting me. Then she got up and got some more beer and sat looking out the window for a long time. I don't know what happened. After a while I gave up and went to sleep.

I guess I should have told her then that it was an Indian thing, the eternal hard-on, the cosmic dick. But I didn't know it then, and wouldn't have been able to say anything anyway, even if I had. I mean, I thought all the guys went on and on. It wasn't till a couple of years or so after her death that I ran across a hilarious letter in Dear Abby from some Anglo dude who wanted to know how to contact Russell Means* or someone at the BIA about Indian men's sexual prowess. Seems his girl was having an affair on the side with some Indian guy from Oklahoma and she'd told the Anglo guy that her Indian lover could go for hours, which she LIKED. Poor dude, he wanted to talk to someone, to some Native guy to find out the secret. He thought maybe we had some drug or meditation or heap big medicine that made us undeflatable! I can tell you from personal knowledge, it sure wasn't Viagra! Hah. We laughed about that column for years. I even sent a copy of it to my uncle out at Chinle. Thought he had some particular information to impart to the poor white guys—a lovelorn column for wannabe hard-ons! AAIII!! Now I think about it, someone should have told the poor dude to pray to Kokopelli, the humpback horny god. You know, they show him all sweet and cute, sort of like a beetle version of Bambi. But he lost his dick only after Old Man Missionary and the tourist trap industry got to him. Now he's a *bilagáana.* Whitewashed, cloroxed, calcimined.

---

* Russell Means is one of the founders of and activists in the American Indian Movement (AIM).

Happily, the next day, Janis was full of beans again. She wanted to go out, see the sights. "Let's take the cable car," she said. "Let's go to City Lights and get some cool books. Let's go to Chinatown and get exotic eats. Let's cruise the scene."

It was early afternoon by that time, and as I recall the sky was bright and the sea breeze was blowing wild. It was my favorite kind of day, and I was glad to get out into it. We hooked a cable car at the bottom of Taylor and Powell and soared over the hill. She jumped off at Chinatown, me right behind, and we zigzagged our way through the crowds of Chinese out shopping. She was wowed by the live ducks, chickens, and fish for sale. She said she had only had chop suey in Port Arthur where she was from, so we got some pork fried rice and dim sum. Then we decided to head for North Beach, but first I had an idea. She was dressed like somebody from L.A. and while it was usually summertime down there, it was always winter in the City by the Bay. I led her back downtown to Mission and took her into a secondhand store I went to sometimes. Going right to the back I found what I was looking for. A sheepskin-lined jean jacket. Just like one of my brothers had. I paid for it, and gave it to her. She was stoked. "Wow, cool, man," she kept saying, posing in windows, trying herself out for herself as we headed back over to North Beach. Well, anyway, we hung out that day and went to some of the bars that night. She got some books at City Lights, got wired on espresso at Vesuvio's, scored some speed outside the Chelsea where we got some fish and chips wrapped in newspaper and drenched in malt vinegar, just like on Carnaby Street in London.

I lost track of her in Coffee and Confusion, but that was groovy, because I caught a show with Lenny Bruce at the Coffee Gallery and got stoned again and wound up crashing somewhere I don't remember. It was like that, then. I was like that, we were all like that, we who were being carried on that big wind of changing times and new worlds, growing like Topsy in *Uncle Tom's Cabin*. I don't think anyone I knew at the time, either in the city or back home, was ever straight. Not for nearly ten years, anyway. None of us knew what was going on, but we all knew something was, and some of us—maybe all of us—knew when it was over. I knew the day that I heard that Jimi Hendrix was dead. DWB, as they say now: Dead While Black. Then, a couple months later, Janis, the Pearl of Great Price.

I hadn't seen her up close and personal in all those years since our encounter in '61. I went back to the Rez that summer, and went back to college for a while, this time I transferred to San Francisco State. I was still there in time for the riots. That was when the Panthers or some of the protesters stepped on the petunia beds outside BSS. BSS was a good name for the building, although in the aftermath of the protests it became the home of Ethnic Studies, which included Native American, then American Indian, Studies. You know, it was quite a decade, that one. It went from the day they killed Marilyn Monroe until they killed Janis Joplin, about eight years. About eighty centuries, truth be known.

Who did, you ask? Who killed them? I'm not sure who sowed the wind, but of those who tried to cross the incandescent vortex some celebrities, and a lot known only to their communities, inherited the whirlwind. Wind causes fire to heat up and heat up, causes a firestorm, the oxygen does it, gets hotter and hotter, until if you're in the center of it the oxygen gets sucked out of you and you're dead before you can burn. That's what happened to Janis. The fires of change and winds of revolution took our breaths away, took hers. Blowing as hot as she was, it's no wonder she went incandescent in the end. I can still hear her singing in the wind, sometimes, burning alive in the blues.

I don't exactly know all of what went on, what went into those times, to tell you the truth. But, however, the *hatali* know something about it, I'll lay you odds. All I can say for sure, from personal experience, is to echo de Maupassant in *Le Horla*: it was as if an invisible being from an invisible empire had clutched the nation by the throat, and people were dying. Only it wasn't exactly invisible, not if you knew how to see under the sheets. The wind isn't visible, exactly, but when your hair ruffles and your body is almost tossed about in a gale, you sure as heck know something's going on. Right? That wind doesn't recognize human-decreed borders: that's what all the celebrity dead had in common. Janis and Marilyn—they were the gender case: they were about women being sexy, being real, being alive, and that wouldn't do. Not in a world that hates life more than it fears death. Not in a world run by the chronically undead. Hey, there's a name for a rocka-boogie-blues band, aaaiii! See, both of those women thought sexy was, well, sexy, and that sexy was about fun, about personal power, and being alive and well in America. Those women, Janis, Marilyn, so many more were killed because they were alive and kicking, and women aren't allowed to do that in Old Man Missionary's world order. Like fags: you know, queer men don't get slaughtered because straights hate homosexuals. They get iced because The Preacher doesn't like women. Or more to the point, because he doesn't like Female. No way, José. Not alive and sexy, screaming and rasping like a power saw gone mad. Not alive and wiggling and singing "Happy Birthday, Mr. President." Not swaying around the circle-tiered skirt swaying hypnotically in time to the drum, firelight playing on the velveteen shirts, the black hair, the earthtone skin of the women at Squaw Dance.

Why shouldn't people like that be picked off by any means necessary, the quicker the better? Why shouldn't a whole earth be poisoned and paved to make it hold still, be quiet, behave, submit? But the boys in the band, the boys in the studio, the boys in the chair, the boys in the pulpit hate whatever's alive, truly, really alive. They killed god, didn't they? They worship god nailed to a cross, dead, forever and ever unable to move. The divine undead. Here's what's really gonna get you killed: crossing boundaries, busting borders, re-making a world they gotta have all sewn up. Like me. A Navajo roadie making time with *bilagáana* celebs. Living in San Rafael, hanging out in a coffeehouse. Only, I'm not dead. Yet. Maybe because I was raised on the Rez. That's where a person always knows which way the wind blows, and the truth of skinwalkers, and devil winds.

Out there where the ancient stars burn cold, and the ancient gods still come for a visit, we burn our lives away. It's a different kind of fire, uranium mines, radiation, coal mines and gasification plants. We try and try to put out the fires or at least slow them down with booze and dancing, with clan fighting and making mad love. There the sun burns high and long everyday, and nothing is hidden by fogbanks or mist. It's hard and bitter a lot of the time, and we are hard and bitter too. But when there's a squaw dance beneath the wheeling stars and the fires burn around the dance ground, and the women take the men out to dance, well, it doesn't get much better than that. You can watch Morning Star rise with the sun, maybe go home with a pretty woman, ride like Turquoise Woman's son across the land. No *chindis* to trouble the earth, nothing but Beauty, All Around. Too bad the *chindi* made its swath there as well as through more urban neighborhoods.

So that's why I find myself in the Royal, brooding over what I can't change when I could be out there in the wilds of home. Maybe I'm hooked on waiting for Gabriel's horn to join Miles and Coltrane in the mother of all riffs. Or seeing if Raphael can heal what is so wounded, so lost, so far away from home. I think that for Janis like for so many of us in this spirit-starved time, glamour was like oxygen. We have to have it to live, but in the end it burns us out. After all the years, it seems to me that it wasn't drugs, it wasn't the scene. It wasn't the soul-sucking, life-eating skinwalkers who stalk the Bay as they stalked L.A. those fateful nights, all those years ago.

It was the time that did her in, did us all in, I guess. A time that swirled madly for a while on the plain of our lives then disappeared.

Chindi. The white-hot blues.

Aho.

Deer Woman

Paula Gunn Allen

Two young men were out snagging* one afternoon. They rode around in their pickup, their Ind'in Cadillac, cruising up this road and down that one through steamy green countryside, stopping by friends' places here and there to lift a few beers. The day was sultry and searing as summer days in Oklahoma get, hot as a sweat lodge.

Long after dark they stopped at a tavern twenty or thirty miles outside of Anadarko, and joined some skins† gathered around several tables. After the muggy heat outside, the slowly turning fan inside felt cool. When they'd been there awhile, one of the men at their table asked them if they were headed to the stomp dance.‡ "Sure," they said, though truth to tell, they hadn't known there was a stomp dance that night in the area. The three headed out to the pickup.

They drove for some distance along narrow country roads, turning occasionally at unmarked crossings, bumping across cattle guards, until at length they saw the light of the bonfire, several unshaded lights hanging from small huts that ringed the danceground, and headlights from a couple of parking cars.

They pulled into a spot in the midst of a new Winnebago, a Dodge van, two Toyotas, and a small herd of more battered models, and made their way to the danceground. The dance was going strong, and the sound of turtle shell and aluminum can rattles and singing, mixed with occasional laughter and bits of talk, reached their ears.

"All right!" Ray, the taller and heavier of the two exclaimed, slapping his buddy's raised hand in glee.

---

* A slang term that means cruising to pick up women.

† "Skins" is slang for "redskins," which is slang for Indians.

‡ The stomp dance originated with the Creek (Muscogee) people, but became a part of Western Cherokee cultural practice after the Trail of Tears and arrival in Oklahoma. At this time, the Cherokee Green Corn Ceremony has been replaced by the stomp dance, which is usually held during late August and early September.

"Gnarly!" his pal Jackie responded, and they grinned at each other in the unsteady light. Slapping the man who'd ridden along with them on the back, the taller one said, "Man, let's go find us some snags!"

They hung out all night, occasionally starting a conversation with one good-looking woman or another, but though the new brother who had accompanied them soon disappeared with a long-legged beauty named Lurine, the two anxious friends didn't score. They were not the sort to feel disheartened, though. They kept up their spirits, dancing well and singing even better. They didn't really care so much about snagging, but it gave them something to focus on while they filled the day and night with interesting activity. They were among their own, and they were satisfied with their lives and themselves.

Toward morning, though, Ray spotted two strikingly beautiful young women stepping onto the danceground. Their long hair flowed like black rivers down their backs. They were dressed out in traditional clothes, and something about them—something elusive—made Ray shiver with a feeling almost like recognition, and at the same time, like dread. "Who are they?" he asked his friend, but Jackie shrugged silently. Ray could see his eyes shining for a moment as the fire near them flared suddenly.

At the same moment, they both saw the young women looking at them out of the corners of their eyes as they danced modestly and almost gravely past. Jackie nudged Ray and let out a long, slow sigh. "All right," he said in a low, almost reverent voice. "All right!"

When the dance was ended, the young women made their way to where the two youths were standing, "Hey, dude," one of them said. "My friend and I need a ride to Anadarko, and they told us you were coming from there." As she said that she gestured with her chin over her left shoulder toward a vaguely visible group standing across the danceground.

"What's your friend's name?" Ray countered.

"Linda," the other woman said. "Hers is Junella."

"My friend's name's Jackie," Ray said, grinning. "When do you want to take off?"

"Whenever," Junella answered. She held his eyes with hers. "Where are you parked?"

They made their way to the pickup and got in. It was a tight fit, but nobody seemed to mind. Ray drove, backing the pickup carefully to thread among the haphazardly parked vehicles that had surrounded theirs while they were at the dance. As he did, he glanced down for a second, and thought he saw the feet of both women as deer hooves. Man, he thought. I gotta lay off the weed. He didn't remember he'd quit smoking it months before, and hadn't had a beer since they'd left the tavern hours before. The women tucked their feet under their bags, and in the darkness he didn't see them anymore. Besides, he had more soothing things on his mind.

They drove companionably for some time, joking around, telling a bit about themselves, their tastes in music, where they'd gone to school, when they'd graduated. Linda kept fiddling with the dial, reaching across Junella to get to the knob. Her taste seemed to run to hard-core country and western or what Ray privately thought of as "space" music.

Linda and Junella occasionally lapsed into what seemed like a private conversation, or joke; Ray couldn't be sure which. Then, as though remembering themselves, they'd laugh and engage the men in conversation again.

After they'd traveled for an hour or so, Linda suddenly pointed to a road that intersected the one they were on. "Take a left," she said, and Ray complied. He didn't even think about it, or protest that they were on the road to Anadarko already. A few hundred yards farther, she said, "Take a right." Again he complied, putting the brake on suddenly as he went into the turn, spilling Junella hard against him. He finished shifting quickly and put his arm around her. She leaned into him, saying nothing, and put her hand on his thigh.

The road they had turned onto soon became gravel, and by the time they'd gone less than a quarter of a mile, turned into hard-packed dirt. Ray could smell water, nearby. He saw some trees standing low on the horizon and realized it was coming light.

"Let's go to the water," Linda said. "Junella and I are kind of traditional, and we try to wash in fresh running water every morning."

"Yeah," Junella murmured. "We were raised by our mother's grandmother, and the old lady was real strict about some things. She always made sure we prayed to Long Man* every day. Hope it's okay."

Jackie and Ray climbed out of the truck, the women following. They made their way through the thickest of scrub oak and bushes and clambered down the short bank to the stream, the men leading the way. They stopped at the edge of the water, but the young women stepped right in, though still dressed in their dance clothes. They bent and splashed water on their faces, speaking the old tongue softly as they did so. The men removed their tennis shoes and followed suit, removing their caps and tucking them in the hip pockets of their jeans.

After a suitable silence, Junella pointed to the opposite bank with her uplifted chin. "See that path?" she asked the men. "I think it goes to our old house. Let's go up there and see."

"Yes," Linda said, "I thought it felt familiar around here. I bet it is our old place." When the women didn't move to cross the shallow river and go up the path, the men took the lead again. Ray briefly wondered at his untypical pliability, but banished the thought almost as it arose. He raised his head just as he reached the far bank and saw that the small trees and brush were backed by a stone bluff that rose steeply above them. As he tilted his head back to spot the top of the bluff, he had a flashing picture of the small round feet he'd thought he'd seen set against the floorboard of the truck. But as the image came into his mind, the sun rose brilliantly just over the bluff, and the thought faded as quickly as it had come, leaving him with a slightly dazed feeling and tingling that climbed rapidly up his spine. He put on his cap.

Jackie led the way through the thicket, walking as rapidly as the low branches would allow, bending almost double in places. Ray followed him, and the women

---

* In Cherokee lore, Long Man is a spirit being who controls rivers and streams.

came after. Shortly, they emerged from the trees onto a rocky area that ran along the foot of the bluff like a narrow path. When he reached it, Jackie stopped and waited while the others caught up. "Do you still think this is the old homestead?" he quipped. The women laughed sharply, then fell into animated conversation in the old language. Neither Ray nor Jackie could talk it, so they stood waiting, admiring the beauty of the morning, feeling the cool dawn air on their cheeks and the water still making their jeans cling to their ankles. At least their feet were dry, and so were the tennies they'd replaced after leaving the river.

After a few animated exchanges, the women started up the path, the men following. "She says it's this way," Linda said over her shoulder. "It can't be far." They trudged along for what seemed a long time, following the line of the bluff that seemed to grow even higher. After a time Junella turned into a narrow break in the rock and began to trudge up its gradual slope, which soon became a steep rise.

"I bet we're not going to Grandma's house," Jackie said in quiet tones to his friend.

"I didn't know this bluff was even here," Ray replied.

"It's not much farther," Junella said cheerfully. "What's the matter? You dudes out of shape or something?"

"Well, I used to say I'd walk a mile for a camel," Jackie said wryly, "but I didn't say anything about snags!" He and Ray laughed, perhaps more heartily than the joke warranted.

"This is the only time I've heard of Little Red Riding Hood leading the wolves to Grandma's," Ray muttered.

"Yah," Linda responded brightly. "And wait'll you see what I'm carrying in my basket of goodies." Both women laughed, the men abashedly joining in.

"Here's the little creek I was looking for," Junella said suddenly. "Let's walk in it for a while." Ray looked at Jackie quizzically.

"I don't want to walk in that," Jackie said quickly. "I just got dry from the last dip." The women were already in the water walking upstream.

"Not to worry," Junella said. "It's not wet; it's the path to the old house."

"Yeah, right," Ray mumbled, stepping into the water with a sigh. Jackie followed him, falling silent. But as they stepped into what they thought was a fast-running stream of water their feet touched down on soft grass. "Hey!" Ray exclaimed. "What's happening?" He stopped abruptly, and Jackie plowed into him.

"Watch it, man," the smaller man said. He brushed past Ray and made after the women, who were disappearing around a sharp turn.

Ray stood rooted a moment, then hurried after him. "Wait up," he called. His voice echoed loudly against the cliff.

As Ray turned the corner he saw Linda reaching upward along the cliff where a tall rock slab leaned against it. She grasped the edge of the slab and pulled. To the men's astonishment it swung open, for all the world like an ordinary door. The women stepped through.

Ray and Jackie regarded each other for long moments. Finally, Ray shrugged and Jackie gestured with his outspread arm at the opening in the cliff. They followed the women inside.

Within, they were greeted with an astonishing scene. Scores of people, perhaps upward of two hundred, stood or walked about a green land. Houses stood scattered in the near distance, and smoke arose from a few chimneys. There were tables spread under some large trees, sycamore or elm, Ray thought, and upon them, food in large quantities and tantalizing variety beckoned to the men. Suddenly aware they hadn't eaten since early the day before, they started forward. But before they'd taken more than a few steps, Linda and Junella took their arms and led them away from the feast toward the doorway of one of the houses. There sat a man who seemed ancient to the young men. His age wasn't so much in his hair, though it hung in waist-long white strands.

It wasn't even so much in his skin, wrinkled and weathered though it was beneath the tall-crowned hat he wore. It was just that he seemed to be age personified. He seemed to be older than the bluff, than the river, than even the sky.

Next to him lay two large mastiffs, their long, lean bodies relaxed, their heads raised, their eyes alert and full of intelligence. "So," the old one said to the women, "I see you've snagged two strong young men." He shot a half-amused glance at the young men's direction. "Go, get ready," he directed the women, and at his words they slipped into the house, closing the door softly behind themselves.

The young men stood uneasily beside the old man who, disregarding them completely, seemed lost in his own thoughts as he gazed steadily at some point directly before him.

After maybe half an hour had passed, the old man addressed the young men again. "It's a good thing you did," he mused, "following my nieces here. I wonder that you didn't give up or get lost along the way." He chuckled quietly as at a private joke. "Maybe you two are intelligent men." He turned his head suddenly and gave them an appraising look. Each of the young men shifted under that knowing gaze uncomfortably. From somewhere, the ground, the sky, they didn't feel sure, they heard thunder rumbling. "I have told everybody that they did well for themselves by bringing you here."

Seeing the surprised look on their faces, he smiled. "Yes, you didn't hear me, I know. I guess we talk different here than you're used to where you come from. Maybe you'll be here long enough to get used to it," he added. "That is, if you like my nieces well enough. We'll feed you soon," he said. "But first there are some games I want you to join in." He pointed with pursed lips in the direction of a low hill that rose just beyond the farthest dwelling. Again the thunder rumbled, louder than before.

A moment later the women appeared. Their long, flowing hair was gone, and their heads shone in the soft light that filled the area, allowing distant features to recede into its haze. The women wore soft clothing that completely covered their bodies, even their hands and feet. It seemed to be of a bright, gleaming cloth that reflected the light at the same intensity as their bald heads. Their dark eyes seemed huge and luminous against skin that somehow gave off a soft radiance. Seeing them, both men were nearly overcome with fear. They have no hair at all, Ray thought. Where is this place? He glanced over at Jackie, whose face mirrored his own unease. Jackie shook his head almost imperceptibly, slowly moving it from side to side in a gesture that seemed mournful, and at the same time, oddly resigned.

Linda and Junella moved to the young men, each taking the hand of one and drawing him toward the central area nearby. In a daze Ray and Jackie allowed themselves to be led into the center of the area ringed by heavily laden tables, barely aware that the old man had risen from his place and with his dogs was following behind them. They were joined by a number of other young men, all wearing caps like the ones Ray and Jackie wore. Two of the men carried bats, several wore gloves, and one was tossing a baseball in the air as he walked. Slowly the throng made their way past the tables and came to an open area where Jackie and Ray saw familiar shapes. They were bases, and the field that the soft light revealed to them was a baseball diamond.

The old man took his place behind first base, and one of the young men crouched before him as a loud peal of thunder crashed around them. "Play ball!" the old man shouted, and the men took up their places as the women retired to some benches at the edge of the field behind home plate where they sat.

The bewildered young men found their positions and the game was on. It was a hard-played game, lasting some time. At length, it reached a rowdy end, the team Jackie and Ray were on barely edging out the opposition in spite of a couple of questionable calls the old man made against them. Their victory was due in no small measure to a wiry young man's superb pitching. He'd pitched two no-hit innings and that had won them the game.

As they walked with the other players back toward the houses, the old man came up to them. Slapping each on the back a couple of times, he told them he thought they were good players. "Maybe that means you'll be ready for tomorrow's games," he said, watching Jackie sharply. "They're not what you're used to, I imagine, but you'll do all right."

They reached the tables and were helped to several large portions of food by people whose faces never seemed to come quite into focus but whose goodwill seemed unquestionable. They ate amid much laughter and good-natured joshing, only belatedly realizing that neither Linda nor Junella was among the revelers. Ray made his way to Jackie and asked him if he'd seen either woman. Replying in the negative, Jackie offered to go look around for them.

They agreed to make a quick search and rendezvous at the large tree near the old man's house. But after a fruitless hour or so Ray went to the front of the house and waited for his friend, who didn't come. At last, growing bored, he made his way back to the tables where a group had set up a drum and was singing lustily. A few of the younger people had formed a tight circle around the drummers and were slowly stepping around in it, their arms about each others' waists and shoulders. All right!

Ray thought, cheered. "49s."* He joined the circle between two women he hadn't seen before, who easily made way for him, and smoothly closed the circle about him again as each wrapped an arm around his waist. He forgot all about his friend.

When Ray awoke the sun was beating down on his head. He sat up, and realized he was lying near the river's edge, his legs in the thicket, his head and half-turned face unshielded from the sun. It was about a third of the way up in a clear sky. As he looked groggily around, he discovered Junella sitting quietly a few yards away on a large stone. "Hey," she said, smiling.

"How'd I get here?" Ray asked. He stood and stretched, surreptitiously feeling to see if everything worked. His memory seemed hesitant to return clearly, but he had half-formed impressions of a baseball game and eating and then the 49. He looked around. "Where's Jackie and, uh—"

"Linda?" Junella supplied as he paused.

"Yeah, Linda," he finished.

"Jackie is staying there," she told him calmly. She reached into her bag and brought out a man's wristwatch. "He said to give you this," she said, holding it out to him.

Ray felt suddenly dizzy. He swayed for a moment while strange images swept through him. Junella with no hair and that eerie light; the woman that was some pale tan but had spots or a pattern of soft gray dots that sort of fuzzed out at the edges to blend into the tan; the old man.

He took a step in her direction. "Hey," he began. "What the hell's—" but broke off. The rock where she sat was empty. On the ground next to it lay Jackie's watch.

When Ray told me the story, about fifteen months afterward, he had heard that Jackie had showed up at his folks' place. They lived out in the country, a mile or so beyond one of the numerous small towns that dot the Oklahoma landscape. The woman who told him about Jackie's return, Jackie's cousin Ruth Ann, said he had come home with a strange woman who was a real fox. At thirteen, Ruth Ann had developed an eye for good looks and thought herself quite a judge of women's appearance. They hadn't stayed long, he'd heard. Mainly they packed up some of Jackie's things and visited with his family. Ray had been in Tulsa and hadn't heard Jackie was back until later. None of their friends had seen him either. There had been a child with them, he said, maybe two years old, Ruth Ann had thought, because she could walk by herself.

"You know," Ray had said thoughtfully, turning a Calistoga slowly between his big hands, a gesture that made him seem very young and somehow vulnerable, "one

* 49s are social songs and dances associated with courting.

of my grandma's brothers, old Jess, used to talk about the little people* a lot. He used to tell stories about strange things happening around the countryside here. I never paid much attention. You know how it is. I just thought he was putting me on, or maybe he was pining away for the old days. He said that Deer Woman† would come to dances sometimes, and if you weren't careful she'd put her spell on you and take you inside the mountain to meet her uncle. He said her uncle was really Thunder, one of the old gods or supernaturals, whatever the traditionals call them."

He finished his drink in a couple of swallows and pushed away from the table we were sitting at. "I dunno," he said, and gave me a look that I still haven't forgotten, a look that was somehow wounded and yet with a kind of wild hope mixed in. "Maybe those old guys know something, eh?"

It was a few years before I saw him again. Then I ran into him unexpectedly in San Francisco a couple of years ago. We talked for a while, standing on the street near the Mission BART‡ station. He started to leave when my curiosity got the better of my manners. I asked if he'd ever found out what happened to Jackie.

Well, he said that he'd heard that Jackie came home off and on, but the woman— probably Linda, though he wasn't sure—was never with him. Then he'd heard that someone had run into Jackie, or a guy they thought was him, up in Seattle. He'd gone alcoholic. Later, they'd heard he'd died. "But you know," Ray said, "the weird thing is that he'd evidently been telling someone all about that time inside the mountain, and that he'd married her, and about some other stuff, stuff I guess he wasn't supposed to tell." Another guy down on his luck, he guessed. "Remember how I was telling you about my crazy uncle, the one who used to tell about Deer Woman? Until I heard about Jackie, I'd forgotten that the old man used to say that the ones who stayed there were never supposed to talk about it. If they did, they died in short order."

After that, there didn't seem to be much more to say. Last time I saw Ray, he was heading down the steps to catch BART. He was on his way to a meeting and he was running late.

---

* The Cherokee "Little People" (or *Yunwi Tsundi*) are very small (about knee-high) spiritual beings, similar to European fairies, but with long hair reaching to the ground. They live in caves or woods and spend a great deal of time making music (drumming) and dancing. They are usually good-hearted and helpful. They are invisible to humans unless they choose to be seen.

† Deer Woman, a familiar figure among the Native people of the Southeastern United States, is a spiritual being who takes the shape of a beautiful woman, renowned for luring men away from family and community.

‡ BART stands for the Bay Area Rapid Transit, a train in the San Francisco Bay Area.

Beth E. Brant
(1941–)

*"Whether it comes directly from the
storyteller's mouth and she writes it
down or someone writes it for her,
the story has to be told."*

Beth Brant, Introduction to *That's
What She Said: Contemporary
Poetry and Fiction by Native
American Women*

Turtle Gal

Beth E. Brant

Sue Linn's mama was an Indian. She never knew from where, only that Dolores wore a beaded bracelet: yellow, blue, and green beads woven into signs. Burnt out from alcohol and welfare, Dolores gave up late one afternoon, spoke to her daughter in an unknown language, and put the bracelet around her girl's skinny wrist where it flopped over her hand. She turned her face to the wall and died. November 4, 1968.

Sue Linn watched her mother die, knowing by instinct that it was better this way. Better for Dolores. But her child mind, her nine-year-old mind, had not yet thought of the possibilities or penalties that lay in wait for little girls with no mother. She thought of her friend, James William Newton, who lived across the hall. She went and got him. He walked Sue Linn back to the room where her mother lay dead.

"Lord, lord, lord, lord," the old man chanted as he paid his respects, covering the still-warm woman with the faded red spread. His tired eyes, weeping, looked down at the child standing so close to him. "Go get your things now, little gal. Bring everything you got. Your clothes, everything."

With his help, Sue Linn removed all traces of herself from the darkening apartment. James William made a last, quick search, then told the child to say good-bye to her mama. He waited in the hall, his face wrinkled and yellowish. His hand trembled as he reached into his pants pocket for his handkerchief, neatly folded. He shook the thin, white cloth and brought it to his eyes where he wiped the cry, then blew his nose.

Sue Linn stood beside the bed she and her mother had shared for as long as the girl could remember. She pulled the spread from her mother's face and looked intensely at Dolores. Dolores's face was quieter, younger looking. Her broad nose seemed somehow more delicate, and her dark lashes were like ink marks against her smooth, reddish cheek. Sue Linn felt a choking move from her stomach up through her heart, her lungs, her throat and mouth. With an intake of harsh breath, she took a lock of her mother's black hair in her small fist. She held on, squeezing hard, as if to pull some last piece of life from her mother. She let go, turned away, and closed the door behind her. James William was waiting, his arms ready to hold her, to protect her.

Together, they opened his door, walked into the room that was welcoming and waiting for their presence. African violets sat in a row along the windowsill, their purple and blue flowers shaking from the force of the door being closed. Sue Linn went to touch the fuzzy heart leaves, wondering once again what magic the old man carried in him to grow these queer, exotic plants in the middle of a tired, dirty street.

James William put aside the bag filled with Sue Linn's belongings and told the child to sit in his chair while he went to call the ambulance. "Don't answer the door. Don't make no sounds. Sit quiet, little gal, and I be's back in a wink." He hugged the child and went out the door.

Sue Linn sat on James William's favorite chair, a gold brocade throne with arms that curved into high, wide wings. She stared out the window. She looked past the violets, past the ivy hanging in a pot attached to threads, dangling fresh and alive in front of the glass. She looked onto the street, the avenue that held similar apartment buildings, large and grey. Some had windows knocked out, some had windows made bright by plastic flowers. Some had windows decorated with a cross and Jesus Is My Rock painted on from the inside. The Salvation Army complex stood low and squat, the lights beginning to be turned on, bringing a softening sheen to the beige cement. The air was cold, the people on the street pulling their coats and jackets closer to their bodies as they walked, hunched over in struggle past the Chinese restaurants, the grocery, the bars, the apartments. Cars made noise—the noises of rust, of exhaust pipes ready to fall off, of horns applied with angry hands. Buses were unloading people, doors opening to expel faces and bodies of many shapes and colors. The avenue seemed to wander forever in a road of cement, tall buildings, people, machines, eventually stopping downtown, caught up in another tangle of streets and boulevards.

James William walked down the three flights of stairs to the payphone in the lobby. He called the operator to report the dead woman, walked back up the three flights of stairs, his thoughts jumping and beating against his brain as his heart lurched and skipped from the climb. When he entered his room the child turned to look at him. "They be here soon, child. Now we not lettin' on you here with me. We be very quiet. We lets them medical peoples take care a things. We don't say one word. Ummhmm, we don't say a word."

He came to the window and watched for the ambulance that eventually came screaming to the curb. Two white men, their faces harried and nervous, got out of the ambulance and entered the building. A police car followed. The cops went into the building where the super was arguing with the medics.

"I don't know nothin' about a dead woman! Who called you? Who did you say she was?"

The officers hurried things along, the super angrily getting out his keys. "If it's 3D, then it's that Indian. She's all the time drinkin' and carryin' on. Her and that sneaky, slant-eyed kid ain't nothin' but trouble. Who did you say called in? Nobody let on to me!"

On the third floor, cops, medics, and super formed a phalanx around the door to 3D. Knocking and getting no answer, they unlocked the door and entered the room. Up and down the hall, doors were opened in cracks. Eyes looked out, gathering information that would be hoarded and thought about, then forgotten.

"Anybody know this woman?" the cops shouted in the hall.

Doors closed. Silence answered. One of the cops pounded on a door. A very old woman opened it, a sliver of light behind her.

"Do you know this woman in 3D? When was the last time you saw her?"

Her dark brown face resettled its lines as she spoke. "I don't know her. She was an Injun lady. One a them Injuns from out west, I guess. I don' know nothin'.."

The officer waved his hand in disgust. He and his partner started down the stairs, their heavy black shoes scratching the steps, the leather of their holsters squeaking as they rubbed against the guns.

James William stood, his ear pressed to the door. Sue Linn continued to stare out the window. There were sounds of feet moving away, sounds of hard breathing as the body of Dolores was carried down the three flights of stairs and into the cold November twilight.

James William Newton turned from the door. He was eighty years old. He was a singer of the blues. He was the prince of Georgia Blues. He was Sweet William. He went to the kitchenette and put the kettle on to boil. He moved slowly to the cupboard, taking out a pot and settling it on the tiny stove. Everything surrounding Sweet William was small and tiny like him. The table, covered in blue oilcloth, was just big enough for two. Little wooden chairs were drawn tight to the edge of the table, waiting for his hands to arrange the seating. The one window in the kitchenette was hung with starched white curtains trimmed in royal blue rickrack. A single wall was papered in teapots and kettles, red and blue splashed on a yellow background. The wall was faded from age but still looked cheerful and surprising. A cupboard painted white held thick dishes and the food. Rice, red beans, spices, cornmeal, salt, honey, and sugar. A cardboard box placed on the cracked yellow linoleum contained potatoes and onions, the papery skins sometimes falling to the floor, coming to rest by the broom and dustpan leaning against the teapot wall.

On the first night of Sue Linn's new life, she watched Sweet William work in the kitchen, her eyes following his round body as he walked the few steps across the linoleum, taking leaves out of a tin box, placing them in a brown pot, pouring the whistling water over the tea. He replaced the lid on the teapot, removed a tea cozy from a hook, and placed this over the pot. The child, ever fascinated by Sweet William's routine, his fussy kitchen work, his hands dusting and straightening, felt comforted by the familiar activity. Often James William made supper for the girl. Cooking up the rice, a towel wrapped around his fat waist, mashing the potatoes, adding canned milk and butter. Sometimes, there was ham hocks or chitlins. The hot, pungent dishes were magic, made from Sweet William's hands and the air and salt.

James William sang quietly as he busied himself with the pot of soup. His eyes grabbed quick looks toward the chair and the thin, golden child who watched him with blank eyes. Little folds of flesh covered her eyelids which rapidly opened and closed. Sitting like that, so still, her eyes blinking, blinking, she reminded the old man of a turtle he'd seen a long time ago, home in Georgia.

Poking around in the marsh, he and his friends had found a spotted turtle upside-down, struggling to put itself right. He had picked up the turtle and looked at its head, pulling in, eyefolds closing over the eyes in panic, opening, closing, staring at him. He had set the turtle on its legs, where it continued on. The boys had laughed at the creature's slow journey. James William remembered the turtle, remembered his friends—the sweetness of them. Memories like this appeared in a haze. When they came to him, he clutched at them, holding onto each moment—afraid he would never see them again. He stood in the kitchenette and recalled the day of the turtle. He called forth the weather, so hot and lush, you could hold the air in your hand and feel it wet on your skin. He called forth the smells of the marsh—a green smell, a salty smell. He recalled the reeds, pulled from the mud and stuck between their lips, the taste of bitter grass mingling with another taste of sweet—like the stick of licorice his daddy had once brought him from town. He tried to call forth his friends, their names, their brown-and-tan colors, but the memory was fading. Yet, he remembered the black skin of Isaac, his best friend of all. Remembered when Isaac held his arm, the thin fingers spread out looking like molasses spilled against his own yellow, almost white-looking arm. Isaac.

"Isaac?"

Stirring the soup, he sang bits of song culled from memories of his mama, church, and memories of the band—Big Bill and the Brown Boys. Tunes spun from his lips. Notes and chords played in his throat, starting somewhere in his mind, trickling down through his scratchy voice box, coming out round, weeping, and full. Sweet William sang, his face shifting as he wove the music in and out of his body. His head moved and dipped. His shoulders jerked and shrugged to emphasize a word, a phrase. To Sue Linn, it was as pleasurable to watch Sweet William sing as it was to listen. His words and music were almost always the same. Words that came from a heartache, a home with no furniture.

"Lord, what I gonna do with this here child? Now listen up, girl. You gonna be my little gal. We be mama and little gal. We be a family. Ummhmm, anybody ask, you be mine. It ain't gonna be easy. Old James William here, he gots to think of some heavy talkin' to fool them peoples what snoopin' around here. Them government types. Yes ma'am, James William gots to think of some serious talk. Lord! Old man like myself with a child. A baby! I tells you, you know I never be's married. Least-wise, not no marriage like the government peoples thinks is right. Just me and Big Bill, movin' with that band. Me bein' a fool many a time over some sweet boy what talks with a lotta sugar but don' make no sense. But that Big Bill, he were some man. Always take me back, like I never did no wrong. Yes ma'am, I be a fool for a pretty boy. But I always got a little work. Workin' on them cars sometime. Child, I swear the metal in my blood! I still hear that noise. Whoo, it like to kill me! That noise, them cars hurryin' along the line, waitin' for a screw here, a jab there. But I worked it. I worked it. Yes I did. And me and Big Bill, we make a home. Yes we did. We did. And before the sugar and the high bloods get him, we make a home. We was a family, that fine man and me. Ummhmmm.

"Now look at her sit there with them turtle eyes. She can't talk. Now listen here, baby. You mama at rest now, bless her sorry little life. You got you another kinda mama now. I take care my baby. You mama so peaceful now. With angels and the In-dians. She make that transition over, ummhmm. She be happy. Now, I gots to make this here turtle gal happy. You gots to cry sometime, child. Honey lamb, you gots to cry! If you don' grieve and wail, it get all caught up in you, start to twist your inside so bad. Girl! It hurt not to cry. You listen to this old man. Sweet William, he know what he talkin' about."

I sing because I'm happy
I sing because I'm free
His eye is on the sparrow
And I know he watches me.

The old man began his song in a whisper. As he ladled out the soup into bowls, he switched from hymn to blues, the two fitting together like verse and chorus. He nodded his head toward the child, inviting her to sing with him. Sue Linn's thin voice joined James William's fat one.

Heaven's cryin', seem like the rain keep comin' down
Heaven's cryin', seem like the rain keep comin' down
That heaven don' let up
Since my baby left this mean ole town.

They sang together. They sang for Dolores. They sang for Big Bill. They sang for each other. Blues about being poor, being colored, being out of pocket. Blues about home—that sweet, hot, green-and-brown place. Home was a place where your mama was, waiting on a porch, or cooking up the greens. Home was where you were somebody. Your name was real, and the people knew your name and called you by that name. It was when you left that home that your name became an invisible thing. You got called new names—Nigger, Bitch, Whore, Shine, Boy. It was when you left that home you started to choke on your name and your breath and a new kind of blues was sung.

The old man came from the kitchen and picked the child up in his arms, set her on his lap in the brocade chair, covered them with his special afghan, and the two rocked and swayed.

"She like a bird, no weight on her at all, at all. I do likes a rock in this old chair. It help a person think and study on things what ails us. Yes ma'am, just a rockin' and a studying on them things."

Sue Linn's tears began. Soon she sobbed, the wails moving across the room, coming back in an echo. James William sang, crooned, wiped her eyes and his with the dry palms of his hands.

"My baby. My turtle gal. Lord, I remember my own mama's passin'.' It hurt so bad. She were a good woman, raisin' us ten kids. My daddy workin' his body to an early grave. It hurt when a mama die. Seem like they should always just go on bein' our mama. You mama, she try her best. She were a sad woman. She love you, little gal. And I loves you. We be a family now. Big Bill! You hears that? A family. Sue Linn Longboat and James William Newton. Now ain't they gonna look twict at this here family? I tell you. I tell you! It be alright, my baby girl. It be alright."

Sue Linn stopped crying as suddenly as she had started. Her thin face with the slanted eyes, small nose, and full lips subdued itself. "But Sweet William, I hear people talk about heaven. My mom didn't believe in it, but where will she go now? I don't know where she is. And sometimes... sometimes she said she wished I never was born."

The girl stared into the old man's face, trusting him to give her the answers. Trusting him to let her know why she ached so much, why she always felt alone and like a being who didn't belong on this earth. His skin was smooth, except for the cracks around his eyes and down his cheeks, ending at the corners of his mouth. His eyes were brown and yellow and matched the color of his skin, like mottled corn, covered with hundreds of freckles. He had few teeth except for a startlingly white stump here and there. When he opened his mouth to sing, it looked like stars on a black map. His lips were wide and brown. His nose was flat, the nostrils deep.

"Baby, I don't know 'bout no heaven. My mama truly believed it. But I thinks this here story 'bout pearly gates and all is just a trick. Seem like they ain't nothin' wrong with this here earth. The dirt gonna cover your mama and that be alright with her. She miss the sky and the wind and the land. Told me plenty a times. Seem like, compared to that heaven where the peoples hang playin' harps and talkin' sweet, this here earth ain't so bad. You mama, she be mighty unhappy in a heaven where they ain't no party or good lovin' goin' on. Seem like that heaven talk just a way to gets the peoples satisfied with the misery they has to bear in this here world. Once you gets to thinkin' that a reward waitin' on you for bein' poor and colored, why it just beat you down more. You don' stops to think 'bout doin' somethin' 'bout it right here, right now. Ummhmm, them white peoples, they thinks a everything. But there be a lot they don' know. Everything don' always mean every thing! I do believe Dolores more at rest in the brown dirt. And lord, child, from jump every mama wish her children never be born sometime! That's a fact. Ummhmm. Honey, she love you. She just too full a pain to remember to tell you.

"It just like me and Big Bill. Why, they be days we forgets to say, 'Big Bill, you my onliest one. James William, you sure one fine man.' Then you gets to thinkin' hey, this man don' love me no more! And you gets afraid to ask, 'cause you thinkin,' that's his duty to remember. Then you gets mad and sad all together and it get all mixed up and then you speakin' in shortness and evil kinda ways. You forgets that everybody be carryin' his own pain and bad things. The disrememberin' be a thing that happen though. We be foolish, us peoples. Ain' no way gettin' 'round that! Seem like, if we be perfect, we be like them white peoples up there in that heaven they thinks so special. Yes, yes, we be in that white heaven, with the white pearly gates and the white robes, and the white slippers. Child! You ever think 'bout heaven always bein' so white? Lord child! Whooo!"

He laughed and laughed, hugging Sue Linn tight, his chest rumbling in her ear. She laughed too, even though she wasn't sure she knew the joke. But it made her feel better to be sitting in Sweet William's lap, her head pressed to his heart, the afghan of bright colors covering her coldness and fright. She used to laugh with Dolores. Mostly over Dolores's mimicry of the people on the street or in the bars. She had almost become those people, so good was she at capturing a gesture, a voice, a way of holding her body. There was no meanness in the foolery; just fun, just a laugh, a present for Sue Linn.

"Now, my turtle gal, this old colored man be talkin' more than his due. I says, after a song and a good cry, they ain' nothin' better than hot soup and peppermint tea. I thinks I even gots a little banana cake saved for you."

They unfolded from the brocade chair and went to the table. The tiny round Black man of light skin. The tiny, thin girl of gold skin and Indian hair, her body wrapped in the afghan crocheted by Sweet William's hands. As James William poured the tea, his white shirt dazzled the girl's eyes. She watched his short legs walk slowly to the stove, his small feet wearing the felt slippers he never seemed to take off. He was wearing his favorite pants—grey flannel with handsome pleats and small cuffs at the bottom. He was wearing the only belt Sue Linn had ever seen him wear—a wide alligator strip with a buckle of solid silver, round and etched with the words Florida Everglades. It had been a gift from Big Bill so many years ago, the date and reason for the gift were lost in James William's memory. He only remembered Big Bill's face as he handed the belt to Sweet William, the pale mocha of his skin flushing and reddening as he pushed the tissue-wrapped gift toward James William, saying, "Here, honey. For you. A gift." James William's starched, white shirt had cuffs that were turned back and fastened with silver-colored links, a red stone gleaming in the center of each piece of metal. Sue Linn stared at the stones that seemed to signal on-off-stop. Red means stop....

She had learned that in school when she started kindergarten. That was four years ago. She was in third grade now, a big girl. She liked school. At least, she liked it when she went, when her mom remembered to send her. When Sue Linn felt safe to ask Dolores to braid her long hair without making the woman cry. When Dolores was in a good mood from having extra money and bought Sue Linn plaid dresses, white socks, and shoes that were shiny and had buckles instead of laces. She talked loud at these times, talked about how her baby was just as good as anybody, and anyway, she was the prettiest kid in school by far. Sue Linn had a hard time understanding this talk. Everyone in school wore old clothes and shoes with laces. It didn't make sense. Maybe it had to do with the picture magazines that showed up around the apartment. The people on the shiny pages were white and stood in funny poses. They wore fancy clothes and coats made from animals. They looked like they were playing statues, which Sue Linn had played once with the kids at school. It was a scary feeling to stop and stand so still until the boss kid said you could move. She liked it though. It made her feel like she was invisible. If she were really a statue, she'd be made out of wood or stone—something hard.

Sort of like the statues at the place her teacher, Miss Terrell, had taken them. Miss Terrell called the giant building a museum and said the statues were sculptures. She pointed out one made by a Black man. She took them to see a display case that had Indian jewelry resting on pieces of wood, only Miss Terrell called it Native American art. Sue Linn thought of her mother's beaded bracelet and stared at the glass case. It made her want to cry for a reason she couldn't even begin to think about. She remembered the Indian case for a long time after. She told her mom about it, and Dolores said it would be nice to go there; she had gone there once, she thought. But they never talked about it again. No, Sue Linn was not a statue. She was bony and covered with soft, gold skin and black hair that was coarse and reached below her shoulder blades. She practiced statues at home, standing on the worn green couch, trying to see herself in the wavy mirror on the opposite wall.

"Getting stuck on yourself, honey? That's how I started. A grain of salt, honey. That's what we need to take ourselves with. We're just bones and skin, honey. Bones and skin."

The child thought her mother much more than bones, skin, and salt. She thought Dolores was beautiful and was proud to walk with her on the avenue. The day they got the food stamps was one of the best days, for a while. Dolores was sober on those days. She would sit at the card table making lists and menus. Dolores labored hard on those days, looking through her magazines, cutting out recipes for "tasty, nutritional meals within your budget." Sue Linn stayed close to her mother on days like that, fascinated by Dolores's activity.

"How would you like chicken vegetable casserole on Monday? Then on Tuesday we could have Hawaiian chicken. I found a recipe for peanut butter cookies. It says here that peanut butter is a good source of protein. Would you like Dolores to make you cookies, baby? Maybe we could make them together." Sue Linn shook her head yes and stood even closer to her mother. Shiny paper with bright colors of food lay emblazoned on the table. Sue Linn was caught by Dolores's words, her magic talk of casseroles and cookies. Writing down words that came back as food. Food was something real yet mysterious. Food was something there never was enough of. Sue Linn ate a free lunch at school. Always hungry, eating too fast, not remembering what she ate, just eating then being hungry again.

Each morning Miss Terrell asked if anyone had forgotten to eat breakfast, because she just happened to bring orange juice and graham crackers from home. Miss Terrell must be magic because there was always enough for everyone. Miss Terrell was black, almost pure black like the stone set in the school door proclaiming when it was built (1910) and whose name it was built to honor (Jeremy Comstock). Marble, yes, that's what Miss Terrell called it. Black marble, that was Miss Terrell's skin. Her hair was cut close to her head and curled tightly against her scalp. James William's hair was like this, but more bushy, and his hair was white while Miss Terrell's was black with a red cast in the sunlight. She wore red lipstick, sometimes purple to go with the dress with white and pink dots on the sash. Her clothes were beautiful. Blue skirt and red jacket. Green dress with gold buttons. Her shoes were red or black shiny stuff with pointy, pointy toes and little wooden heels. Miss Terrell was tall and big. Some of the boys whispered and laughed about Miss Terrell's "boobs." Sue Linn saw nothing to laugh about, only knowing that boys giggled about sex things. She thought Miss Terrell's chest was very wonderful. It stuck out far and looked proud in a way. When she told this to Sweet William, he said, "Child, that Alveeta Terrell be a regular proud woman. Why wouldn't her chest be as proud as the rest of her? You lucky as can be to have proud Miss Alveeta Terrell be your teacher!"

One time, and it was the best time, Miss Terrell had come to school in a yellow dress over which she wore a length of material made from multicolored threads of green, red, purple, yellow, and black. She called it Kente cloth and told the class it was woven in Africa and the people, even the men, wore it every day. She said she was wearing this special cloth because it was a special day. It was a day that Black people celebrated being African, and even though they might live in all kinds of places, they had come from Africa at one time. Then she showed them a map of Africa and traced lines running from that continent to North America, to the West Indies, to South America, to just about everywhere. Amos asked, if Africa was so special, why did the people leave? Miss Terrell said that the people didn't leave because they wanted to, but because these other people—Spanish, British, American, and French—had wanted slaves to work on their lands and make things grow for them so they could get rich. And these same people killed Indians in North America to get land. And these people had captured Africans as if they were herds of animals. They had put them in chains and shipped them to land where their labor was needed. Some Africans had died trying to escape, some from hunger, thirst, and disease, but some had stayed alive to reach the new land that was a stranger to them.

The children pondered on these facts before raising their hands to ask questions. Miss Terrell answered in her sure voice. She knew everything. She told them about Denmark Vesey, Nat Turner, John Brown, Crispus Attucks, whose last name meant deer because his mama had been a Choctaw Indian. She told them about Touissant-Louverture, about the Maroons in Jamaica, about Harper's Ferry. She told them about the Seminoles and Africans in Florida creating an army to fight the U.S. soldiers and how they had won the fight! Sue Linn's mind was so filled with these wondrous facts, she dreamed about them that night. And it came to her in the dream that Miss Terrell was a food-giver. Her thoughts and facts were like the graham crackers she laid out on her desk each morning. They were free to take, to eat right at that moment, or to save for when one got really hungry. The next morning, Sue Linn copied down her dream in the little notebook she carried with her everywhere. "Miss Terrell is a food-giver." She told Sweet William, who agreed.

Food stamp day. Dolores making something out of nothing. What did it mean? Everything meant something. This she had learned on her own, from the streets, from being a kid. She wanted to talk with Dolores about this, but was too shy.

Dolores was ready. Sue Linn puttered at the table, stalling for time, prolonging the intimacy with her mother. Sue Linn was not ready for the store. It happened every time. Dolores got sad. The store defeated her. It was a battle to see how far down the aisles she could get before giving up. The limp vegetables, the greenish-brown meat, the lack of anything resembling the food in the magazines. Sue Linn sensed it before it happened. The faint shrug of Dolores's shoulders, the shake of her head as if clearing it from a dream. Then they proceeded fast, Dolores grabbing at things that were cheap and filling, if only for a few hours. The little girl tried calling her mother's attention to funny people in the store, or some fancy-packaged box of air and starch. Anything, please, please, to get that look off her mother's face. That look of fury and contempt. That look of sadness and loss. They would end up with a few things like bread, canned corn, and maybe, hamburger. All her food stamps gone, they'd put the groceries away and Dolores would go out and not return until the next day with a few dollars and a raging headache.

Dolores picked up her lists and stamps, placed them in her purse, a beige plastic bag with her initials stamped in gold letters: D.L., Dolores Longboat. She went to the wavy mirror and, with her little finger, applied blue eye shadow because "you never know who we'll meet." She brushed her black hair until it crackled with sparks and life across her wide back. Dressed in too-tight jeans, a pink sweater frayed and unraveling at the bottom, her gold-tone earrings swinging and dancing, she defied anyone or anything to say she didn't exist. "Let's go."

Sue Linn took hold of her mother's hand and stared up at Dolores, as if to burn the image of her mama into her brain, as if to keep the scent of lily-of-the-valley cologne in her nose. The brown eyes shaded in blue looked down at her child. Dark eye watched dark eye—two females locked in an embrace of color, blood, and bewildering love. Dolores broke the intensity of the moment, cast her eyes around the apartment, committing to memory what she had to come home to. Tightening her hold on Sue Linn's hand, she said once again, "Let's go." She set the lock and the two went out into the street.

Sue Linn's eyes closed with this last memory. Her head nodded above the soup. James William rose from the table and pulled the bed down from the wall. Straightening the covers and fluffing the pillow, he made the bed ready for the child's tired body and heart. He picked her up and carried her the few feet to the bed. Taking off her shoes, he gently placed the girl under the blanket and tucked the pillow under her head. He placed the afghan at the foot of the bed, folded and neat.

James William Newton—Sweet William—went to his chair and sat in the nighttime light.

He could see the piece of the moon through a crack between two buildings across the street.

"Ole moon, what you think? I gots this here child now. Them government peoples be wantin' to know where this child be. Or is they? Seem like the whereabouts of a little gal ain' gonna concern too many a them. Now, I ain' worryin' 'bout raisin' this here turtle gal. It one a them things I be prepared to do. But Moon, we gots to have a plan. I an old man. This here baby need me. Yes, ma'am. There gots to be some providin' to do. Big Bill? Is you laughin' at me? It be a fix we in. Ummmhmmm, a regular fix. Big Bill? I needs a little a that talk you always so ready with. Honey, it ever be a wonder to me how a man could talk so much and still make sense like you done! I sittin' here waitin' on you, honey. Sweet William, he waitin' on you."

He sat through the night, refilling his cup many times. His memories came and went like the peppermint tea he drank. His lips moved in conversation and song. Sometime before dawn he laughed and murmured, "Thank you, honey. You always was the bestest man." He drank his last cup, rinsed it, and set it upside-down in the sink. He settled his body on the blue davenport, the afghan pulled up to his shoulders. He looked one more time at the sleeping child, her dark hair hiding her face in sleep.

"Child, sleep on and dream. Sweet William, he here. Me and Big Bill take care of our baby, turtle gal. You be alright. Yes, ma'am, you be alright."

He closed his eyes and slept.

Swimming Upstream

Beth E. Brant

Anna May spent the first night in a motel off Highway 8. She arrived about ten, exhausted from her long drive through farmland, bright autumn leaves, the glimpse of blue lake. She saw none of this, only the grey highway stretching out before her. She stopped when the motel sign appeared, feeling the need for rest, it didn't matter where.

She took a shower, lay in bed, and fell asleep, the dream beginning again almost immediately. Her son—drowning in the water, his skinny arms flailing the waves, his mouth opening to scream with no sound coming forth. She, Anna May, moving in slow motion into the waves, her hands grabbing for the boy but feeling only water run through her fingers. She grabbed frantically, but nothing held to her hands. She dove and opened her eyes under water and saw nothing. He was gone. Her hands connected with sand, with seaweed, but not her son. He was gone. Simon was gone.

Anna May woke. The dream was not a nightmare anymore. It had become a companion to her, a friend, almost a lover—reaching for her as she slept, making pictures of her son, keeping him alive while recording his death. In the first days after Simon left her, the dream made her wake screaming, sobbing, arms hitting at the air, legs kicking the sheets, becoming tangled in the material. Her bed was a straitjacket, pinning her down, holding her until the dream ended. She would fight the dream then. Now, she welcomed it.

During the day she had other memories of Simon. His birth, his first pair of shoes, his first steps, his first word—Mama—his first book, his first day of school. His firsts were also his lasts, so she invented a future for him during her waking hours: his first skating lessons, his first hockey game, his first reading aloud from a book, his first....But she couldn't invent beyond that. His six-year-old face and body wouldn't change in her mind. She couldn't invent what she couldn't imagine.

She hadn't been there when Simon drowned. Simon had been given to her ex-husband by the courts. She was judged unfit. Because she lived with a woman. Because a woman, Catherine, slept beside her. Because she had a history of alcoholism.

The history was old. Anna May had stopped drinking when she became pregnant with Simon, and she had stayed dry all those years. She couldn't imagine what alcohol tasted like after Simon was born. He was so lovely, so new. Her desire for a drink evaporated every time Simon took hold of her finger, or nursed from her breast, or opened his mouth in a toothless smile. She had marveled at his being—this gift that had emerged from her own body. This beautiful being who had formed himself inside her, had come with speed through the birth canal to welcome life outside her. His face red with anticipation, his black hair sticking straight up as if electric with hope, his little fists grabbing, his pink mouth finding her nipple and holding on for dear life. She had no need for alcohol. There was Simon.

Simon was taken away from them. But they saw him on weekends, Tony delivering him on a Friday night, Catherine discreetly finding someplace else to be when Tony's car drove up. They still saw Simon, grateful for the two days out of the week they could play with him, they could delight in him, they could pretend with him. They still saw Simon, until the call came that changed all that. The call from Tony saying that Simon had drowned when he fell out of the boat as they were fishing. Tony sobbing, "I'm sorry. I didn't mean for this to happen. I tried to save him. I'm sorry. Please, Anna, please forgive me. Oh God, Anna. I'm sorry. I'm sorry."

So Anna May dreamed of those final moments of a six-year-old life. And it stunned her that she wasn't there to see him die when she had been there to see him come into life.

Anna May stayed dry, but she found herself glancing into cupboards at odd times. Looking for something. Looking for something to drink. She thought of ways to buy wine and hide it so she could take a drink when she needed it. But there was Catherine. Catherine would know, and Catherine's face, already so lined and tired and old, would become more so. Anna May saw her own face in the mirror. Her black hair had streaks of grey and white she hadn't noticed before. Her forehead had deep lines carved into the flesh, and her eyes, her eyes that had cried so many tears, were a faded and washed-out blue. Her mouth was wrinkled, the lips parched and chapped. She and Catherine, aged and ghostlike figures walking through a dead house.

Anna May thought about the bottle of wine. It took on large proportions in her mind. A bottle of wine, just one, that she could drink from and never empty. A bottle of wine, the sweet, red kind that would take away the dryness, the withered insides of her. She went to meetings but never spoke, only saying her name and "I'll pass tonight." Catherine wanted to talk, but Anna May had nothing to say to this woman she loved. She thought about the bottle of wine: the bottle, the red liquid inside, the sweet taste gathering in her mouth, moving down her throat, hitting her bloodstream, warming her inside, killing the deadness.

She arranged time off work and told Catherine she was going away for a few days. She needed to think, to be alone. Catherine watched her face, the framing of the words out of her mouth, her exhausted eyes. Catherine said, "I understand."

"Will you be alright?" Anna May asked her.

"Yes, I'll be fine. I'll see friends. We haven't spent time with them in so long, they are concerned about us. I'll be waiting for you. I love you so much."

Anna May got in the car and drove up 401, up 19, over to 8 and the motel, the shower, the dream.

Anna May smoked her cigarettes and drank coffee until daylight. She made her plans to buy the bottle of wine. After that, she had no plans, other than the first drink and how it would taste and feel.

She found a meeting in Goderich and sat there, ashamed and angered with herself to sit in a meeting and listen to the stories and plan her backslide. She thought of speaking, of talking about Simon, about the bottle of wine, but she knew someone would stop her or say something that would make her stop. Anna May did not want to be stopped. She wanted to drink and drink and drink until it was all over. *My name is Anna May and I'll just pass.*

Later, she hung around for coffee, feeling like an infiltrator, a spy. A woman took hold of her arm and said, "Let's go out and talk. I know what you're planning. Don't do it. Let's talk."

Anna May shrugged off the woman's hand and left. She drove to a liquor outlet. Vins et Spiriteaux. *Don't do it.* She found the wine, one bottle, that was all she'd buy. *Don't do it.* One bottle, that was all. She paid and left the store, the familiar curve of the bottle wrapped in brown paper. *Don't do it.* Only one bottle. It wouldn't hurt. She laughed at the excuses bubbling up in her mouth like wine. Just one. She smoked a cigarette in the parking lot, wondering where to go, where to stop and turn the cap that would release the red, sweet smell before the taste would overpower her and she wouldn't have to wonder anymore.

She drove north on 21, heading for the Bruce Peninsula, Lake Huron on her left, passing the little resort towns, the cottages by the lake. She stopped for a hamburger and, without thinking, got her thermos filled with coffee. This made her laugh, the bottle sitting next to her, almost a living thing. She drank the coffee driving north, with her father—not Simon, not Catherine—drifting in her thoughts. Charles, her mother had called him. Everyone else called him Charley. Good old Charley. Good-time Charley. Injun Charley. Charles was a hard worker, working at almost anything. He worked hard, he drank hard. He tried to be a father, a husband, but the work and the drink turned his attempts to nothing. Anna May's mother never complained, never left him. She cooked and kept house and raised the children and always called him Charles. When Anna May grew up, she taunted her mother with the fact that her Charles was a drunk. Why didn't she care more about her kids than her drunken husband? Didn't her mother know how ashamed they were to have such a father, to hear people talk about him, to laugh at him, to laugh at them—the half-breeds of good-old-good-time-Injun Charlie?

Anna May laughed again, the sound ugly inside the car. Her father was long dead and, she supposed, forgiven by her. He had been a handsome man back then, her mother a skinny, pale girl, an orphan girl, something unheard of by her father. How that must have appealed to the romantic that he was. Anna May didn't know how her mother felt about the life she'd had with Charles. Her mother never talked about those things. Her mother, who sobbed and moaned at Simon's death as she never had at her husband's. Anna May couldn't remember her father ever being mean. He just went away when he drank. Not like his daughter who'd fight anything in her way when she was drunk. The bottle bounced beside her as she drove.

Anna May drove and her eyes began to see the colors of the trees. They looked like they were on fire, the reds and oranges competing with the yellows and golds. She smoked her cigarettes, drank from the thermos, and remembered this was her favorite season. She and Catherine would be cleaning the garden, harvesting the beets, turnips, and cabbage. They would be digging up the gladioli and letting them dry before packing the bulbs away. They would be planting more tulips. Catherine could never get enough tulips. It was because they had met in the spring, Catherine always said. "We met in the spring, and the tulips were blooming in that little park. You looked so beautiful against the tulips, Simon on your lap. I knew I loved you." Last autumn Simon had been five and had raked leaves and dug holes for the tulip bulbs. Catherine had made cocoa and cinnamon toast, and Simon had declared that he liked cinnamon toast better than pie.

Anna May tasted the tears on her lips. She licked the wet salt, imagining it was sweet wine on her tongue. "It's my fault," she said out loud. She thought of all the things she should have done to prevent Simon's leaving. She should have placated Tony; she should have lived alone; she should have pretended to be straight; she should have never become an alcoholic; she should have never loved; she should have never been born. Let go! She cried somewhere inside her. "Let go!" she cried aloud. Isn't that what she learned? But how could she let go of Simon and the hate she held for Tony and herself? How could she let go of that? If she let go, she'd have to forgive—the forgiveness Tony begged of her now that Simon was gone.

Even Catherine, even the woman she loved, asked her to forgive Tony. "It could have happened when he was with us," Catherine cried at her. "Forgive him, then you can forgive yourself." But Catherine didn't know what it was to feel the baby inside her, to feel him pushing his way out of her, to feel his mouth on her breast, to feel the sharp pain in her womb every time his name was spoken. Forgiveness was for people who could afford it. Anna May was poverty-struck.

The highway turned into a road, the trees crowding in on both sides of her, the flames of the trees almost blinding her. She was entering the Bruce Peninsula a sign informed her. She pulled off the road, consulting her map. Yes, she would drive to the very tip of the peninsula and it would be there she'd open the bottle and drink her way to whatever she imagined was waiting for her. The bottle rested beside her, and she touched the brown paper, feeling soothed, feeling a hunger in her stomach.

She saw another sign: Sauble Falls. Anna May thought this would be a good place to stop, to drink the last of her coffee, to smoke another cigarette. She pulled over onto the gravel lot. There was a small path leading down to the rocks. Another sign: Absolutely No Fishing. Watch Your Step. Rocks Are Slippery. She could hear the water before she saw it.

She stepped out of the covering of trees and onto the rock shelf. The falls were narrow, spilling out in various layers of rock. She could see the beginnings of Lake Huron below her. She could see movement in the water coming away from the lake and moving toward the rocks and the falls. Fish tails flashing and catching light from the sun. Hundreds of fish tails moving upstream. She walked across a flat slab of rock and there, beneath her in the shallow water, saw salmon slowly moving their bodies, their gills expanding and closing as they rested. She looked up to another rock slab and saw a dozen fish congregating at the bottom of a water spill—waiting. Her mind barely grasped the fact that the fish were migrating, swimming upstream, when a salmon leapt and hurled itself over the rushing water above. Anna May stepped up to a different ledge and watched the salmon's companions waiting their turn to jump the flowing water and reach the next plateau.

She looked down toward the mouth of the lake. There were others, like her, standing and silently watching the struggle of the fish. No one spoke, as if to speak would be blasphemous in the presence of this. She looked again into the water, the fish crowding each resting place before resuming the leaps and the jumps. Here and there on the rocks, dead fish, a testimony to the long and desperate struggle that had taken place. They lay, eyes glazed, sides open and bleeding, food for the gulls that hovered over Anna May's head.

Another salmon jumped, its flesh torn and gaping, its body spinning until it made it over the fall. Another one, the dorsal fin torn, leapt and was washed back by the power of the water. Anna May watched the fish rest, its open mouth like another wound. The fish was large, the dark body undulating in the water. She saw it begin a movement of tail. Churning the water, it shot into the air, twisting its body, shaking and spinning. She saw the underbelly, pale yellow and bleeding from the battering against the rocks, the water. He made it! Anna May wanted to clap, to shout with elation at the sheer power of such a thing happening before her.

She looked around again. The other people were gone. She was alone with the fish, the only sound besides the water was her breath against the air. She walked further upstream, her sneaker getting wet from the splashing of the salmon. She didn't feel the wet, she only waited and watched for the salmon to move. She had no idea of time, of how long she stood waiting for the movement, waiting for the jumps, the leaps, the flight. Anna May watched for Torn Fin, wanting to see him move against the current in his phenomenal swim of faith.

Anna May reached a small dam, the last barrier before the calm water and blessed rest. She sat on a rock, her heart beating fast, the adrenalin pouring through her at each leap and twist of the salmon. There he was, Torn Fin, his final jump before him. She watched, then closed her eyes, almost ashamed to be a spectator at this act, this primal movement to the place of all beginning. He had to get there, to push his bleeding body forward, believing in his magic to get him there. Believing, believing he would get there. No thoughts of death, of food, of rest. No thoughts but the great urging and wanting to get there, get *there*.

Anna May opened her eyes and saw him, another jump before being pushed back. She held her hands together, her body willing Torn Fin to move, to push, to jump, to fly! Her body rocked forward and back, her heart madly beating inside her chest. She rocked, she shouted, "Make it, damn it, make it!" Torn Fin waited at the dam. Anna May rocked and held her hands tight, her fingers twisting together, nails scratching her palms. She rocked. She whispered, "Simon. Simon." She rocked and whispered the name of her son into the water, "Simon. Simon." Like a chant. *Simon. Simon. Simon.* Into the water, as if the very name of her son was magic and could move the salmon to his final place. She rocked. She chanted. *Simon. Simon.* Anna May rocked and put her hands in the water, wanting to lift the fish over the dam and to life. As the thought flickered through her brain, Torn Fin slapped his tail against the water and jumped. He battled with the current. He twisted and arced into the air, his great mouth gaping and gasping, his wounds standing out in relief against his body, his fin discolored and shredded. With a push, a great push, he turned a complete circle and made it over the dam.

"Simon!" Torn Fin slapped his tail one last time and was gone, the dark body swimming home. She thought...she thought she saw her son's face, his black hair streaming behind him, a look of joy transfixed on his little face before the image disappeared.

Anna May stood on the rock shelf, hands limp at her sides, watching the water, watching the salmon, watching. She watched as the sun fell behind the lake and night came closer to her. Then she walked up the path and back to her car. She looked at the bottle sitting next to her, the brown paper rustling as she put the car in gear. She drove south, stopping at a telephone booth.

She could still hear the water in her ears.

Diane Glancy
(1941–)

*"Native American storying is an
act of gathering many voices to
tell a story in many different ways.
One voice alone is not enough
because we are what we are in
relationship to others, and we each
have our different way of seeing.
Native American writing is also
an alignment of voices so the story
comes through."*

Diane Glancy, *The Cold
and Hunger Dance*

minimal indian

Diane Glancy

Now it happened in the twelfth month that James and Crowbar visited Renah, James's sister. They were there to never lift a hand. Just their fork expecting something on it.

The two men drove from Nail, Arkansas, along Highway 16 to Red Star, where Renah had her cabin nearly built into the hills. Her goats and a few hens. A woodpile. Some rusted auto parts Crowbar was thinking of asking for his salvage yard he called Trucks and Stuff.

If he could find them under the snow.

And Renah rising early to cook, cooked until after sundown thinking already what to have the next day. Asking for nothing but a trip to the cemetery with a Christmas basket for the parents' graves. If her brother, James, and his friend, Crowbar, had made it across Highway 16 from Nail, they could give her a lift to the graveyard.

What were they doing here anyway? Expecting their Christmas fruitcake and curls of pork-rinds early?

The two men sat at the kitchen table. James stirred his coffee with fury and chopped the eggs on his plate.

Renah cleared her hands.

We open the morning with prayer.

Even before their first bite was swallowed.

EEEEEeeeee. Renah jumped on the curled edge of the linoleum floor when the Spirit moved her. She skitted across the floor in a holyghost dance. James and Crowbar just looking at her with their mouthfuls of eggs and toast. Even when she prayed quietly, you could hear James chewing. He might choke, you know, with a mouthful of breakfast. He had to get it down. Crowbar nudged him. But James kept chewing.

You can't hear what she says when you chew. James told him.

It was true. Crowbar tried it.

But Renah kept moving in the Spirit.

And sure enough, soon you could see the drizzling stars dry up. And soon you could see the morning coming from a long way off. Over the curls of cabin smoke. The pine trees and acorns. The morning sun round as an egg basket.

But soon James and Crowbar went back to eating. The truth of the matter was, the ceiling in Arkansas was too high for them. Somewhere up near under heaven, Renah said. They lost interest before they saw too far.

The men lived according to their own ways which were somewhat limited and shortsighted. But they could see the blue sweep of sky across the window.

James. Renah said when she'd prayed.

Whad?

I'd like to take a Christmas basket to the graves.

Id snowed, he said.

I want to go anyway.

Go f' 't. James said.

Renah hummed as she boiled rinse water for the dishes.

James had hoped Crowbar would be a brother-in-law. Renah was not an un-handsome woman, but how could he hand her to Crowbar, bible-brained as she was? She had black curls kept tight to her head. White skin. A skinny, black-haired, white-skinned woman. One of the strains of back-hill Cherokee. Whose mouth even turned up with the curve of a squirrel tail.

Crowbar owned his business, Trucks and Stuff, on the edge of Nail, Arkansas.

He had, after inventory:

2 pick-ups
  or what was left of them
a backhoe
a twenty-year-old bus used by a preacher friend of Renah's
a Kenworth cab that parted from its trailer on some back curve
  with stubs of grass and dirt still hooked in the door
a rail-fence to keep out trespassers
  mostly now fallen
a house with a lean-to
an assortment of
crank shafts
fenders
doors
struts
springs
shocks
engine parts
who knew what else
maybe not even Crowbar
the Trucks and Stuff sign by the road
a satellite dish

and a fifteen-year-old James McAdoo for Sheriff sign in his yard.

Politics was still the latest.

Bigger than satellite dishes.

Crowbar would be a good husband for Renah.

James didn't know why Renah never married. Maybe no one asked her. No. That wasn't true. There was Sam Jackson from Sam's Bait and Tackle over on Bull Shoals who had asked her.

And there was the traveling tool salesman.

Family meant something to Renah. She had their photos lined up on the kitchen walls and along the top of the pie safes and on lace doilies that their grandmother had tatted. Hairpin lace or something like that. The old women always had their hands going. Back and forth like a litter of birds in the trees. All chirped up all the time.

A regular backhoe at anyone who passed. Dredging up.

Renah could do it. You got the whole story from her. Whether you wanted it or not.

The only thing she cut off, when she was behind the camera, was the heads in the photos, or at least above the nose so you kind of had to guess who it was by their trousers or dress.

She was a good woman though.

After breakfast, Renah fed the hens and goats, and James and Crowbar drove Renah to the cemetery in the snow.

Renah had her Brownie camera with her.

She decided she wouldn't get out of the car, but honked James and Crowbar in the direction they should go with the Christmas basket for the parents. Since James couldn't remember. Or couldn't find the graves under the cover of snow.

Over this way.

Honk.

Now that.

Honk.

Not that way.

Honk.

Renah motioned them one way then another. Back to the left. There James.

Honk.

In the car, Renah was warm as if she'd never left her cast-iron bed in the kitchen all heaped with her string-tied rag-quilts in the darkest purples and browns and maroons.

James and Crowbar swept snow from the graves.

Renah took a photo of James and Crowbar placing the basket.

I wasn't even turned around. Crowbar said.

Won't make no difference. James answered. There'd be nothin' of us from the ears up in her picture anyway.

The car radio played Christmas music as they drove back to the road.

Then an advertisement for Burleen's hair salon.

An evangelist saying hallelujah to the snow-covered morning.
And the Singing Starbrites!
Those sisters:
Juanita
Bonita
Corita
Dorita.
Their mother spit 'em out like peas.
James waved to a car that passed. Another Cherokee. A marginal Indian to the ones powwowing and migrating and buffaloing on the plains.
The Cherokee had been a robed and turbaned tribe with curled-handled pipes, writing and reading the letters of Sequoyah's syllabary.*
Full of superstitions and little-people tales,† unless they'd been converted to Christianity. Even at that, they were still full of both worlds. Sometimes conjuring. Sometimes singing hymns. Not knowing anything about being an Indian.
But a somewhat farming
backyard-hung-with-quilts
canning-jar-cellared-for-a-long-winter
vegetable-patched-in-summer
few-hogged
sort of folk.
Dry goods on the shelf
a bag of material scraps in the corner
egg baskets
apple baskets
one and two pie baskets
berry baskets
potato baskets
market baskets
froes
mallets
draw-knives
string
strips of oak and willow for more baskets
bittersweet

* A syllabary is a set of written characters in which each character represents one sylla-
   ble. Sequoyah created a syllabary (a phonetic alphabet) for the Cherokee language.
† The Cherokee "Little People" (or *Yunwi Tsundi*) are very small (about knee-high)
   spiritual beings, similar to European fairies, but with long hair reaching to the
   ground. They live in caves or woods and spend a great deal of time making music
   (drumming) and dancing. They are usually good-hearted and helpful. They are
   invisible to humans unless they choose to be seen.

sage

herbs hanging by the woodstove

What kind of Indian that?

Their backwoods jamming was enough to keep a regular Indian out.

James and Crowbar hadn't been converted, Renah knew. She remembered them climbing out the vestibule window of the New Covenant Church.

That's why they'd come to Red Star from Nail! The Spirit had delivered them to Renah for another chance to be saved. Hallelujah. She tossed in the seat as they drove back toward her cabin.

Especially when they came over the hills, and saw into the distance of Arkansas.

They still almost could see the smoke from the old Cherokee pipes in the winter fog rising off the ice in the streams and farmponds.

She told James and Crowbar how the ancestors had walked from the southeast on a forced march. Most kept going to Oklahoma. But theirs stopped here.

Except for the hand of God they wouldn't have made it.

It was a haunted land. A magical kingdom of animal transformations and mutations of borders. Too much knowledge of the old ways. When no one would talk about it. That's what they did. And a Christian God to whom they had to make a commitment. Who could come for them anytime.

There could be a revolution in Arkansas from the suppression of the old ways. Anytime. Gunshot heard nightly. Everyone digging in. Like squirrels spread-legged in the yard. Trying to uncover.

The Cherokee seemed like everyone else. Maybe another language leaping out once in a while. Little people under the house. Chimney smoke dancing on its front legs over the yard. Its hind legs in the air. But God waited for their decision. Just like everybody else.

I can see up into heaven, Renah said. Just up to God's ears. I can see his son Jesus standing by his throne, a halo bright as an egg yolk hanging over his head. A book on how to *save the lost* under his hand. I can see God's old truck parked behind his throne. I can see the long white hair that hangs to his shoulders. I just can't see his face.

James looked at Crowbar.

We'd be BLIND if we did. Renah's voice was rising again like heat from the wood stove, if they'd been in her kitchen instead of James's car. We can't stand the sight of purity. Here on earth. In these plank-floored cabins and leaning fields. The low roofs and high floors.

Yo, James said. It feels sometimes like my head is going to meet my knees when I'm sitting at your table.

The roofs leaks snow, Renah told James. If it warms up, I'll have to get the buckets, James. Otherwise I see it coming through like the joy of heaven.

Yes.

The former and latter rain often fell all day in buckets on Renah's floor. Maybe James and Crowbar could repair the leaks.

Maybe Renah could marry, and her husband could fix it.

James ate an apple from the basket as they listened to Renah.

Got another one? Crowbar asked.

The men chewed.

An apple works just like a piece of toast, James said.

It was another day under God's grace. He must be in his hip boots and fishing gear. Warming his truck in his garage. Yes God had it wrapped up. Had his inventory in line. His family photographs on the wall. His angels with their bright wings. Renah could almost see their faces, thought she could hear their wings beating like a fan belt.

EEEEEeeeee.

How those Starbrites could sing:

Juanita

Bonita

Corita

Dorita.

Wuuh. Whhuuu. James and Crowbar could see their voices up there on the stage.

Around a curve in Newton County, just east of the Boston Mts., a farmer's truck loaded with chickens crossed the center line and hit James and Crowbar and Renah head-on.

There were chicken feathers and splintered chicken crates everywhere.

Renah stood up and shook herself off. Well, she was light as a feather herself. She walked down the road. Where was she going? What happened?

She saw James and Crowbar dazed in the truck.

Hens were flying up to heaven on their little wings like snow. Renah didn't know they could fly. Up over Arkansas. Past the woodcarvers in their cabins. Past hog farmers and turkey barns. The rocky soil. Logging trucks. Her goats and hens. She even saw the steam from the Dardanelle Nuclear Power Plant on Interstate 40. The dam that Renah spelled d.a.m.b. whenever she said it. That's the way you heard it around her. She wouldn't have it any other way.

And there was some sort of funny tag on her ear.

Renah even saw heaven spread out before her like hills in the distance of Arkansas. The trees were the heads of everyone who had called the name of Jesus.

And now she could see GOD.

She could see HE looked a little like Floyd Buber, her father's old friend.

She turned to tell James and Crowbar.

But they had their heads caught in the fork of a tree. And the Spirit of the air wouldn't let them pass.

They suddenly looked monkey-faced, and disappeared. Renah cried out, and tried to rush after them, but she heard the angels singing.

She saw the very face of GOD. Not just ears and nose as she imagined she'd seen his body on the throne. But a whole forehead full of stars. A nose with two garages. A mouth like the opening of a backwood cave. Some sort of engineering design on his face. Well, he was a regular computer chip. She'd seen a magazine in a doctor's office once. A complicated crossroads of veins and connectives. A numbered face full of more than she could recognize at first. A whole being full of life and love.

The Starbrites had been right.

The bait date she ended with Sam Jackson when she told him of her love for GOD, and he took off the next day back to Bull Shoals.

The traveling tool salesman likewise.

But this God. And there was his son. He was the one who waited for her. He was in his old jeans down there at the end of the road where she now walked. Just like her vision had seen.

Stamp Dance

Diane Glancy

For Jim Moore

Uncle Al teased him. "Here Mack, you want to go somewhere?" He put a canceled postage stamp in his hand.

Mack looked at the small square. "Marianne Moore American Poet 1887–1972 25 USA." He read. "What does she do?" Mack asked.

"Mails things." Uncle Al gave his usual lack of information.

But Mack didn't let Uncle Al go.

"Electric bills. 'Sorry I can't marry you today' letters. 'Buy more magazines and become a millionaire.'" Uncle Al was pleased with himself.

Now Mack acted uninterested.

"You know the mailboxes? The Post Office with the flag where you went with your ma when your daddy was overseas?"

Mack looked at him.

"Where you went for food stamps."

Now Mack knew. But he didn't remember Marianne Moore.

"She might have been there and you never saw her." Uncle Al laughed at himself and Mack wondered what was up.

"Yes, but I couldn't see what my mother did over the counter," Mack said.

Mack held Marianne Moore in his hand. She had a pink face and a rose at her collar. A light shined up in her face. He looked at the dark blue background around her. Royal blue.

But what did Poet have to do with Marianne Moore? He got the post office part. But what did *e* and *t* stand for if she was a mail handler? Why didn't it say Pomh? Marianne had her hand to her cheek.

Uncle Al put another canceled stamp in Mack's hand. It wasn't Marianne Moore at all, but a bird. In fact, it was an eagle.

"Why's an eagle crowded on a stamp?"

"There's lots of things on stamps." Uncle Al poured the last of the milk in a glass for himself. "There's whole stores that sell stamps," Al said. "Nothing but. There's lots of birds and animals. Whole series of them."

"How did you get to one of those stores?" Mack wondered. "And what are they for if you can buy stamps at the post office?"

"Well, there's collectors." Mack's friend, Billy, told him in Mack's attic room. "They keep them in books in drawers. Foreign stamps. Old stamps."

Mack had never heard such things.

"They make special books with plastic pages and you put the stamps in them."

"Why?"

"Just to collect them."

"How do you get them?"

"The same as you get everything. You buy them."

Mack tasted the back of Marianne Moore. Some of the glue was still shiny. It was so the stamp would stick to the letter. Mack held it in his hand. The dirt under his fingernails made thin black curves.

Mack sat in the attic room after Billy left. The oak tree and the street light raked at the window in the eave. Mack had a box under his bed, and a helmet on the wall with a horsehair tail. He didn't know where it came from. Maybe one of Uncle Al's girlfriends.

The back corner of Marianne Moore was still sticky. He stuck it to his bedpost. He wished he had a book to put it in. He wished he had a drawer for the book with the one stamp in it. He kept his socks and underwear in the box under his bed.

When Mack's mother went for money orders to pay the bills, Mack begged to go with her. Mack had hated to go in the past. Before she got a job. When they lived on food stamps. She'd yell at him for wandering away from her in line. She'd yell at him for standing on her shoes. She didn't know why Mack didn't stay with Uncle Al, except Mack always wanted to go places.

"United States Post Office." He read the large letters on the building. He saw the flag. He knew the Post Office was a place connected to the government. He knew it was a place connected to the world. It was even connected to life because the Post-Office man had given his mother the food stamps. And it was connected to war and death because it was where his father had come to sign up for the army. The Post Office was where Mack and his friend, Billy, would register when they turned eighteen.

But Mack's father made it back from Viet Nam. When Uncle Al called him "missing in action," it was the war in the city he meant. In whatever there was that called men away from their families and out into the streets never to come back again. Mack wasn't sure where or why but he heard stories of how his ancestors roamed the prairies following buffalo. Now they couldn't hunt. There was even the notice of the annual Indian shoot that appeared in spear-fishing season. The joke was, they were supposed to be hunted.

The stamps were like angels that took things away. But where was Marianne Moore? The large marble corridors echoed with people's coughs and footsteps.

Mack saw the large open-mouthed canvas sacks waiting on racks to be closed and taken to the trucks on the loading dock. He watched the customers buying stamps, mailing packages and letters. In a corner was a "slippery when wet" sign. Two small posts held a rope that looped lazily on the floor. The shiny marble corridor began to slither with its brown and gray patterns. Mack thought of the snake he'd seen on the science table in school.

The square boxes along the wall were like the apartments where his friend, Billy, lived. They were like Indian cliff-dwellings his teacher showed him in a book. There was mail in some of the boxes. It leaned at the same angle in every box and reminded Mack of snow on the window of his attic room in the winter.

At school Mack wrote an essay on "My Stamp Collection." He used words like "perforated." His teacher told Mack she'd save her stamps for him and praised his paper.

When he saw stamps on envelopes in the crooked tin wastepaper basket in the office, he wanted to steal them. Even Uncle Al still blessed him with an occasional canceled stamp he tore from an envelope.

But Mack wanted a new stamp. Not one always crossed with bars. He told Uncle Al that he and Billy would go to the store for his lottery ticket if he'd give them a nickel. Uncle Al even gave Mack several pennies for staying out of his room for a while. It made Uncle Al's girlfriend laugh.

Mack told Billy he wanted to go to the Post Office one day after school. "You can come," Mack said as he counted his money.

Billy said he could go, but on the first day Mack planned the trip to the Post Office, Billy came crying to the door of the school. He had lost his glove and would get beat when he got home, he said. His father would be waiting.

They walked back to Billy's locker. They asked in the office. They walked through the halls. Mack told Billy he'd go with him to Billy's father, but Billy wouldn't let him. Mack was afraid to go to Billy's house anyway. They should cover his father with stamps and send him somewhere.

It made cold fish swim up Mack's spine.

"Candied Pike," Uncle Al called that feeling. Mack started out on his own, but he walked a long time and never found the Post Office. His footsteps on the walk made him think of the fists of Billy's father.

When Mack got home, he asked his mother where the Post Office was, and he had been going in the right direction. He just hadn't gone far enough.

The following week Mack asked Billy again to walk to the Post Office with him, but Billy couldn't. His father would find out about it, and he'd get beat again. Billy couldn't do anything. Mack had seen the cut under the Band-Aid over his eye.

It was twelve blocks to the Post Office. Mack counted them this time. They wouldn't miss him at home. They might think he was under the plaid bedspread on his rumpled bed where he slept when he stayed up too late. Or they would think he was hiding out with Billy after his father hit him again. Sometime they could climb through Mack's attic window up the oak tree to the roof and sit against the chimney.

Mack peered into the Post Office. The large corridors. The echo. There was always a line. His heart pounded. Someone behind him opened the door and pushed him in. He walked slowly to the people who stood like they were going to the lunchroom.

"Next," the people behind the counter kept saying in their uniforms. Yes, the Post Office was a very important place. It kept you alive or sent you away. Whatever it chose to do. Mack stood straight in line. He watched people move up to the counter one by one. How restless he had been when he'd come with his mother. How often she had told him to stand still as she waited.

Mack looked at the stamps in the display case. Why hadn't he seen them before? There were birds, dinosaurs, badgers, fish. There were ships, trains. There were even airplanes. Bombers and jets that took people far away. There were famous men, even Indians. Or their war bonnets, at least. There was even, yes, Marianne Moore! Without the bars on her face. Looking at him with her hand to her cheek just like his teacher standing over his desk. Post Office Elementary Teacher. That's what the "Poet" meant on her stamp.

Suddenly the "next" was for him. He didn't know what to do. The woman behind him nudged him forward. "It's your turn," she said.

Mack walked to the counter and looked up to the man. His heart pounded again. "How much are stamps?"

"$12.50 for a sheet of fifty. $25.00 for one hundred."

Mack stood with his mouth open. The man spoke so fast Mack couldn't hold it in his head.

Marianne would be watching with that teacher-look on her face.

The man held up a sheet of stamps. "There are fifty on a sheet for $12.50."

A sheet of stamps? No one told him they came in sheets. What would anyone do with that many stamps? Who had that much money? Mack couldn't think what to do. He held up his hand with the sweaty money. Several nickels and many pennies.

"You want just one stamp?"

Mack nodded his head.

"Any particular kind?"

"No." Mack said.

The man looked through his drawer.

The Indian war bonnet. Mack wanted to say.

"I—" Mack tried to speak and the man looked at him. He thought everyone across the counter and everyone in line behind him was looking. "The headdress—" Mack pointed, and the man handed Mack the feathered war bonnet.

"Next," the man said.

If Mack saved his money forever, he wouldn't be able to buy a sheet of stamps. Why would anyone want that many? How could there be that many people to mail letters to? Mack didn't know anyone to write to.

But maybe he did.

Mack knew he could trust stamps. He would write a letter to his father wherever he was. The stamp would find him. Mack would write to his father to come home even if he beat him. Though he wouldn't. Not Mack's father. Mack would share the attic room with him. The dark plaid bedspread. They could watch their white breath rise together in the winter like the vapor trail of a faraway plane above the dark walls that curved like the dirt under fingernails.

Mack revised his "My Stamp Collection" essay. He would send it to his father too. Now he knew that stamps came in large squares like the map of their state sectioned off in counties the teacher had on the schoolroom wall. She talked to them about geography with her hand to her face. The sheets could be pulled apart like Mack's family had been. Billy said it was better that Mack didn't have a father.

That night Mack drifted off into sleep thinking of the stamps he had collected on his bedpost. In a dream the stamps were wings of white, creamy birds. They blew off the bed in flocks like geese he'd seen lift from a lake. Then they changed their flight and came back. They landed and lifted again and their movement over the water was a stamp dance. Everything was shimmering. Even Billy waved to him with dinosaur stamps on his face instead of the school-nurse's Band-Aids.

Yes, Mack had to show Billy the Post Office. They could go on long migrations setting out across the world. In one of those open-mouthed sacks they could go anywhere.

An American Proverb

Diane Glancy

We live with acts of God. But God isn't in it like us. Not in any way. He's the one who owns the land allotments, the words. He sends the little people* to mess up our lives.

What do we know? Born into this world. Driven up the hill to school. Licked like postage stamps.

If we look at the blue sky's curtain hiding us from the hunting grounds, we can't know it yet or who would be left to stay?

Sometimes I think I should still be writing him.

Now I have to get up in the night and go into the little rollaway on the back porch. Even in winter, I sleep there. Once he woke almost glowing. The field he said the field. Helicopters flying and men screaming. The guns. Viet Cong running over them, men gurgling in their own blood, arms and hands and legs shot off not yet dead and he saw by god the acts of God. He saw the angels sweating. They wore headbands and guns on their backs between their wings. They rode horses with braided tails and war masks.† They lifted the dying onto their horses and rode off. Up past old cattle trails, the buffalo herds stampeding like comets.

When you're so far away you don't know what's going on anymore. That's the way I like it. It's why I stay here. The only other place I'd like to go is space. Up there in the hereafter. I don't think much of the little blue speck down there in the bottom of the well like a stone. Turning in the waters as if it were something.

---

* The Cherokee "Little People" (or *Yunwi Tsundi*) are very small (about knee-high) spiritual beings, similar to European fairies, but with long hair reaching to the ground. They live in caves or woods and spend a great deal of time making music (drumming) and dancing. They are usually good-hearted and helpful. They are invisible to humans unless they choose to be seen.

† In the old days, warriors braided their horses' tails to indicate that they were riding into battle.

Ha.

It's time to do things in a different way. Tear up old standards. Barriers.

We're not supposed to do what it seems like we should be doing. But follow sometimes the trail even when it seems not right. Flying a helicopter by instrument flight. You have to fight against your instincts. You think you're going straight and you're traveling in circles.

"Will you get off the paper when I'm trying to read it?"

"What do you want?"

"A Sunday morning without the dizzies. The bomb drop."

He meck ta.

Sometimes he wanders blind in space. I see his eyes smell the campfire and I know he's nearing home. I feel it with my heart.

No they can't push us around. We stand our ground. We're the watchdog of the world. The sayers of the way life is.

Anna Lee Walters
(1946–)

"I guess that songs, prayers, and
stories are our old folks, too. I mean
they speak to us through their own
voices and say the same thing, too. I
guess it's up to us to listen and
to learn."

Anna Lee Walters, "The
Buffalo Road" in *Here First:
Autobiographical Essays by Native
American Writers*

Buffalo Wallow Woman

Anna Lee Walters

My name is Buffalo Wallow Woman. This is my real name. I live on the sixth floor of the whiteman hospital, in the mental ward. This is not the first time I have been in a mental ward, I know these places well. I wander through this one like a ghost in my wrinkled gown. My feet barely brush over the white tile floor. The long windows reflect the ghost that I have become: I am all bones and long coarse white hair. Nevertheless, there are slender black iron bars on the windows to prevent my shadow from leaving here. Bars on sixth-story windows puzzle me. On the other side of the bars, the city lays safely beyond my reach, the wrath of the ghost of Buffalo Wallow Woman.

Bars or not, I plan to leave this ward tonight. I've already been here too long. This place makes me ill, makes my heart pause and flutter. Sometimes it makes me really crazy. I told that to those in white, but they refused to listen, with the exception of one. I said, "Hospitals make me sick! Here my strong heart is weak." In response, one of them shrugged, another frowned suspiciously. A nurse replied, "Now, Mrs. Smith, you don't want to hurt our feelings, do you?"

Well, that made me grab her arm and dig my long fingernails into it. I wanted to scream, but I controlled this urge and said calmly, "What's that you called me? My name is Buffalo Wallow Woman." She and I stared each other in the eyes for five minutes before we separated: she to her mindless patients, and me to my room to locate the clothes I ought to wear when I escape from here.

My clothes are missing. Why would someone take a ghost's clothing? My possessions are so old. My moccasin soles consist only of patches by now, but I don't care. They take me where I want to go. I look at my feet stuffed into polyfoam and I hunger for beautiful things that are no more.

The closet is empty. Perhaps my clothes were never there. Perhaps I really am a ghost now. Perhaps I did not live at all. I look in the window to reassure myself—my spirit shimmers and fades, shimmers and fades. Am I deceased or alive? At this moment I really don't know.

I float down the hall, going from room to room. I search each one. Because I am a ghost, I go where I please. No one takes me seriously. Those who see me stare for a minute and decide to ignore the bag of bones and wild white hair that I have become. They underestimate me. They do not believe that I am really here. Down the hall and back again I haunt the ward. My clothes are not anywhere on this floor. I return to my room, climb up the bed like a large clumsy child. I am waiting for nightfall, hours away, to make my departure. After all I've been through, this brief wait is nothing to Buffalo Wallow Woman.

Through the barred window, clouds fly rapidly to the north. They call to me. By name they know me. *Buffalo Wallow Woman,* they whisper through the glass and the bars to remind me who the old bag of bones is and why I am here. I lift my head and square my sagging shoulders.

Far away, I hear a melody flow toward me. It is from my people's golden age and it has found me in this insane place where I am now held without respect or honor. A thousand years ago, or yesterday, in the seasons of my youth, my people danced and sang to the cloud beings in spectacular ceremony as the cloud beings gathered to shoot arrows of zigzag lightning and fiery thunderbolts across the sky. The cloud beings darkened to spirals of purple and dark red. They all twisted and turned in space like the mighty and powerful beings they truly were. And in the torrents of rain to fall later, slapping down upon the earth, filling the dry beds there to overflowing, my people lifted their heads and drank the rain thirstily. Afterward, with that taste still in their mouths, they sang in unison, "O you! That mystery in the sky!"

Miraculously, the words return to me in this alien room. I feel the wind of those clouds blow across my face, the raindrops splash the crown of my head one at a time. My face and hair feels soaked with rain. I lift my face and open my mouth. I sing, *"Hey yah hah O!"*

My voice is as small as a red ant. It is swept away in the noises coming from the vent, crushed under the hospital sounds of announcements and rolling carts and beds going back and forth in the hallway. My room is suddenly quiet and dry. The clouds are disappearing in the sky, too. Bah! There is no magic in man-made places like this. This is why Buffalo Wallow Woman always brings it with her.

I look at my wrinkled hands. They are wide and large-boned. My nails are faded yellow and longer than they need to be. I wish I could hold a birchbark rattle with painted streaks of blue lightning on it in my idle fingers. I would shake it this way and that, in the manner of my people. They lifted their rattles to the cloud beings and shook them softly in that direction. To show the departing cloud beings that I remember who they are, their magnificent splendor and power, and also who I am, I stand on the step to my bed and face them. I lift the imaginary rattle and shake it just so. A soft hiss emanates from it.

Behind me, someone says, "Mrs. Smith."

I see part of him in the window. He is the doctor who arrives each day to study me, but now I am tired of him and I think he is tired of me as well. Nothing has been exchanged between us, and he always arrives at times like this. I look at the bars before I look at him.

I think of the animals my men have taken in communal hunts before there were grocery and convenience stores. The beautiful glassy eyes of a dozen soft-brown deer people stare at me from the walls of this room. They look me right in the eye, but I do not flinch. They say, *Buffalo Wallow Woman, here we are.* I see the trail of their last misty breaths arch up into the sky—rainbows they are. I hear a shaggy buffalo bull as he turns his great frame to face me. I see the dust rise in smoky spirals under his trotting hooves as he charges toward me. His breath is hot steam on my face.

Then come the human sounds, the footsteps, a pumping heart, blood rushing to the face, and the promised words of appeasement to the animals as they silently fall with a shattering thud, offering themselves to us. For this ultimate gift, we offered everything in return, our very lives were traded on the spot, and those animal people taught us thousands of prayers and songs to honor their spirits and souls from then on. In that way, they permitted us to live, and they too lived with us. That is how we mutually survived all those years. The man behind me, the man who is here to help, doesn't know this.

He occupies the chair near the door.

"Do you come with prayers?" I ask. I turn to face him. The eyes of the deer and buffalo people surround us. They wait for his answer.

He is tall and angular with dark hair standing straight up. His eyes are foreign to me, colorless and jumpy, as if they must run somewhere. He glances behind him, over his shoulder. I am the one suspended here, but he acts trapped too. "If you come with prayers, I'll talk to you," I say, trying to figure out this odd creature whose habitat I do not know. Each day his behavior and appearance has become more unsettled. His presence disturbs the room.

He decides to speak. His voice booms at me. "Mrs. Smith, do you know how long you've been here? Do you understand that you have made no progress at all?" He is angry at me for being here.

I refuse to answer for this. I zip my lips together but I face him head-on. I have time, lots of time. I can outwait him. I become the ghost again. I start to disintegrate before him.

"Now don't do that!" he orders. He rubs his eyes and runs a hand through his wiry hair. His eyes dart everywhere. His breathing is rapid. He manages to hold his eyes in one place for a few seconds and he forcibly calms himself. He moves closer to me.

"All right, Buffalo Wallow Woman, if that's who you say you are, how did you get here? Do you know where you are?" He is still brusque and impatient, but he has called me by my real name and I must reply. My body becomes more solid and earthly again. I lean toward him.

"Do you come with prayers?" I venture again in my small voice.

"What kind of prayers?" he asks.

"Prayers to the spirits of those whose fate is in your hands." My voice is like the red ant again, crawling quietly across the room.

"What do you mean? I don't understand," he says while his eyes jump all over.

"You have no prayers then?" I persist.

"No!" he says.

"It is as I feared," I answer, turning away from him. "That is why I must leave here. Ghosts and spirits long for them. The hearts of human beings cannot beat steadily without them for long either. I know my own can't." I stand on the stepstool to move down to the floor.

"You aren't going anywhere. You don't know where you are, let alone who you are!"

We are almost the same height now. I stand before him, and he observes me from his throne.

"Where are my clothes?" I ask in my most rational voice. "I am going to leave here tonight."

He ignores me.

"You're very ill," he says with a frown. "You have no family, no one to take care of you. With your bad heart, you may not last long outside of here."

This time there is something in his voice I haven't heard before, but I want him to go. I seal my lips, and he sees immediately what I have done. He stands and goes. The room settles again.

For several weeks, there has been one in white here who is unlike this doctor and the others. Today she will appear when the sun reaches the third bar in the window. It will be soon now. In the meantime, I decide to haunt the hallway once more. I've covered its distance at least a dozen times each day for the last three months. It is the only exercise the patients have. I think of wolves in zoos, running in circles inside their cages, as I leave my room.

Today I look carefully at the occupants of each room and those people in the hall-way. There are thin walls separating the two, skinny lines that distinguish the patients from the staff. I can't tell them apart except by their clothing. If truth be known, the doctors and staff may be more quirky than the others. We patients just show our quirkiness.

In Room 612 sits a skeleton with frozen eyes. I am drawn to it, magnetized by its forceful pull. "I am a ghost," I confess to it. The skeleton does not move at all. Something whispers to me that its spirit is gone. I look around the room for it but I am the only ghost here. I leave 612 and go across the hall.

The man there is waiting for me. He embraces me tenderly and strokes my wild white hair. He calls me Grandmama and weeps on my gown. I sit down beside him, we stare into each other's souls while he holds my hand. He babbles at me, I nod. He weeps until his eyes are bright red. Then, exhausted, he lays down on his high bed. Asleep, he relaxes his grip on me and I move on.

Two nights ago, a hysterical young woman was brought into the next room. There she sits now, sullen and old before her time. Her wrists are wrapped in white bandages. I pause at the door. She raises a hand and a finger at me. "I am a ghost," I say. "That means nothing to me."

My words anger her. She rises abruptly to rush at me but hesitates after a step or two to clutch her belly and groan. It is then I notice the rise of it under her gown. I go to her rescue and she leans on me, breathing hard. Her eyes are scared.

"You would kill your child?" I ask as she bends into me. The moment passes, and she is able to stand on her own.

"Not my child," she says, "me!" Then she looks at me and adds, "I thought you were a ghost."

"I am," I repeat. This is our introduction to one another.

There is a loud disturbance in the hall, scuffling and a shouting exchange of words. One of the hospital staff is wrestling a middle-aged man. I and the young woman go to the door to watch. All the way down the hall, different colored faces appear in the doorways of each room like wooden masks. The faces are expressionless and blank, like those on the street.

The patient is overpowered and wrestled to the floor before our eyes. A silver needle punctures his arm. After the initial outburst of anger, the whole scene takes place in silence. The patient is lifted up, whisked away. The staff quickly tidies the area as if nothing happened and the hall clears. Seconds later, no one remembers what just occurred.

Only the young woman and I remain. She asks if the incident really took place. I say, "That's what will happen to all of us if we don't do what they say." The girl frowns at the bars on the windows. She has just discovered them.

"When you leave here, you must live," I say. "If you don't see to your child, it could end up here."

The girl is confused. She looks at her bandaged wrists and again at the bars. She rubs her belly. I leave her there, alone and troubled. I make my way down the hall, looking in on each person in each room along the way.

Most everyone, patients and staff alike, look right through me. My presence is not acknowledged at all. Quite unexpectedly, from deep within me, I feel the wrath of Buffalo Wallow Woman for this indignity. My blood begins to boil. It is hot and dangerously close to making me explode! My heart flaps against my chest, voices caution me.

I pause and reflect on this feeling. That old fire still burns? Rage, this overpowering, is still a part of Buffalo Wallow Woman? How very strange. I thought that I had given up this human feeling years ago, the very first time I went into a mental hospital. I mutter my thoughts aloud and head toward my room.

Back there, Tina awaits. She is nervous, frantic, because of what I am about to do. Her soft voice is usually a coo. Now it is high and squeaky.

"Where were you?" she asks tensely. "For a minute I thought maybe you had already gone." She rushes toward me and embraces me.

I pat her tiny hand. "It's not time yet." I go to my bed, climb upon it and say, "My clothes are gone, but where I am going, clothes don't matter I guess."

The first day Tina walked into my room I knew who she was. It was evident in her dark hair and high cheekbones, though her skin was more fair than mine. But where it really showed was in her behavior and her usually carefully chosen words. She was such a tiny thing. She carried bed pans past my door all day before she finally came in.

She read my name on the door and over the bed. "Mrs. Smith," she said, "I'm Tina. I'll be your evening nurse until you leave here, or until the shifts change in a few weeks, whichever comes first."

I stood at the door and watched her adjust my bed.

"It's Buffalo Wallow Woman, Tina, not Mrs. Smith," I responded, "and I am a ghost."

"I know," she replied seriously, "I've heard."

She gave me a red lollipop from a pocket and asked, "Why are you here, Buffalo Wallow Woman, if you don't mind me being so direct?"

I tore the shiny wrapper off the lollipop and stuck it in my mouth. I didn't answer. I sucked on the candy and counted the bars on the window, the way I did with the doctor when I wanted him to leave.

"Why are you here, Buffalo Wallow Woman?" she asked again.

I sucked the candy hard and motioned that my lips were sealed. I climbed on the bed, sure that she would leave.

Instead, she pulled out a wire hairbrush from the nightstand and answered with a mischievous smile, "If I ask you four times, and if you really are Buffalo Wallow Woman, then you will have to tell me, won't you?"

She began to comb my hair, pulling my head here and there. "Ghost hair is hard to comb," I said, as if this was our secret.

She replied, "You are not a ghost, Buffalo Wallow Woman. Do ghosts like lollipops?"

"Ghosts like a lot of earthly things," I said. "That's what often keeps us here."

"Why are you here, Buffalo Wallow Woman?" she asks a third time, and I knew then that I wanted someone like her, someone important, to know.

She braided my hair tightly around my head. Her fingers flew.

"I'm lost, Tina," I said. "I'm caught between two worlds, a living one and a dead one. This is the dead one," I motioned out in the hall, "right here. And this is the root of my illness. I have to return to the living one in order to be whole and well."

Tina's fingers stopped a second. She chuckled, "This is the dead one? How do you figure that?"

"Look around," I answered. "There is no magic here because everything is dead. I think that only ghosts are capable of surviving here."

Before I realized it, she asked me the fourth time. "Why are you here, Buffalo Wallow Woman?" She pulled a chair close to me as if she really planned to listen.

I decided to tell. I composed my thoughts for a moment and then began. "I am the ghost of Buffalo Wallow Woman. Do you know what a Buffalo Wallow is, my child?"

Tina nodded. "A watering hole, or something like that?" She reached over and held my hand as I spoke. Her hand was half the size of mine.

I asked, "Do you want to know about my name?" She nodded again.

"The name was taken about a hundred winters ago most recently, but I suppose it is older than that. It came out of a time when the animal people still had possession of the world. Then, they were the keepers of all sacred things.

"Wallows are shallow depressions in the earth that were made by most animals when they rolled around there and lay down. Several large ones are still visible today. They usually surround water holes or later become them because of the shallow bowls they eventually form. Today most of them, of course, are gone. They have either blown away, or towns or other things sit on top of them.

"The marshy areas that the wallows were, or became, often dried up as the summer days grew hot and long. Each, in turn, disappeared. Some time ago, there was one large wallow with water, a buffalo wallow, left. All the others had turned to dust. It was a precious thing to all life then, especially to a standard or lost human being. One day, there appeared on the horizon of that sacred place, a lost woman, on foot and traveling alone. The buffalo people stood up one by one when they saw her approach. They saw her stumble and fall from either weakness or illness, and the searing heat of the sun. Near the wallow, she collapsed and failed to rise again. One of the old buffalo bulls told two younger ones to go to her aid. The young bulls trotted through the evaporating marsh to the ailing woman. Behind them, where their hooves sunk into the marsh, pools of water began to gurgle and bubble up. They trotted around the stranger in circles until she lay in a dirty pool of water, but she was cooled and revived. Afterward, she received more help from the buffalo people and then was able to travel on. She took the name Buffalo Wallow Woman out of humility to the buffalo people, out of gratitude for her life. She understood that it was the buffalo people and the spirit of the wallow who gave her humility and gratitude, as well as her life. These were the lessons she had learned in the hands of the buffalo people."

Tina expected more. I promised, "Tomorrow, I'll finish if you still want to know."

The next day she arrived in the afternoon and brought with her a dark green leaf of Indian tobacco and a small red tin ashtray. She lit the tobacco and burned it in the tray. The odor of that one small curled leaf filled the mental ward, but it was not enough to take away all the pain and fears contained on this floor. She hid the tray in the drawer just before another nurse popped in the room to ask what was burning.

Tina shrugged her shoulders and winked at me. "Would you mind if I called you something other than Mrs. Smith or Buffalo Wallow Woman? Where I come from we don't call each other by such names. One seems too formal and the other too sacred. Would I offend you if I called you Grandmother?" she asked politely.

I gazed at her with admiration and answered, "That would not offend me, my child. That would honor me. And if this is your plan and decision, then I must call you grandchild, if that's the way it is to be."

Tina offered her hand to me and I took it. This is the way we joined forces. When her schedule permitted, I resumed my story.

"Buffalo Wallow Woman died in the year of the great smallpox epidemic, near the very place she had been saved as a younger woman. This time, she and others who were sick isolated themselves from the remainder of the people and, therefore, did not receive formal burials.

"As a young girl of perhaps eleven or twelve winters, I visited this place unexpectedly. At the time, I didn't know who Buffalo Wallow Woman was or her story. I had been traveling by wagon with my family through an unfamiliar stretch of open plains country that was partly frozen but was beginning to thaw in a sudden burst of sunshine. When the wagon became bogged down in deep gray clay, the men got off to dig out the back wheels. I, too, climbed off and noticed a place to the side of the wagon trail that tugged at me. It was a very large shallow pool covered with ice. Its size was perhaps half a city block. Birds were soaring overhead and chirping at me. I watched them dip toward the frozen pool and fly away in flocks. Soon my family had dug out the wagon and were ready to leave. By evening we had reached our destination, and I thought that I had already put the shallow pool out of my mind.

"But that night I dreamed of it. I saw it in all the four seasons. There were buffalo at the pool's edges, and their reflections were in the water with the clouds and sky. Other animals were also there, such as bears, deer, and all species of birds.

"Every night I dreamed of the pool, and it seemed to be speaking to me. Then one night, Buffalo Wallow Woman visited me in my dreams and in a mysterious way told me who she was and what had happened there. She said that she had not died after all, and that in another world she had learned that she never would. She said this was all true and because it was, our people had never lied to us. They understood everything all along.

"She told me that it was an old spirit who had called me to the watering hole, the same spirit that guided her there each time she was close to death, and for this reason, she and I were tied together by it. The same spirit had called the buffalo people, the bird people, and all the others who came to drink, because that spirit made no distinction between the life of a buffalo, a cloud, a mountain, a stone, or a human being. It was the same indescribable force, no matter what form it took.

"At my tender age, it was truly remarkable that I actually understood what Buffalo Wallow Woman said. It was wonderful that I understood she had claimed some invisible part of me, and I claimed some part of her, and I accepted our relationship without question. I could not understand with my head, though. I grasped it at the level of and at the center of my heart. I understood that I had been thirsty but didn't know it myself, and I had gone to the wallow so that my soul might drink. The spirit of the wallow knew me better than I knew myself."

Tina didn't press for more right then. She was quiet, staring outside at the evening sky. The room was quiet. We didn't speak about me again for several days. Then she came into the room and sat down without a word. She waited for me to continue.

"All my life, I have been told by the whiteman that I am crazy, my child," I picked up where I left off, "because I see things that other people do not. I hear voices that no one else does. But the craziest thing I do, they tell me, is take these visions and voices seriously. This is the way of all Buffalo Wallow Women, I suppose. I structure my life around the visions and voices because it pleases me to honor them this way. I am never alone because of this. It is my inheritance from Buffalo Wallow Woman, from my own flesh and blood, from the visions I have received, and from my identity as this kind of person.

"But each day the doctor asks me if I know who I am, and I have to bear this outrage. He also asks me if I know where I am. He talks about 'reality.' He tells me to face it, that this is, after all, a new time which has no room for Buffalo Wallow Women. His questions, pretensions, and arrogance are ludicrous to me. I feel that he is more ill than I am. I am Buffalo Wallow Woman! Wherever I go, the spirits go with me.

"I am suspect and feared because I admit that I am a ghost. This is dangerous, I am told. It is the one thing the doctors have said that I know to be true. I am dangerous. I am dangerous because my craziness may spread from me to another and on and on. I am dangerous because I still have some rage left about what's happened to me over the years. It's not entirely squelched yet, although I've tried to empty it out of me. This surprises even me at the moment. And I am dangerous because I have great destructive powers within me that I haven't used yet.

"For instance, I can kill with my eyes if I so desire. I can shoot out poison and make my victims squirm with agony. There's all kinds of poison for this, but most come from pure hate. I can use words in incantations that will steal the soul, the spirit, the will, and mind away."

Tina looked at me mischievously. Before she could speak, I said, "Now don't say a word until you walk through this ward, look closely at every patient, and are able to explain how they became that way!"

We ended here, and Tina left. That night, laying in the dark, I decided to ask Tina to help me escape from this unbearable indignity of forced confinement. A few days passed before I voiced my question.

I said, "Tina, my child, I am going to escape from here, I am going to fly away. When the time comes, I would like you to be there, to help me at the very last."

Tina replied, "If you are a ghost, why can't you just go?"

"It's not that easy. Some earthly person has to release me, you see."

She stood at the window staring at the iron bars. She turned around and asked, "You can really do it?"

I nodded.

She took a deep breath and crossed her heart like a small child. "O.K.," was all she said.

Now that the time is here, Tina seems reluctant to have me leave. She's had weeks to prepare, but her eyes are actually moist and red.

"Tell me I am doing the right thing," she says. "I mean, you're my patient, what am I doing?"

She is panicky. She flutters all around.

"You and I, my child, are more than patient and nurse, much more than that. Don't make our kinship so small, so insignificant. This is the stuff that links the whole chain of life together, old to young, grandchild to grandmother, and on and on."

It is dark outside. Not even the bars on the window can be seen. I climb off the bed. My nightgown floats loosely around me.

Tina is watching me. She has a large brown sack with her. When she speaks, her voice is calm. "I brought everything you asked of me, and something that I thought of myself." She takes out a thin red flannel blanket from her package, folds it in half, and puts it at the foot of the bed. "This is for you," she says.

"Thank you, my child," I answer, touched by her thoughtfulness. I pick up the blanket and hold it to my heart.

"What do you want me to do?" she asks. I see her hesitate before she moves.

I lift the blanket and ask her to lay it on the floor.

"Sit here." I point to one end of the blanket. She takes her sack with her. I sit down at the other end.

"Now," I say, "I want to speak to you before I leave. Please, child, put those things between us."

Tina lays out a pouch of green tobacco and cigarette papers, and the red ashtray. She puts a beaded butane lighter inside the tray.

I ask her to turn out the fluorescent lights over us. Only a soft light comes from the bathroom. The door to it is half closed. Then I ask her to take my hair down and pull off my shoes.

We sit together in silence for a long time, gathering our thoughts together for the last thing we are about to do for one another.

Finally, I am ready. I say, "My child, you are the answer to a prayer, the prayer of Buffalo Wallow Woman. To find you in a place like this is very sweet to someone like me. I feel a stab of victory for Buffalo Wallow Woman, for though she is a ghost, you are alive and are as strong and thoughtful as she has ever been.

"You came to me with open arms and received a ghost in them, and you did not flinch at anything I said. All of it you took in, in your strong, gentle way. You have been taught well. I have told you everything—good things, ugly things, sacred things, and unholy things. We have even sung together. You have given me honor and re-spect in a way that only kin can pay. In exchange for that, kin to kin, grandmother to grandchild, I want to include you in my prayer tonight.

"Everything I have told you these past few weeks is the truth, you know. Some-times we ghosts are full of rage and anger, such as I have been at certain times, but the ghost of Buffalo Wallow Woman can only speak the truth, even when it hurts, as it sometimes does.

"Anyway, I thank you, my child, for the honor you have brought me, by listening to me, by singing with me, by calling me your grandmother, by praying for me tonight, and by setting me free.

"I have spent a lifetime in and out of this insane place that the doctors call reality, or the real world. I have spent a lifetime waiting to be set free, because no one else but you could do it for me. This is what we mean to each other. This is what life means.

"These are my parting words to you, my child. Do you wish to say anything?"

Tina nods her head. I can almost hear the movements. The spirit people have come into the room. They surround us.

"You don't understand," she says. "I'm not what you want me to be. I have flaws. I went to school. I can't speak my language because of this. I don't want to live in poverty the way my family does. I'm weak, and worst of all, I'm not very spiritual."

She pauses, threatening to break into tears.

"And I agreed to this because I thought you would change your mind. I didn't think you would really go through with it. I never thought I would actually be here right now."

"But you are here," I answer. "You are here with the ghost of Buffalo Wallow Woman. Most of us never know what we will do at a certain moment until that moment arrives. Then we know. Do you have doubts now?"

"Not doubts," she says, "but lots of sadness."

"This is not a bad thing, Tina," I say. "Soon you will feel like singing out, *Hey yah hah O!*" I say. "I promise you that you will feel it in you."

I pick up a cigarette paper and the Indian tobacco and began to roll a smoke. I give it to Tina. I say, "When I have gone, you must light the smoke, then blow a puff to the earth and sky and then to the four directions. Then you must say in a clear voice, 'I offer this smoke for the spirit of my grandmother, Buffalo Wallow Woman. May she be forever at peace and may she forever live in nature all around me.' You must say this, Tina, not only think it."

The spirit people make noises all around me. Some of them are in the darkness, others are in the light.

Tina is flustered, but she acknowledges my directions.

I close my eyes and begin my prayer. "O Mystery of Life! The time has come for Buffalo Wallow Woman to depart," I say to the spirits in the room, the spirits that follow me everywhere. They agree with my words. Their voices answer Yes in chorus. I continue. "I want to leave this world without anger or hate, for in this final moment, I want none of that to remain. I leave this world to my grandchild sitting here. May she love it and care for it as much as her elders did. My final requests are that you spirits accept me and take me home, and that in my departure, you watch over my grandchild here."

My heart flaps against my breastbone. I feel it pause, flutter, and thump my breastbone again. I open my eyes. The room is cold. The spirits are everywhere. There are deer people, buffalo people, and cloud beings—so much life in one little room! They chant and sing.

I am strangely weightless and transparent. I feel myself break up into a fine, wet mist. Then, I am looking down from the ceiling. Tina sits alone. I see my body lying across the floor, a bag of old bones and long wild white hair.

Tina is holding the smoke. Her hand shakes violently. She looks up at the ceiling, takes a deep breath, and steadies herself. She picks up the beaded butane lighter and lights the sacred smoke. She tries to speak. Her words are timid and frightened. She clears her throat and starts again.

She says it all perfectly, word for word. The spirits answer joyfully, Yes! Yes! They turn to me and say, *Buffalo Wallow Woman, now you are free. No bars shall ever hold you again.*

The spirits guide me to the window, but now it is my turn to hesitate. I look back at Tina, my grandchild. She is sitting there all alone. She looks troubled and sad.

We'll always be here, the spirits say, and I nod. Then, as we begin to slip through the bars, I hear little Tina sing, *"Hey yah hah O!"*

Las Vegas, New Mexico, July 1969

Anna Lee Walters

Rosa Lopez sat in a rocking chair, staring out one of the long narrow windows to the mountains west of Las Vegas. Everything outside was a thick green though the sky was filled with dusty summer rain.

She was frail now, as thin as the wood in the frame of the rocking chair, as limp as the dainty handkerchief she kept in the pocket of her dressing gown. It was a long, dark gown with white lace around her neck and at her wrists. Her feet were covered in the same color. A crocheted coverlet lay across her lap.

The room was massive, dwarfing her against the afternoon haze pouring through the wispy, ivory curtains. A large, soft, maroon rug covered most of the floor area, and dark, heavy, polished pieces of furniture filled the walls and corners. The bed was under the long, skinny windows.

She had been sitting where she was for perhaps two hours, staring out the window, and waiting. Death was certain now, as certain as the light spray of rain on the windowpanes. After nearly one hundred years of living, Rosa didn't mind it too much.

She began to undo the bun that her hair was styled into. Her movements were painstakingly deliberate. Her hair was white, as white as the lace around her neck. She lifted a heavy brush from the dressing table and slowly began to brush out her long hair.

Finally, she put the brush down and stared at her hands. They were brown and wrinkled. She picked up the heavy hand mirror and hesitantly peeked into it. Her face was ancient. The black eyes gazed into the mirror for a long time, and then she put the mirror down.

Rosa hadn't said much in the last eight years, only the few words that were necessary in day-to-day life. She had spent much of that time in thought, reflecting on her long life, her three children, and two husbands. At times, she could not completely remember all of her life. These gaps did not alarm her though, because sooner or later everything came back to her. Today was one of those days when her memory was crystal clear. She ached from remembering almost everything.

She hadn't thought of Taos for a long time. Today the image of Taos Pueblo loomed up before her. How could she remember after so long? Nearly eighty years. She was a lithesome eighteen-year-old, and the Taos man who became her husband was nearly thirty. She could feel the strength of him even now, the firm muscles in his arms and back. He wore long braids. What was his name? She couldn't remember. She should remember his name!

Rosa winced, how could she forget? Her teary eyes found the mountains outside the window again. Raindrops slid down the windowpanes.

His name was on the tip of her tongue. There were two children, Maria and Domingo. She remembered the weight of them in her belly, the odor of milk on them. The girl was born shortly after the marriage, within a year or two. The boy came later, perhaps four years.

Those children lived past middle age. The girl died at the age of sixty. What year was that? 1949? 1948? The boy died more recently, as an old man. Rosa always remembered him as a boy, a dear boy. She'd outlived both of her first two children. A hundred years. Rosa had had a hundred years. It was more than enough.

The face of her first husband darted across Rosa's mind again. His eyes were light liquid brown; he had crooked smile. What was his name?

Rosa had actually lived in the pueblo for a brief time, maybe five years, with her husband and children. Then he was killed on the eastern plains in circumstances she never fully comprehended. Her children stayed in the pueblo and she went to Española after that, to work for a family there. Sitting in the hard rocking chair now, Rosa could feel the two warm children in her arms as she prepared to leave them in Taos with her husband's family. They did not cry out when she left. They waved.

Rosa was lonely then. It seemed that for most of her life, Rosa was lonely. As a child, she had grown up in the care of several families, all of whom had shown her tender kindness and charity. But something had always been missing. In this void, Rosa was often lonely.

She knew nothing about her own mother and father. None of the families, in whose temporary care she lived, discussed them with her, though at times the faces of her foster families held inscrutable expressions when they looked at her, but then they were careful to smile very brightly at her, and Rosa's own doubts vanished then.

Maria was the only constant in her early life, the Indian woman, Maria. Rosa never knew what tribe Maria was, and Maria never volunteered this information. It was funny that Rosa hadn't spoken to Maria for sixty years, and yet at the same time there wasn't a day that went by that Maria wasn't there in her memory. Even in these last few years, when the memory lapses became serious, Maria stayed secure somewhere inside Rosa's head and heart.

Maria was strange, enigmatic, to Rosa, and their relationship, though somehow bound together forever, was indefinable. Rosa even now wasn't sure what she felt for Maria. Maria, with her dark eyes, and long black hair, in the earliest memories. Maria must have been in her early forties then. Later, Maria's hair was white as Rosa's was now.

Rosa lifted the heavy mirror again and looked at herself. Yes, Maria *did* look like this. The white hair *and the eyes too*? Rosa put the mirror down.

In Rosa's first memory of Maria, when Rosa was about five or six, the two were running. It was dark and Rosa ran after Maria as if life itself depended upon it. As Rosa ran, she called Maria by another name. What was it? Maria, a night shadow, turned and lifted the child, Rosa, and carried her. Rosa bounced in Maria's arms. Maria smelled of food and smoke. Had she been cooking? Why were they running?

Maria had always been near, close by to Rosa. Rosa saw that now. When Rosa lived with different foster families, Maria was a distant shadowy figure who followed Rosa everywhere.

This vivid recall was suddenly overpowering and exhausting to Rosa. It was also threatening somehow. She leaned her head back and rested it on the high frame of the chair.

A voice came from the kitchen. Rosa looked over her shoulder to see Anita put a tea kettle on the stove. Rosa studied Anita, who had once been a handsome woman. In her sixties now, Anita was still a striking woman, despite being a little overweight.

"Anita," Rosa called. "Anita."

The woman in the kitchen came to Rosa.

"I was thinking of Maria," Rosa said in Spanish; her voice was not strong.

Anita sat down on the bed. She wore a surprised look on her face.

"Maria?" she asked. "The Maria from Taos Pueblo. We haven't seen her for a long time."

"No, Anita," Rosa said, "That is another Maria, your half-sister, a younger one. I've never told you about the older one, the other Maria. She died just before you were born in the same year. You were born in 1900, no?"

Anita nodded.

Rosa continued. "Maria was about sixty-five when she died. Your father, Santiago, knew her though."

"Who was this Maria, Mama?" Anita asked curiously. Rosa didn't look well.

"I really don't know, Anita. But now I think that she was somebody important to me." Rosa whispered, her voice cracked.

"You said you had no family, Mama. No mother, no father. You yourself have often said that." Anita carefully watched Rosa whose face was drained of color. Alarmed, she asked Rosa more softly, "You want to talk about Maria?"

One tear rolled down Rosa's face. Anita wanted to hold Rosa but did not.

"Anita, Maria was an Indian woman." Rosa wiped the solitary tear from her face.

"Yes?" Anita asked expectantly.

"The first person I have a memory of is Maria. All my life, the first half of my life, Maria was there, not close, but always apart from me. When I was a child we were in Taos together, then later Española, and then Santa Fe. She was always there. Even after Santiago and I came to Las Vegas, Maria followed us."

"What happened to her, Mama?" Anita asked.

"I don't know. I don't know anything about her except that she spent her life alone. To the day she died, she was alone. She was not lucky like me to have found a man like Santiago, your father. And so late in life. I was over thirty. After Taos, I thought my life was ruined..." Rosa smiled a girl-like smile.

"Santiago was good for me. And then I had you—when I was an old woman too! Life should not be spent alone. I think Maria's was. There was a sadness about her.

"The day that Maria died, she walked to our first little house in the early dawn. She was old then. Santiago built that house for me, Anita. It still stands. Maria came into the house, appearing to be very tired, and carrying cornmeal, which she had ground the day before. She set the meal on the table and then sat down beside Santiago.

"'Rosa,' Maria said, 'After today, you will not see me again.'"

"Maria spoke to Santiago and me about her life then. She did not often do this. Her life had been long and very hard, but Maria said she had lived the best she could. She also said that sometimes she had been lonely, very lonely, but somehow she had survived it."

Rosa stopped here, picked up the mirror again, and gazed at herself. Anita was frightened at Rosa's weak appearance.

"Mama," Anita said, "let's eat. You haven't eaten all day." When Rosa did not object, Anita went into the kitchen, poured tea and cut a melon in two. She returned carrying a tray to Rosa, who was still studying herself in the mirror.

Anita served Rosa, placing the saucer and teacup on the dressing table. Then she sat down on the bed again and said, "Mama, Maria is gone. Don't think about her."

Rosa looked up at Anita and then at the melon and cup of tea. She drank the tea, and then said heavily, "On that last day, Maria told me a truth and a lie."

"What was it?" Anita asked.

"Maria said that she was there on the day that I was born. She said that my mama died in childbirth the day that I was born and Maria said that she then promised to look after me. She promised this to my mother. Maria said that I did not scream when I entered this world, but my mother wept, she said." Rosa quieted.

"And your father? Did Maria tell you about this man?" Anita asked.

Rosa said no. She picked up the hand mirror again and looked into it.

"Mama, what lie did Maria tell you?" Anita asked. "Was it about your mother? Who was your mother, Mama?"

Rosa held the mirror on her lap. Her eyes brimmed with tears.

"Come here," she told Anita.

Anita went to Rosa who held up the mirror and told Anita to look inside. Rosa bent and looked in the mirror. The only thing she saw was her own face and Rosa's.

Rosa said, "Anita, *that is Maria* in there. She is older than Maria lived to be, but it is Maria."

"What are you saying, Mama?" Anita gasped.

"Maria was my mother, Anita," Rosa said tearfully. "I didn't know it until today, this afternoon sometime."

"Why?" asked Anita. "Why didn't she tell you, Mama?"

"I don't know," Rosa said as the tears flowed freely down her face. "Go away, Anita, for a little while please. I must be alone. This is a shock to me somehow though there is really no reason to be surprised. No reason at all."

Anita hugged Rosa and then disappeared into another part of the house.

Rosa sat the rest of the day alone, with Anita peeking in on her from time to time. Most of Rosa's thoughts were of Maria. Maria cooking. Maria praying. Maria seldom laughing.

Toward dusk, Anita entered the room. Rosa watched her turn on the lights and pull the bed covers down. Then Anita gently lifted Rosa and guided her toward the bathroom, and then to the bed. When Anita had helped Rosa change to a night-gown, and put her under the covers, Anita sat down on the bed, beside Rosa. She took Rosa's hand in her own. She did not intrude on Rosa's thoughts, but looked into Rosa's eyes for a long time.

Rosa asked one question, "Why didn't Maria tell me, Anita?"

Anita patted Rosa's hand and let it go. She left the room.

Outside the narrow windows, the rain stopped, night came. For a while, Rosa's memories kept her awake. She tried to remember her Taos husband's name. But try as she might, his name escaped her. Then, once more, she saw his brown eyes staring into hers. His eyes were hypnotic, lulling her to sleep. In this peaceful state, she remembered his name, Manuel. She smiled. Then about two hours later, Rosa died quietly, in this sleep.

Apparitions

Anna Lee Walters

Wanda looked at the distorted reflections of herself and her mother as they passed in front of the store window wishing for a Maytag washing machine and a vacuum cleaner with at least six attachments, though their house had no throw rugs, let alone a thick carpet like the one shown in the store window. Wanda was shorter than her momma, and her mother was short alongside of the other promenading figures moving past the store window. There were other differences, too. Wanda's momma wore a black-and-white checkered housedress and long braids held together by a red rubber band. Wanda was a younger version of her mother in a cotton print dress and faded light blue tennis shoes. Wanda's momma wore moccasins over her flesh-colored stockings. The other figures, apparitions in the tinted store glass window, looked Wanda and her momma up and down as they passed the mother and daughter. The men wore summer suits and white shoes, while the women wore high-heeled shoes. Their coiffures were nestlike: a strand of hair never strayed out of place, even in the summer breeze.

Wanda turned away from the glass window to a woman standing beside her looking at something inside the display. Wanda looked her up and down. The woman wore spiked heels and a pink knitted dress. The red-brown nest was in place upon her head. Her lips were red, and her eyes were purple just above the lids. She carried a large handbag which she then raised to open. Wanda realized the woman was looking at herself in the window. The woman pulled out a chrome-colored tube and applied some more red to her mouth. Then the woman turned to Wanda and gazed at her for a few seconds. "Hi honey," the woman said. Wanda didn't answer. She just stared at the nest that was the woman's hair. The woman frowned and looked to Wanda's momma, who was counting change in a small beaded coin purse. The woman dug into her boxlike handbag again and stared tentatively at Wanda. Impulsively, she grabbed one of Wanda's hands and pressed a fifty-cent piece into it. Then she held her red lips tightly together in a straight horizontal line and marched off, her spiked heels clicking on the hot cement.

They were mostly quarters inside the coin purse. The little pouch bulged out when Wanda's momma snapped the top shut. She put the coin purse inside her housedress pocket and the weight of the quarters made the pocket fabric pull down on one side of it. Then Wanda's momma took out a headscarf, neatly folded, from the other pocket of her housedress. At one corner of the scarf was a knot which she began to untie. Wanda watched.

There were one dollar bills in the knot. There were four of them. Wanda's momma lifted her eyes to Wanda with a smile and said, "Over seven dollars, Wanda. It's more than enough."

Wanda held out the fifty-cent piece to her momma. Wanda's momma said, "Where'd you get that?"

"That woman who was here," Wanda said.

"Well, come on, Wanda," her mother said. "We have to get back home to fix your daddy's supper because he's got to work again tonight." She pushed Wanda's fifty-cent piece away.

Wanda followed her mother down the street amidst the clicking of high heels and the brush of tailored summerwear. Wanda watched the apparitions in the brown and pink-tinted store window glass. The apparitions moved about curiously on the smooth glassy surface, entering one side and disappearing on the opposite side.

The huge sign hanging from a bank building corner said that it was three o'clock and 92 degrees. Following that came a long message about investing in certificates and saving for the future. Wanda did not read it, though she knew most of the words. She was in the third grade.

She plodded along after her mother. At the department store, Wanda's mother stopped and waited for Wanda to enter. It was cold inside the store. Again, Wanda followed her mother to a counter that said LAY-AWAYS HERE.

"Yes," a young woman with horn-rimmed glasses said to Wanda's momma.

"Well," Wanda's momma said, "I came to pay off my lay-away." Wanda's momma's voice was naturally quiet. She was soft-spoken.

The woman behind the counter did not know that. She said harshly, "You'll have to speak up if you want help around here." She looked Wanda and her mother up and down, her eyes lingering on Wanda's momma's braids and moccasins.

Wanda's momma grimaced slightly, but she raised her voice to accommodate the woman behind the counter. She said, "I came to pay off my lay-away."

The woman frowned and turned away to search a stack of files. She found the right group of files and asked, "Name?"

Wanda's momma asked, "What?"

The store clerk turned and put a hand on her bony hip and said very loudly, "I asked you your name. Can't you hear?" Other customers nearby lifted their eyes curiously to the store clerk and Wanda's momma.

Wanda's momma answered, "My name is Marie Horses."

ANNA LEE WALTERS

The store clerk answered, "Horses? It figures." She quickly pulled out a yellow sheet of paper and said, "You owe $4.50 on that."

Marie Horses untied the handkerchief knot and laid the four dollar bills on the counter. The store clerk watched incredulously. Marie Horses then took out two quarters from her coin purse and laid them down.

The store clerk disappeared through a curtain hanging behind her and returned carrying a package. She set it down before Wanda and her mother.

Wanda's momma said, "I'll be putting something else in lay-away today." She waited to see if the woman had heard, but the clerk gave no indication that she knew Wanda and her momma were alive.

Wanda's momma led the way again down the tiled aisles to the shoe department. They passed plastic shower curtains and towels hanging from brightly colored plastic rods. These things Marie Horses touched. In the fabric section, she stopped and went to touch some white satin cloth. It was smooth under her fingers, and she lay the cloth against her face. She smiled with delight at the feel of the satin on her face.

Once in the shoe section of the store, the two people, mother and daughter, sat down in low, orange chairs. This part of the store was carpeted. Wanda's momma reached down and ran her fingers over the carpet texture.

The man who came out of another curtain at the back of this store section was quite tall and middle-aged. His eyes were on the package Marie Horses carried. He said, "Can I help you? If not, those chairs are for paying customers." When he said *paying*, he said *PAY-YING*. He'd had it with people coming in to sit down for a few minutes to cool off.

"Yes," Wanda's mother answered. "The girl needs shoes. See?" Marie Horses showed the tear in one of Wanda's tennis shoes. She said, "I sewed it twice. Bloodied myself with the needle. Can't sew it anymore."

The man measured Wanda's foot in a metal contraption. He studied the measurement, then turned to Marie Horses. "How much money you want to spend? The amount of money you can spend is going to rule out certain things. How much money you have?"

Marie Horses blushed ever so slightly. The man did not notice. She said, "It's all right. I have money. I'm going to put them on lay-away for the girl."

He was looking at a rack of merchandise behind him, and he pulled a pink tennis shoe off the display. Along with that, he pulled a white plastic shoe with buckles. Then he disappeared into the curtain again.

He carried several pairs still in boxes when he returned. He deposited all the boxes in front of Wanda.

Wanda lifted her foot with the white sock so that he could slip one of the shoes on her. He told her, "Stand on it." Wanda stood in the stiff shoe.

He felt her left toe, and then he put his hand on her left calf. He kept his hand there. He said, "How does that shoe fit you?" Wanda didn't say anything. He moved his hand to her knee and held her there. Wanda's dress hem covered his hand. He told Wanda to sit down again and he put the other shoe on Wanda's other foot. This time he placed both of his hands on Wanda's legs. His hands were on Wanda's knees. "Those shoes fit all right?" he asked.

Marie Horses sat studying the shoes, not aware of the place the salesman's hands lingered. Wanda would not look at her mother's face. The salesman moved his hands up to Wanda's thighs, and all the time he talked about the shoes Wanda wore. Finally his hands came out of Wanda's dress, and he pulled off the shoes.

The salesman turned to Marie Horses now, giving her his full attention. He said, "Ma'am, if you're going to put these shoes on lay-away, you'd better go see the lady at the Department to see if it will be all right. Me and the girl here will keep trying the shoes on until we find a pair that fits."

Marie Horses thought about this and said, "The lady knows already."

The salesman frowned and said, "Well, no one told me. Someone will have to tell me before I let you carry these shoes off." Marie Horses turned red in the face. She got out of her chair and padded down the tiled aisles again in her moccasined feet.

Wanda wanted to run after Marie Horses, but the salesman glared at her, and one of his hands tightly pinched one of her knees. The other hand dug into the flesh behind her other knee. He released one hand with a silent warning and took another shoe out of a tan shoebox.

Wanda looked around. There was no one else in this part of the store.

Again, the man pushed Wanda's foot into the plastic shoe. Then he forced the other foot into the other shoe. Again, he told her to stand, while his hands moved from her knees to her thighs. He was talking to her. Wanda didn't know what he said. Then his hands went higher to Wanda's pink underpants. His fingers jabbed her. Still he talked about the shoes. Wanda tried to move away from him. He grabbed her viciously on one of her thighs, and his eyes glared into hers. His other hand slipped beneath Wanda's underwear.

The closest saleslady was at a counter a few aisles over, straightening clothes that customers had ruffled through and then not purchased. Marie Horses was walking toward Wanda and the salesman, but she was quite a distance away. Wanda raised her hand to motion to Marie Horses. The salesman understood what Wanda was trying to do. He pulled on her thighs, and Wanda sat down hard on the chair before she realized it. Marie Horses was then only a few feet away. The salesman left the shoes on Wanda and stood beside her. His face became blank and expressionless. He held his hands clasped together behind his back. Wanda watched him. He looked like the other apparitions in the store glass windows outside. His nice summerwear rustled when he moved, and his white shoes made no sound on the carpeted floor.

Marie Horses said to him, "The lady said for you to bring the shoes over to her when you are ready." To Wanda, Marie Horses said, "You like those shoes, honey?" Wanda didn't reply.

The salesman said, "Those shoes fit her fine."

Wanda took off the shoes by herself and wrapped them in the tissue paper in the shoebox. She still had the fifty-cent piece in her hand. The salesman took the box to the lady at the counter. He said, "Doris, got a ticket for you to write up over here."

The lady he spoke to was the same one who had dealt with Wanda and Marie Horses earlier. When Doris didn't respond to him, Marie Horses told him, "That lady can't hear too good. You have to speak up to her." The shoe salesman left Wanda and Marie Horses there with the shoebox.

Eventually, Doris came over to them and prepared the sales ticket. She collected $3.50 from Wanda's momma. Then the two, mother and daughter, left the store and went out into a hot burst of wind.

Wanda was quiet, looking at her mother from time to time with a hard-to-read expression on her face. Marie Horses noticed. She asked Wanda, "You want to spend your fifty-cent piece before we go home?" Wanda looked at the shiny coin in her sweaty hand. She shook her head no and let the coin drop through her fingers. It rolled down the sidewalk past Marie Horses's moccasins and stopped a few feet away with a ping. It glittered in the four o'clock sun. Wanda didn't retrieve it. Neither did Marie Horses. Their reflections went from store window to store window as they made their way out of town. After a few minutes, Marie Horses turned to Wanda and asked, "Honey, you like coming into town?"

"No," Wanda said emphatically.

"Me neither," Marie Horses said, and they walked on in silence.

Janet Campbell Hale
(1947–)

*"If it is to be real and true, if you
are to write the deep-down truth
and have it understood the way you
intend, then you must concentrate
all your energy, must throw off
pretensions and bare your soul,
write with the utmost sincerity and
intensity whatever it is you want to
say, right down to your very core."*

Janet Campbell Hale, *Bloodlines*

Claire

Janet Campbell Hale

A person has to watch her step when she is an inmate of an old people's home. Especially if her mind happens to be clear. Especially if she loathes the so-called home and resents the son who brought her to Oakland, California, who insisted, after his father died three years ago, that she live with him. "Come home with us, Ma," he said. "You can't live all alone out in the country. We love you. We would love having you. Let us look after you." (She was grief-stricken at the time; after all, she and Sam, who were married some fifty odd years, were as close as two people could be.) Her mind was clouded when she agreed to leave Idaho and its harsh climate for sunny California, when she agreed to leave her home and everything that had ever meant anything to her, even her dog. At the time it seemed the rational thing to do.

She *was* old, after all, at seventy-six. (Now she was three years older.) And it was true that the winters were hard and she didn't know how she would manage without Sam. And then there was the case a year or two before of the old widow who was beaten to death by a gang of teenagers. The girl who testified against the others in exchange for immunity told how they knocked at the old woman's door and asked to use her telephone. Their car had broken down, they told her, and they needed to call a tow truck. The old woman let them in and, turning her back to them, said, "The phone is in here. Just follow me." One of the girls stabbed the old woman in the back, but she braced herself in a doorway and didn't fall. The girl pulled the knife out of the first wound and stabbed her again. This time she fell and the other girls began kicking her and pounding her with their fists as she, realizing now what was happening, began to pray: "The Lord is my shepherd, I shall not want." She was dead before she could finish her prayer.

That heinous crime had occurred in the next county less than a hundred miles from Claire's home. They did it, the one who testified said, because they wanted to see what it felt like to kill someone, and they had decided, some weeks before, that their victim would be either a young child or an elderly person. The weekend before they'd gone to Northtown Mall in Spokane hoping to find a child who was not being watched carefully whom they could lure away. No luck there. They didn't know the old woman who became their victim, whose name was Mrs. Olson, but their school bus passed her house twice a day on school days. They'd seen her working in her garden and sitting on her front porch. They'd never seen anyone else with her and figured she must live alone. Elderly widows who live alone aren't unusual.

"Remember poor Mrs. Olson," Claire's son, Ozzie, had said, and that was enough, finally, to make up her mind. But Maybelle never wanted her mother-in-law in her home. After she found Claire's journal, she wanted her out.

Claire began keeping a journal about a month after she first came to her son's home. She was used to Sam, to telling him her most intimate thoughts, telling him what she had seen or heard and what her impressions were. Without Sam she found her thoughts floating away before she got a good look at them. At first her journals were a substitute for the good company she was used to. She talked to her journal, that is, to herself, rather than to no one at all. The journal writing gave her a sense of control. Her life otherwise was so much out of her control now that she'd become dependent upon her son and his wife.

Maybelle had gone into her room, she said, to give it a more thorough cleaning than Claire was obviously capable of giving it. And she found the journals right there in the top dresser drawer in ten brightly colored spiral notebooks. Claire's writing was, according to Maybelle, "Full of bitching and pissing and moaning." (Maybelle was not the most refined woman in the Bay Area.) "She doesn't like our house. She called our walls Pepto Bismol pink. She doesn't like California. It's too crowded and she misses the seasons. Hah! What an ingrate your mother is! After we opened our home to her." Maybelle issued an ultimatum to Ozzie: "Either she goes or I go!" Of course Claire was the one who went.

"I was a fool to have listened to you, Ozzie," she said to her son on the drive to Loma Vista. "I would prefer returning to my own home."

"Don't start in, Ma. You know you can't live alone. You need someone to look after you full time now. Remember poor Mrs. Olson."

Ozzie, the eldest of her three boys, was no spring chicken himself. His hairline receded just a bit and he had a double chin and a pot belly. A high school and college football player, he had gone to fat in middle age. He was a grandfather himself now. "It's okay, Ozzie. I'll be better off in the home." She was never that fond of Maybelle, and no doubt Maybelle knew. She wondered why Ozzie hadn't married a girl from back home or one of the girls who was his college classmate instead of a brassy blond white girl who worked at a hamburger stand near the UCLA campus. But then who was she to question Ozzie's odd choice?

Now, firmly ensconced at Loma Vista, Claire knew better than to rock the boat in any way. She kept no journal as there was even less privacy than at Ozzie's. She tried to keep quiet and cause no stir, to be as unobtrusive as she could be. She didn't want anyone to know how she felt. She could end up like one or the other of the McIvers.

Henry and Martha McIver were the only married couple she ever encountered at Loma Vista. Mr. McIver didn't try to hide his anger. "We were doing just fine, Martha and me, on our own. Our son just got tired of waiting for us to pass away and decided to put us here and grab control of our house and land, while he's still young enough to enjoy it. We were fine. Our grandson came every other Saturday to help with the yard work and any heavy lifting we needed to have done. True, my driver's license was revoked last year because my vision and reflexes aren't that good anymore, but we don't need to drive. Our neighbors give us lifts into town. The supermarket delivers for seniors. Sonny Boy has another thing coming if he thinks he can get away with this!" McIver's lawyer paid him a couple of visits at the home (he was going to sue the son and he was going to sue Loma Vista Nursing Home, he said, for false imprisonment).

But the thing was, McIver was eighty-nine, and no matter how lucid of mind or spry of body, no court would rule in his favor... no court would agree with him that he would be fine living on his own. And then there was Martha. Though "only" eighty, Martha, beginning shortly after the birth of their only child, frequently suffered from depression and now began to show signs of senility.

One day their grandson told Henry he worried about them. His father was worried, too, that the old people couldn't manage on their own anymore. To set his mind at ease, Henry confided in the young man.

"No need to worry none about us. None at all. See, your grandmother and I know we're getting on and it might come to our not being able to manage. We made a pact. If the going gets too rough and it appears we can't handle it anymore, well, keep it to yourself now, don't mention it to your dad, but we decided we're going to check out together. Not some hideous way, now, so don't be afraid of any 'grisly finds,' but easy-like. Get in our car in the garage and start the motor. Take some pills. Just go to sleep. Something real easy-like. So don't worry about us." The grandson did tell their son. All in all, it didn't seem likely to Claire that any judge would find in Henry and Martha's favor.

"And when we get out of here, one of the first things I'm going to do is sue this damned place for false imprisonment!" Henry said.

Martha didn't carry on like Henry. (Didn't "bitch" as Maybelle would say.) She paced the floor and wrung her hands and refused to eat. She hyperventilated, and then they made her take deep, slow breaths into a paper bag.

"The poor dear," Mrs. Lacey, one of the attendants, told Claire. "He's got her all upset with his rantin' and ravin'. He's got some attitude that one. Well, I'll let you in on a little secret, Miz LaFromme, he ain't gonna be kept here much longer, the old coot. We're gettin' rid of 'im! See how he likes them apples!" And they did get rid of him, striking in the middle of the night with no warning.

"They came into our room and told him he was run-down and needed a vitamin shot," Martha told Claire the morning following her husband's abduction. "He said no he didn't want a shot of anything, and they were nuts if they thought he believed for one split second that they had vitamins there. He was no fool. They held him down and forced it on him, him cussing them out all the while."

"Get the hell away from me, you bloody gorillas," Claire had heard him yell, no doubt at the Santos brothers. The burly Santoses' arms were all covered with thick black hair. Of course old McIver had no hope of fighting them off. They sedated him and then carried him away on a stretcher.

"When I asked them where they were taking my husband they just said, 'Someplace else.' I don't know how I'll live without him."

"Oh, you'll do just fine without that cantankerous old bugger," Mrs. Lacey, who was in Claire's room making beds, said. Claire wanted to say something smart like, "Who asked you, you old bugger?" but she didn't dare say a word. Matilda, her roommate who died recently, sometimes talked back to them and she suffered for it. They wouldn't answer her when she clicked the red button that lit a light at the desk signaling she needed assistance. They often didn't bring her meal tray until last, when the food was cold. And if she spoke to them they would ignore her as if she were invisible and inaudible. They wrote reports and stuck them in her file and gave them to her children to read when they visited, and Matilda's children would confront her as though she were a bad little girl. "So you've been giving them a hard time here. Shame on you! When are you going to straighten yourself up and act right?" they'd demand and Matilda, her face flushed, would look down at the floor.

Claire knew better than to speak her mind at Loma Vista. She took comfort in thinking they—Mrs. Lacey, the Santos Brothers, and the mean head nurse—would be old themselves one day. Mrs. Lacey and the head nurse were already middle-aged. They were not creating good karma for their old ages. They would suffer for their meanness to the helpless elderly under their care. But Claire wouldn't be around to see it.

At night Martha cried in her sleep making odd yowling sounds, like a cougar.

"Good Lord Almighty," Mrs. Sullivan, Claire's new roommate, said when she heard. "What on earth is that? Sounds like a damned banshee!"

"That's just poor Martha in the next room crying in her sleep. She can't help it."

"Can't help it, eh? We'll see about that! I'm talking to the management. It's outrageous. Medicare and my son and daughter aren't paying out good money so that I will be kept awake by shrieking. Poor little Martha isn't going to get away with it."

After that night the yowling stopped. Claire wondered how Martha controlled herself. Maybe, she thought, Martha kept herself awake all night. They were all fearful, or should be (including Mrs. Sullivan, though she didn't realize it yet), of rocking the boat. They were, after all, powerless, and it didn't pay to make waves.

Four days after McIver's abduction, Martha somehow made it past all the watchful eyes on floors one, two, and three to the roof. Claire wondered whether Martha dove off the roof, then, as soon as she arrived, or did she take in the view for a minute or two (but she would have been wary of being caught), did she hesitate before taking the leap, did she have to work up her nerve? Or was it easy for her ... did she have the heart for it? Did she do it with surety that that was the right thing, the only reasonable thing to do? Martha jumped. Or dove. Or stepped off the roof into the air.

Claire happened to be standing at her window looking out at that moment. She saw Martha pass her window. It was very, very sudden and there was no scream;

she made no sound of any kind. Claire saw the body hit the ground and heard the "thud" it made upon impact.

Later, after the ambulance took the corpse away, Claire snuck out into the courtyard. She knelt on the grass beside the spot where Martha had landed. Such a small person, yet she had left an impression on the ground. The grass lay flattened. Claire pressed the palm of her hand into the impression. "Now you're free, Martha dear," she whispered.

"Hey, you crazy old bat, what do you think you're doing?" Mrs. Lacey grabbed her roughly by the arm and pulled her to her feet. It reminded her of the nuns when she was a little girl back on the reservation and forced to go to Catholic mission school. The nuns treated children like that, grabbing, manhandling, scolding. She never dreamed she would spend her old age in the same way she had spent most of her childhood, under lock and key, keeping her guard up at all times, being rudely spoken to and physically abused. Mrs. Lacey pulled and pushed, all the while scolding. "You know better than that, Miz LaFromme. You know good and well you're not allowed outside without supervision. I'm going to have to file a report on you now. And, of course, your son will be told. We'll tell your son you're not to be trusted, you sneaky little thing, you damned old weasel you. Just about had me fooled, but you're like all the rest. Can't trust a one of ya' damned coots."

That was when she first heard her own voice whispering: "*You've got to get out of this place. If it's the last thing you ever do.*" Yes. But how? Probably every inmate of Loma Vista had heard at one time or another that same voice in their head, their own voice saying the same thing. Did anyone ever succeed in running away? she wondered. "*You've got to get out of this place!*" it said again, no longer a mere whisper, but with conviction.

"Yes," she agreed silently. "Yes."

Ozzie visited her every first Sunday of the month. When he came again she brought the subject up.

"I wish I had never let you talk me into leaving home, son. I would have been all right. I had Mike. You know Mike is a good dog." Mike was their young Doberman whom Sam had trained to attack anyone who might threaten them. But he could be gentle, too. She'd given Mike to her nephew, Joe Whitehawk, and his little boy, Billy, when she left Idaho.

"Don't start in, Ma. We've been over this a dozen times. No old lady can live out in the country all alone."

"Well, some do."

"And some are found dead in their houses."

"Everyone dies. Better to die in my own house I would think than..."

"Ma! That's enough! You must have someone to look after you. That's all there is to it."

She thought of telling him about the death of her last roommate, before Mrs. Sullivan. Matilda—Mrs. Krenshaw—who had shared Claire's room for two years.

The last night of her life Matilda took very ill. Claire went over and touched her forehead. "You're burning up!" she said. Matilda shivered so hard her sheet and blanket slipped off. Her eyes rolled back. "I'm going to get help, Matilda." Her friend opened her eyes a moment and seemed to focus on Claire's face.

"You can't go home in this storm, Grace," Matilda said. "I'll tell the boys to bed your horses down and I'll get you some bedding." Matilda was delirious. Claire hated to leave her and clicked first Matilda's red button, and then, when the staff didn't respond, her own. Still they didn't answer and did not appear. She replaced the blanket and sheet, covering her friend though she knew they would be shivered off again right away.

Claire walked to the desk and told them Mrs. Krenshaw was seriously ill. They acted as though they hadn't heard her. She thought of calling an ambulance but knew there would be big trouble for both Matilda and herself if she dared do that.

Claire stayed by Matilda's side. She soaked washcloths in cold water and put them on Matilda's forehead and replaced them when they warmed with fresh cold ones. She wished she had aspirin to give her. That would bring the fever down, but they weren't allowed to have any sort of medications at Loma Vista except for what was doled out by the staff several times a day. "Don't leave me, Grace. I'm frightened," Matilda said, reaching out. Claire took her hand and held it, patted it. She knew Grace was Matilda's sister who had died in childbirth many, many years ago.

"Don't worry. I'm here. I won't leave. I'm right here." About three A.M., when Matilda hadn't spoken for an hour, Claire heard the death rattle. She wondered why it was called that. It was more like a gurgle than a rattle. Anyway she knew what it meant. Matilda opened her eyes and looked at Claire. Claire felt that Matilda recognized her this time. Then she closed her eyes and was gone.

Claire went to the front desk and told the fat, freckle-faced, red-haired black nurse on duty that Mrs. Krenshaw had passed away. "We don't have time for that now," she said, irritated that Claire was bugging her. She'd been reading a book, which Claire could tell by the cover illustration of an extremely handsome man embracing a very attractive young woman in a low-cut gown was a cheap romance. Maybelle, her daughter-in-law, devoured such books. "Go back to bed!"

Just before they brought the breakfast trays, around seven o'clock, the Santos brothers finally came and got Mrs. Krenshaw's dead body and took it away. That's how they looked after old people at Loma Vista Nursing Home.

"Look, Granny Claire," Buddy, Ozzie's grandson, said, holding up a new crayon drawing, "do you like it?" Buddy, who was eight, usually came with Ozzie. Her *tupiya*.* The one bright spot in all of this was that she had gotten to know her *tupiya*. Buddy, who was very fair-skinned, had dark brown curly hair and large grey-hazel eyes. No one would ever take him for an Indian. It didn't matter. He was her dear *tupiya*.

---

* Coeur d'Alene Salish, meaning both "great-grandparent" and "great-grandchild."

"Bring it here, let's have a look." She blinked back her tears.

The drawing appeared to be of two people sitting in a giant cup which was on a giant saucer. One figure wore a baseball cap, the other had two long braids. Both wore wide grins. She and Buddy were often the subjects of his drawings. "Is that us?" he nodded. "Why are we sitting in a cup? Is someone going to drink us?"

"No. We're at Disneyland and here we're riding the Mad Hatter's Tea Party. Next we're going to Pirates of the Caribbean."

"We sure look happy."

"We are."

"Ma, I have to go make a phone call, okay. I'll be back in a few minutes. You stay with your Gran, Buddy."

"His *tupiya*," Claire corrected her son, who ignored her.

"Okay," Buddy said. As soon as Ozzie left the room, Buddy said in a very quiet voice, just barely above a whisper, "Gran, I have something to tell you. Don't tell nobody, okay? I've got a plan."

"Okay."

"When I grow up, I'm going to come here and break you out."

"How will you do that?"

"I'll bring a disguise of some kind. We'll walk right out the front door. Then we'll run away. They'll never find us."

"Where will we go, Buddy?"

"I don't know. I was thinking maybe L.A."

"Why L.A.?"

"Because it's far away. Because it's real big. And because it's close to Disneyland. After I get a job we'll go to Disneyland on my days off. We'll have a good time."

"Sounds good to me, Buddy. Sounds great. And thanks. I feel better now knowing I'm not going to be stuck in this place forever." Buddy smiled. One of his front teeth was missing. Maybe he wasn't eight. Maybe he was seven.

That was the second time she heard her own voice saying, "*You've got to get out of this place. And you're going to have to do it all yourself. Nobody is going to rescue you. You can't wait for Buddy to grow up. You have to do it, Claire. You're all you've got.*"

Yes. She already knew. *She* was all she had.

"I love that picture of us in a teacup, Bud. You know what, I'm not going to tape this one to the wall. I'm going to keep it in my pocket so I can take it out and look at it whenever I want." One wall was covered with Buddy's drawings. Mrs. Sullivan said they were an eyesore and when Claire refused to take them down, Mrs. Sullivan said she was going to complain, was going to change rooms if she had to. Claire was making waves. She was afraid of being taken away in the night as Henry McIver was to "someplace else." Claire had to get out.

That very evening, just before dinner was brought in, Claire stole into the room of a man named Arthur, "Hi, Arthur. How're you doing?"

Arthur narrowed his watery eyes and looked her up and down.

"What do you want?" he asked. He was a skinny little man about her size.

"I want to borrow some clothes from you, okay?" Claire said, opening the old man's locker. So spare and neat.

Arthur was not in his right mind, like many, perhaps most, of the inmates of Loma Vista. He saw goblins and giant nuns and rodeo clowns traipsing around his room at odd hours. Sometimes he thought he was still a soldier in France. Sometimes he thought he was a young husband and father and talked about his kids and his job at the factory. Some days Arthur thought he was in a POW camp and would refuse to speak at all except to give his name, rank, and serial number.

Nobody would believe Arthur if he told them Claire had come into his room, opened his locker door, selected a sports coat, a pair of trousers, a cotton dress shirt, and a vee-neck pullover sweater (all of which she knew were there since she'd seen him decked out in these clothes when his children came to visit, which was only once a year at Christmas). And besides, he didn't appear to recognize her today. Maybe he thought she was an enemy soldier.

Arthur's clothes fit her nicely, except for the shoes, which were much too big. Damn! Well, she had a pair of walking shoes, no heels, very plain. Maybe they would pass for men's shoes. She took the folded crayon drawing Bud had given her, the one depicting the two of them happily riding in giant cups at Disneyland, and put it in the inside pocket of the sports coat.

Claire decided she would make her break after they collected the dinner trays. They were busy then and wouldn't be around again until late evening. And her cantankerous roommate, Mrs. Sullivan, always took a bath after dinner.

The dinner trays were brought. Mrs. Sullivan ate her dinner. Then she took a clean towel from her locker, a bar of soap, her robe. Claire couldn't let her leave just yet. She needed Mrs. Sullivan to be gone right after the trays were collected. She had to dress, then make good her escape. Timing was important.

"Mrs. Sullivan, tell me, are you sleeping well now?" Mrs. Sullivan frowned at her.

"Why, yes, I am. Thank you. And I don't think I'm to blame, not at all, for your friend's death. She was the one who chose to jump off the roof. I was within my rights complaining about that horrid noise she made at night."

"Of course, Mrs. Sullivan. Of course. Nobody thinks you're to blame. You need your rest. We all do." Mrs. Sullivan left the room as the attendant swept in and swept the trays away. Claire closed the door behind them. She couldn't lock it, though. Loma Vista doors had no locks on them. She dressed quickly in Arthur's clothes and her leather walking shoes and looked at her reflection. "Not bad, if I do say so myself," she said. She looked like a man, except for the long braids. They might be a giveaway down here. You didn't see men, like up on the reservation, in long braids. Maybe she could get a hat somewhere and pin them up under it. For now, though, she was ready. This was it.

The upper half of the window opened outward. She was very slim and, for an old person, very agile. She made it out onto the ledge. Though they were on the first floor, still, it was about a twenty-foot drop. She got down on her knees and got hold of the ledge with both hands and let her body slide down the outer wall. This way it was only about a ten-foot drop and, with any luck, she would fall into the flower beds where the earth was damp and soft. She did. She kept close to the ground and to the building. She cut across a park and kept walking.

She could feel and hear her heart pounding. Her body, sensing her excitement, sent adrenaline to her aid to help her out. Fight or flight. She would rather take flight than put up a fight. Oh, the giddiness! The exhilaration!

Claire spent her first night of freedom under a park bench beside Lake Merritt. She didn't get much rest; it was too cold and damp and she was too excited. Towards daybreak she did doze off for just a short while, an hour or forty-five minutes. But she couldn't let them find her sleeping under a park bench.

It was time to wake up, go downtown, find a pawn broker, and sell her diamond ring. But it would be a couple of hours yet before the stores opened. She thought of Buddy. If she were successful in her escape, she would, most likely, never see Buddy again. What would he think when he passed the nursing home on his way to school this morning and saw that she wasn't there waiting for his smile and wave as she did every weekday morning? She decided she would double back a bit and try to see Buddy one last time, try to intercept him on his way to school. She didn't even know where his school was located exactly. She would have to take a chance.

She waited under a tall palm tree in front of a modern, boxy apartment complex of pink stucco. This was just four blocks west of Loma Vista. She tried not to look suspicious.

Loma Vista, housed in a dingy grey concrete-block structure, loomed on a high hill, dominating the landscape. In its dark-grey ugliness it could have been a penitentiary, but one without high walls topped by barbed wire and towers with armed guards. A house of detention for those who committed the crime of getting old. Loma Vista's inmates were *all* on death row with no possibility of a last-minute reprieve.

"*God! I did it! I got away! I got away!*" She spotted her *tupiya* walking towards her. He carried his little tin lunch bucket with Batman's likeness on it. (He'd taken it to the nursing home on one of his visits, when it was new, and showed it to her.) He wore a green-and-yellow baseball cap. Her heart warmed at the sight of him. He was right in front of her when he looked up into her eyes and realized who she was. He smiled, "Grandma Claire! It's you!"

"Shhh! Don't draw attention! I'll walk you to your school. Let's go." And they began walking. How odd. They'd never walked down the street together until now.

"Did you escape? Your disguise is boss! Here, take my cap," he said and handed it to her. She took it and put it on her head. "Perfect fit!"

"Yeah. Now, tuck your braids up under your cap, Gram. There! Now you *really* look like a guy!" The old woman disguised as a man and her now bareheaded great-grandson held hands as they walked briskly down the street on the chilly late summer morning.

In front of the red-brick school the boy hugged her around the waist. She stroked his hair. She almost wept. She loved this little boy so, whom she'd never seen until she came to California with Ozzie and Maybelle. Something good and important had come out of the California fiasco. "I love you, Gran," Buddy said. "Be careful."

"I love you, too, Buddy. And I want you to know I took the last drawing you did for me, of us at Disneyland, you know the one, and just as soon as I get where I'm going I'm going to take it out and tape it to my wall. Don't worry about me. I'm going to be fine. Okay?"

"Okay. And you don't worry about me neither, okay?"

"Okay." Then he went his way and she went hers. Her eyes welled up with tears, but she blinked them back and shed not one. She had to be tough to pull this one off and she was. "*I'm a tough old bird*," she thought to herself. "*A tough old bird. And I'm going to make it.*"

The man at the pawn shop near the Greyhound depot would give her only $100 for her diamond ring. "It's worth at least $2,000," she said.

"Hey! You come waltzing in here with a diamond ring and no I.D. whatsoever and $100 isn't good enough for you? That's my offer, Pops. $100 and no questions asked. Take it or leave it." Claire took it.

She went to the Greyhound depot and purchased a ticket on the local to San Francisco. The important thing now was getting out of town as quickly as possible. If Ozzie or the nursing home were looking for her, they would be checking the buslines for an old woman buying a ticket to Idaho or Washington, and they would be looking for her in Oakland, not San Francisco. She wasn't sticking around.

She had only a ten-minute wait before boarding time. She bought a newspaper and sat down on a bench. She noticed a small wool blanket, blue and green plaid, neatly folded on the bench beside her. She picked it up. She decided to keep it rather than turn it in to lost and found. She could use a blanket. She hoped whoever had forgotten it and left it behind didn't need it too badly.

In San Francisco she bought herself a one-way ticket to Portland, Oregon, and then sat reading her paper and waiting for an hour to pass. Dear Abby was one of her favorite features. "*Dear Abby: I am in love with a wonderful man. I have never been in love before although I am thirty-three. I was my invalid mother's caretaker from the time I graduated high school until last year when she died. When I met my man, I was a thirty-two-year-old virgin. When we had been going together for about six months, he told me he was married and had two young children. As soon as his kids start school, he says, he'll move out of the house and begin divorce proceedings. He hasn't made love with his wife, who is frigid, in well over a year. He actually began weeping as he told me I was the love of his life, that he never imagined he'd ever love anyone so much. He is very religious and believes God gave us to each other. My friends tell me to get out, that he's a low-life and has no intention of getting divorced and marrying me. I love him so much, Abby. I am not sure I want to go on without him. Please help me. Signed, Starved-for-Love in Kansas City.*"

Claire noticed two policemen enter the big waiting room. It was eleven o'clock now and the large depot was very crowded. The cops took a turn around the depot checking things out while Claire pretended to read her paper and furtively watched them. They woke a white-haired bag lady and told her she had to move on. She did.

At the door the bag lady paused and looked back before stepping out onto the street. For just a moment she and Claire made eye contact. Claire wondered how it was the bag lady, nearly as old as she, was allowed to live on her own. No children, she guessed, or at least none who were concerned about her. "Get along there, Granny. Don't wanna have to run you in," one of the young cops called to the bag lady, who went on her way, pushing her supermarket cart full of paper and plastic bags. The cops didn't give Claire a second look.

"Dear 'Starved-for-Love,'" Abby's reply began, *"Not everyone, including me, would agree with you that this man is a 'wonderful guy.' He deceived you. He's cheating on his wife. And don't buy that baloney about no sex in over a year. Get rid of the bum! At first it will be painful, but in the long run you'll like yourself better. The world is full of 'wonderful guys.' Unfortunately your boyfriend's not one of them."*

Claire would hate to have Abby's job. What if "Starved-for-Love in Kansas City" gave the wonderful guy the boot and then found herself utterly bereft and ended up committing suicide? After all, she'd led a terribly sheltered life. She didn't have experience that would teach her pain would pass and life would go on. Maybe that rat of a married man was her only source of love ever.

Claire would hate to have Abby's job, but she wished she had a job of some kind. Who would hire a person her age to do anything? If she drew on Sam's social security benefits, Ozzie would find her and take her back to lockup. Where would she get money? How would she live? *"Focus on the moment, on the road ahead. You are alive and you are free."* At the moment her most pressing problem was a full bladder. First things first.

Not without some apprehension, Claire went to the men's room. She was not surprised to see two men standing at urinals holding their penises and relieving themselves. Claire chose one of the two booths that had doors, but, bad luck, it had no lock. She had to hold the door closed with one hand as she sat on the toilet. *"Kway Elpsh!"* she muttered under her breath. Then, aware she had just spoken the only Coeur d'Alene Salish she'd heard in a few years, she said it again, whispering: *"Kway Elpsh!"* (*"A fine thing I must say!"* she would have said in English were she speaking English.)

When she came out of the little stall with a door that did not latch, she washed her hands. She still wore her gold wedding ring on the third finger of her left hand. Above it, where the diamond ring had encircled her finger for so long, the skin was much lighter, almost white. It showed something important was missing. Nobody looked at her. Nobody at all. It worked! She was a smashing success. She looked at herself in the mirror. She didn't make a bad-looking old coot if she did think so herself. She smiled at her reflection. *"We got out of that place, old man. We did it!"*

The coach bound for Portland pulled out of the stall and headed down Mission Street to the freeway entry and crossed the Bay Bridge and stopped at the Oakland depot to take on more passengers. Claire didn't see Ozzie or any police. A fat middle-aged woman boarded and took the aisle seat beside her.

How thrilling to sail up the road so fast and so free! Everything she saw, the other vehicles, the green hills, the green pastures full of black-and-white spotted cows, all of it was a feast for her eyes! It was as if she had stirred to life again after a long, cold winter's hibernation.

"Pretty day, isn't it," the woman beside her said. Claire nodded. It was. Clear, incredible blue clarity. A pretty day. "My name is June. What's your name?"

Claire, who had always had a deep voice, answered, "Jack."

"How do you do, Jack. Are you going all the way to Portland?" Claire nodded. "Me too. I live in San Francisco. I'm going to Portland to see my daughter. She's going to have a baby. My first grandchild. I'm going to stay on and help her for awhile. Imagine! Me, a grandmother. Hey, do you have grandchildren? Of course, you must. And you probably have great-grandchildren as well, don't you, Jack." Claire nodded again. "Do you live in Portland or are you going there to visit?"

"Live there."

"Oh, do you live alone or do you stay with relatives?"

"Alone."

"Imagine that! At your age! I admire independence. I couldn't help noticing your high cheekbones, Jack. Are you Native American?" Claire nodded again.

"What tribe? Do you say tribe? What tribe do you belong to, Jack?" Claire turned her back on gabby June and said, mumbled, in a deep, manlike (she hoped) voice, "Sleepy. Gonna sleep now."

In Portland June's pregnant daughter and a tall lanky man, probably her son-in-law, met June. Nobody met Claire, of course. She got off the bus and bought herself a hot dog and Coke. Such a long time since she ate anything like that. She slathered mustard onto the dog and wolfed it down. Then she got a chili dog with extra onions and ate it slowly, savoring the intensity. Food at Loma Vista was bland. Many believed old people liked bland food because they had lost their sense of taste. When she was done eating she bought a ticket to Sunnyside, Washington, because the bus to the Yakima Valley was boarding right away and Sunnyside was the first town in the Valley.

Claire couldn't turn her worries off anymore as the bus sped through the night. What would she do? Where would she go? What was going to become of her now that she was free? Her throat constricted. She couldn't go to her own home. Ozzie had rented it to a non-Indian family. The rent helped pay the bills at Loma Vista. Her anxiety grew. Was she insane? A near octogenarian running off like some kid. A kid would lie about their age and sometimes that might work. Maybe Claire could lie about hers, too. How young might she pass for? Nobody ever told her she looked young for her age. Even the rude and nosey June, who was fooled concerning her gender, implied she saw her as a very old person—"*You must have great-grandchildren.*" But she wasn't trying to look young. What could she do to make herself look young? Cut her hair for starters. Buy some fashionable, youthful-looking clothes. Maybe she could dye her hair. It was snow white now, so she could color it whatever shade she wanted and it would take. People always say black, once her natural color, is too harsh for elderly people even if black had once been their natural color. Maybe medium brown would work. And a little makeup. Maybe she could doll herself up and pass for sixty. What sort of job could a sixty-year-old with no job skills or employment record expect to get? Not a great one.

When the bus stopped, still in Oregon, a couple of hours before entering the Yakima Valley, Claire got off, taking her plaid blanket, and didn't get back on again. She had no desire to go to Sunnyside, and getting off would help confuse anyone who might be looking for her. Biggs Junction this place was called, a wide spot in the road where busses coming and going from all kinds of destinations and points of departure across the Northwest stopped to let off and take on passengers. All Biggs Junction consisted of, though, was a trailer house bus depot, a little café, a gas station that was also a repair garage, and a small grocery store.

She sat an hour or so in the depot reading a newspaper. President Kennedy was getting tough with the Russians. Something about Cuba. If push comes to shove, Kennedy would be no pushover. Maybe another war. There were always wars, weren't there? Her horoscope, she was a Capricorn, said, "Romance on the horizon but stars do not favor travel. Best stay home today and for the next few days, Cap." She dozed off a little now and then. Finally she toppled over, lying on her side on the bench, and went to sleep.

She dreamed. *She was at Loma Vista where she lay unable to sleep while Mrs. Sullivan snored away in the bed beside her. White moonlight filled the room. She had a heavy heart as she often did at Loma Vista. Her world was one of bleak desolation. She was strong and healthy for a person her age and her mind was clear and sharp, but what was the point? Where was she going? Why was she here? What had she now to look forward to? She'd had such an odd dream, she thought, the night before: that she stole some clothes from Arthur and disguised as a man ran away. But it was just a dream. Just a dream. She'd never be free again.*

Just then Martha McIver opened the door to her room. "Martha!"

"Shhh," Martha said, holding an index finger to her lips. Oh, yes, of course, we mustn't wake Mrs. Sullivan. Martha walked over to Claire's bed, sat down on the chair beside it, and took Claire's hand.

Whispering, Claire said, "Martha! How are you? I thought you were…gone." Martha shook her head no. "That's what I wanted them to think. I wanted them to think I was dead so they would send me away in an ambulance. That was a fake ambulance, a rented ambulance. Mr. McIver and some friends of his pretended to be a driver and couple of paramedics. Hah! Joke's on them! I'm better off now, Claire, and happy. Mr. McIver and I are together again. I just wanted to tell you good-bye and let you know I'm not really dead. And neither are you, dear: Remember that."

Claire felt so sad. She began to weep as Martha McIver faded away, "Don't leave me again, Martha," but Martha kept fading until she disappeared.

"Sir. Sir. Wake up, sir. Wake up." It was daylight and a janitor gently nudged her shoulder. "Having a bad dream?" Claire nodded.

"Yes," she said in her deepened, faint voice. "Thank you for waking me."

Claire bought a few supplies: matches, a can opener, some cans of ravioli and corned beef hash, a package of hot dogs, a six-pack of soda pop. She read the headlines on a newspaper. Elizabeth Taylor announces her intention to divorce Eddie Fisher and wed Richard Burton. *"About time,"* Claire thought. The news photo showed a very fat Liz. Fat as she was, she was still beautiful. Probably she'd be beautiful when she was eighty.

Claire took the newspaper, too, and off she went down into the ditch next to the road, under the fence, and up the side of a grassy, yellow hill. On and on she hiked farther and farther from Biggs Junction and the highway.

At length she found an old tree that cast a big shadow and there she sat, leaning her back against the gnarled, rough bark as she took a deep breath of fresh, free air. She took a can of soda pop from the six-pack and drank it down. Never had soda pop tasted so fine. At last she was truly, truly free. She needed to be alone awhile, she decided. Alone and not having to watch her step or look over her shoulder for the first time since she left Idaho nearly four years before. Decompress. Breathe fresh air. Be alone in her new freedom. She took hold of a branch and broke it down to the appropriate length to make a walking stick for herself.

For several hours she walked, aided by her fine new walking stick, leisurely taking in the scenery, which was mostly desert. Once she spotted a rattlesnake curled up near a pile of boulders. He blended in quite nicely there. Rattlesnakes were okay, she thought. This one held himself still as could be. He thought she didn't see him. He would not strike at her unless she came near enough to step on him. She had no intention of going near him.

Garter snakes, the little black things with yellow or red stripes down their backs, the nonpoisonous "good" snakes that ate pests were the kind she didn't like. They were always darting around imposing their presence on humans as though they didn't know they were repulsive, as though they thought themselves cute. Rattlers weren't like that at all. They knew how to keep their distance.

When she came to the top of a high hill and saw a winding creek way down yonder, she headed for it and found a good camping place. She took off her clothes and washed her underpants and shirt and pullover sweater and draped them over bushes to dry. She took the elastic fasteners off the ends of her braids and undid them. Her hair fell loose about her shoulders and down to her waist in back.

She waded out just a few feet into the icy cold river, until the water was knee-deep, then she sat down in a spot that had few stones and bathed herself and rinsed her hair.

Oh, the water was so cold it made her teeth chatter. As soon as she felt clean enough, she waded back out of the water and lay on her back on a smooth, flat rock that was very warm. She spread her white hair all around her to dry in the sun. She felt the sun and warm chinook wind on her naked body and laughed a little to herself. This was so fine, this moment, so fine. All was perfect, absolutely perfect. She was alive again and was glad. Life could be good. No, it *is* good. Despite everything, despite heartache and loss and meanness and unfairness and the fact that we all must die, life is good and in these perfect moments we know the goodness.

Such times occurred most often, it seemed, when she was a child. Once, seventy-one years ago, she was perfectly content a whole summer.

Claire was a little girl of seven when the men from the government took her and hauled her away to Catholic mission school, where she was forced to learn to speak English and to read and write and learn about white people's manners and way of life and about Jesus and the Virgin Mary. That was the year after her mother died.

She hated mission school. Most of the children did, but some seemed to adapt easily. Years later when she was one of the "big girls" (thirteen or fourteen) she heard a boy had hung himself in the dormitory and told his friend he would rather be dead than be a white man's Indian.

They weren't allowed to speak their own language at mission school. If they did and were caught, they would be whipped by the priest.

She hated the food. She especially hated spinach, which, if she actually downed it, made her vomit. The nuns, knowing she hated spinach, would watch her the days spinach was on the menu and force her to take a bite of it before she could eat anything else. She would sit with her mouth full of spinach until the meal was over and the children filed out of the dining hall and then spit it out on the ground. And the nuns forced them to drink milk, never catching on that Indians lack the enzyme to digest it. They all, or almost all, had chronic diarrhea because of the milk.

Most of all she hated the nuns who acted like jailkeepers, who acted much the way the attendants at Loma Vista acted towards those who were under their care and at their mercy.

When Claire had been at mission school a whole school year, she found out the children would not be allowed to return to their homes for summer, but would have to stay there and take piano lessons and learn how to embroider and work in the laundry and kitchen and scrub the floors on their hands and knees (mops were never allowed—down on all fours with a scrub brush was more thorough); she decided to run away.

Little Claire kept near the edge of the playground at every recess for days watching for her chance and at last, just two days before classes were to end, an opportunity arrived. Two boys on the other end of the playground got into a fight, a bad fight, rolling around in the dust, bloodying each other's noses. Both nuns on playground duty, the nun on the boys' side and the one on the girls' side, had to break it up. The boys weren't small and they were very strong and very angry and breaking them up wasn't easy for the old nuns. The fight took all their attention and even the attention of most of the children. Claire simply took a few steps backward, left the playground, and disappeared into the woods.

The nuns had their pets who told on the others and were rewarded for their loyalty, were allowed special privileges and were put in positions of authority as "monitors" or "sergeants at arms" and would have others at their mercy as they were at the mercy of the nuns. She had to be careful of them. Good little Catholic snitches earning points with the sisters and maybe even earning points in heaven, who knows. Maybe Claire, when she died, would have to spend some time in purgatory for being such a bad, disobedient little girl, while the sisters' pets would be sent straight to heaven. But that time would pass and then she would be with her mother for all eternity. Time in purgatory wasn't such a high price to pay for keeping one's integrity intact while one lived on this earth. Claire wasn't about to let the sisters mold her into their image.

Claire got away and they couldn't find her. Though she was just eight years old, she slept in the woods all alone that night and it was very, very dark and she was afraid. She slept, nonetheless, because she was exhausted from running all day.

The next day around noon she arrived in her village, but she didn't have a home, really. Her mother, who she always thought of when she thought of home, was dead so long now Claire couldn't remember her face anymore. Her father, always a heavy drinker, had given himself over to it after his wife's death. She found him sitting passed out on the floor, his back propped up against a wall.

Claire went back outside and looked around her village. No children were there except for the very young and one crippled boy her age. "Hey, runaway," the boy called to her. He sat on the little porch of his wooden house—they all had wooden houses now—playing with his dog. "They were looking for you. Maybe they're going to put you in jail now. They told us anybody hiding you would be put in jail. Why don't you go back to your school?"

She saw her great-grandmother, her tupiya, standing in the doorway of her wooden house. She ran to her and when she reached her, Ya-ya embraced her and held her close. "They came to my house and looked around," Ya-ya said in Coeur d'Alene Salish. "Of course I don't have any white people's hiding places: no closets, tables, beds. I could tell they were disgusted because I don't have those things. All I have is that big trunk and they opened it and looked all through it. Disturbed my private possessions which I keep in that trunk. The umbilical cords of all my children, some of them long dead now like your grandmother. I hated them for doing that but I didn't let them know. Who knows what they might do to me if they knew? They told that nosey woman next door to tell me they would be back and if I hid you instead of returning you to them they would lock the two of us up. I pretended I didn't understand. You know what? I'm not scared of them. Not scared of their jail either. But I believe they're coming back so let us hurry now! We've got to get ready and get out of here quickly."

They took the old woman's gentle mare to ride and a small young mule to carry their supplies—their tent and blankets, the kettle and skillet, a little venison jerky. Everything they would need to live in the woods. They rode without a saddle. Claire, always small for her age, was very little at the age of eight. She sat in front of her great-grandmother, who sometimes let her hold the reins. She could remember still how happy she felt when she and her Ya-ya rode out of the village that day, all the neighbors, the nosey woman next door, the crippled boy who wasn't made to attend mission school, even Claire's father, who had staggered outside, all stared at them but said nothing. "Let them tell those men from the government," Ya-ya said in a whisper. "They're too stupid to find us, or too lazy. We'll be safe in the woods for as long as we wish."

The old woman touched Claire's hair now and then and stroked it. Claire knew they couldn't live in the words forever, but that they could elude the government people for a good long time, and no matter what they did to her for running away, she knew it was the right thing to have done. No matter if they whipped her unconscious or locked her up in a little, dark room like they did to the older children when they were caught swearing (in English, of course) or when they got into fights or when they tried to run away.

Whatever they did to her when they caught her, it was worth it to have this time with her beloved tupiya, this sweet period of freedom. She would remember it always.

They rode for several hours, went down by the eastern shore of the lake and there, near the water, found a good place to camp.

They fished and trapped rabbits and squirrels. They picked huckleberries. Tupiya made bread dough and fried it over their fire in the skillet. They had everything they needed. Life was not hard for the first time in a long while.

At night Ya-ya would tell good stories, though summer was not usually storytelling time.* *They both knew they probably would not be together when winter came. "Tell me, Ya-ya, tell me about the frog girl who didn't want to marry Coyote.† Tell me about the time Coyote pretended he was dying and wanted to apologize to the rabbits for always chasing and killing them. And the time he traded places with the sun and ended up telling everyone's embarrassing secrets, including his own. And the time he decided to get rid of Bear once and for all."*

And she would.

They would go for long rides exploring the woods, and Ya-ya would tell her what it was like when she was a little girl Claire's age. She hadn't seen a white person yet at that age, nor had she heard a word of English. They didn't know then what was coming, the wars, and how they would come to be under the rule of the white man and have to do everything the white man wanted.

But Ya-ya didn't mind her wooden house, which was better than the underground winter longhouses by far. Those old longhouses were miserable. Several families living crowded together where it was warm enough to survive but where there was no light except that made by the fire. It smelled bad after a month or so. Sometimes all the members of all the families ended up with lice. Awful. They had to do it because of the harsh winters. But the white man's wooden houses were sturdy and kept out the cold well, and they had windows through which the world outside could be seen. Wood houses, at least in winter, were good, an improvement over the old ways, like many other things the white man brought. Loss of freedom, though, that was no good. People should not have to live this way.

Tupiya's granddaughter was Claire's mother and tupiya told her what her mother was like, as a little girl, as an older girl. She was a beautiful young woman with a mild disposition, not like tupiya's eldest daughter, who was ready to do battle over anything, who liked conflict, who liked to argue and get her own way.

Claire's mother had a quiet disposition, a sweet disposition, and was well-loved by everyone who knew her. But her health was always fragile and there were several times, before she was even grown, when she became very ill and nearly died. When she gave birth to Claire, it was the happiest day of her life. She loved her baby very much. She gave her two names, one after a woman who worked at the agency, Claire, a white woman who was both pretty and kind. The white name she would need in this white world they lived in. The other, She-Is-Free, was what she would call her. In the old days, a mother gave her newborn child such a name, She-Smiles, She-Who-Is-Beloved, but this would not be a true name. It expressed the mother's hopes for her child more than anything else. The child would have to earn her true name when

---

* In most Native North American cultures, winter (not summer) is the storytelling season.

† Coyote is a common form of Native American trickster who is often an amoral character and who educates about and reinforces cultural norms, usually by violating them.

she became a woman. "But we don't live that way anymore," Ya-ya said. "Claire" was the only name Claire ever knew.

"Do you believe in Jesus and God, Ya-ya? Do you think they're real?"

"Maybe. Maybe Jesus and God are real. Maybe they are not all that is real, like they say. Maybe they're right. How do we know? Anyway, it doesn't hurt to believe in their Jesus and God. They love humans and want good lives for them on this earth so that they may have good everlasting lives too. It won't hurt you to go along with their Jesus stories, will it?"

"No. Only they don't act nice like Jesus told them they were supposed to."

"They'll be surprised then, when they die, won't they? Maybe we'll all be surprised when we die."

They knew about the danger. A very little girl and a very old woman all alone might seem like easy prey. Sometimes animals were known to attack and seriously maul humans. But Claire was never afraid of the animals that lurked in the dark or maybe lurked in the dark: bears, cougars, wolverines, and the like. And surely there were more of them back then. But they never saw one dangerous creature, though they did hear cougars crying in the night sometimes, and a few times wolves howling.

"Never mind then. Go back to sleep. They won't bother us. They're in love. They're not interested in us. We aren't good-looking young cougaresses are we? So we've got nothing to worry about."

Coyote's howling didn't bother them, that old buffoon. They were safe from Coyote as long as they didn't trust him and allow him to trick them somehow. They heard him often but saw him not once. He could probably sense they were too smart for him.

The weather turned cold early that year, before the end of summer, and Claire and the old woman weren't able to keep themselves warm enough; they huddled together under their covers inside their tent trying to keep warm. Then the rain began, cold, cold rain drenching them, and there was no way to keep warm and dry. Tupiya got sick. She started coughing and having a hard time of it.

One morning Claire woke up and found tupiya had picked up their camp and loaded the mule. She sat on a log beside the fire drinking coffee from a tin cup. "I think it's time we went back in, don't you?" Claire nodded. It was. The summer of contentment, the fine interlude, was over. Knowing it was over made Claire's throat constrict and ache. She hated the idea of the good time ending and herself returning to the mission.

She could still remember how sad she felt. She couldn't stop time.

Back at mission school she wasn't well received. "If you insist on acting like a little animal, you'll be treated like one," Sister Bernadette said. They kept a close eye on her, kept her locked up tight at night, and she wasn't allowed out on the playground at recess. Neither was she allowed to go home for visits. She couldn't be trusted. She didn't return to her village until she was fourteen and could speak English better than she could speak her own language. By then, of course, her tupiya had died, as she knew she would have. Her father, too, had died. She had just one clear memory of her father: the time she ran away and found him passed out sitting on the floor propped up against the wall in their house. She didn't feel sad that he had died. She felt nothing one way or the other. She didn't know him. Now she never would.

Claire lay on the big flat warm rock facing the sun—her long white hair spread out around her head. She closed her eyes and remembered her *tupiya*. Ya-ya and she were fugitives that summer as she was a fugitive now. She drifted off to sleep.

She slept for hours on that rock in the sun and kept on sleeping when the sun went down. When she woke it was the cold that woke her. It was hard finding her clothes in the dark. The moon was not in the proper position to provide much light. As she felt lightly among the bushes for her clothes she hoped she wouldn't stumble and fall in the dark. That wouldn't be a good way for her adventure to end. Finally she found them. The dry clothes smelled fresh and clean like wind and sun and all the other fresh scents of the country, grass and trees and wildflowers. It felt good to put these fresh garments on her body.

She built a little fire and sat near it heating two hot dogs on a stick in the flames. She was hungry, truly hungry, and the hot dogs tasted better than any she could remember. She stayed awake, snug now, fully dressed, covered with the blanket she found in the Oakland bus depot (was it just yesterday?—it seemed like months and months ago) and with the newspaper with the headline about Elizabeth Taylor's divorce over the blanket. Newspapers were good for keeping out cold. She lay awake and enjoyed being free, smelled the smoke from the fire she'd made, looked up at the stars in the sky above. She'd not seen such a sky in a long while and never thought about it. Never realized she'd missed seeing the sky all filled with stars like this. *Whatever happens now*, she thought, just before closing her eyes and sleeping again, *it's worth it for this.*

Claire spent only two nights camping out alone. Sleeping on the hard ground was really not comfortable for an old person and her bones began to ache; her arthritis acted up.

She woke the first morning with a mild sore throat. By that night it was worse and she had a full-blown head cold. Probably June or someone else on the bus carried the cold germ and gave it to her and she lowered her resistance by camping out in the cold night. Still, it was worth it, worth the delicious taste of freedom.

The second night under the stars she dreamed a destination: she would head for her nephew Joe's house. Joe Whitehawk was a widower with a little boy about Buddy's age. Joe would let her stay as long as she liked. He had her watchdog, Mike, the tough Doberman who had been such a sweet and loving puppy. Sam had trained Mike to be a killer attack dog, to protect his home and the two old people who adopted and loved and took good care of him.

She could help Joe, she thought. He was way off center with his drinking. He was not unlike her own father, a man unable to recover from the death of his young wife, unable to function as he ought. That wasn't good for the boy, Bill. She'd make Joe see, make the boy more comfortable.

She would gently tell Joe he had to pull himself together. She would say to him, "Your son is the motherless child, Joe, not you. He looks to you for strength, to love him and make him feel safe in this world. How can you make anyone safe when you're drunk?" Maybe she could get Joe to take them all camping down by the lake before this summer ended. She would love to do that. Maybe she would tell that boy some Indian stories. She wondered if Joe had told him any.

She walked back to the little place, Biggs Junction (you couldn't call it a town), where the bus depot and convenience store were and she went to the café for a meal. Trucks, great big trucks, were parked in front. Inside she sat at the counter and had a bowl of stew and a cup of coffee and then used the men's room. Actually, there were no women here, except for the waitresses. On her way out, a truck driver who wasn't looking where he was going, talking to his friends over his shoulder as he was leaving, bumped into her and knocked her to the floor.

"Oh, Christ! I'm sorry, mister. Are you okay?" She broke her fall with her hands, landing in a sitting position. The green and yellow baseball cap fell from her head and her long braids tumbled down. She put the cap back on but let the braids stay free. She was nearer Indian country now where you would find a man with long braids, an Indian man, and it was not a strange sight. The trucker held out a hand and she took it and he pulled her to her feet. "Are you all right? Are you sure?" Concerned because of her age. When an old person takes a fall it can be very serious. Claire nodded she was all right. "I could take you to the emergency hospital ten miles down the road if you want. Let's do that. Let them have a look at you."

"I'm not hurt." The cold she had naturally made her voice deeper, a most convincing man's voice. "But I could use a ride. Where you headed?"

"Spokane," he said.

Spokane! That was close, just sixty miles from the northern border of the reservation. "Can you give me a lift?" So it was that Claire rode in a semi all the way from a little truck stop in Oregon to Spokane, Washington. And there she found the Greyhound Depot again and had enough money to buy a ticket to Coeur d'Alene. From there she decided she would hitchhike to the reservation.

She would ask Joe to hide her since she was a fugitive, and Joe would say, "Of course, Auntie. Stay as long as you like." And she would stay with them and maybe she would help Joe turn himself around. She was strong of mind and body, even though she was almost an octogenarian, and still able. She would keep house for them and cook. Pick wild berries and put them up for winter. She'd give the little boy the attention he needed. She would go to them, her nephew and his little boy, and there she'd be welcome and useful. And she would thank God each day she was no longer an unwelcome guest in her daughter-in-law's house and no longer an inmate of Loma Vista.

By the time she boarded the bus to Coeur d'Alene, Claire felt sick for real. Weak. Her throat was so sore it hurt to breathe, and her chest was all congested. But she would be all right once she got to Joe's house and got some rest. Inside the crowded bus it seemed very, very warm to her. Once she was seated she took a good look around. Nobody else seemed uncomfortable. Nobody but her took their jackets off. She leaned her cheek against the green-tinted glass window. It felt so cool, so blessedly cool. The whole world outside looked green now, a sick-looking green like bile a person with an empty stomach throws up when he vomits.

The bus driver announced through a microphone that this coach would stop in Coeur d'Alene and then would be continuing on to Bonner's Ferry. *"Continuing on,"* she thought. *"Shouldn't say that. 'Continuing to Bonner's Ferry' or 'Going on to Bonner's Ferry.'"* The nuns pounded correct grammar into her head so hard it stayed there. How funny that Indians, at least those of her generation who were forced to attend mission school, spoke better English than most white people did. Continuing on. It bugged her.

Claire closed her eyes and saw her beloved husband's face. *"Sam."* He smiled, his face lit by the sun. *"What happens when we die, Sam?" Could be anything. Could be like the Hindus think and we build up karma, good or bad, and get reborn as a queen or a hyena or something according to what kind of life you earned. Could be you turn into a ghost of some kind. That's a possibility.*

Catholics, who don't allow divorce, or do but no remarriage, think you're completely changed in heaven. You're a completely different form concerned with only spiritual things. Nobody cares about husbands or wives or sweethearts anymore. Everyone is all the same. All without gender. Wouldn't homosexuals be the same, too, then? One of her sons was a homosexual, she thought. Either he was a homosexual or a middle-aged man who happened never to have married but had lived with a close male friend for the past fifteen years.

There's no reason why this son, Ernie, should be shut out of heaven. Especially not the Catholic heaven. Except Ernie was not such a good son. He didn't even make the effort like Ozzie did. He visited her for two hours at Loma Vista last Christmas and on Mother's Day he sent a floral arrangement. A lot of the inmates received floral arrangements on Mother's Day and Father's Day instead of visits. Maybe Ernie wouldn't be let right in to Catholic heaven because there he was just across the bay in San Francisco and never phoned his Mom, never tried to see to her needs. Well, Ernie was the youngest of her three boys. Nothing much was ever expected of him as such. Ernie was a bit spoiled. She hoped he wouldn't have to do time in purgatory for being an inattentive son.

Once Mormon missionaries came out to the house and started telling Claire and Sam about the Mormon religion, all their beliefs and whatnot. It was interesting and those two boys, the missionaries, were really nice, very polite. Of course they weren't going to convert, but those boys were so pleasant and she enjoyed their spiel, even though one of the things they said about Indians was silly, she thought.

They thought Indians and all dark-skinned people (except for Negroes who were descended from Cain) used to be white but then their ancestor, Laman, committed a terrible sin so God made him turn brown. And He told Laman that from then on all his descendants would be brown, but one day they would make it up to God and he would forgive them and they would all turn white again. Something like that.

One thing, though, she wished were true that the Mormons had told her about heaven was that everyone in the hereafter would be restored to their prime, that mothers and fathers and children and husbands and wives, all the dearly departed, would find each other again and all be happy. Husbands and wives would have sexual relations in this Mormon heaven and even, if they wished, have spiritual children. She hoped this were true, that she would be young and beautiful once again and she and Sam would be together, have sex with each other the way they used to. That would be so lovely. She wondered if in Mormon Heaven, since they were Mormons and it *was* their heaven, did they practice polygamy?

She thought not. Polygamy used to exist, it seemed, in societies in which there was a surplus of single women due to war or whatever and widows and sometimes orphaned children weren't up to taking care of themselves. Then some man, especially if he were wealthy, would marry more than one woman and provide for all his wives. In heaven, all the kinds of heaven, everyone would have enough. No one would have to compromise themselves in any way. And she was sure her Sam would have no interest in taking another wife, even if it were allowed.

But Sam was not her first husband. Her first husband, whom she'd married when she was seventeen, was George, Sam's brother. George joined the army and was sent over to France. Claire, who was pregnant with Ozzie, stayed with his parents. Sam tried to join the army too, but he had a heart murmur that kept him out. George was killed in the war shortly after Ozzie was born. He never knew he had a son. They sent his body home and gave him a military funeral, draped his coffin with the Star-Spangled Banner, which had only forty-eight stars back then, and folded it in the correct way and gave it to Claire. George was just twenty when he died. Hardly more than a boy.

Claire was sorry her young husband died, but, she was ashamed to admit to herself, she liked Sam more than she had ever liked his brother. Sam married his brother's widow as old-time Indians used to do, because she and her child needed a husband and father to look after them. But Sam told her, not right away, after they were married five years, that he loved her all along, began loving her the minute he laid eyes on her when George brought her home to have dinner with his family, when Claire was just fifteen and recently released from mission school.

Claire lived with a white family in town looking after their children, helping with the housework. That's how she supported herself. She was glad to marry George and begin her own family. She didn't think much of being a household servant, though it beat both mission school and Loma Vista.

But what would she do if heaven was like the Mormons said and she'd get there and there she'd be with two husbands? Probably that sort of thing wouldn't bother Mormons. But Claire didn't want two husbands. What would they do? She would choose Sam, of course. Would George's feelings be hurt? Would he have to be alone then for all eternity? Probably not. Most likely he'd met some nice single woman and they had gotten together and married in heaven.

And then there was Clairice, their only daughter, who died when she was a baby. If her daughter had lived, Claire wouldn't have been sent to Loma Vista. Daughters don't allow their mothers to be put out and not many sons-in-law would make the demands as daughters-in-law were known to do. According to Mormon belief, in heaven little Clairice would grow to adulthood, to her prime. It would be good,

Claire thought, if she and Sam and baby Clairice could all be together and they could raise her and watch her grow. Who knows what it might be like.

Well, she was going to be eighty years old at the end of summer. She would probably find out soon enough. Or maybe she wouldn't. Maybe it would be nothing. The great darkness and only that and their whole lives, and everyone's, would be like drops of water going over Niagara Falls. And their little human lives would really mean only what they made them mean.

She fell asleep and dreamed of Sam, not the young man in his prime, but the old man she buried nearly four years ago. She saw Sam's face in her dream and heard him say, "*Hurry, dear. I'm waiting.*" And then his image faded and she surfaced from her deep sleep, her face pressed against the cold, green-tinted glass. She was in Coeur d'Alene, Idaho.

She got off the bus, a little old lady dressed like a man, and walked out to Highway 95 carrying her plaid blanket, feeling miserable with her cold and sore throat, and she stuck out her thumb. Almost right away a young man in a pickup truck, who was going to Moscow, far south of the reservation, stopped for her.

"You shouldn't be hitchhiking, sir," the young man said, "it's very dangerous. A woman's body was found in the woods just out of Coeur d'Alene last week. Nobody knows what happened, but she was known to hitchhike." Claire nodded and said she knew he was right and she would never hitch a ride again. She hoped she'd never have to.

The young man, who was white, worked for a logging company up north. He worked many hours and there was never enough time. He hoped Claire wouldn't mind that he was going to drive very, very fast, but he was a good driver. He was going to see his girlfriend, who was a student at the university in Moscow. He missed her so much. He just had to see her. But he had to drive back to the camp that very night and he had to get some sleep because he had to be up by five a.m. the next morning. "You don't look so good," he said. "Are you sick? Are you going home now?"

"I'm going to my nephew's house now. I am sick but I'm going to be okay. My nephew will take care of me, take me in to see the doctor if I don't get well after a good night's sleep."

The young man left her at the mailbox at the end of Joe's long drive. "You take it easy now, Pops," he said, and she answered he'd better take his driving easy or he would never see his girlfriend. He grinned. She stepped down out of the cab and he pulled the door closed. They waved to each other and there she was. Almost home.

Joe's little house, at the end of the mile-long drive, was nestled close to a group of pine-forested hills. Between the highway and the house, on both sides of the drive as far as one could see, were wheat fields, oceans of ripe yellow wheat. Smoke rose out of the chimney. Joe's pickup, the same one he'd had when she last saw him, sat in front of the house. She started walking down the road. Claire felt tired, very, very tired. Too tired to want to eat. Too tired to want anything except to lie in a warm, comfortable bed and sleep and sleep and sleep.

Joe, who had just returned from driving Billy to school, stood at the kitchen sink washing dishes. The dogs, the little terrier who had wandered onto the place a few months ago and never left, the arthritic old Lab, and Mike, the Doberman his aunt had given him, alerted him that someone was coming down the road. He picked up his binoculars, which he kept on the windowsill above the sink, because from this location he could see all of the road clearly.

A small, old Indian man with long braids walked down the road towards the house, not at all daunted, it seemed, by the dogs. He'd better go out there and see who it was, keep the dogs from attacking the old fellow. He put on his coat and went out the door, crossed the log bridge over the creek. "Quiet down, you guys. Knock it off. Mike. Theodore. Bennie. Knock it off," he shouted. The dogs knocked it off, for the most part. The old man waved to Joe and Joe waved back, though he didn't recognize him. He was sure the old man was somebody he knew. He did look familiar.

Then the old man took his baseball cap off his head and waved it in the clean, crisp morning air and called out in Coeur d'Alene Salish: "Mike! Mike! *Whui'nech nep I ill ish uss. Ah, Dune.*"* Mike whimpered and then took off running as fast as he could. When Mike reached the old man, the man bent down and hugged Mike around the neck and that fierce, always aloof watchdog licked the old, smiling face.

---

* "Mike! Mike! Come here, boy. Come greet your mom."

Linda Hogan
(1947–)

*"They want us to believe we don't
exist. I realize now that the stories
are eternal. They will go on as long
as there are people to speak them.
And the people will always be there.
The people will listen to the world
and translate it into a
human tongue."*

Linda Hogan, interview with
Laura Coltelli in *Winged Words*

Descent

Linda Hogan

My mother used to say, "You trying to dig a hole to China?" And I guess I was. Every place that I could find a crack of pure earth I'd dig. It was in my mind to escape this world. I'd pretend I was tunneling out of prison or that I'd break into one of the rivers underground and float away from here. I thought a way would break open, and I'd find an entrance to another world and I would enter it free and alone.

Sometimes I see things as they were before this world, in the time of first people. Not just before the building of houses, the filling in of land, the drying up of water, but long ago, before we had canoes and torches and moved through the wet night like earthbound stars, slow and enchanted in our human orbit, knowing our route because, as Ama said, it had always been our route. I see this place from in the beginning when it was an ocean of a world. Even sky was a kind of water. Land not yet created. And then a breeze of air, an alive wind, swept through, searching for something to breathe its life into and all it could do was move the water in waves and tides, and water didn't stand up, although it spoke.

It was before there were ants that survived the floods by gluing sticks together to make rafts that will float. At first, there was not even a stone. It must have been that a dreaming god, a begetter of some kind, dreamed up something solid and rooted. Then, that first island floated up like limestone from the ocean floor, the way it is now, in this time, and it began to breathe. Soon, green ferns pushed up their first coils from the ground and opened. The frogs emerged from mud and the island in the sea was breathing. The wind breathed through all of this. And all this was before anyone thought of heaven. The time might have been the age of the first trees, tall cypress or the mangrove trees that form land now.

In this watery, foggy world of one color and only the breeze of life, the great anhinga bird with its open, drooping wings, broke through the watery sky world with its beak, broke it like the shell of an egg. It, the sun bird, they call it, sat in light and draped its wings, and these wings, Ama said, called down the sun. And that first view of the sun from this world must have been as beautiful as it was blinding. And as the great bird rested, the panther entered through the broken shell, the hole of creation, all golden eyes and secret pride and lithe stillness, walking as if every cell of its muscular body was breathed awake and healthy. She, Sisa, God of Gods, entered this world with grace and sunlight and beauty. It was a world filled with the wind, with life-creating air. And everything in it began to breathe and move.

People used to believe that what rises up from the ground, or falls from the sky, opens its eyes and is alive, like first walkers and trees and birds. Now it seems it is the whole world that has fallen. Not the way light falls on the trunks of trees, not just shade and shadow cast by the light of sun, either, not even the first beginnings of life down in the tangle of roots and seeds. It has all fallen, this poisoned, cut world. It has fallen in a way that means this place is taken down a notch. Unloved and disgraced and torn apart. Fallen, that's what this world is. And betrayed.

Some say we, too, are fallen. We are Taiga Indians and no one has heard of us. We are a small tribe and we are swamp people. Once the Tocobagas were to the north of us. Calusas to the west. Tequestas with their pottery marked like kernels of corn to the east. Most of the other tribes, Seminoles, Mikosukkes, do not remember us now, but the old people say that, like them, we are related to the panther, Sisa, one of the first people here. And I am related to the panther, also. I'm from the people of the Panther Clan, which makes me a grandchild or niece to Sisa. Like Janie Soto and Annie Hide, my mother's cousin, I come from the Panther Clan on my mother's side. This is my ancestry. We are its descendants, all of us. We, my family, clan, and me, are one-third of the number of Taiga Indians still in this world. I don't like to think about this very much because it is too large for me, but sometimes this knowledge falls on me like misery.

I'm still digging when Donna drives up in her boyfriend's blue car and it's a sight, the roof dented in from a tree branch, the hood pitted with hail. I lean the shovel against the steps.

Donna gets out of the car like a queen and walks toward me. Her hair is curled and it lays softly about her face. She's pretty under her makeup. For a while she is quiet and I am, too, before she moves toward the car and opens the door for me. "Come on," she says. "But take off those muddy boots."

I am still wearing Ama's muddy boots and they look filthy with earth, and I realize I must have slept with them on. I take them off and leave them by the door. I run back to the house for my shoes.

She's quiet for a while after I get in the car, but then the first thing she says is, "On our way back, we saw Janie Soto. The day after the hurricane. Just before they got the roads cleared." The first words out of her mouth. "We came looking for you. She was limping down the road. From making a phone call is what I think she told Mom, but she didn't say it in English."

Soto lives up above Kili Swamp where the other people, mostly old people, live. Soto, the woman who never goes to town or comes close to the world outside that invisible boundary line of Indian land. A woman who wanted Ama to live up at Kili with them. The woman who'd do anything, Mama says, anything at all to get us all back.

I want to ask Donna more, because it makes me nervous that Soto, the woman who is in charge of everything that happens with the panther, was this close to Ama and me. I wonder, does she know?

"She'd been making a phone call. I guess." Donna laughs a little, with tension. "It surprised us because she must have walked all that ways on her wooden leg and she could hardly walk, she was so tired, what with carrying a bag so big with one hand and with her cane in the other hand. We gave her a ride partway home."

"What were you doing there?" I ask.

"We were looking for you." She reaches over and touches me on the hand, but in a hesitant way, and I try to place where we were when they got to Ama's house, and I think I must have been in bed, dead tired, but where was Ama? I didn't even hear a knock on the unhinged door.

"She sat in the back and never said another word to us."

It isn't like Janie Soto to come this close to town. She wants to avoid the town people. All of the swamp people do.

Janie Soto is the old woman who is head of our clan and she has a wooden leg that is made of a tree that used to bloom. I heard that after she first started wearing the leg, it leafed out and blossomed. Green leaves grew from it. She walked with it that way, the tree still believing it was alive. And whenever I think of her, that's what I see in my mind's eye, the wooden leg sprouting leaves, budding with leaves and flowers even as she walks. Mama said that in the Bible, in Numbers, Aaron had a staff that bloomed and because of it he was made the first priest of Israel. Janie Soto herself is something like a tree, the clothing she wears is always dark green and brown. And she always wears the red beads, coral I think, that came from another place. She got them in a trade that was made between our tribe and another from before the time the Spanish arrived.

"We looked all over for you. Mama was in a panic," Donna says, both to let me know she loves me and to take sides with Mama against my thoughtlessness. "Mama thought you were killed in the storm. We drove over as close as we could get, four times, but at first the trees were on the roads. Then we got there but the house was empty. And later we thought someone had been there but we couldn't find you. Then Mama called the police."

I make her repeat this and I look at her while she talks. Not because there is a distant sound of chain saws but because I can tell by the tone of her voice, before she even tells me, that she and Mama both know about the panther and me and Ama. There's something in her voice, a suspicion or doubt. I imagine it was the police that told them where to find me, not that they'd have looked anywhere else. And I suppose Janie Soto knows and that's why she came along the road to Ama's. Janie

Soto, I believe, might know what happened to the panther by her blood alone, they are that connected.

Then, she is silent. She doesn't have to talk. I know what she's thinking. It feels like the car is full of her thoughts. I can almost hear them. She wonders how I could do this thing. She wonders why. Now and then she looks at me with a weak little half-smile. She fidgets with her necklace, a gold heart on a chain. She knows what me and Ama have done even though she never comes right out and says it, but she looks at me different than ever before and she always will, the rest of our lives. I know this.

I feel the pulse in my neck. "What did they say? Did Janie Soto say what she was doing there?" My only words. Because I think if she was this close to the edge of town there must have been a good reason for it. But maybe someone was hurt by the storm.

"No. She was quiet but she was carrying a feather. A white feather."

"What kind of feather was it?" Although I know that Donna would not be able to identify any feather.

"It might've been a swan." She makes a turn. "And her bag. She was carrying a bag that seemed a little heavy. She didn't say anything except when we asked if she'd seen you and she just smiled at us. Something like a smile. Mama thought maybe she didn't understand us, so Mama tried to speak Taiga and asked her a lot of questions all the while we drove her up toward Kili Swamp, but Janie just sat there holding the bag on her lap and the feather in her hand. She had trouble getting her leg in and out of the car. We didn't make it all the way there to Kili because of the trees blown down across the road. Trees are still falling, you know. They get the roads open and then another tree falls. We had to let her out to walk the rest of the way. I offered to help her or carry the bag but she wouldn't have it."

I hardly hear a word Donna says or even the traffic of cars passing. I watch the world pass by as we drive, the broken, windblown world. I think of Ama and me tracking and moving in the almost-wilderness. Now what we did seems like a dream, like it could never happen here so close to the red-roofed houses and shopping centers set down here on the top of the ground, and not so far from Ama's either. I could almost forget there is a horse I need to finish burying and that Methuselah has fallen straight away from centuries of holding on to life.

And then Donna says, "What do you think she was doing this close?" She adjusts the mirror as if to see Janie Soto on the road behind us.

"Maybe someone was hurt."

But I weigh all this in my own mind and know it's not the case. When did the people up at Kili ever ask for help? I imagine old Janie trying to walk across the tree limbs and bodies of birds and fish swept out of the waters.

Donna turns on the car lights as if it is night. It isn't, although there is a feel of something like night. She is trying to see through some kind of darkness. All along the few miles to Mama's, I see what has happened to the world. Things have been ripped up. Street signs are bent, trees thrown down. From a water pipe, all that's left of a home, water is pouring. Fences are down, balconies torn away, cars are twisted wreckage. There is a cloud of smoke or fog hanging over the cane field and the workers' houses are a shambles from the storm, nothing about them was built to hold in the first place. The sun reveals the despair of the broken world, the stark unconcealed limestone glaring, the water and the ruined fruit trees. Men work like ants, trying to repair the damage, stopping to wipe their foreheads with rags, to smoke a cigarette. In jeans, white T-shirts, sweating, they work just when you'd have thought all work would have come to an end.

A heron flies over in the hot, musty air, its wings bent back, neck at an angle. I watch its flight, the suspension of it, the way it hangs in air, legs out behind it.

We go past where the land has been cleared and drained. It's only a few miles from Ama's house. I can run it in a short time, but there's a world of difference. The Indian land is still wet and fertile. But all the other land is poison now, like the pestilence of Mama's Bible that entered the houses as if to claim the firstborn sons.

At my mother's, in the streets of houses, there is only a thin green line of ancient trees remaining just behind the buildings. As we drove up, I see Mama and Herm are airing out the tornado cellar and in spite of myself and the storm, I smile. It is Herm's idea, to have a cellar in the torrents of falling rain even though it's the kind of water-soaked, flooded land that makes such a cellar impossible and yet he dug it out himself, cemented the walls, and they go into it, all of them, at his urging, his memory of Oklahoma storms and twisters, because he is convinced it's safer. But sometimes he has to use a sump pump to get water out of it. And the roots of trees are always trying to break in. Still, it's the only thing I like about him, that as unrealistic as the cellar is, he worries about Mama's safety part of the time.

"Thank God," my mother says, hugging me, as soon as I walk in the door. "We looked all over for you."

A towel and newspaper sit on the floor by the door so we won't leave footprints all over the house. She has never grown accustomed to the dirt, mud, and clay of this place, even though she's lived nowhere else. "Take off those shoes. You'll track in mud." The next words my mama says even though she's been afraid for me. Cleanliness is next to godliness, Mama always says. She's godly enough and her house is neat as a pin; it seems sharpened to a point.

I am thrown back into the world too fast and I reel from it. Inside my mother's house, the washing machine is running. The lights are on even though it is light outside, as if there is something dark fallen all around us that can't be seen but that everyone knows is here. The same kind of darkness that made Donna turn on her car lights in broad daylight.

I sit down in my mother's kitchen by habit, looking at the gray linoleum tiles of the floor, not saying a word. But the air is thick with everything that's not said. Outside the kitchen window is the devastation, the despair, the stark, unconcealed breaking of things. The fruit trees are ruined, oranges on the ground, but the house itself is untouched, at least it seems that way, unlike the houses with their roofs blown "all to tarnation," as my mother says, their walls pushed inward, pulled outward.

"I was worried sick about you," she says. Now that I am safe, she's able to be angry.

I say nothing. I only nod a little, not so much at Mama, but looking around the house where I have always lived. Nothing seems familiar, not the television, the blond coffee table, the school photographs of me and Donna. I can hardly concentrate on her words because it all looks new to me, as if I've never seen it before.

I look around my mother's house and nothing is familiar. It's as if I have never lived here. I see the world this place has come from. I see the walls of the fallen forest, the floor of clay dissolving in time.

"The sheriff told me what happened," Mama says, almost gentle. She is looking at me and I realize how I look. I am dirty and disheveled and wearing Ama's clothes because mine still hang in the tree. My arms are scratched, my nails broken and filled with black dirt. All this in her clean little kitchen. But I am thinking also about Janie Soto and how on her one good leg she got to the phone at the gas station over trees and branches and blown-in building parts. And I am thinking of the Spanish horse and what to do about burying it, and that I need to get back and take care of the goats and chickens that live at Ama's.

"Why?" my mother says.

She means why did I do it.

This house seems lonely and sad. And I look at Mama and try to listen. She's telling me what I already know. "There's a law, the government has a law against it."

"I know."

"You're in deep water." She's getting shrill now. "Do you know that? For killing that panther."

I nod at her.

"It wasn't your idea, was it? It was hers. It must have been Ama's. No one would ever believe you could do such a thing. People are coming to town from all across the country to investigate this and write it up; they've already called here eleven times to ask about you. They know you were with her."

I don't ask how.

"It was endangered, you know."

I nod at her.

"You knew that. I know you did."

Some people have even called to tell how evil I am and it's in all the newspapers, bigger than life. My photograph they got from the high school, illegally, Ama's from right after she was arrested and went to the jail.

"I don't know how they could put your picture in the paper. You're too young. Isn't that wrong?" my mother asks. "They're not supposed to do that, are they? I thought it was against the law." She rattles on, nervously.

I sit in my mother's kitchen, looking down.

"I can't believe you'd do this," Mama says. "You've got such a tender heart. You get mad at the way Herm fishes."

It's true. I do, for him leaving them on a stringer, keeping them alive until they're in the sink. I think it's cruel.

She says, "For all I knew you were in your boat at the bottom of one of the canals or lakes. And the way the river's flowing, you could have gotten washed all the way to kingdom come."

And Herman, my stepfather, says, "This time you've really done it, they're putting you in the newspaper, and some reporter's been calling here to talk to you."

He doesn't say, as usual, "I ought to backhand you."

My mother: "They shouldn't have done that."

"It's a federal crime," he says.

Then to me Mama says, "You weren't to blame. But you should listen to your father."

"He's not my father," I say, sounding more angry than I feel.

Now he says it. He says, "I ought to backhand you. I went without good shoes for you. I glued my shoes together for you girls. Now you're dragging us in the mud."

"Ama's a bad influence," my mother says, like it explains everything away.

I can't tell her—she would never understand—that it was an old story we must have followed, that we were under something that felt like a spell, that what I followed wasn't Ama, and that Ama followed something that wasn't her either. It wasn't that Ama was claiming something, but that something was claiming her. Ama would never have done this otherwise and neither would I. It wasn't even so simple as a mercy killing, even though, judging by the look of the cat, that was cause enough. It's not like me at all to believe in any such nonsense as stories or forces that would take over a person but it's the closest I can come to truth and reason. She was acted on. But outside, the rain starts to fall again, and as it does, it runs over this small square house and begins the long, slow process of disintegrating it, rotting it away. For this I am glad.

Without saying another word, I get up and draw a bath for myself and this is when I feel how dead tired I am. My muscles ache. My eyes burn with fatigue and unfallen tears. I get my robe off the hook on my bedroom door and I lock the door and get into the water, and see the scratches on my arms and legs and close my eyes and lay back in the hot water wondering what it would have been like in the earlier days to have been scratched by panther claws. I stay in the water a long time until it is time to go to bed. For a change, no one knocks on the door or complains.

I dry off and put some talcum powder on my body, under my small breasts and beneath my thin arms, and I tie the robe and go into my small room without saying good night, and I go to bed smelling fresh as lilies, those little flowers that bloom for only a day before they wither and the petals fall down seedless. I can hear everyone in the living room watching TV. They are together, as if to show that now I am outside this family. I am the source of their problems. I have brought them closer together, joined them in their judgment of me. I lie down on my back. My bed is more narrow than I remember, the house more small, as if I've outgrown it. I look at the moving shadows of the trees cast on the wall by a streetlight that, miraculously after the storm, is one of the few still working. The shadows are dancing over me. I can still smell the cat, the sharp odor, the damp fur, the smell of cut flesh and blood, all still with me like it's become my skin, and I am steeped in it. All around me are the houses, with people watching television and eating their snacks, and I am in the trees.

Later, in the middle of the night, I wake up. My shadow is on the wall of the room in this, my mother's house. I get up at once and look out at the bushes and they are glowing in the dark with foxfire, after the storm. Like a burning bush in Mama's Bible. I am so deeply tired and I'm sweating but my skin feels cold and I cover myself and lie back down and fall asleep. Sleep is another sinking down and it is a deep sleep in which I dream of people who do not yet know they are human. Maybe they are only now being born. It includes me, this cast of people, and there are the four women singing and they are the future, not the past, like I first thought. In the dream I am a green branch beginning to bloom, to grow something strong and human and alive.

Once when I was younger I went out and sat under the sky and looked up and asked it to take me back. What I should have done was gone to the swamp and bog and ask them to bring me back because, if anything is, mud and marsh are the origins of life. Now I think of the storm that made chaos, that the storm opened a door. It tried to make over the world the way it wanted it to be. At school I learn that storms create life, that lightning, with its nitrogen, is a beginning; bacteria and enzymes grow new life from decay out of darkness and water. It's into this that I want to fall, into swamp and mud and sludge, and it seems like falling is the natural way of things; gravity needs no fuel, no wings. It needs only stillness and waiting and time.

In the early morning, before it's even light, I get out of bed before everyone else is up and dress quickly, soundlessly, pulling on my jeans, and I go out the door and close it quietly. I take a shortcut past the houses, behind them, through trees. Some have fallen and are hard to pass. I head back to Ama's house before anyone will miss me. I think I should finish burying the horse.

Outside, it's a chaotic, disordered world where I could break a bone with more ease than not. I watch for downed wires. The birds are not yet singing or fussing about. The sky is overcast and I think of the storm, of looking up and seeing the circle of clear night and stars in the silent eye of that storm only a few days ago, and how I entered something so calm as to be unearthly and it could have killed me if it wanted to.

I see Ama's little hutlike house from the black trees, more dilapidated than before. She has not returned, as I already knew, because she has no bail, no recognizance, although Mama said they would keep her there for her own safety. There are people who hate her for what she's done.

When I see the Spanish horse, I am surprised it has hardly started to decay. The vines have already started growing across it. That's how hungry they are, these foreign vines, that's how fast they grow. I take the shovel handle and wrap it with cloth because it has started to splinter and it's still wet. Then I begin once again to dig. Because it's early and it has been cool, only a few slow-moving flies are near the horse.

Willard's white horse, too, is still at Ama's. It comes out of the trees and watches me. It's a true witness, the only one. I feel guilty in its eyes. I stop digging a moment, put down the shovel and go over to it. It's so dirty, I fill the bucket Ama washed in with water from the little cistern and pour the water over it and wash clean its sides with my bare hands. It curves its neck around and breathes on me, its breath sweet with chewed grasses, its dark eyes looking at me. It doesn't want to go back to Willard's. Maybe he's beat it and it's not so stupid as everyone thinks horses are, but I decide to take it back because I know they'll blame Ama for it. From now on, everything that goes wrong, every single thing, is going to be blamed on Ama.

I lead the horse back to Willard's. It seems like such a short distance when only a night or two earlier this space between places seemed far away and forever. I prop up Willard's fallen gate to try to keep his white horse at home. And then I return and dig once again at the hole, digging down centuries toward what is lost and covered up.

I wonder who is missing this horse. Maybe they think it is still alive, that it ran away in terror and will go wild out in the swamps like the Spaniard Cabeza de Vaca, the explorer who wandered these places for years. But no one has yet stepped forward to claim it.

It's not quite deep enough, the hole, and I am already tired. I dig down into roots and limestone, packs of clay. The hole I dig fills with water and I have to get into the chalky brown water and stand in it to dig. It's not deep enough but I am tired and so wet I stay in it partway and see if I can dig underneath the horse enough to get it partway down, my jeans wet and muddy, and then mound it over with stones. Then I get out and push it, as if I've lost my reason and think I have strength, but I can't budge the mud-caked horse that is solid as wood. I dig around the horse, close to it, thinking I can dig the hole out larger, until I can get the horse to fall into it, and I'm sweating and the flies are starting to swarm as the sun rises and I hear the sound of shovel, rock, water.

Smelling the wet earth, I know that somehow the police will dig this hole up again later, believing it is where Ama hid her gun, or hid the panther. Maybe they will know the hole is fresh and dug by me and believe I have taken whatever was buried there, that I have stolen evidence. And even knowing this, I dig until my back hurts.

And finally, I think I can get the horse in and then, just then, a ledge of earth breaks off and the horse falls in with me, on me. I scream out and rush to pull myself back away from the horse, rushing out of the water, leaving one shoe underneath the horse, solid as wood, and then I sit, catching my breath, looking around me at the world that has been torn out of its ground, and the sun rises across the land. I sit, simple, plain, alive. Like a lizard in the sun, eyes closed and alive. I am still these few moments before I pour water over my arms and clean the mud off. Then, just then, the birds all come awake at once and they make such a clatter, a noise of life, that I, who have had trouble hearing since the storm, I hear them clear and sharp, their songs descending to touch me. I go inside and leave my remaining shoe beside the door and put on Ama's boots. The house is dark and smelling of earth and root and decay.

Two worlds exist. Maybe it's always been this way, but I enter them both like I am two people. Above and below. Land and water. Now and then.

Bush's Mourning Feast

Linda Hogan

Sometimes now I hear the voice of my great-grandmother, Agnes. It floats toward me like a soft breeze through an open window.

"The house is crying," I said to her as steam ran down the walls. The cooking stove heated the house. Windows were frozen over with white feathers and ferns.

Bush said the house could withstand it. She had black hair then, beautiful and soft. She stepped out into the cold and brought in an armload of wood. I caught the sweet odor of it and a wind of cold air as she brushed by me. She placed a log in the stove. It was still damp and when the flame grabbed it, the wood spat and hissed.

I didn't for a minute believe the house could withstand it. I knew already it was going to collapse. It was a wooden house, dark inside, and spare. The floors creaked as she swept about. The branches of trees scraped against the windows like they were trying to get in. Perhaps they protested the fire and what it lived on.

Bush unjointed the oxtails and browned them in suet. She worked so slowly, you would have thought it was swamp balm, not fat and backbone, that she touched. I thought of the old days when the oxen arrived in black train cars from the dark, flat fields of Kansas, diseased beasts that had been yoked together in burden. All the land, even our lost land, was shaped by them and by the hated thing that held them together as rain and sunlight and snow fell on their toiling backs.

The shadows of fish floated in the sink. Bush did her own hunting then, and she had a bag of poor, thin winter rabbits. She removed their fur the way you'd take off a stocking. She dredged them in flour. In the kitchen, their lives rose up in steam.

Day and night she worked. In her nightclothes, she boiled roots that still held the taste of mud. She stirred a black kettle and two pots. In her dark skirt, she cut onions. I didn't understand, until it was over, what it was she had to do. I didn't know what had taken hold of her and to what lengths she must go in order to escape its grip.

She folded blankets and clothing and placed them on the floor in the center of that one dark room. She took down the curtains, shook out the dust, washed them in the sink, and hung them on lines from wall to wall. All the while, bones floated up in broth the way a dream rises to the top of sleep.

Your mother entered my dreaming once, not floating upward that way, but crashing through, the way deer break through ice, or a stone falls into water, tumbling down to the bottom. In the dream, I was fishing in Lake Grand when the water froze suddenly like when the two winds meet and stop everything in their paths, the way they do in waking life, the way they left a man frozen that time, standing in place at the bank of Spirit River. In the dream I saw your mother beneath ice in the center of the lake. I was afraid of her. We all were. What was wrong with her we couldn't name and we distrusted such things as had no name. She was like the iron underground that pulls the needle of a compass to false north.

Whatever your mother was in that dream, whatever she is now, it wasn't human. It wasn't animal or fish. It was nothing I could recognize by sight or feel. The thing she was, or that had turned into her, pulled me toward it. I was standing, still and upright, drawn out that way to the terrible and magnetic center of what I feared. I slid across the glaring surface of ice, standing like a statue, being pulled, helpless and pale in the ice light. Old stories I'd heard from some of the Cree began to play across my mind, stories about the frozen heart of evil that was hunger, envy, and greed, how it had tricked people into death or illness or made them go insane. In those stories the only thing that could save a soul was to find a way to thaw the person's heart, to warm it back into water. But we all knew your mother, Hannah Wing, stood at the bottomless passage to an underworld. She was wounded. She was dangerous. And there was no thawing for her heart.

Bush, the wife of your grandpa, had struggled with your mother's cold world. She tried to keep you with her, to protect you from the violence that was your mother. There was the time she heard you crying in the house when you were not there. I heard it, too, your voice, crying for help, or I would not have believed her. It was a chilling sound, your soul crying out, and Bush turned desperate as a caged animal. She fought for you.

In that battle with what amounted to human evil, Bush didn't win, but she didn't lose either. It was a tie, a fragile balance that could tip at any time. That was the reason she cooked the mourning feast. That was why she baked the bread and soaked corn in lye and ashes until it became the sweetest hominy, and who would have believed such a caustic thing could sweeten and fatten the corn? That was why she cooked the wild rice we harvested two years earlier, and the rice was the most important thing because you had gone with us that fall day. You were all wrapped in cotton, with netting over your face so that the little bugs and dust wouldn't bother you as we drifted through the plants, clicking the sticks that knocked rice into the boat.

The last thing Bush did to prepare her feast in honor of you was to open the jar of swamp tea, and when she did, I smelled it. It smelled like medicine to me. It smelled like healing. It reminded me of the days when the old women put eagle down inside wounds and they would heal.

Bush is a quiet woman, little given to words. She never takes kindly to being told what to do. So while she prepared the feast, I let her be, even when she did a poor job on the rice soup. I knitted and sat in the chair by the window and looked outside, straight at the face of winter. There was a silence so deep it seemed that all things prepared for what would follow, then and for years to come, the year you returned to us, the years when the rest of us would be gone, when the land itself would tremble in fear of drowning.

The windows were frozen over, so it was through ice that I saw them coming, the people, arriving that cold Sunday of the feast. Across ice, they looked like mere shadows against a darkening winter evening. Wind had blown snow from the surface of the lake, so in places the ice was shining like something old and polished by hands. Maybe it was the hands of wind, but the ice shone beneath their feet. I scraped the window with my fingernails and peered out. It wasn't quite dark, but Jarrell Illinois, gone now, wore a miner's headlamp and the others walked close to him, as if convinced that night had fallen. As they drew closer, I saw that their shadows and reflections walked alongside them like ghosts, or their own deaths that would rise up one day and meet them. So it looked like they were more. My breath steamed the window, I remember. I wiped it again for a better look.

Some of the people were wrapped in the hides we used to wear, or had blankets wrapped around them. They walked together like spirits from the thick forest behind winter. They were straight and tall. They were silent.

"Here they come," I said. Bush, for a change, was nervous. She stirred the iron pot one last time, then untied her hair. It was long and thick. Hair is a woman's glory, they say. Her glory fell down her back. The teakettle began to sing as if it remembered old songs some of us had long since forgotten. Its breath rose up in the air as she poured boiling water over the small oval leaves of swamp tea. The house smelled of it and of cedar.

"Look at that," I said. "They look beautiful."

Bush bent over the table and looked out the window as the people came through a path in the snow. The air shimmered in the light of the miner's lamp and a lantern one woman carried. Bush wiped her hands on her apron. Then they came through the door and filled up the crying house. Some of them stamped their feet from the habit of deep snow, their cheeks red with cold. They took off their boots and left them by the fire. They greeted us in a polite way. Some of them admired the food or warmed their hands near the stove. All of them looked at the pictures of you that sat on the table. After greeting us, they said very little. They were still uncomfortable around Bush even after all those years. She was a misplaced person. She'd come there to marry my son, Harold. They had never understood her and how love was the one thing that kept her there. To get them to her banquet, she'd told them this was her tradition, that it was the only thing that could help her get over her grief from losing you. There wasn't one among us who didn't suspect that she'd invented this ceremony, at least in part, but mourning was our common ground and that's why they came, not just for her, but out of loyalty for the act of grief.

Bush put a piece of each of the different foods in her blue bowl for the spirits, wiped her hands on her apron, and took the bowl outside. I could see through the doorway how heat rose from the bowl like a prayer carried to the sky, begging any and all gods in the low clouds to listen. The aching joints of my hands told me it was a bone-chilling, hurting cold, the worst of winters. Bush held up the bowl for sky to see, for the spirit of ice, for what lived inside clouds, for the night wind people who would soon be present because they lived on Fur Island and returned there each night. I could barely make out her shape in the newly swirling snow, but when she came back in, she smiled. I remember that. She smiled at the people. It was as if a burden was already lifted.

One by one the people took their places, settling into chairs or on the couch that was covered with a throw I had made, or they sat at the long table. They hadn't been there before, and so they looked around the small, now-stripped house with curiosity. The wood and wallpaper were stained where rain had seeped through.

When Bush served up the food, it came to me that I didn't want to eat. I was a large woman then, I love my food, but I must have known that eating this meal would change me. I only picked at it.

At first, we hardly spoke, just small talk, and there were the sounds of forks on plates, spoons in bowls. There were silences when the wind died down, and all you could hear was snow hitting against the wood of the house, dying against the windows, tapping as if it was hungry and wanted in. I remember thinking of the island where she lived, the frozen waters, the other lands with their rising and sloping distances, even the light and dust of solar storms that love our cold, eerie pole.

We had moose meat, rice, and fish. The room was hot. There were white-haired people, black-haired people, and the mixed-bloods—they wore such colorful clothes. Frenchie was there, dressed in a blue dress. It was low-cut and she wore rhinestones at her neck, and large rubber boots. We were used to her way of dress, so we didn't think it was strange attire. We just believed she was one kind of woman on top and another below the waist.

It was so damp and warm inside that the wallpaper, full of leaves, began to loosen from the moist walls. It troubled my mother, Dora-Rouge, who sat with her back against the wall. She was always an orderly woman and accustomed to taking care of things. And she wasn't as bent as she is now, so when Bush wasn't looking she tried to stick the wallpaper back up, holding edges and corners with her hands until it became too much for her, and she gave up and went back to taking the fine bones out of her fish.

Jarrell Illinois—he was a good man—took some tobacco out of the tin and pinched it into his cheek and smiled all around the room.

In that one day it seemed that the house grew smaller. It settled. The floors sloped as if they knew the place would soon be abandoned, the island quiet and alone with just its memory of all that had happened there, even the shipwreck of long ago.

I don't know how to measure love. Not by cup or bowl, not in distance either, but that's what rose from the iron pot as steam, that was the food taken into our bodies. It was the holy sacrament of you we ate that day, so don't think you were never loved. It's just there was no way open between us after the county sent you back to Hannah, and however we tried, we never saw you again after that.

We ate from evening through to near light, or as light as it gets in winter. The fire cast shadows on the walls as the old men picked the bones, then piled them up like ancient tellers of fortune. They ate the bowls empty, clear to the bottom. By then, people were talking and some even laughing, and there was just something in the air. That night, in front of everyone, Bush cut her long hair. The way we used to do long ago to show we had grief or had lost someone dear. She said it held a memory of you. She said that hair had grown while you were living on the island with her. She said she had to free that memory.

When the dishes were all piled up, she went to the middle of the room where she had placed her earthly goods, then in a giveaway, she gave each diner present some part of her world. It was only your things she parted with unwillingly, holding them as if she dreaded their absence, and now and then a tear would try to gather in her eye, but she was fierce and determined. She gave away your handmade blanket, T-shirt, shoes, socks—gave one here, one there. Some of the people cried. Not only for her, but for all the children lost to us, taken away.

She gave away her quilts, and the hawk feathers that had survived both flood and fire. She gave the carved fish decoys my son Harold had made. They were weighted just right to drop through ice and lure many a slow and hungry winter fish. No one else had weights as good as those. She gave away her fishing poles and line, and her rifle. She gave away the silverware. At the end she stood there in her white sleeping gown, for she'd even given what she wore that day, the black skirt, the sweater.

With all the moisture of cooking and breath, the door froze shut, and when the people were ready to leave, John Husk struggled to open it until finally it gave. When they went through it each person carried away a part of her. She said it was her tradition. No one questioned her out loud or showed a hint of the doubt I knew they felt.

They came to love her that night. She'd gone to the old ways, the way we used to live. From the map inside ourselves. Maybe it reminded us that we too had made our own ways here and were ourselves something like outcasts and runaways from other lands and tribes to start with.

They left through the unstuck, pried-open door. Night had turned over. The white silence of winter was broken by the moaning, cracking sound of the lake.

I remained, but I watched the others walk away with their arms full. Going back that morning, in the blue northern light, their stomachs were filled, their arms laden with blankets, food, and some of the beaver pelts Bush had stolen and been arrested for—from the trappers who had trespassed the island. Anything that could be carried away, they took. Frenchie pushed a chair before her across the ice, leaving the track of wooden legs in shining lines. Beneath her coat, she wore Bush's black sweater over the dress and rhinestones. But the most important thing they carried was Bush's sorrow. It was small now, and child-sized and it slid its hand inside theirs and walked away with them. We all had it, after that. It became our own. Some of us have since wanted to give it back to her, but once we felt it we knew it was too large for a single person. After that your absence sat at every table, occupied every room, walked through the doors of every house.

The people walked through the drifts that had formed when the wind blew, then they seemed to merge with the outlines of the trees. I was worried that Frenchie might fall into the warm spot where the lake never freezes. Others had fallen before her.

Bush went outside to get the bowl. It was empty and there were no tracks. Or maybe the wind had covered them. But a bowl without its soup is such a hopeful thing, and like the bowl, Bush was left with emptiness, a place waiting and ready to be filled, one she could move inside and shape about her. And finally, she was able to sleep.

The next evening, Bush said it was time for me to leave. "Go on," she said, handing me my coat and hat. I hesitated. She had little more than a few pieces of firewood and some cooking pots. She had given away even the food. She saw me look about the house at what wasn't there. I sipped hot tea. We'd slept near each other for warmth the night before, my bear coat over us. Once Bush sat up and said, "This coat is singing." I told her it was just the sound of ice outside the door. I must have looked worried. "I'll be fine," she said, holding up the coat to help me into it.

But I said, "What about me? It's getting close to dark." She wasn't fooled. She knew I walked late at night just to hear the sounds of winter and see the sky and snow. I was always a great walker. She handed me my gloves and hat. I left unwillingly. It was all I could do to go out the door. I felt terrible leaving her in all that emptiness. I guess it was her sadness already come over me. I wanted to cry out but I knew the wind, on its way to the island where it lived, would freeze my tears.

I took my time getting home. Above me there were shimmering hints of light. I remember thinking how the sky itself looked like a bowl of milk.

Then one night, worry got the best of me. I laced up my boots and went back over the frozen water. She was thinner, but she looked happy, and she didn't argue when I opened this bear coat I've always worn and wrapped it around the two of us and walked her back to the mainland. The only sound was our feet on ice, the snap and groan of the lake. We were two people inside the fur of this bear. She said she could see the cubs that had lived inside and been born from this skin, and I said, "Yes."

Leslie Marmon Silko
(1948–)

"I will tell you something
about stories,
[he said]
They aren't just entertainment.
Don't be fooled.
They are all we have, you see,
all we have to fight off
illness and death.

You don't have anything
if you don't have the stories."

Leslie Marmon Silko, *Ceremony*

Storyteller

Leslie Marmon Silko

Every day the sun came up a little lower on the horizon, moving more slowly until one day she got excited and started calling the jailer. She realized she had been sitting there for many hours, yet the sun had not moved from the center of the sky. The color of the sky had not been good lately; it had been pale blue, almost white, even when there were no clouds. She told herself it wasn't a good sign for the sky to be indistinguishable from the river ice, frozen solid and white against the earth. The tundra rose up behind the river but all the boundaries between the river and hills and sky were lost in the density of the pale ice.

She yelled again, this time some English words which came randomly into her mouth, probably swear words she'd heard from the oil drilling crews last winter. The jailer was an Eskimo, but he would not speak Yupik to her. She had watched people in other cells, when they spoke to him in Yupik he ignored them until they spoke English.

He came and stared at her. She didn't know if he understood what she was telling him until he glanced behind her at the small high window. He looked at the sun, and turned and walked away. She could hear the buckles on his heavy snowmobile boots jingle as he walked to the front of the building.

It was like the other buildings that white people, the Gussucks,* brought with them: BIA and school buildings, portable buildings that arrived sliced in halves, on barges coming up the river. Squares of metal paneling bulged out with the layers of insulation stuffed inside. She had asked once what it was and someone told her it was to keep out the cold. She had not laughed then, but she did now. She walked over to the small double-pane window and she laughed out loud. They thought they could keep out the cold with stringy yellow wadding. Look at the sun. It wasn't moving; it was frozen, caught in the middle of the sky. Look at the sky, solid as the river with ice which had trapped the sun. It had not moved for a long time; in a few more hours it would be weak, and heavy frost would begin to appear on

* Derived from a Russian word, Gussuck is a local word for "white man."

the edges and spread across the face of the sun like a mask. Its light was pale yellow, worn thin by the winter.

She could see people walking down the snow-packed roads, their breath steaming out from their parka hoods, faces hidden and protected by deep ruffs of fur. There were no cars or snowmobiles that day; the cold had silenced their machines. The metal froze; it split and shattered. Oil hardened and moving parts jammed solidly. She had seen it happen to their big yellow machines and the giant drill last winter when they came to drill their test holes. The cold stopped them, and they were helpless against it.

Her village was many miles upriver from this town, but in her mind she could see it clearly. Their house was not near the village houses. It stood alone on the bank upriver from the village. Snow had drifted to the eaves of the roof on the north side, but on the west side, by the door, the path was almost clear. She had nailed scraps of red tin over the logs last summer. She had done it for the bright red color, not for added warmth the way the village people had done. This final winter had been coming even then; there had been signs of its approach for many years.

She went because she was curious about the big school where the Government sent all the other girls and boys. She had not played much with the village children while she was growing up because they were afraid of the old man, and they ran when her grandmother came. She went because she was tired of being alone with the old woman whose body had been stiffening for as long as the girl could remember. Her knees and knuckles were swollen grotesquely, and the pain had squeezed the brown skin of her face tight against the bones; it left her eyes hard like river stone. The girl asked once what it was that did this to her body, and the old woman had risen up from sewing a sealskin boot, and stared at her.

"The joints," the old woman said in a low voice, whispering like wind across the roof, "the joints are swollen with anger."

Sometimes she did not answer and only stared at the girl. Each year she spoke less and less, but the old man talked more—all night sometimes, not to anyone but himself; in a soft deliberate voice, he told stories, moving his smooth brown hands above the blankets. He had not fished or hunted with the other men for many years, although he was not crippled or sick. He stayed in his bed, smelling like dry fish and urine, telling stories all winter; and when warm weather came, he went to his place on the river bank. He sat with a long willow stick, poking at the smoldering moss he burned against the insects while he continued with the stories.

The trouble was that she had not recognized the warnings in time. She did not see what the Gussuck school would do to her until she walked into the dormitory and realized that the old man had not been lying about the place. She thought he had been trying to scare her as he used to when she was very small and her grandmother was outside cutting up fish. She hadn't believed what he told her about the school because she knew he wanted to keep her there in the log house with him. She knew what he wanted.

The dormitory matron pulled down her underpants and whipped her with a leather belt because she refused to speak English.

"Those backwards village people," the matron said, because she was an Eskimo who had worked for the BIA a long time, "they kept this one until she was too big to learn." The other girls whispered in English. They knew how to work the showers, and they washed and curled their hair at night. They ate Gussuck food. She lay on her bed and imagined what her grandmother might be sewing, and what the old man was eating in his bed. When summer came, they sent her home.

The way her grandmother had hugged her before she left for school had been a warning too, because the old woman had not hugged or touched her for many years. Not like the old man, whose hands were always hunting, like ravens circling lazily in the sky, ready to touch her. She was not surprised when the priest and the old man met her at the landing strip, to say that the old lady was gone. The priest asked her where she would like to stay. He referred to the old man as her grandfather, but she did not bother to correct him. She had already been thinking about it; if she went with the priest, he would send her away to a school. But the old man was different. She knew he wouldn't send her back to school. She knew he wanted to keep her.

He told her one time, that she would get too old for him faster than he got too old for her; but again she had not believed him because sometimes he lied. He had lied about what he would do with her if she came into his bed. But as the years passed, she realized what he said was true. She was restless and strong. She had no patience with the old man who had never changed his slow smooth motions under the blankets.

The old man was in his bed for the winter; he did not leave it except to use the slop bucket in the corner. He was dozing with his mouth open slightly; his lips quivered and sometimes they moved like he was telling a story even while he dreamed. She pulled on the sealskin boots, the mukluks with the bright red flannel linings her grandmother had sewn for her, and she tied the braided red yarn tassels around her ankles over the gray wool pants. She zipped the wolfskin parka. Her grandmother had worn it for many years, but the old man said that before she died, she instructed him to bury her in an old black sweater, and to give the parka to the girl. The wolf pelts were creamy colored and silver, almost white in some places, and when the old lady had walked across the tundra in the winter, she was invisible in the snow.

She walked toward the village, breaking her own path through the deep snow. A team of sled dogs tied outside a house at the edge of the village leaped against their chains to bark at her. She kept walking, watching the dusky sky for the first evening stars. It was warm and the dogs were alert. When it got cold again, the dogs would lie curled and still, too drowsy from the cold to bark or pull at the chains. She laughed loudly because it made them howl and snarl. Once the old man had seen her tease the dogs and he shook his head. "So that's the kind of woman you are," he said, "in the wintertime the two of us are no different from those dogs. We wait in the cold for someone to bring us a few dry fish."

She laughed out loud again, and kept walking. She was thinking about the Gussuck oil drillers. They were strange; they watched her when she walked near their machines. She wondered what they looked like underneath their quilted goose-down trousers; she wanted to know how they moved. They would be something different from the old man.

The old man screamed at her. He shook her shoulders so violently that her head bumped against the log wall. "I smelled it!" he yelled, "as soon as I woke up! I am sure of it now. You can't fool me!" His thin legs were shaking inside the baggy wool trousers; he stumbled over her boots in his bare feet. His toenails were long and yellow like bird claws; she had seen a gray crane last summer fighting another in the shallow water on the edge of the river. She laughed out loud and pulled her shoulder out of his grip. He stood in front of her. He was breathing hard and shaking; he looked weak. He would probably die next winter.

"I'm warning you," he said, "I'm warning you." He crawled back into his bunk then, and reached under the old soiled feather pillow for a piece of dry fish. He lay back on the pillow, staring at the ceiling and chewed dry strips of salmon. "I don't know what the old woman told you," he said, "but there will be trouble." He looked over to see if she was listening. His face suddenly relaxed into a smile, his dark slanty eyes were lost in wrinkles of brown skin. "I could tell you, but you are too good for warnings now. I can smell what you did all night with the Gussucks."

She did not understand why they came there, because the village was small and so far upriver that even some Eskimos who had been away to school did not want to come back. They stayed downriver in the town. They said the village was too quiet. They were used to the town where the boarding school was located, with electric lights and running water. After all those years away at school, they had forgotten how to set nets in the river and where to hunt seals in the fall. When she asked the old man why the Gussucks bothered to come to the village, his narrow eyes got bright with excitement.

"They only come when there is something to steal. The fur animals are too difficult for them to get now, and the seals and fish are hard to find. Now they come for oil deep in the earth. But this is the last time for them." His breathing was wheezy and fast; his hands gestured at the sky. "It is approaching. As it comes, ice will push across the sky." His eyes were open wide and he stared at the low ceiling rafters for hours without blinking. She remembered all this clearly because he began the story that day, the story he told from that time on. It began with a giant bear which he described muscle by muscle, from the curve of the ivory claws to the whorls of hair at the top of the massive skull. And for eight days he did not sleep, but talked continuously of the giant bear whose color was pale blue glacier ice.

The snow was dirty and worn down in a path to the door. On either side of the path, the snow was higher than her head. In front of the door there were jagged yellow stains melted into the snow where men had urinated. She stopped in the entry way and kicked the snow off her boots. The room was dim; a kerosene lantern by the cash register was burning low. The long wooden shelves were jammed with cans of beans and potted meats. On the bottom shelf a jar of mayonnaise was broken open, leaking oily white clots on the floor. There was no one in the room except the yellowish dog sleeping in the front of the long glass display case. A reflection made it appear to be lying on the knives and ammunition inside the case. Gussucks kept dogs inside their houses with them; they did not seem to mind the odors which seeped out of the dogs. "They tell us we are dirty for the food we eat—raw fish and fermented meat. But we do not live with dogs," the old man once said. She heard voices in the back room, and the sound of bottles set down hard on tables.

They were always confident. The first year they waited for the ice to break up on the river, and then they brought their big yellow machines upriver on barges. They planned to drill their test holes during the summer to avoid the freezing. But the imprints and graves of their machines were still there, on the edge of the tundra above the river, where the summer mud had swallowed them before they ever left sight of the river. The village people had gathered to watch the white men, and to laugh as they drove the giant machines, one by one, off the steel ramp into the bogs; as if sheer numbers of vehicles would somehow make the tundra solid. But the old man said they behaved like desperate people, and they would come back again. When the tundra was frozen solid, they returned.

Village women did not even look through the door to the back room. The priest had warned them. The storeman was watching her because he didn't let Eskimos or Indians sit down at the tables in the back room. But she knew he couldn't throw her out if one of his Gussuck customers invited her to sit with him. She walked across the room. They stared at her, but she had the feeling she was walking for someone else, not herself, so their eyes did not matter. The red-haired man pulled out a chair and motioned for her to sit down. She looked back at the storeman while the red-haired man poured her a glass of red sweet wine. She wanted to laugh at the storeman the way she laughed at the dogs, straining against the chains, howling at her.

The red-haired man kept talking to the other Gussucks sitting around the table, but he slid one hand off the top of the table to her thigh. She looked over at the storeman to see if he was still watching her. She laughed out loud at him and the red-haired man stopped talking and turned to her. He asked if she wanted to go. She nodded and stood up.

Someone in the village had been telling him things about her, he said as they walked down the road to his trailer. She understood that much of what he was saying, but the rest she did not hear. The whine of the big generators at the construction camp sucked away the sound of his words. But English was of no concern to her anymore, and neither was anything the Christians in the village might say about her or the old man. She smiled at the effect of the subzero air on the electric lights around the trailers; they did not shine. They left only flat yellow holes in the darkness.

It took him a long time to get ready, even after she had undressed for him. She waited in the bed with the blankets pulled close, watching him. He adjusted the thermostat and lit candles in the room, turning out the electric lights. He searched through a stack of record albums until he found the right one. She was not sure about the last thing he did: he taped something on the wall behind the bed where he could see it while he lay on top of her. He was shriveled and white from the cold; he pushed against her body for warmth. He guided her hands to his thighs; he was shivering.

She had returned a last time because she wanted to know what it was he stuck on the wall above the bed. After he finished each time, he reached up and pulled it loose, folding it carefully so that she could not see it. But this time she was ready; she waited for his fast breathing and sudden collapse on top of her. She slid out from under him and stood up beside the bed. She looked at the picture while she got dressed. He did not raise his face from the pillow, and she thought she heard teeth rattling together as she left the room.

She heard the old man move when she came in. After the Gussuck's trailer, the log house felt cool. It smelled like dry fish and cured meat. The room was dark except for the blinking yellow flame in the mica window of the oil stove. She squatted in front of the stove and watched the flames for a long time before she walked to the bed where her grandmother had slept. The bed was covered with a mound of rags and fur scraps the old woman had saved. She reached into the mound until she felt something cold and solid wrapped in a wool blanket. She pushed her fingers around it until she felt smooth stone. Long ago, before the Gussucks came, they had burned whale oil in the big stone lamp which made light and heat as well. The old woman had saved everything they would need when the time came.

In the morning, the old man pulled a piece of dry caribou meat from under the blankets and offered it to her. While she was gone, men from the village had brought a bundle of dry meat. She chewed it slowly, thinking about the way they still came from the village to take care of the old man and his stories. But she had a story now, about the red-haired Gussuck. The old man knew what she was thinking, and his smile made his face seem more round than it was.

"Well," he said, "what was it?"

"A woman with a big dog on top of her."

He laughed softly to himself and walked over to the water barrel. He dipped the tin cup into the water.

"It doesn't surprise me," he said.

"Grandma," she said, "there was something red in the grass that morning. I remember." She had not asked about her parents before. The old woman stopped splitting the fish bellies open for the willow drying racks. Her jaw muscles pulled so tightly against her skull, the girl thought the old woman would not be able to speak.

"They bought a tin can full of it from the storeman. Late at night. He told them it was alcohol safe to drink. They traded a rifle for it." The old woman's voice sounded like each word stole strength from her. "It made no difference about the rifle. That year the Gussuck boats had come, firing big guns at the walrus and seals. There was nothing left to hunt after that anyway. So," the old lady said, in a low soft voice the girl had not heard for a long time, "I didn't say anything to them when they left that night."

"Right over there," she said, pointing at the fallen poles, half buried in the river sand and tall grass, "in the summer shelter. The sun was high half the night then. Early in the morning when it was still low, the policeman came around. I told the interpreter to tell him that the storeman had poisoned them." She made outlines in the air in front of her, showing how their bodies lay twisted on the sand; telling the story was like laboring to walk through deep snow; sweat shone in the white hair around her forehead. "I told the priest too, after he came. I told him the storeman lied." She turned away from the girl. She held her mouth even tighter, set solidly, not in sorrow or anger, but against the pain, which was all that remained. "I never believed," she said, "not much anyway. I wasn't surprised when the priest did nothing."

The wind came off the river and folded the tall grass into itself like river waves. She could feel the silence the story left, and she wanted to have the old woman go on.

"I heard sounds that night, grandma. Sounds like someone was singing. It was light outside. I could see something red on the ground." The old woman did not answer her; she moved to the tub full of fish on the ground beside the workbench. She stabbed her knife into the belly of a whitefish and lifted it onto the bench. "The Gussuck storeman left the village right after that," the old woman said as she pulled the entrails from the fish, "otherwise, I could tell you more." The old woman's voice flowed with the wind blowing off the river; they never spoke of it again.

When the willows got their leaves and the grass grew tall along the river banks and around the sloughs, she walked early in the morning. While the sun was still low on the horizon, she listened to the wind off the river; its sound was like the voice that day long ago. In the distance, she could hear the engines of the machinery the oil drillers had left the winter before, but she did not go near the village or the store. The sun never left the sky and the summer became the same long day, with only the winds to fan the sun into brightness or allow it to slip into twilight.

She sat beside the old man at his place on the river bank. She poked the smoky fire for him, and felt herself growing wide and thin in the sun as if she had been split from belly to throat and strung on the willow pole in preparation for the winter to come. The old man did not speak anymore. When men from the village brought him fresh fish he hid them deep in the river grass where it was cool. After he went inside, she split the fish open and spread them to dry on the willow frame the way the old woman had done. Inside, he dozed and talked to himself. He had talked all winter, softly and incessantly, about the giant polar bear stalking a lone hunter across Bering Sea ice. After all the months the old man had been telling the story, the bear was within a hundred feet of the man; but the ice fog had closed in on them now and the man could only smell the sharp ammonia odor of the bear, and hear the edge of the snow crust crack under the giant paws.

One night she listened to the old man tell the story all night in his sleep, describing each crystal of ice and the slightly different sounds they made under each paw; first the left and then the right paw, then the hind feet. Her grandmother was there suddenly, a shadow around the stove. She spoke in her low wind voice and the girl was afraid to sit up to hear more clearly. Maybe what she said had been to the old man because he stopped telling the story and began to snore softly the way he had long ago when the old woman had scolded him for telling his stories while others in the house were trying to sleep. But the last words she heard clearly: "It will take a long time, but the story must be told. There must not be any lies." She pulled the blankets up around her chin, slowly, so that her movements would not be seen. She thought her grandmother was talking about the old man's bear story; she did not know about the other story then.

She left the old man wheezing and snoring in his bed. She walked through river grass glistening with frost; the bright green summer color was already fading. She watched the sun move across the sky, already lower on the horizon, already moving away from the village. She stopped by the fallen poles of the summer shelter where her parents had died. Frost glittered on the river sand too; in a few more weeks there would be snow. The predawn light would be the color of an old woman. An old woman sky full of snow. There had been something red lying on the ground the morning they died. She looked for it again, pushing aside the grass with her foot. She knelt in the sand and looked under the fallen structure for some trace of it. When she found it, she would know what the old woman had never told her. She squatted down close to the gray poles and leaned her back against them. The wind made her shiver.

The summer rain had washed the mud from between the logs; the sod blocks stacked as high as her belly next to the log walls had lost their square-cut shape and had grown into soft mounds of tundra moss and stiff-bladed grass bending with clusters of seed bristles. She looked at the northwest, in the direction of the Bering Sea. The cold would come down from there to find narrow slits in the mud, rainwater holes in the outer layer of sod which protected the log house. The dark green tundra stretched away flat and continuous. Somewhere the sea and the land met; she knew by their dark green colors there were no boundaries between them. That was how the cold would come: when the boundaries were gone the polar ice would range across the land into the sky. She watched the horizon for a long time. She would stand in that place on the north side of the house and she would keep watch on the northwest horizon, and eventually she would see it come. She would watch for its approach in the stars, and hear it come with the wind. These preparations were unfamiliar, but gradually she recognized them as she did her own footprints in the snow.

She emptied the slop jar beside his bed twice a day and kept the barrel full of water melted from river ice. He did not recognize her anymore, and when he spoke to her, he called her by her grandmother's name and talked about people and events from long ago, before he went back to telling the story. The giant bear was creeping across the new snow on its belly, close enough now that the man could hear the rasp of its breathing. On and on in a soft singing voice, the old man caressed the story, repeating the words again and again like gentle strokes.

The sky was gray like a river crane's egg; its density curved into the thin crust of frost already covering the land. She looked at the bright red color of the tin against the ground and the sky and she told the village men to bring the pieces for the old man and her. To drill the test holes in the tundra, the Gussucks had used hundreds of barrels of fuel. The village people split open the empty barrels that were abandoned on the river bank, and pounded the red tin into flat sheets. The village people were using the strips of tin to mend walls and roofs for winter. But she nailed it on the log walls for its color. When she finished, she walked away with the hammer in her hand, not turning around until she was far away, on the ridge above the river banks, and then she looked back. She felt a chill when she saw how the sky and the land were already losing their boundaries, already becoming lost in each other. But the red tin penetrated the thick white color of earth and sky; it defined the boundaries like a wound revealing the ribs and heart of a great caribou about to bolt and be lost to the hunter forever. That night the wind howled and when she scratched a hole through the heavy frost on the inside of the window, she could see nothing but the impenetrable white; whether it was blowing snow or snow that had drifted as high as the house, she did not know.

It had come down suddenly, and she stood with her back to the wind looking at the river, its smoky water clotted with ice. The wind had blown the snow over the frozen river, hiding thin blue streaks where fast water ran under ice translucent and fragile as memory. But she could see shadows of boundaries, outlines of paths which were slender branches of solidity reaching out from the earth. She spent days walking on the river, watching the colors of ice that would safely hold her, kicking the heel of her boot into the snow crust, listening for a solid sound. When she could feel the paths through the soles of her feet, she went to the middle of the river where the fast gray water churned under a thin pane of ice. She looked back. On the river bank in the distance she could see the red tin nailed to the log house, something not swallowed up by the heavy white belly of the sky or caught in the folds of the frozen earth. It was time.

The wolverine fur around the hood of her parka was white with the frost from her breathing. The warmth inside the store melted it, and she felt tiny drops of water on her face. The storeman came in from the back room. She unzipped the parka and stood by the oil stove. She didn't look at him, but stared instead at the yellowish dog, covered with scabs of matted hair, sleeping in front of the stove. She thought of the Gussuck's picture, taped on the wall above the bed and she laughed out loud. The sound of her laughter was piercing; the yellow dog jumped to its feet and the hair bristled down its back. The storeman was watching her. She wanted to laugh again because he didn't know about the ice. He did not know that it was prowling the earth, or that it had already pushed its way into the sky to seize the sun. She sat down in the chair by the stove and shook her long hair loose. He was like a dog tied up all winter, watching while the others got fed. He remembered how she had gone with the oil drillers, and his blue eyes moved like flies crawling over her body. He held his thin pale lips like he wanted to spit on her. He hated the people because they had something of value, the old man said, something which the Gussucks could never have. They thought they could take it, suck it out of the earth or cut it from the mountains; but they were fools.

There was a matted hunk of dog hair on the floor by her foot. She thought of the yellow insulation coming unstuffed: their defense against the freezing going to pieces as it advanced on them. The ice was crouching on the northwest horizon like the old man's bear. She laughed out loud again. The sun would be down now; it was time.

The first time he spoke to her, she did not hear what he said, so she did not answer or even look up at him. He spoke to her again but his words were only noises coming from his pale mouth, trembling now as his anger began to unravel. He jerked her up and the chair fell over behind her. His arms were shaking and she could feel his hands tense up, pulling the edges of the parka tighter. He raised his fist to hit her, his thin body quivering with rage; but the fist collapsed with the desire he had for the valuable things, which, the old man had rightly said, was the only reason they came. She could hear his heart pounding as he held her close and arched his hips against her, groaning and breathing in spasms. She twisted away from him and ducked under his arms.

She ran with a mitten over her mouth, breathing through the fur to protect her lungs from the freezing air. She could hear him running behind her, his heavy breathing, the occasional sound of metal jingling against metal. But he ran without his parka or mittens, breathing the frozen air; its fire squeezed the lungs against the ribs and it was enough that he could not catch her near his store. On the river bank he realized how far he was from his stove, and the wads of yellow stuffing that held off the cold. But the girl was not able to run very fast through the deep drifts at the edge of the river. The twilight was luminous and he could still see clearly for a long distance; he knew he could catch her so he kept running.

When she neared the middle of the river she looked over her shoulder. He was not following her tracks; he went straight across the ice, running the shortest distance to reach her. He was close then; his face was twisted and scarlet from the exertion and the cold. There was satisfaction in his eyes; he was sure he could outrun her.

She was familiar with the river, down to the instant ice flexed into hairline fractures, and the cracking bone-sliver sounds gathered momentum with the opening ice until the churning gray water was set free. She stopped and turned to the sound of the river and the rattle of swirling ice fragments where he fell through. She pulled off a mitten and zipped the parka to her throat. She was conscious then of her own rapid breathing.

She moved slowly, kicking the ice ahead with the heel of her boot, feeling for sinews of ice to hold her. She looked ahead and all around herself; in the twilight, the dense white sky had merged into the flat snow-covered tundra. In the frantic running she had lost her place on the river. She stood still. The east bank of the river was lost in the sky; the boundaries had been swallowed by the freezing white. But then, in the distance, she saw something red, and suddenly it was as she had remembered it all those years.

She sat on her bed and while she waited, she listened to the old man. The hunter had found a small jagged knoll on the ice. He pulled his beaver fur cap off his head; the fur inside it steamed with his body heat and sweat. He left it upside down on the ice for the great bear to stalk, and he waited downwind on top of the ice knoll; he was holding the jade knife.

She thought she could see the end of his story in the way he wheezed out the words; but still he reached into his cache of dry fish and dribbled water into his mouth from the tin cup. All night she listened to him describe each breath the man took, each motion of the bear's head as it tried to catch the sound of the man's breathing, and tested the wind for his scent.

The state trooper asked her questions, and the woman who cleaned house for the priest translated them into Yupik. They wanted to know what happened to the storeman, the Gussuck who had been seen running after her down the road onto the river late last evening. He had not come back, and the Gussuck boss in Anchorage was concerned about him. She did not answer for a long time because the old man suddenly sat up in his bed and began to talk excitedly, looking at all of them—the trooper in his dark glasses and the housekeeper in her corduroy parka. He kept saying, "The story! The story! Eh-ya! The great bear! The hunter!"

They asked her again, what happened to the man from the Northern Commercial store. "He lied to them. He told them it was safe to drink. But I will not lie." She stood up and put on the gray wolfskin parka. "I killed him," she said, "but I don't lie."

The attorney came back again, and the jailer slid open the steel doors and opened the cell to let him in. He motioned for the jailer to stay to translate for him. She laughed when she saw how the jailer would be forced by this Gussuck to speak Yupik to her. She liked the Gussuck attorney for that, and for the thinning hair on his head. He was very tall, and she liked to think about the exposure of his head to the freezing; she wondered if he would feel the ice descending from the sky before the others did. He wanted to know why she told the state trooper she had killed the storeman. Some village children had seen it happen, he said, and it was an accident. "That's all you have to say to the judge: it was an accident." He kept repeating it over and over again to her, slowly in a loud but gentle voice: "It was an accident. He was running after you and he fell through the ice. That's all you have to say in court. That's all. And they will let you go home. Back to your village." The jailer translated the words sullenly, staring down at the floor. She shook her head. "I will not change the story, not even to escape this place and go home. I intended that he die. The story must be told as it is." The attorney exhaled loudly; his eyes looked tired. "Tell her that she could not have killed him that way. He was a white man. He ran after her without a parka or mittens. She could not have planned that." He paused and turned toward the cell door. "Tell her I will do all I can for her. I will explain to the judge that her mind is confused." She laughed out loud when the jailer translated what the attorney said. The Gussucks did not understand the story; they could not see the way it must be told, year after year as the old man had done, without lapse or silence.

She looked out the window at the frozen white sky. The sun had finally broken loose from the ice but it moved like a wounded caribou running on strength which only dying animals find, leaping and running on bullet-shattered lungs. Its light was weak and pale; it pushed dimly through the clouds. She turned and faced the Gussuck attorney.

"It began a long time ago," she intoned steadily, "in the summertime. Early in the morning, I remember, something red in the tall river grass. . . ."

The day after the old man died, men from the village came. She was sitting on the edge of her bed, across from the woman the trooper hired to watch her. They came into the room slowly and listened to her. At the foot of her bed they left a king salmon that had been slit open wide and dried last summer. But she did not pause or hesitate; she went on with the story, and she never stopped, not even when the woman got up to close the door behind the village men.

The old man would not change the story even when he knew the end was approaching. Lies could not stop what was coming. He thrashed around on the bed, pulling the blankets loose, knocking bundles of dried fish and meat on the floor. The hunter had been on the ice for many hours. The freezing winds on the ice knoll had numbed his hands in the mittens, and the cold had exhausted him. He felt a single muscle tremor in his hand that he could not stop, and the jade knife fell; it shattered on the ice, and the blue glacier bear turned slowly to face him.

Mistaken Identity

Leslie Marmon Silko

"Of course the real man they called Geronimo, they never did catch. The real Geron-imo got away," old Mahawala said late one night when Calabazas was half-asleep. Although the small cook fire at their feet had died down to a few coals and there was no moon, he could still see the faces of these old-timers well enough in the light of the stars and the wide luminous belt of the Milky Way. High in the mountains, the old ones claimed they were that much closer to the clouds and the winds. They claimed people of the mountain peaks got special attention from the planets and moon. Cala-bazas had looked at each face trying to determine in an instant if this was a joke or not. Because if it was a joke and he appeared to take it seriously, they would have him. And if it wasn't a joke, and he laughed, they would have him too. But when Calabazas realized the old ones were serious about this Geronimo story, he had given in.

Old Mahawala started out, and then the others, one by one, had contributed some detail or opinion or alternative version. The story they told did not run in a line for the horizon but circled and spiraled instead like the red-tailed hawk. "Geronimo" of course was the war cry Mexican soldiers made as they rode into battle, counting on help from St. Jerome. The U.S. soldiers had misunderstood just as they had misun-derstood just about everything else they had found in this land. In time there came to be at least four Apache raiders who were called by the name Geronimo, either by the Mexican soldiers or the gringos. The tribal people here were all very aware that the whites put great store in names. But once the whites had a name for a thing, they seemed unable ever again to recognize the thing itself.

The elders used to argue that this was one of the most dangerous qualities of the Europeans: Europeans suffered a sort of blindness to the world. To them, a "rock" was just a "rock" wherever they found it, despite obvious differences in shape, density, color, or the position of the rock relative to all things around it. The Europeans, whether they spoke Spanish or English, could often be heard complain-ing in frightened tones that the hills and canyons looked the same to them, and they could not remember if the dark volcanic hills in the distance were the same dark hills they'd marched past hours earlier. To whites all Apache warriors looked alike, and no one realized that for a while, there had been three different Apache warriors called Geronimo who ranged across the Sonoran desert south of Tucson.

Strategists for both the Yaquis and the Apaches quickly learned to make use of the Europeans' inability to perceive unique details in the landscape. Although the Indians hired as scouts by the white armies were not so easily fooled, still the confusion of the white officers and their arguments with the scouts time and again gave the Apache and Yaqui women and children opportunities to escape their pursuers. The trick was to lead the chase to rocky terrain cut by narrow, deep arroyos. The longer the soldiers rode up and down the steep terrain, the more exhausted and afraid they became.

So the Apache warrior called Geronimo had been three, even four different men. The warrior of prominence and also of controversy among other Apaches had been born in the high mountains above the river now called Gila. This man had not been a warrior but had been trained as a medicine man. As the wars with the Americanos and Mexicans had intensified, and the ranks of the warriors wanted men, the medicine man had begun riding with them on the raids. His specialty had been silence and occasionally, invisibility. With his special skills, the raiders had been able to move so silently not even the Apache scouts who worked for the U.S. cavalry had been able to hear the raiders walk past their bedrolls.

The old Yaquis liked to tell stories about the days when their beloved mountain canyons used to shelter the four Geronimos. They discussed the strange phenomenon of the Geronimo photographs and of course other matters, such as how best to exploit the weakness of the whites.

First they had settled back over mutton ribs supplied by the youngest of the three "Geronimos." They each told their most strange or amusing experience with American colonels or Mexican captains who believed they had captured the notorious "Geronimo." Denials or attempts to explain the mistaken identity were always rejected angrily by the white men. "*You* are that murderer! The savage beast Geronimo!" the white men would bellow. Explanations or denials had only been further proof of guilt for the soldiers.

General Crook had been careful to engage the services of the traveling photographer stationed in Tombstone. The photographs had been for national publicity to maintain Crook's support among the territorial congressional delegations in Washington. The old people, who generally could not agree on the details of anything that had happened more than a minute or two before, had been unanimous about the photograph. Calabazas remembered he had repeated the word *photograph* to Mahawala, and one of the other old people mimicked his tone of dumb surprise. At the meeting of the three Geronimos, naturally there had been discussion of photographic images. All of them, even Red Clay, the final Geronimo who died in Oklahoma, had been photographed at one time or another. Sleet, the youngest of the Geronimos, had been photographed, during a stay at Fort Apache when General Crook and the Indian agents had attempted to get the War Department to order the forcible removal of white squatters from mountain land that had already been promised to Sleet and his people.

The photographer who made the photograph had been at Fort Apache for a number of weeks by the time he learned from the camp mulemaster which of the Apaches was "Geronimo." The photographer had perfected his Arizona-desert backdrop and had time enough to commission Apache women to create a huge feathery warbonnet unlike any headpiece the Apaches had ever seen, let alone worn. Sleet had dressed exactly as the photographer directed, then stood slightly to one side so that the long, trailing cascade of chicken and turkey feathers could be fully appreciated in the profile view.

Big Pine had been photographed around the same time. By then the photographer's warbonnet had disappeared, and Big Pine had posed instead with a .45–70 across his lap. The rifle had no firing pin and the barrel had been jammed with an iron rod because Big Pine and his band had been arrested at their camp west of Tucson and even the small children had been locked in manacles and shackles. The locks and chains were "punishment" for "breaking away" from the Fort while Washington made a final determination of their ancestral homelands. Big Pine had tried to explain to the Indian scouts and interpreters that he was not "Geronimo," that the one they were looking for was probably Sleet, and his band of warriors, who were headed for the border. Big Pine offered as proof their tidy little camp. Anyone could see, Big Pine said patiently, this camp had taken months to build, and that the venison drying in the sun had taken weeks of patient hunting. All this proved he and his band of women and children could not have just escaped from Fort Apache and gone there. The half-breed Apache scout knew Big Pine was truthful, and Sleet's band had headed for Mexico. But the Indian scouts had discovered that American army officers did not like complications. The Indian scouts had already determined that if they ever revealed that mistakes had been made, and that there were probably three or maybe even four Apache warriors called Geronimo, all of the Apache scouts might be court-martialed and hanged. Every hotshot young captain had come to the Arizona and New Mexico territories eager to be the man who captured and brought in Geronimo. Cash bonuses were constantly offered to the army scout or enlisted man whose efforts led to the taking of Geronimo dead or alive.

The man who had been born at the headwaters of the Gila River in New Mexico and who had spent years as a medicine man before assuming certain duties on raids had gone by different names. He had been photographed in a group picture some years before with Nana, Mangaas Coloradas, and Jute. He was known to the Yaquis in the mountains of Sonora as Wide Ledge, which the Yaquis understood to be the meaning of his Apache name. But Yaquis also understood that a person might need a number of names in order to conduct all of his or her earthly business.

The discussion of the photographic image centered upon the group photograph, which Wide Ledge had been shown by a young U.S. cavalry officer. Wide Ledge recalled that the young white man had pointed to the flat paper. Here the chorus of voices in the darkness had quickened, and Calabazas knew they were nearing what they considered to be the heart of the story of the four Geronimos. Wide Ledge, old Mahawala told Calabazas emphatically, had done a lot of thinking and looking at these flat pieces of paper called photographs. From what he had seen, Wide Ledge said, the white people had little smudges and marks like animal tracks across snow or light brown dust; these "tracks" were supposed to "represent" certain persons, places, or things. Wide Ledge explained how with a certain amount of training and time, he had been able to see the "tracks" representing a horse, a canyon, and white man. But invariably, Wide Ledge said, these traces of other beings and other places preserved on paper became confused even for the white people, who believed they understood these tracks so well. Wide Ledge had actually observed a young soldier fly into a rage at the photographer because the soldier said the image on the paper did not truly represent him. The soldier's friends had examined the photograph, but among themselves they could not agree. The photographer only wanted to be paid.

The secret, as a Yaqui or Apache might already have guessed, was that the black box contained a huge quartz crystal that had been carefully cut, polished, and mounted inside the black wooden box. Wide Ledge had had a chance to look through the flat, polished crystal; a boulder nearby had taken on a great many different forms while Wide Ledge looked through the lens. Wide Ledge said he was just beginning to have an understanding of the big polished crystal when the photographer saw him under the black cloth and began shouting at him.

Each of the so-called Geronimos had learned to demand prints of themselves as payment for posing. At meetings in the mountains they had compared photographs. The puzzle had been to account for the Apache warrior whose broad, dark face, penetrating eyes, and powerful barrel-chested body had appeared in every photograph taken of the other Geronimos. The image of this man appeared where the faces of the other Geronimos should have been. The old man called Nana by the whites studied the photographs and conferred with his acquaintances, elderly people who had ranged in the mountains even before the Apache Wars. The identity of the Apache in the photograph could not be determined, but a number of theories were advanced by both Apaches and Yaquis concerning the phenomenon; the light of the polished crystal, the light of the sun, and the light of the warrior's soul had left their distinctive mark with the Apache face white people identified as Geronimo.

Opinion had been divided over the dangers of allowing a photographic image to be made. Could the face and body that kept appearing in place of the three Geronimos be evidence that at some earlier photographic session, the soul of an unidentified Apache warrior had been captured by the white man's polished crystal in the black box and was now attempting to somehow come back? If so, why did this warrior's soul appear only in connection with the three Apaches white people called Geronimo?

Well, there were many interesting questions surrounding the strange polished crystals in the white men's black boxes, Sleet said. Why bother with speculations and arguments over whether the crystal always stole the soul or only did so when white men harbored certain intentions toward the person in front of the camera. The point was, Sleet reminded Wide Ledge and Big Pine, whites on both sides of the border were hunting the Apache called Geronimo. U.S. newspapers from Tucson to Washington, D.C., had the biggest headlines in the blackest ink Sleet had ever seen, demanding death for Geronimo. Wide Ledge was the oldest and most tired of the three Geronimos. Constant movement through rough desert country and the endless scattering of the women and children had exhausted this "Geronimo." He had been ready to "go in" until the bootlegger in the whiskey wagon from Tucson had shown him that same newspaper. The bootlegger had read the big words to him, Wide Ledge said, and that had scared all of them. If they were going to die, to have their heads chopped off and their skins tanned for chair cushions, Wide Ledge and all his people had agreed, they would not make it easy for the whites. The people would crawl back into the stony crevices and cling fiercely like scorpions.

Old Pancakes

But while the three Apaches had been meeting to discuss the confusion of the whites over "Geronimo," news came that Old Pancakes had surrendered to U.S. troops in Skeleton Canyon. Old Pancakes had been the best customer the Tucson bootleggers had ever had. Old Pancakes bragged that the bootleggers in Tucson protected him from the army; Old Pancakes would only "surrender" his tiny band long enough to rest, fatten up, then they would escape again. Old Pancakes bragged he was fighting his own personal war, for his right to drink when and what he wanted to drink, and as much as he wanted to.

Wide Ledge and Big Pine did not see why this news should concern them. But the young boy who had brought the news of Pancakes's surrender stood before the three Geronimos and seemed to have something more to tell them. Sleet told the boy not to be afraid to tell them whatever it was. Well, Old Pancakes had really done it. Old Pancakes had claimed he was the warrior called Geronimo. The Indian scouts doubted the story, but the attaché to General Miles had heard the name Geronimo. The attaché accused the scouts of withholding critical intelligence information. It was no secret General Miles wanted to do what his rival Crook had failed to do, namely, bring in the ferocious criminal Geronimo and make the territories safe for white settlement.

Thus Old Pancakes had finally been able to use his skills as a liar and joker to seize the opportunity to save the others. Old Pancakes had released all his men and women of fighting age early in the campaigns. For years Pancakes managed some-how to guide his small band of old women and small children left in their care, to one or two campsites in the Santa Rita Mountains south of Tucson.

The boy reported that Old Pancakes had not expected the Geronimo trick to work because he was such an old man and he had no warriors with him anymore, and he spent most of his time dozing under shady trees in Skeleton Canyon or one of the other canyons in the Santa Ritas. But Pancakes had not counted on army politics. Even when the scouts failed to convince the attaché and the general that

Pancakes was an impostor, Pancakes had been certain once the wagon carrying him in shackles and chains reached Tucson, General Miles and his aide would be set straight by other seasoned army personnel.

But as the troops with their captive arrived in Tucson, a strange thing occurred. A stagecoach load of East Coast journalists who had arrived a few days before came running out of bars and whorehouses. The only word Old Pancakes heard was "Geronimo!" Pancakes watched the bootlegger come out of his yard where the wooden vats of fermenting liquor were poured into oak barrels. Pancakes watched the face of his old friend who had made vast fortunes off the Apache Wars. Out came the townspeople who held contracts to supply the U.S. cavalry troops with hardtack, beans, and meat. Pancakes watched the faces of the Tucson city fathers.

Pancakes's good friends, the white fathers of Tucson, realized the Army's mistake but the swarms of journalists at the telegraph station and the army greatly outnumbered them. The news of Geronimo's capture had been telegraphed to the entire U.S. By then, Pancakes had begun to be frightened by his joke. He could see he was not going to be turned loose, with all forgiven as a big misunderstanding. When the bootlegger and other Tucson dignitaries told the army they had the wrong Apache, General Miles revealed to the press there had been cooperation between some white men and the marauding Apaches. Although Miles did not say so, the implication had been the white businessmen in Tucson might have reasons for alleging Miles had captured the wrong Apache.

Within three days the president of the United States had sent a telegram to General Miles, rewarding him with another star. By then Old Pancakes had been locked up in Fort Lowell, and he realized the bootlegger and all the others could not stop what was happening. Pancakes's last hope had been the skepticism of two reporters—one from the *New York Times*, and the other from the *Washington Post*. They had studied photographs in the general's dossier on Geronimo. The general reminded them the photographs were from years before. As they could see from Pancakes's appearance, the years of relentless pursuit had taken their toll. The reporter from the *Times* had a proposal. Would the general allow the captive Geronimo to be taken out the back door of the brig to be photographed? The man from the *Times* had already engaged the photographer. Miles, who was concerned that reporters might in some way tarnish his moment in history, reluctantly agreed. Miles remarked that he'd had nightmares since they had brought Geronimo from Skeleton Canyon. In the general's dreams, Geronimo had brushed away shackles and leg irons as if they were cobwebs, and walked away, disappearing as the troops looked on, paralyzed by an invisible force. For more than fifteen years, five thousand U.S. troops, costing $20 million, had stomped through cactus and rock to capture one old Apache man more sorrowful than fierce.

"And what do you think?" old Mahawala had said, pointing her arthritic finger so it nearly touched Calabazas's forehead. "What do you think? What did Old Pancakes see when they showed him the picture of 'Geronimo's' surrender?" They had all been grinning at Calabazas, waiting for him to pick up where old Mahawala left off. Calabazas opened the last beer and began:

Old Pancakes did not go in much for photographs anyway. He held the photograph in his hands and turned it slowly around and over, sniffing it and sneezing from the strong smell of the chemicals. All the white men watching Pancakes would have laughed; the East Coast journalists would have laughed harder than the Americano soldiers or the general, who was probably glancing nervously at the brushy slopes of the rocky foothills above the fort, watching nervously for the legions of war-painted Apaches he'd dreamed of the night before. The journalists loved the ease with which this savage desert and its savage creatures so effortlessly yielded front-page copy.

Hours later, after the plate was developed, they compared it to the wiry old man standing in front of them. Old Pancakes had never been defiant, but he had never given up anything he cared about either. He stood before them refusing to admire the piece of paper covered with brownish spots and smudges. The lieutenant and the major thought it was not a good likeness and turned to the photographer to ask for another shot. But the photographer said he wasn't being paid by them, he was being paid by the gentleman from the *New York Times*. If the gentleman from the *Times* was satisfied, that was that. Of course there was little resemblance between Old Pancakes and the image of the Apache that appeared in the photograph.

"And so the three Geronimos suddenly were safe again." Old Mahawala gave a grin as wide as a full moon.

"There," she said to Calabazas, "you have heard that one again." Calabazas had nodded. A lot of Yaqui stories about Apaches were not so good or amusing. Until the white men came, they had been enemies; sometimes they had raided one another. Of course, as they later reminded one another, the raids and the scattered deaths were not at all the same as the slaughters by U.S. or Mexican soldiers.

Calabazas had asked if any Yaqui ever claimed to know the identity of the Apache whose face kept appearing in the photographs. But old Mahawala and the others had only shaken their heads and begun to gather up the empty beer bottles to wash and reuse for home remedies. Then an old uncle had hobbled over to Calabazas. The face in all the photographs had belonged to an ancestor, the soul of one long dead who knew the plight of the "Geronimos." The Apaches were nervous about the dead and the activities of their souls, but the Yaquis were not. The Yaquis had extensive experiences with just such occurrences. The spirit of the ancestor had cast its light, its power, in front of the faces of the three "Geronimos." Calabazas had been fascinated, and he asked the old man if the spirit had entered those warriors. "Oh, no!" the old uncle had said, waving his arms and shaking his head. "*That* is something else again! Very different! Not so good!" The spirit could move in and out easily through a crystal rock, that was all, the old man assured Calabazas. So a camera could not steal the soul as some people fear. A camera could not steal your soul unless you were already letting it go in the first place. But Calabazas had never forgotten the last thing his old uncle had said that night: "Of course in the hands of a sorcerer, who can say what might happen. Don't take any chances. Look where poor Old Pancakes ended up."

Patricia Riley
(1950–)

*"My grandmother, this woman who
had lived her entire life in denial
of her Indianness, blessed me in
the only way she knew how, with
a memory and a story that would
eventually enable me to find my
way home to my Cherokee roots."*

Patricia Riley, Introduction to
Growing Up Native American

Damping Down the Road

Patricia Riley

Carnel sat in the old front porch swing with her left leg tucked up under her skirt and pushed off with her right foot. The day was hot and still, the silence broken only by the creaky, sawing sounds that the chains made and the dull gentle thud of wood against wood when the back of the swing hit the house. It was the kind of repetitious noise that annoyed her mother, she knew, but to Carnel, it was soothing. Its rhythm matched her dreaming mood. The oppressive August heat made it difficult to do much of anything else.

It seemed to Carnel that she had passed almost the entire summer rocking slowly back and forth in the porch swing, picking off dried and curling pieces of its faded, flaking paint, watching the clouds of red dust rise up off the road as cars passed on their way to town. Dreaming. Looking for secret meaning in the patterns the flakes formed on the grey concrete. Sometimes, a small breath of a breeze came up and blew the patterns away before she could read what was in them, but today the lack of wind allowed the flakes to arrange themselves the way they wanted. Carnel could almost make out a face looking back at her. One eye was open and the other closed. She was just about to wonder out loud whose face it could be when her mother opened the screen door and broke her concentration.

"Carnel," she said. "Stop that infernal banging. I need you to go around the side of the house and unkink the hose for me so I can water down this road."

Carnel stood up and looked at her older sister, Ruby, who had suddenly replaced her mother at the door.

"She's damping down the road again," Carnel said. "Isn't this an exercise in, whachamacallit, futility, Ruby? It's just gonna dry up again in twenty minutes like it always does. It doesn't make good sense to me."

"Did you say that loud enough, Carnel? You want her to hear you?" Ruby whispered and rolled her eyes skyward with an exasperated look that spoke of having had this conversation before.

"You know you can't tell Mama nothin'. And if she hears you try, you're gonna catch hell like you did the last time. Besides, you know that Mama's on a mission and whenever she is you can't do a damn thing about it except sit back and watch."

Ruby was three years older than Carnel. Being fifteen going on sixteen had made her overly fond of spicing her conversation with dots and dashes of profanity. She thought it made her sound more mature. Carnel thought it made her sound more like poor white trash.

"Mama hears you running your mouth that way, I won't be the only one that catches it."

Carnel wrinkled her nose at Ruby and stomped off to do as she was told, secretly hoping that her mother had heard what Ruby said, even if it meant that she had heard what came before. Ruby could get on her nerves sometimes. Carnel loved Ruby, it was true. She was her sister and it was hard not to love a sister. These days, though, it seemed that Ruby didn't care much about anything but boys and what clothes she was going to wear to school the next day, and hairdos. Ruby cared a whole lot about hairdos. She went to sleep every night with her hair all wrapped up in giant brush rollers. How she slept at all was a mystery to Carnel who had tried it once herself and hated the way the prickly brushes stabbed her scalp all night. She hadn't slept for more than five minutes at a time. The next morning when she tried to take them out, her hair was all tangled in the brushes. She remembered having to pull and pull to get them out. Ruby had called her a dummy. Carnel guessed she must have been one because, after all that pain and trouble, the curl only lasted for all of forty-five minutes. It had started to droop on the way to the bus stop. By the time she was halfway across town, the curls had turned to waves. When she finally climbed the school steps, it was perfectly straight again, as if she had never bothered with it at all. And after that, she never did. To Carnel, it just didn't make good sense to try to force a thing to be what it didn't want to be and she felt good about the fact that her father agreed with her.

"It is what it is and what it is is straight. Good old Indian hair," Eli said and smiled at his wife while ruffling Carnel's hair.

Nettie humphed.

"What she needs is a good perm," she said.

When Ruby heard that she got all excited. "Oh, Mama," she cried. "Can I have one, too?"

"I don't want a perm," Carnel said. "I like my hair just fine the way it is."

"But I do, Mama. I want one," Ruby wheedled. "I want a perm, and I want to dye my hair. I want to dye it blonde. The boys at school like the girls with blonde hair better. Can I get a perm and dye it blonde, Mama?"

"Have you lost your mind completely?" Carnel asked. She never dreamed that Ruby would go so far, but here it was. Ruby was jumping on the idea like a duck on a June bug.

"Bleach, Ruby, not dye," Nettie said. "I imagine you can. You'll be sixteen soon. We'll go and do it tomorrow if you like."

Carnel took a deep breath and let it go. She was grateful to have escaped. Ruby, on the other hand, was in heaven. She danced around the kitchen in an ecstasy of anticipation. Dreams of hard-bodied football players vying for her attention filled her head.

When she came home from the beauty shop the next day, her hair was short, curly, and platinum blonde. Everywhere she went, people told Ruby how nice she looked, now that she was all curly and blonde, but Carnel had a different view of things. To her, the new and improved Ruby looked like an old washed-out dishrag.

Although she and Ruby were often at odds over one thing or another, Carnel knew that what Ruby had said about their mother was true. Nettie was on a mission. It was her own private battle against the natural world. Against the way things were. Against the way things wanted to be. She was a devoted disciple of change. A true believer. To Nettie, if you didn't like a thing you changed it somehow so that it would suit you better. It didn't matter what it was. If Nettie didn't like it, if for some reason it got on what she called her "bad side," she was going to change it, and that philosophy extended to everything in the world around her. People, too, as her attitude toward the rest of her family often bore out. But it was the red dirt road, with its neverending clouds of dust that sifted under closed doors and around window sills that attracted her attention every summer. To her the road was out to get her. She was its Captain Ahab. It was her Moby Dick. There was no mistaking the fact, that the road had most definitely gotten on Nettie's "bad side."

Looking back, Carnel could see that the signs of her mother's troubled relationship with the road had always been there, and that what finally happened to her most cherished possession just turned her smoldering dislike into a sublime hatred. Nettie's aversion had begun to surface six years earlier, shortly after she and her husband, Eli, had bought the place on Old Birch Road. The house was a plain white clapboard with green trim, selling at a reasonable price, one they could almost afford. Part of the reason it had been so reasonable was because it fronted on a road at the edge of town that the county had somehow managed to overlook during its paving project. But that was part of the reason that Carnel's father liked the place so much and wanted to buy it. He said its red dirt reminded him of home.

Before they moved there Eli told his girls that, although living on a red dirt road might seem to have some disadvantages, it had its good points, too. It all depended on how you chose to look at it as to which was which. At the time, Nettie had only shaken her head and continued packing boxes, sighing now and then as she carefully folded tissue paper around the treasured lace tablecloth her mother's mother had brought with her when she came from Ireland. But not too long after they moved in, the spring rains began and the road filled up and flooded over. Carnel's mother stood in front of the living room windows and watched as the water continued to rise. She began to fuss and fume, and before long, her anger and frustration spilled around the family creating a flood of its own.

"Is this one of the good points, Eli?" Nettie asked, aiming a sullen glare at her husband.

Eli didn't answer. He just smiled at his wife and bent to pull on his high-top fishing boots for the third time that day.

"Mama," Carnel said. "Daddy says that when it rains our road dreams that it's a river. I think that must be true, don't you? It's rushing along right now as if it were the Brazos."

"Eli, why do you keep filling her head with all that nonsense?" Nettie asked. "Roads can't dream. That road's nothing more than a bunch of dead dirt pounded flat. And Carnel, if you believe any different, then you're just as crazy as he is."

"Carnel," Eli said, ignoring the question and the comment. "Run outside to the garage for me and bring back that big flat-faced shovel. I'm going out there and dig another trench so some of that water will drain off into the trees."

"For God's sake, Eli," Nettie said. "At least come back through the back door, and take your boots off outside on the porch. I don't want that damn red mess tracked all over my floors like it was the last time."

While Carnel ran to retrieve the shovel, Nettie walked into the kitchen and began banging pots and pans around. A sure sign that she was more than fed up with what she called "that road nonsense." Ruby joined her, and Carnel could hear the two of them talking together as she passed beneath the kitchen window. It was then that Carnel decided that she must be crazy and accepted it, if that was what it truly was, because she believed her father was right. The red dirt road was a living thing every bit as much as she was. She knew it. It was far more than the lifeless dirt pounded flat that her mother believed it to be. It had a life of its own. It could dream, and it could turn itself into a river, or dry itself up into a fine powdery dust whenever it felt like it. You only had to live with it awhile to see that what her father said about the road was true.

Besides watching the road transform itself into a river, Carnel thought that the road had other advantages, too. After each spring rain, when the water finally went down and the road had turned itself into a soft mass of glistening red clay, Eli took Carnel out to the edge of the road and dug out bucketfuls of the sticky stuff to make things with. While Nettie and Ruby watched television in the living room, and complained about them muddying up her clean kitchen floor with all their daubs and dabs of clay, he and Carnel would spend hours at the kitchen table fashioning small pots and a menagerie of turtles, swans, and snakes until they had enough to fill a cardboard box. Then Eli would carry the box full of their handmade treasures out to the storage shed in the backyard where he would carefully place them on a shelf to dry. When winter came, Eli would bring their creations back inside and fire them in the fireplace. He would keep the fire going day and night until each piece was properly cured. After the fire died and the pieces were cool enough to handle, he gave Carnel the animals and pots that she had made for her to keep in her room. He put the ones he'd made in the shed because Nettie didn't like what she referred to as "tacky things like that" cluttering up her otherwise tastefully decorated house. She told Eli, on more than one occasion, that what Carnel chose to do with her own room was up to Carnel, but she wasn't going to have anything she didn't approve of spoiling the looks of the rest of her house.

Carnel was baffled by her mother's rigid disapproval of the things she and her father made together out of the wonderful red clay from the road. She cherished each and every little pot, each and every fanciful creature. She lined them all up on a shelf her father made especially for her to keep them on and loved them fiercely. To her they represented what was true and magical about the red dirt road they lived beside, and she marveled that a road like that could have so many different and wonderful personalities. But her most favorite piece of all wasn't one she had made herself. It was a small turtle fashioned by her father and given to her as a Christmas present when she was ten. She had admired it as he was making it and was delightfully happy when he gave it to her. From that time on, every night before she went to sleep, Carnel would gently take the turtle down from the shelf and spend a few minutes enthralled by the intricate patterns her father had carved on the turtle's shell. If she stared long and hard enough at it, she thought she could see a whole world spinning on the tiny turtle's back. But the turtle was gone now because a little over a year after her father had given it to her, Ruby had gotten mad at Carnel and thrown a shoe at her head. Carnel had ducked and the shoe continued on across the room, finally hitting the shelf, knocking the little turtle to the floor where it broke. Carnel tenderly gathered the pieces together, wrapped them in a handkerchief, and put them safely away in her underwear drawer. Every now and then, she took a piece out and held it in her hands, remembering how the turtle had been. Ruby laughed at her. "You're crazy," she said. "Just like Daddy." It seemed as if Ruby always agreed with her mother's lopsided take on things. Sometimes she wondered why her mother had ever married her father, if she thought he was crazy. She'd asked her mother about it not so long ago.

"For love, Carnel," Nettie said. "For love. But I thought I was getting one thing, and I wound up getting another. I thought I was getting a practical man with his feet on the ground. What I got was a head-in-the-clouds dreamer."

Carnel could guess what her mother meant by that because she knew that her mother didn't like the stories that her father used to tell her and Ruby when they were younger. But she didn't think her father's storytelling was a bad thing. She'd loved those stories about Corn Woman and the Lucky Hunter, and the way that the tricky old rabbit could almost always talk himself out of any trouble he got into. She loved those stories more than anything. She was sorry that Nettie had eventually made her father stop telling them. But she was sorry for her mother, too, because, after that, her father had told her another story. It was about what had happened to her mother when she was sent away to a Catholic boarding school in Arkansas.

Eli said that when Nettie was a girl she had loved those stories, too. Every year she'd looked forward to the time when her Cherokee relatives would come for a visit because that meant it was storytelling time. She'd curl up in her Grandma Mary's lap and listen quietly as all the aunts and uncles told their favorite stories, filling the air around her with their words and laughter. But the summer that Nettie turned thirteen, her Grandma Fiona decided that she should be sent away to St. Helen's so that she would receive a proper education. She loved Nettie, she said, and wanted the very best for her, so that when she grew up she could prosper as much as she deserved. Knowing that the family couldn't afford the price of the tuition, Grandma Fiona paid for it herself from part of her savings that she had tucked away.

At first, Nettie had been thrilled at the idea of going to school so far away from home, and the summer couldn't pass fast enough to please her. It was an adventure to her and she couldn't imagine when she left just how much she would miss her family. But Nettie's sense of adventure began to slowly wear away as days turned into weeks and the weeks into months. She often left her bed at night to stand at the window of her dormitory room and look longingly in the direction of the home she'd left behind. As time passed, the hollow space she felt inside her stomach grew so big that she felt as if it would never go away. To console herself, she thought about the stories, and how it was when the family was all together. Since she often seemed so thoughtful and withdrawn, the girls she shared her room with felt sad for her. They began to ask questions about Nettie's home and the family she missed so much. Nettie responded to their friendship, and it wasn't long before she began to share the special stories with her new friends. She told them about how Corn Woman made food out of her own body. How she loved the Cherokee people so much that she gave her life so that they could live, and that she came back to life again so that she would always be there for the people to talk to and ask for help. She painted word pictures for them so that they could see the wonderful magical lake where the animals went to bathe when they were sick or injured and how they came out of the water whole and healed again. Sharing these stories with her roommates made Nettie feel closer to her home and family.

The girls delighted in the stories Nettie told. They had never heard stories like these before and encouraged her to tell them more. Soon, the storytelling sessions became a nightly event, and girls from other rooms began to crowd in and listen, too. That was when Sister Mary Celeste became suspicious. As she patrolled the house late one night, making sure that all the girls were in their beds and asleep, she heard the sound of girlish laughter and excited talking coming from Nettie's room. Tiptoeing softly, so as not to be heard, she came up to the door, leaned in, and pressed her ear gently against it. Nettie was right in the middle of telling about the evil witch, Awl-finger, and the way that she lured unsuspecting children into her murderous clutches.

"You never know," Nettie said. "She can look like any kind of person. That's why my Grandma Mary says you should never talk to strangers. Sometimes she takes the shape of a kind, old woman. That's how she fools them. She calls them over and pets them and combs their hair. When they start to trust her and fall asleep in her lap . . . ZAP! . . . that's when she stabs them right in the heart, or in the back of their neck. Either way, those kids are done for. Then, she steals their liver and eats it because it has a kind of soul in it, and she wants to add the years of their lives to her own. But it isn't only kids she goes after. She'll go after grown-ups, too, sometimes. She has a witch hunger and she can never get enough so she kills and kills and kills. If she could, she would eat the souls of everybody in the whole world. That's how hungry she is to live forever. So, I'd be careful who I talked to from now on if I were you."

Nettie was just about to sing the song that went along with the story when the door burst open and Sister Mary Celeste swooped into the room. Everyone screamed and jumped about two feet. Pale and trembling all over, Sister Mary Celeste rushed over to where Nettie was sitting on the floor and pointed towards the center of Nettie's chest with a long, bony forefinger. She was shaking so hard that she could barely speak.

"Filth," she sputtered. "Filth and abomination. How dare you tell such vile things to these girls?"

Nettie was so startled and confused that she couldn't move. As she looked into the nun's contorted face, it seemed as if she was looking right into the eyes of the evil Awl-finger herself.

"Sister," she croaked. "I was only warning them about..."

"Not another word," the nun screamed. "You get up from there this instant and come with me. We're going to have a little visit with Sister Superior. She knows how to deal with the likes of you."

Nettie must have failed to move fast enough to suit the nun because Sister Mary Celeste suddenly reached down, wound one of Nettie's thick, dark braids around her wrist, and yanked her up by the hair.

"I mean now, Missy!" she said and pulled Nettie out of the room. The other girls had begun to sniffle and cry by then, and Nettie continued to hear their frightened voices as Sister Mary Celeste propelled her down the hall.

When they reached the Superior's office, Sister Mary Celeste left Nettie alone for a few minutes to ponder her fate. Nettie didn't know what to expect. She worried that she might be expelled from school. Although that might be a disappointment to Grandma Fiona, Nettie almost wished it would happen that way. If it did, at least it meant that she could go home, and she wouldn't have to come back anymore. But that wasn't what happened. What happened was a great deal worse.

Nettie could see that the Superior, Sister Mary Mathilde, was agitated the moment she opened the door. Her face had several creases in it that betrayed that she had been sleeping when she was called, and was none too happy about having been awakened in the middle of the night.

"Down on your knees," she ordered.

Nettie complied without a word. She thought she knew what was coming next because she had heard about something like this happening to another girl who had been expelled the year before.

Sister Mary Mathilde opened her desk drawer and took out a small plastic bottle of holy water. She removed the square, black stopper and began to circle Nettie slowly, all the while sprinkling her with the blessed fluid.

"This will drive the devil out of you," she said as she began to pray for the salvation of Nettie's wayward soul.

Nettie endured it, humiliated, but confident that it would be over soon. She expected that she would be told she was expelled and to call her folks and make arrangements to leave for home on the next morning's bus. But when Sister Mary Mathilde finished her prayers, she had something different to say.

"Here at St. Helen's we have certain religious standards to uphold," she began. "Those standards do not include the telling of filthy heathen stories to your school-mates. Such stories are inspired by the devil. They are evil and will not be tolerated. Am I being clear? They will not be tolerated, and neither will you if you persist in telling them. Do you understand what I am saying to you? Answer me!"

"Yes, Sister," Nettie murmured. I understand what you're telling me."

"Good," she said. "Because it is very important that we understand one another. It is very important that we be very clear. I had considered expelling you, but I have decided that you will be allowed to stay, but that does not mean that you will escape punishment. You will do three days detention, alone, in the basement. You will do your penance in total darkness to remind you of the darkness you have brought upon your immortal soul. You will eat only once a day, in the evening, and your supper will be a plain piece of white bread and a cup of water. While you are there, you will contemplate the sin you have committed this night in the sight of God, and you will ask Him for His loving forgiveness. When your detention is over and you are allowed to rejoin the other girls, I expect to see a change in your behavior. You may go now and begin your atonement."

Eli said he never knew exactly what had happened to Nettie while she was locked up in the basement of the convent school, but he knew that whatever happened there must have been bad because Nettie refused to talk about it. He also knew that Net-tie had changed enormously because her mother had told him once that she was a completely different person when she came back from that place. She seemed sad all the time, and nervous, jumping at every little sound. Nettie's mother had called all the aunts and uncles and invited them for a visit to cheer Nettie up. She knew how much Nettie had always loved their company and the nightly storytelling sessions. But when the family arrived, Nettie hardly smiled at all, and when the storytelling began, she ran to her room with her hands clapped over her ears. She refused to speak to anyone, or to come out again. When her mother went back to check on her a while later, she found Nettie sitting on the bed, rocking slowly back and forth, with a vacant look in her eyes. In her hands, she clutched the white lace tablecloth her Grandma Fiona had brought from Ireland and given Nettie for her hope chest. Tears were running down her face, but she wasn't making a sound. Eli said that he thought that she had never gotten over whatever it was that happened to her in that basement. He didn't say any more, but Carnel thought that she had heard enough to begin to make some sense out of her mother's often puzzling behavior, especially in regard to the red dirt road.

Although the spring flooding was a source of annual irritation for Carnel's mother, it was a particular event that happened one summer four years ago that finally drove her into the fits of impotent rage that led to the practice of damping down the road. Things started out slowly at first. Nettie began cussing the road and the way the dust flew up and settled on everything within its reach every time a car sped past the house. She thought if she kept the doors and windows closed the dirt wouldn't be able to get in, but she was wrong. It sifted under the doors and around the windows, leaving its trace on everything it touched, and Nettie felt it did that just to defy her efforts at keeping it out. Nettie had a surprising way of taking things personally. Finally, the road committed an unforgivable sin. It happened on one of Nettie's wash days. Nettie always divided what wash she had to do into "colored days" and "white days." She liked doing things that way. Orderly. It was a habit she had picked up from the nuns. Everything she did had its own special day. A day for vacuuming, a day for washing windows, and on and on. The day that things finally hit the fan for Nettie was on one of her "white days."

She had just hung up a load of white things that included sheets, pillowcases, and, her most prized possession, the white lace tablecloth that her grandmother had given her. Nettie only used the tablecloth on holidays and special occasions, like when she had church company, or relatives came to stay from out of town. The rest of the time, she kept it hidden away in a cedar chest where it would be safe from the mouths of hungry moths, and the insistent sifting of the dreaded red dust.

Nettie always chose her wash day carefully, so she waited for days when the sun was hot and the wind was still to avoid the red dust settling on whatever it was that she had washed before it had a chance to dry. She had a good sense for the weather, and was usually successful. Usually, whatever was on the line dried quickly and safely. But the day the terrible thing happened, everything went wrong.

That day she washed and rinsed her beloved tablecloth by hand in the kitchen sink using Ivory soap, as she always did, because the lace was far too delicate and fine to be thrown in the washing machine with some old regular harsh detergent. She lifted the cloth out of the rinse water with the care that was ordinarily reserved for infants and the very aged. She wrung it out, gently and slowly, her eyes glowing with pride and affection. Holding it just so, she carried it outside, and hung it to the left of the sheets and pillow cases, and fastened it into place with six clothespins that had been chosen scrupulously for their smoothness and lack of splinters. Then, she returned to the house. She was tired. At the moment, she wanted nothing more than to get herself a cold drink, and rest her aching, heat-swollen feet.

The girls were already ensconced on the couch watching General Hospital. It was a Friday. The day of the cliffhanging episode. A small, soft breeze lifted the living room curtains ever so slightly, which didn't cause much of a stir, but when a sudden large gust of wind sent them billowing out into the room like Salome's veils, Carnel saw her mother's head snap up. She was listening for the sound of cars coming up the road, but all she could hear was the sound of the sheets popping in the wind. She smiled at first.

"Maybe, this isn't such a bad turn of events," she said. "Those sheets might dry real fast in a stiff, hot wind."

Carnel blinked her eyes at Ruby. She couldn't believe what she had just heard. It wasn't like her mother at all. Carnel guessed that she must have been lulled into a false sense of security because it was Friday, and the road never had much traffic on Fridays until after five o'clock when people returned from work, or went to the store to do their weekend shopping.

"Mama?" Carnel questioned.

"Yes, I know, Carnel," she replied. "But it's early yet and the wash will dry real quick now with this wind. I think the wash is safe enough, and I'm just too tired today to go back out there and take it all down again." Sometimes Nettie did take it down, and when she did, the house turned into something that resembled an Arctic landscape. First, Carnel would spread several layers of brown butcher's paper across the tops of the chairs, sofa, and tables to prevent the furniture from coming into direct contact with the still damp sheets. When the preparations were all taken care of, the sheets would be brought in, ceremoniously carried by Nettie and Ruby with one of them at each end. The sheets were then draped carefully across the furniture and smoothed with quick hands before any wrinkles could form. But drying the sheets this way sometimes took all day and no one enjoyed it. You couldn't do much of anything, or even find a comfortable place to sit, while the sheets were occupying the living room.

Since it was such a misery and an inconvenience, and because she was so very tired, Nettie just couldn't bring herself to move from where she was comfortably curled in her favorite easy chair. She decided that she was just going to stay put and relax. But not too much time had passed before Carnel noticed that her mother's forehead had formed itself into a small crimped frown.

"Carnel, if you please," she said. "I would deeply appreciate it if you would run on outside and check on that wash for me. I'm worried that the sheets might get wound around and tangled in the clothesline. You know I don't like wrinkles, and pay special care to the tablecloth, Carnel. If it's all wound up, don't yank on it or it'll tear. You just come back and get me and I'll fix it myself."

"Ok, Mama," Carnel said and ran outside. That was why she was there to see it when it happened.

Carnel had untangled all the sheets and was standing back admiring what she had done, feeling grateful and relieved because her mother's special tablecloth had somehow emerged unscathed and not tangled at all. That was when she heard it coming up the backside of the hill. She could tell by the growl and whine of the engine that it was moving fast. Carnel looked up and saw a huge cement truck cresting the top of the hill. For a second or two, Carnel found herself running in a panic from one end of the clothesline to the other. She knew she couldn't stop what was about to happen even if she tried, but she had to try. Her eyes flew to the precious tablecloth that had traveled all the way from Ireland in the bottom of her great-grandmother's trunk. Try as she might, she couldn't unpin it fast enough to get it loose. Her fingers grew thick and clumsy, and tangled uselessly in the clothespins. She only managed to unfasten two of the six pins her mother had pinned in place before it was all over.

The sound of the truck grew louder and louder, gradually intensifying to an ear-splitting roar, as it finally rattled and rumbled past the house and on to its next destination.

Carnel's eyes widened with despair and horror as she watched the momentous cloud of red dust that followed in the truck's wake being driven by the wind straight toward the clothesline. There wasn't a thing that she could do except watch as the red dirt settled and stained all of the white things. But the worst was what had happened to her mother's white lace tablecloth. It was completely ruined, covered by a film of red dust that turned to mud almost as soon as it had settled.

Carnel heard a small whimpering sound behind her. She knew it was her mother. Even before she turned around to face her, Carnel knew that Nettie had seen it happen, too. Carnel looked into her mother's eyes and saw the look of helpless defeat that widened and fixed them in a horrified stare. Nettie was standing stiff as a statue with both hands stretched out in front of her, as if to ward off what had already happened. Her face had gone as white as the tablecloth had been moments before, and the freckles across the bridge of her nose stood out in stark contrast to her sudden paleness. A slow fountain of tears spilled down her cheeks, and her mouth was frozen in the rounded shape of a startled and disbelieving "O." Finally, Carnel put her arm around her mother's shoulders, as if their roles had been reversed, and gently led her back inside the house. She hardly knew what else to do.

Following the tablecloth tragedy, Nettie stayed in her room for three days and three nights. She emerged from her bedroom at sunrise the morning of the fourth day, and began to formulate her battle plan. Eli watched as she stirred her morning coffee. Her expression was distant and preoccupied. After watching her for awhile, Eli decided it might be a good idea if he made breakfast himself.

"Want some eggs and bacon, Nettie?" he asked. "I'm cookin' this morning."

But Nettie didn't answer. She just sat there stirring and stirring. When Eli kissed her cheek and left for work, she hardly noticed.

Carnel woke up at 8:30 that morning. It was already 102 degrees and her mother was nowhere to be found. Not in the kitchen, not in the living room and not in the backyard. Finally, Carnel thought she heard the sound of water running somewhere in the front yard. She opened the door to look out, thinking that it was probably her mother watering the iris and lantanas that grew along the porch front. She was more than a little surprised to see her mother standing at the edge of the yard in an old house dress, wearing a huge straw hat, and watering the road with a determined vengeance.

That is how it had begun, and every summer since, Nettie watered the road with religious dedication. Every day of every summer, Nettie organized her life around the road, damping it down exactly every four hours, around the clock. Her battle with the road was constant and precise, and she was determined never to allow it to beat her again.

Thinking back on all these things made Carnel tired. She could feel the weight of her thoughts and memories pressing down on her, breaking open a lonely place inside her heart that she didn't know how to fill. She wished her father was home so she could talk to him about the way she felt, but he had left early in the summer to take a job in an oil field near Houston. He wouldn't be back for another visit until September. Her father made good money in the oil fields, and always sent plenty home for his family, but it was hard to have him away for such long stretches of time.

Carnel returned from untangling the hose for her mother and settled herself once more in the old porch swing. As she resumed studying the patterns the flakes of paint made on the concrete, she saw the same face she had seen before, but she still couldn't make out who it was or what it might mean. It was a little after eight o'clock now, and the mosquitoes were coming out. Carnel swatted at them as they swarmed around her face, and watched as her mother watered the road. Inside the house, she heard the phone ring and Ruby's rapid footsteps as she ran to answer. Carnel was sure it was her father. He called as often as he could. She couldn't wait to hear the sound of his voice. Carnel watched as Ruby opened the screen door and leaned out to call her mother.

"Mama," she said. "There's a man wants to talk to you on the telephone."

Carnel saw her mother lay the hose down and walk around the side of the house to turn off the water. She waited until her mother came up the steps, and then she followed her inside. She and Ruby fidgeted while Nettie picked up the phone and said, "Hello." They were hoping that maybe their father had decided to come home ahead of schedule, that the man on the other end of the line was a friend of his letting their mother know that he was on his way. But Nettie only said a few words before her face went white the way it had the day the special tablecloth was ruined, only Carnel could tell that this was worse because her mother sat down hard and sudden, as if she had been shot. A low moan escaped her lips and she began to sob.

Ruby walked over to her mother and took the phone out of her hand and replaced it in its cradle. Whoever had been on the line had hung up. Ruby reached out for Carnel's hand and squeezed it. No one had to tell them anything. They knew that only death could make a person act the way their mother was acting now. Realizing that their mother needed them more than ever, Carnel and Ruby bit back their tears. Together, they led Nettie into her room. Carnel held her as Ruby removed the damp and dirty house dress and replaced it with a clean, fresh nightgown. Then, the girls helped her into bed and took turns bathing her face with cool water, telling her over and over how much they loved her, how everything was going to be alright. They needed more than anything to believe that what they said was true, and they didn't want Nettie to see how desolate and frightened they really were. When Nettie finally fell into a deep and exhausted sleep, Ruby and Carnel went to their own rooms in search of whatever rest the two of them could find. Carnel held Ruby's hand for a long time until her sister finally cried herself to sleep exhausted by grief as her mother had been.

Finally, alone in the darkness, Carnel felt her own tears begin to well up, fierce and hot, behind her eyes, and she felt her heart begin to break. She didn't know how she would ever be able to stand it, now that her Daddy was gone. He was the one who held them all together. He was the one who always knew just the right words to say to heal a hurt. And she was hurting now, worse than she had ever hurt before, and she didn't see how that could be healed, ever.

Carnel guessed she must have cried herself to sleep, too. She awoke suddenly a little before dawn to the sound of her mother's house shoes whispering as they approached her bed. Nettie placed a hand softly on her daughter's shoulder.

"Carnel," she said. "This is for you. I was wrong, Baby. I was so completely wrong."

It was too dark to see what her mother was talking about, but she could feel the intricate figures her father had carved on the tiny turtle's back and the broken lines now filled with the glue her mother had used to put it back together. Carnel felt overwhelmed with love. She put her arms around her mother's waist and hugged her hard. They stayed like that for awhile, feeling the love that they had for each other settle around them like a blanket.

After Nettie returned to her room, Carnel listened as the red dust filtered through the screens of her open bedroom windows. Hearing the soft, shushing sound that the dust made, Carnel knew that by morning a fine, red film would cover everything. She inhaled long and deeply, took the red dust in, allowed it to fill her up. She tasted it on her tongue, and ground it between her teeth when she finally slept again. And that night, she dreamed she was a river, red, and rushing towards a destination that she couldn't yet see.

Wisteria

Patricia Riley

It was half past seven in the morning and Eddie T. was already up and stirring an enormous black pot full of the bright yellow squash she planned to can that day. She hummed absentmindedly as she wiped the perspiration from her ancient face with the edge of her rose-embroidered apron. Though the hour was early, the kitchen already had the feel of mid-afternoon due to the hickory fire that blazed inside the antique wood stove where Eddie T. continued to do all of her cooking. In the storage shed behind the garden, a modern "radar range" languished new and never lifted from its crate. It had been a gift from her daughter-in-law, Jessie, but Eddie T. mistrusted the new stove's shiny chrome and doubted its ability to brown the crust just right on a fresh loaf of bread. She felt this way, at least in part, because Jessie had chosen the appliance. Everyone within smelling distance of Jessie's farm knew that she burned most everything she turned her hand to. Eddie T. never ceased to be amazed at how far the charred smell of burned beef and biscuits could travel on an evening breeze. It only made sense that such a person could not be relied upon to make an intelligent decision about something that was meant for cooking.

Justine crept up to the back door, pressed her face softly against the screen, and quietly watched her grandmother's preparations. Eddie T. moved back and forth along the kitchen counters with thoughtful precision. Carefully, she poured boiling water from a copper kettle into the tall round jars that sat like sentinels in dishpans of battered enamel. Justine knew she had to wait until Eddie T. was completely engrossed in her work or she wouldn't have a chance of making it past her undetected. If luck was truly with her, which it never had been before, she would be able to sneak inside quietly, make her way to the table unobserved, and be there, sitting smugly, when her grandmother turned around from the sink. It was a kind of cat-and-mouse game the two of them played whenever Justine came to visit, which was almost every day, except for Sunday. These days, Jessie kept her daughter to herself and away from Eddie T. on the Lord's day.

Justine blamed the enforced Sunday boycott on the TV preachers her mother had listened to during a two-week bout with the flu. Before that, her mother had been a fan of three, sometimes four, soap operas that she somehow managed to work into her hectic daily routine. Being ill, however, changed all that. Confined to bed, her mother had little else to do but watch whatever came on the TV. She had started out by intending to increase her soap opera consumption, but then something happened. Something that her mother reverently referred to now as "the mighty hand of God." On day three of the flu, three for the Trinity, her mother swore, an unprecedented thunderstorm of the most severe electrical variety had hit Harrison County and knocked out the local programming. When the ozone finally cleared, the only station that remained operational was a religious network broadcasting from out of Tennessee. It had to be a miracle.

Justine's father, Tom, told her that he figured the combination of the flu and the thunderstorm must have put Jessie in immediate touch with her own mortality because by day seven of vomiting and the green apple trots, Jessie had suddenly acquired what could only be described as a religious personality and rapidly converted to three-times-a-day Bible study and absolute churchgoing on a strict Sunday basis. This practice, as designed, was no doubt intended to be spiritually beneficial. However, in Jessie's case it provoked an intolerant streak a mile wide and five-hundred years deep. After six steady weeks of study groups and Sunday sermons, the hellfire-and-brimstone kind, her face took on a fevered expression and her eyes began to gleam with unnatural light. At the drop of a hat, she would launch into long and impassioned sermons to whoever was within hearing distance, willing or otherwise, on why Eddie T.'s was no fit place for a young girl on Sunday mornings. In fact, Justine knew that if her mother had been allowed to have things entirely her way, visits with her grandmother would be limited to Saturday afternoons, when the rest of the family dropped in to check on the old woman and have their traditional Saturday family suppers. Those visits, at least, could be controlled, taking place as they did under Jessie's newly righteous and ever watchful religious eyes. She eagerly oversaw every suspected nuance or contrary word in a conversation with the protective tenacity of a bulldog guarding the sanctuary door. Justine's father, Tom, sat on the other side of the fence. He continued to insist that no harm was being done and that as far as he was concerned, Justine should spend as much time as possible with her grandmother.

In his secret thoughts, Tom regretted ever having listened to the disparaging things his schoolteachers had said about his people and their ways. They had made him feel backward and ashamed of who he was and where he came from. Most of all, he wanted Justine to grow up proud of herself and her people. He knew his mother had a lot to offer on that score and he thought he ought to give a listen to the things she said more often himself.

Jessie naturally took a dim view of her husband's attitude. She rebuked him regularly, called him "stiff-necked," compared him to some Philistine people, and prayed to God not to smite him. In her eyes, his failure to capitulate put all their souls in jeopardy. The entire state of affairs left her flustered because even though Tom professed to be a Christian, nothing she could say, do, or quote from Scripture would convince him that his mother was a heathen.

Often, late at night, Justine lay in bed listening to the endless, usually one-sided, argument over whether or not Eddie T. was an endangerment to Justine's tender young soul.

"Why, Tom, Eddie T. don't even pray to God," Jessie cried. "I myself have come upon her a number of times standing in the woods, waving her hands about and calling on the sun and moon and stars. Even the river one time. God only knows who or what else she calls on. Anybody that does that is a heathen and a heathen's domain is no place for my daughter on Sunday mornings. Or any other morning for that matter. And I will say it. I don't care if she is your mother. I have a right to my opinion and a right to raise my child as I see fit. A heathen is a heathen and children need to be protected from that kind of thing."

"She prays to God, Jessie. She just does it in her own way is all."

Justine's father seldom answered his wife's diatribes directly, though he often shook his head over them. He hated most any kind of conflict, pure and simple, and avoided it as much as possible. Usually, he just listened until Jessie blew herself out and then went off on a walk somewhere while she simmered down. But even though he eventually compromised with her about the Sunday visits, purely for the sake of the temporary domestic peace, he remained firm about Justine's freedom to visit every other day of the week.

Eddie T. always looked forward to Justine's visits. She enjoyed the little games they played together. They kept her on her toes, and let her know that even though she was almost eighty-seven years old, she still had her wits about her. From the corner of her eye, she could see Justine's shadow now as it fell across the doorstep and into the room.

"Mornin', Liz." Eddie T. cackled and turned to face the small girl, who had tried so hard and unsuccessfully to make herself silent and unobserved. "Durned if you don't look like the spittin' image of Liz Taylor this mornin'."

"It's the haircut." Justine smiled at the old woman and opened the screen door. "Mama had it done. I liked it long, myself, but you know Mama. She says it tangles too much and, besides, long hair isn't stylish these days. She told Arleen at the Beauty Barn that she wanted something particularly stylish and this turned out to be it."

"Well, it looks okay, so don't get yourself worked up. Anyway, we got more important fish to fry. I found somethin' special out back of the yard this mornin'." Eddie T. looked sideways at her granddaughter and motioned for Justine to follow her back outside. "I can show you, but you got to promise not to mention it to your mam. You know how she feels about some kinds of things. It'll have to be our secret."

"Okay, Gramma," Justine said and smiled. It seemed as if they shared a lot of secrets these days since her mama had gone over to the TV preachers.

The old woman crossed the overgrown expanse that she called "the yard" and stopped beside a huge, out-of-control wisteria bush, heavy with pungent lavender blossoms.

"Mmmm, last blooms of the season. Smell that perfume. Sure smells good, don't it?" Eddie T. smiled at Justine, revealing toothless gums, which she quickly tried to hide.

"You came so early I didn't get a chance to put my choppers in," she said.

Justine took a deep breath of the flowered air and held it in as long as she could, reluctant to let go of the heavy, sweet smell.

"Gramma," she said, "you know I don't care if you got your teeth in or not."

"Yeah. You might not, but I do. I used to be pretty once."

"Still are." Justine tugged at the old woman's skirt. "Prettiest old lady in three counties, I bet."

Eddie T. chortled behind her hand. "We won't ever know the truth of that one, Miss Priss, since they ain't no beauty pageants for old toothless ladies in these parts."

"We'll start one of our own. It'll be a first."

"Um-hmm, I can see a king-size pitcher of that already."

The old woman took Justine's small hand in her own and led the way through the thick tangle of undergrowth behind the yard and on into the bordering woods. The tall oak trees provided shade and home to a wide variety of creatures and served as a kind of an outdoor pharmacy for the old woman. Eddie T. had taken the girl there many times and taught her where to look for roots and plants that were good for healing any number of common complaints from sore throat to fever.

"Somebody sick?" Justine asked. She knew that her grandmother was often asked by some of her neighbors to gather and prepare plant remedies. Most of the people Eddie T. knew couldn't afford the price of a town doctor.

"No, not this time. I told you this was somethin' special. Somethin' you almost never see."

"Did that old mama squirrel finally have some squirrel babies, is that it?"

Justine's eyes jumped with excitement at the thought. That was something she could tell the kids about at school, and her own mama, too. Then again, Justine thought she probably ought to keep that one to herself as well. Her mother could go on for hours about how squirrels carried rabies and wasn't it just like Eddie T. to expose her daughter to the perils of familiarity with savage disease-carrying rodents.

"Look over there where that blackberry bush is twinin' around that stump and you'll see what I'm talkin' about."

Justine scrunched her eyes and studied the area, but all she could see was an old broken-off oak tree and blackberry vines trying to turn brown from the summer's heat and not enough rain.

"I don't see anything so special about a tree stump and some dying berry vines, Gramma." Justine kicked at the ground in disappointment. "What am I supposed to see?"

"Look beside the stump, Justine, not at it. See that circle of grass all mashed down?" Eddie T. pointed at a spot about two feet in diameter that appeared to have been deliberately trampled down.

"Uh-huh," Justine said, still not seeing anything special about a spot of mashed grass.

"There's little people* out back here, Justine, and sometimes they get together and hold a dance. They must have had one of them dances right there just last night."

"Little people? Really? Mama says there ain't no such thing as little people, Gramma."

"Well, I'm not gonna say that your mam is wrong, Justine, 'cuz that wouldn't be right. I guess for some people, and your mam's probably one of 'em, there ain't any. That's 'cuz they let them die inside their minds a long time ago, I expect. But there's always been little people livin' in these old woods since time immemorial. That's what the old folks told me when I was a girl and I know it's true. Sometimes late at night I could hear them singin' songs. They must have been dancin' back then, too. I used to get up out of bed and go to the cabin door and see way off in the woods little lights flickerin' through the leaves. Those old-time Cherokees always said they was there. They called them the *Yunwi Tsundi*."

"If you been knowing this such a long time, Gramma, how come you never told me before today?"

"Well, mostly because I always get in trouble with your mam, or get you in trouble with her, but also because I wanted to wait until the time was right to tell you."

"How come now is the right time to tell me, Gramma?"

"Well, I'm not as young as I used to be, Justine. I'm an old lady. I have had a responsibility to these little people for a long time now. I remember them, you see. It's our obligation to do that."

"How do you remember them, Gramma? What does that mean?"

"Oh, I leave things for 'em. Little snacks of food mostly, sometimes tobacco and beads when I got 'em, and wisteria flowers when they're bloomin'. They like them blossoms. My mam called them things offerings. Just to let them know that we ain't forgot about 'em. That we know they're out there livin' on. But like I said, Justine, I'm gettin' to be an old lady now and I know I won't be on this old earth much longer."

"I wish you wouldn't say things like that, Gramma. You make me sad."

"Shush. Ain't nothin' to be sad about, Child. Things got to grow old and die when their time comes, just like them wisteria. And dyin' ain't all that much anyway. It's all a part of the cycle. What's old just naturally got to make room for them that's new. It's the way things is. If it weren't there'd be too many things walkin' around chokin' up the earth. Us what's old just got to move on and make a place for you to stand in this world. All things gotta die, Child, that's just the way of it. It ain't as bad

---

* The Cherokee "Little People" (or *Yunwi Tsundi*) are very small (about knee-high) spiritual beings, similar to European fairies, but with long hair reaching to the ground. They live in caves or woods and spend a great deal of time making music (drumming) and dancing. They are usually good-hearted and helpful. They are invisible to humans unless they choose to be seen.

as all that, because nothin's ever really gone even when it dies. It's kind of like a snake sheddin' its skin: you just wiggle on out of the old dried-up part and leave it behind. You wipe them eyes. We'll go on back to the house now. We got Saturday supper to think about, but you got to promise me to remember them little people when I'm gone, Justine. And bring 'em some of that wisteria once in a while. They like that."

Justine grabbed the old woman's hand and held it as if she never wanted to let go. "I promise, Gramma," she said, "I promise."

Late that night, the weather turned and a wind blew up out of the north that keened around the doors and rattled the windows of Eddie T.'s house. It thundered so hard and long that jelly jars tumbled off the cellar shelves and broke on the old stone floor.

Safe at home, Justine stretched and snuggled, warm beneath the quilts her grandmother had given her. She watched the long oak branches skitter and scrape against her bedroom window and thought about how they sounded like nightbirds calling to each other across the darkness. The last thing Justine remembered before she fell asleep was the wind whispering secrets to her in a language she couldn't understand and a streak of light that blazed and sped across the southern sky.

The next day, Eddie T.'s kitchen stood quiet and empty. The usual open door remained closed and locked. And for the first time there was no smell of fresh-made coffee hanging in the morning air. The ashes in the ancient black stove stood gray and cold. In the tiny room next to the kitchen, the old woman never stirred. And way out back of the house, near the woods, something small sobbed as it moved slowly and heavily among the suddenly silent trees.

Joy Harjo
(1951–)

"Stories create us. We create ourselves with stories. Stories that our parents tell us, that our grandparents tell us, or that our great-grandparents told us, stories that reverberate through the web."

Joy Harjo, "A Laughter of Absolute Sanity," interview with Angels Carabi in *The Spiral of Memory*

The Reckoning

Joy Harjo

Everyone has their own version of the world I tell myself as I wait on the Central Avenue sidewalk while Larry disappears behind the Starlight Motel to take a piss. The vacancy sign flashes on and off. Closing hour traffic jams the street. I imagine everyone taking off for the forty-nine,* squeezed into cars and pickups with cases of beer under their legs heading in a caravan to the all-night sing on West Mesa. Each direction is a world and each world has its own set of rules, its own hierarchy of gods and demigods, its own particular color. I am painting a series based on the four directions, but I am stalled. It has been months since I've painted.

When I was five my mother began standing me on a chair to wash dishes after dinner because I couldn't otherwise reach. The front of my dress was usually soaked when I finished. "Don't get your dress wet like that; it means you'll marry a drunk." Yet night after night after dinner she would drag a chair to the sink and my dress would soak no matter my efforts otherwise. Every morning I wake up with a hangover after trying to keep up with Larry I remember the wet stomach of my dress. I then promise I will let him go. I know I cannot save him, but to let him go feels unbearable.

This morning Larry mentioned that his cousin was coming into town from California and wanted to have dinner before heading out to the pueblo. Would I like to go to Alonzo's for pizza with them? A wedge of tension cut the air between us. I tried to ignore it. Last night he said he was going to quit drinking again and Alonzo's is one of his favorite bars. I watched as he fried the bacon and stirred the eggs, as he placed them in a perfect arrangement on our plates. He cooked as deftly as he honed out an argument or turned a piece of silver into the wind. I poured Joe Junior a glass of milk and wrapped a sandwich for his lunch. He fidgeted, running his Hot Wheels cars up and down his chair, across the table, faster and faster in response to the tension. "Stop it!" I yelled, surprised at the vehemence in my voice. He put his head down on the table and began slowly kicking the table leg. I told myself then that I could use a break.

* A forty-nine is a Native social dance.

That night after cleaning the house and walking guiltily by my easel I took Joe Junior to the babysitter. He liked going to Larry's sister's house because she had twin boys his age so I didn't mind leaving him for the night. When I handed him over with his pack of clothes, toys and snacks I hugged him close, savoring his freshly shampooed hair. I felt bad for yelling at him this morning. He saw the twins peeking around the corner and wriggled free. Larry's sister was roasting chile and had just pulled out of the oven a fresh batch of those little fruit pies her people make. She offered me some.

"And take some for Larry, too," she said. When she said her brother's name worry flickered across her forehead. I was worried too, but to entertain all the reasons would cause an avalanche. I would prefer to stay here with Joe Junior in Larry's sister's warm house, to wash dishes and set the table and visit, but the zigzag of anxiety went way back, over tortuous territory. If I followed the source it would slam me back into childhood, to my father staggering in drunk, beating my mother, the shame and hate in him burning, burning. Then he'd hit my brothers. And then me whom it was said he loved most. He'd save me for last, when his anger was ashes, when the fire was hottest. And then he'd hold me, "Sugar, Sugar" he'd croon, the tears so thick they made a lake on the linoleum floor.

There is a world of mist in which my father now lives. It is beyond the Milky Way, but it is also as close as my voice to your ear. I have often seen my father in the middle of the night when I am painting. Or when I have tucked his grandson in after he has fallen asleep. He is just the other side of the spin, the same frequency as moonlight. He's held here by disappointment, by the need to speak. He tells me he loves me and asks if I will forgive him. I do not say anything. "You're a dreamer," my mother says when I tell her, "just like your father. And you won't ever get it together until you decide to deal with the real world." She is an elected tribal official and she teaches Sunday school every week. She has a mission in her small world. She wants to make sure there are rules and that they are enforced.

The first time Larry hit me was on a Saturday night like this one. We hadn't been together long. We were still amazed we had found each other. We were partying away not at Alonzo's, but at the Feathered Dancer on the other side of town. He was talking politics with his buddies while I played pool with my best friend Jolene and some other students in the backroom. I kept feeding the jukebox with quarters, playing the Rolling Stones, "wild horses couldn't drag me away" over and over again. He was down about the anniversary of the death of his best friend a few years ago. That should have been a warning to me. This man had been his idol. He had been the only man from his pueblo to finish law school and he fought the U.S. legal system by any means possible, including his fists. But he couldn't fight alcohol. He was taken down by drink, his body found in a field weeks after his death. His grieving brothers were honoring him by drinking to oblivion and they were getting rowdy. I tried to ignore them and kept shooting the solids into the pockets, just as I had ignored my father when he and his friends partied, argued and played. I knew the routine. There was a high and then there was a low.

Every small hair on my neck was on alert. "Fuck you," I heard Larry yell. We ran in from the pool tables to see what was the matter. Larry aimed a pitcher of beer at his cousin Leno's head. It missed and smashed into the bar mirror. There was a terrible crash. We all scattered as the bartender called the police. Larry refused to go; instead, he decided to climb the fence to the roof of the bar. Leno and I tried to stop him. He punched me and I went down. He climbed to the roof and jumped, then stood up like a defiant child, without a scratch, and walked away, the sound of approaching sirens growing loud and shrill.

I should have left him then, instead I caught a ride back with Jolene who tried to convince me to stay at her place. "No, I want to get the sad good-bye over with," I told her. The next morning he apologized profusely. This will never happen again, he promised as he made us breakfast of his specialty: chorizo and eggs. He came back from the 7-Eleven with a newspaper and a bouquet of wilted flowers. I told him to pack his bags, to get out.

"No," he said. "How can we make a better world for the people if we cannot hold it together in our own house?"

I convinced myself that we owed it to ourselves to keep trying. I found excuses. He was taken over by grief for his buddy, I told myself. And most of the time he wasn't like that, I reasoned. I took him back.

The next few weeks were tender and raw. Carefully he planted a garden in the small yard behind the apartment with my son. He worked obsessively. He held fire in his hands and he crafted a bracelet to bridge the hole in our universe. I believed he didn't mean to lose control. I believed that he loved me.

"So did your father," Jolene reminded me. "You've gone and married your father."

"I haven't married him yet. I will never get married again," I laughed.

I didn't want to hear her and after that I talked to Jolene only when I had to, at rallies, at Indian center meetings. She was a distant reminder of prickly truth, a predictor of trouble. I watched her disappear on the horizon as I turned to tend to my shaky world. When he asked me to marry him, I said yes.

We were nervous the day we headed up to Santa Fe in a borrowed car to get married. I had never planned to marry anyone and this would be my second. The first had been to Joe Junior's father. Larry had gotten grief from his parents for shacking up with a girl who wasn't from his tribe. Marriage would make me one step closer to acceptable.

It was a perfect spring day as we headed north. Joe Junior stayed at Larry's sister's place and was excited about getting to help make the wedding cake. A small reception was planned for the next day. We'd just passed the city limits when the Ranchero Bar came into view, poised on the reservation line. All the windows were painted and broken glass mixed with gravel in the parking lot. Larry pulled the car over and parked. "Let's go in, just for a beer," he said. "To celebrate." It had been a few months since he had stopped drinking, after the punching incident. He already had enough jewelry for a show and had attracted a dealer who talked New York and Europe markets. We had been happy.

"No. You can't drink."

"One drink will not hurt me, or you either," he said as he opened his door. "We have a lot to celebrate."

"Okay, you promised," I reminded him.

"I promise," he said.

One beer turned into a pitcher because these were his brothers, he announced eloquently to the bar. The pueblo farm workers sitting around him smiled at me and nodded their heads. "It's time to go," I urged him under my breath, all the while smiling at his new friends.

"I can't turn down a drink because I would offend them," he whispered to me, looking at me sharply because I should know better. Obviously he wasn't afraid of offending me.

I sipped my beer and felt my heart sag in disbelief. This was my wedding day. If I had another drink I wouldn't hear the voice telling me to get out, to get out now. I poured myself another beer from the pitcher, matching Larry drink for drink to the delight of Larry's new friends. The day stumbled into oblivion. I have a faint memory of dancing a ranchera in front of the jukebox with a cowboy, and of a hippie girl coming into the bar and sitting on Larry's lap. "It's part of my job," he told me once after I had yanked a blonde girl off him and demanded he come home with me. He had pocketed the girl's phone number as he slid off the stool and followed me. He had a reason for everything.

We didn't make it to Santa Fe to get married. I tore up the marriage license and tossed it like confetti over him and his drinking partners, confirming that I wasn't the kind of girl his pueblo parents wanted for his wife. His mother would never embarrass his father in that manner no matter what he did to her. I left him with the borrowed car and hitchhiked back. I called Larry's sister and told her the wedding was off and I'd pick up Joe Junior tomorrow when I could pull myself together. I could not think; I could not paint. I looked up the Women's Center in the student directory. What would I say to them? Do you have a crisis center for idiots? I missed Jolene and my friends, but I had too much pride to call them now. I dialed my mother's number and hung up. She would just say, "I told you so."

It is now two thirty in the morning and the avenue is quiet. Larry should have been back by now. The small desk light in the motel office makes me feel lonely. I feel far away from everything. There's that ache under my ribs that's like radar. It tells me that I am miles away from the world I intended to make for my son and me. I imagine my easel set up in the corner of the living room in our apartment, next to Joe Junior's box of toys. I imagine my little boy asleep in my arms. I imagine having the money to walk up to the motel office to rent a room of my own. I know what I would do.

First I would sleep until I could sleep no more. Then I would dream. I fly to the first world of my mother and father, locate them as a young married couple just after the war, living with my father's mother, in her small house in Sapulpa. I am a baby in my mother's arms, cooing and kicking my legs. Then I am a girl on my father's shoulders as he spins and dances me through the house drunk on beer stolen from the bootlegger. I hold on tight. I hear my mother tell him to be careful, let me down. We are all laughing. He spins until I am in high school and I have won the art award. Then I am a teenage mother. "A new little Sugar," he says as he holds his grandson and sings to him. Then I am standing with my mother at my grandmother's funeral, singing those sad Creek hymns that lead her spirit to the Milky Way. My father can't be found in time for the funeral. Then he's next. The centrifugal force of memory keeps moving through the sky, slowly sifting lies from the shining truth.

My mother told me that if you go to sleep laughing you will wake up to tears. My father's mother told me that to predict the shape of the end of something take a hard look at the beginning.

"I'm not interested in marriage or finding yet another man to break my heart," I remember telling my friend Jolene as we stood in the heat in front of the student union the day I met Larry. The tech people were making racket while they set up the microphones and tables for the press conference. I had just gotten over Joe Junior's father. He left me before the baby was born, even took the junk car, drove off dragging it behind his cousin's truck to his mother's house in Talihina.

"Well, there are always women," she said nodding toward a table that had been set up by the Women's Resource Center. They were passing out information on their services. I walked by the Women's Center every day on my way to work at the Indian Center after classes. Once I stopped to visit on my way to an organizational meeting. I had heard a speaker from their center address students on the mall about women's rights and it occurred to me that our centers could link up in an action. But the day I walked in with my son in hand I got the distinct feeling that Indian women with children weren't too welcome. I had never gone back.

"Women would certainly open up our options," I agreed with Jolene and we laughed. We thought it was funny, but we agreed that as women we spent most of our time with each other, took classes together and cried on each others' shoulders in the shifting dance of creation and destruction.

It was a fine-looking contingent from the National Council on Indian Rights who made their way to the makeshift stage. They were modern-age warriors dressed with the intent of justice in their sunglasses and long black hair. "There is my future," I said lightly and nodded to the Pueblo man whose hair was pulled back in a sleek ponytail. I watched as he balanced his coffee and unclasped his shoulder bag of papers. He felt familiar at the level of blood cells and bones though I didn't know him. I had heard him holding forth before at meetings and had seen him in passing on campus.

"Who is he?" Jolene knew everyone because her father was a name in local Indian politics.

"His name is Larry. He's an artist," she said, "a fine artist. He makes jewelry. Be careful. Women love him and are always chasing him." I could see why and I could not stop watching him as he read the press release demanding justice and detailing how it could occur. He was as beautifully drawn as he was smart.

As we stood in the hot sun listening to the prepared statements I was suddenly aware of the fragility of life, how immensely precious was each breath. We all mattered—even our small core fighting for justice despite all odds. And then the press conference was over. That day would become one of those memories that surfaced at major transitional points like giving birth and dying. I would feel the sun on my shoulders, hear the scratch of the cheap sound system and feel emotional. I would recall a small Navajo girl in diapers learning how to walk, her arms outstretched to her father. I would remember picking up my son at the daycare across campus, his bright yellow lunchbox shaped like a school bus.

That night at the impromptu party after the strategy meeting I watched from the doorway of the kitchen of Jolene's cousin's apartment as Larry easily rolled a cigarette with his hands. His hands were warm sienna and snapped with the energy of his quick mind, his ability to shape metal. He lit a cigarette and blew smoke with his perfect lips in my direction. The lazy lasso hung in the air between us. I passed him a beer as I was the end of a brigade passing out beer from the cooler in the kitchen.

"So who are you, Skinny Girl?" I kept passing and throwing beer to the rest of the party as he talked, pretending to ignore him.

"You must be one of those Oklahoma Indians," he said. I had been warned that he was used to getting what he wanted when it came to women.

"Come on over here and sit next to me, next to an Indian who is still the real thing." I considered hitting him with a beer for that remark. These local Indians could be short-sighted in their world.

"Why would I want to?" I retorted. "Besides, you look Mexican to me." His eyebrows flew up. His identity had never been challenged, especially by a woman he was interested in.

"We're full-bloods. We haven't lost our ways."

"And what does that mean? That my people have?" I questioned. "Then why do you have a Spanish last name?" Of course I knew the history but he had pissed me off, still I couldn't help but notice his long eyelashes that cast shadows on his cheeks. I caught the last beer and opened it, stood close enough for his smell to alert my heart.

"All tribes traveled, took captives and were taken captive." I emphasized "captive" and leaned in to take a puff on the cigarette he offered me. Jolene waltzed over and grabbed my arm, dancing me to the living room in time to the music in order to save me. I didn't talk to him again until I headed out the door with my ride, two other first-year students. We were buzzed on smoke and flying sweetly.

"Hey girl," he shouted from the corner as I reluctantly made my escape. "I'm going to get you yet."

It happened quickly. When I got home that night there was a message that my father had died. Joe Junior and I left for a week. When we returned Larry met us at the bus station with flowers and toys. He took us for breakfast at the Chuckwagon and then we went home together. It wasn't long after my father's death that I dreamed a daughter who wanted to be born. I had been painting all night when she appeared to me. She was a baby with fat cheeks and then she was a grown woman, with a presence as familiar as my father's mother. She asked me to give birth to her.

I was in the middle of finals and planning for a protest of the killing of Nava
drunks by white high school students on weekends for fun. They had just
questioned and set free with no punishment.

"This is not a good time," I said. "And why come into this kind of world?"
Funny, I don't remember her answer but her intent was a fine unwavering line that
connected my heart to hers.

I walk behind the motel to look for Larry. He isn't anywhere, but I find his shoes
under a tree where he has taken them off. And ahead of them, like two dark salaman-
ders, are his socks. A little farther beyond is his belt, and then a trail of pants, shirt and
underwear until I am standing in the courtyard of the motel. My stomach turns and
twists as I consider all the scenarios a naked and drunk Indian man might get into in
a motel on the main street of the city.

I hear a splash in the pool. He's a Pueblo; he can't swim. I consider leaving him
there to his fate. It would be his own foolish fault, as well as the fault of a society
that builds its cities over our holy places. At this moment his disappearance would
be a sudden relief. Strange that it is now that I first feel our daughter moving within
me. She awakens me with a flutter, a kick. I don't know whether to laugh or cry.
I never told Larry about the night she showed up to announce her intention, or how
I saw her spirit when she was conceived wavering above us on a fine sheen of light.
Behind her my father was waving good-bye. The weave pulled tighter and tighter, it
opened and then he was gone.

the snake

Joy Harjo

The backyard patio had become the oasis for the neighborhood birds. The crows, starlings, sparrows, and pigeons met there early every morning for gossip, their morning baths, and their first meal of the day, attracted by the dog's food and water supplies. As with all creatures, some left refreshed and got on immediately with the business of the day, while others couldn't get enough dog chow or gossip as they lazed around all afternoon, hopping around the patient and lonely dog who didn't seem to mind the noisy gathering or sharing his food and water.

One day the very busy humans who lived there thought things had gone too far. The dog's fresh water had become the bathing system for hundreds of birds, and though the birds ate relatively little they scattered dog food all over the patio and made a terrible clutter. The humans were tired of cleaning up bird mess and the clatter of gossip broke their sleep and set their teeth on edge. So they had a meeting to figure out what to do.

Snakes were one of the most feared enemies of the birds and they were few and far between in this city. Cats were the most common enemy, one they battled daily, but no cat would venture into the dog's territory. He was a huge dog and his greatest weakness was chasing cats. He would break off a leash, leap over the wall at the sight of a cat. It was a compulsion with him, though he never got close enough to catch one. He convinced himself it was the chase that really mattered. It was deeply satisfying like nothing else. So as the birds talked, lazed, and bathed he dreamed about chasing cats.

    The humans decided to buy a huge rubber snake to frighten the birds. They weren't sure it would work but they were willing to try anything. That night they curled the snake into an alert circle next to the food and water supplies. The next morning they awoke to the alarmed cries of the birds, who were disturbed at the presence of this predator next to their favorite hangout. The birds cried "snake" in their various languages and gathered in the largest tree high above the house, above the patio, dog, and humans and now the invader snake, which had ruined their prized meeting place. They discussed the situation for several hours, sent scouts down to see if they could find out anything about the kind of snake it was, where it came from, its intentions, and its plans for leaving. The snake was silent, stealthy and so controlled it could appear dead. These were the most dangerous.

Now the birds would have to go back to their old routine in which they raided dog and cat dishes in scavenger groups of two and three birds all over the neighborhood. It was a tricky business to run the gauntlet of cats, and humans, particularly the young human males. In this house they were protected by the dog, who had actually learned their names and inquired after their families. And the humans had been tolerant in the beginning.

The dog didn't fear snakes; he didn't see any reason for alarm. The snake didn't bother him, nor was he too friendly. He came to miss his bird friends, who, though they were often a nuisance, even standing on his back and wakening him while he was in the midst of a particularly delicious dream chase, were his friends. The humans were glad that the snake trick had worked but had to admit they missed some of the storytelling of the birds, particularly that of the crows, whose language was closer to human languages.

For a long time the birds stayed away, though sometimes they would fly by the patio, nostalgic for the good times, the stories that seemed to naturally arise after a good meal, a good bath.

The oldest crow, who happened to be the wisest (and this isn't always the case), had this gut feeling that something was strange about this snake who suddenly appeared on the patio. He was like the others who when they saw the snake were guided by the primordial knot in the brain that said "run." There was no thinking involved, instinct took over the muscles, brain, and heart.

He, too, like the others would reminisce about the good times. That was the place he had met his favorite wife, a beautiful shiny one who had a gift for finding prized bits of food. She always gave him the best pieces and they had great times together the few years they had and loved watching the sunrise together. She was killed by a cat who stalked her while she scavenged the trash cans in the alley. He never paired with anyone else after that, preferred to contemplate the deeper meaning of life and picked the scab of his sorrow as he lived at the edge of his crow community.

He knew this wasn't all there was, this struggle for food, territory, and survival in a city that kept churning up more trash. Dreams came to him and gave insight into the history of crows and possibilities for their evolving place in this world. The respect for his knowledge grew in the birds' world, even as he contemplated the appearance of the snake, an event that destroyed a happy rhythm in their lives.

No one thought to further question the identity of the snake, to understand why the snake did not move and kept silent vigil at the water and food oasis. The old crow decided to solve the mystery. He knew he would die soon and he was too wise to fear death. If it be by snake, so be it.

Without the knowledge of the others the crow began to keep vigil and stood on a chair in the patio watching this snake. The humans saw him, perceived him thinking, measuring and weighing the curled snake. Even they were impressed by the wisdom in his eyes, the careful way he observed and pondered the monster that had changed his world.

He walked around the snake, then touched the dreaded enemy and stepped back, blinking his eyes as he waited for the strike. He touched the cold snake again. Nothing! He then kicked at the snake. Again, nothing! This snake was not alive, never had been; they'd been fooled by the humans. Before traveling to call a meeting to tell the others he stopped for a bite to eat, a bath, and a visit with the dog, who greeted him warmly.

The bird meeting went long into the night and ended with a bitter disagreement and a separation between those who thought the crow was lying, because they had seen the snake themselves and they were going to believe what they saw, and those who believed the wisdom of the crow and prepared to return to their beloved meeting place. Those who thought the crow was lying wished to protect their friends they thought were foolish for wishing to believe what they considered a lie. When they could not garner agreement they turned and walked away and were never seen again by those who believed.

The next morning a few birds were gathered at the meeting place though they were raw with the hurt of the separation. They bathed, ate of the plentiful dog food nuggets, and recounted the history of the place and discussed what they had learned.

The humans saw that the crow had discovered the secret of the snake and took it back into the house. They often looked for the wise crow and would catch a glimpse of him once in a while; then there came a time they never saw him again.

And it was never quite the same in that neighborhood for the crows, pigeons, starlings, and sparrows, or the humans and the dog, who missed his old crow friend. But there were new creatures born: human, dog, and bird, and they were always told the story of the birds and the snake.

The Woman Who Fell from the Sky

Joy Harjo

Once a woman fell from the sky. The woman who fell from the sky was neither a murderer nor a saint. She was rather ordinary, though beautiful in her walk, like one who has experienced freedom from earth's gravity. When I see her I think of an antelope grazing the alpine meadows in mountains whose names are as ancient as the sound that created the first world.

Saint Coincidence thought he recognized her as she began falling toward him from the sky in a slow spin, like the spiral of events marking an ascension of grace. There was something in the curve of her shoulder, a familiar slope that led him into the lightest moment of his life.

He could not bear it and turned to ask a woman in high heels for a quarter. She was of the family of myths who would give everything if asked. She looked like all the wives he'd lost. And he had nothing to lose anymore in this city of terrible paradox where a woman was falling toward him from the sky.

The strange beauty in heels disappeared from the path of Saint Coincidence, with all her money held tightly in her purse, into the glass of advertisements. Saint Coincidence shuffled back onto the ice to watch the woman falling and falling.

Saint Coincidence, who was not a saint, perhaps a murderer if you count the people he shot without knowing during the stint that took his mind in Vietnam or Cambodia—remembered the girl he yearned to love when they were kids at Indian boarding school.

He could still see her on the dusty playground, off in the distance, years to the west past the icy parking lot of the Safeway. She was a blurred vision of the bittersweet and this memory had forced him to live through the violence of fire.

There they stood witness together to strange acts of cruelty by strangers, as well as the surprise of rare kindnesses.

The woman who was to fall from the sky was the girl with skinned knees whose spirit knew how to climb to the stars. Once she told him the stars spoke a language akin to the plains of her home, a language like rocks.

He watched her once make the ascent, after a severe beating. No one could touch the soul masked by name, age and tribal affiliation. Myth was as real as a scalp being scraped for lice.

Lila also dreamed of a love not disturbed by the wreck of culture she was forced to attend. It sprang up here and there like miraculous flowers in the cracks of the collision. It was there she found Johnny, who didn't have a saint's name when he showed up for school. He understood the journey and didn't make fun of her for her peculiar ways, despite the risks.

Johnny was named Johnny by the priests because his Indian name was foreign to their European tongues. He named himself Saint Coincidence many years later after he lost himself in drink in a city he'd been sent to to learn a trade. Maybe you needed English to know how to pray in the city. He could speak a fractured English. His own language had become a baby language to him, made of the comforting voice of his grandmother as she taught him to be a human.

Johnny had been praying for years and had finally given up on a god who appeared to give up on him. Then one night as he tossed pennies on the sidewalk with his cousin and another lost traveler, he prayed to Coincidence and won. The event demanded a new name. He gave himself the name Saint Coincidence.

His ragged life gleamed with possibility until a ghost-priest brushed by him as he walked the sidewalk looking for a job to add to his stack of new luck. The priest appeared to look through to the boy in him. He despaired. He would always be a boy on his knees, the burden of shame rooting him.

Saint Coincidence went back to wandering without a home in the maze of asphalt. Asphalt could be a pathway toward God, he reasoned, though he'd always imagined the road he took with his brothers when they raised sheep as children. Asphalt had led him here to the Safeway where a woman was falling from the sky.

The memory of all time relative to Lila and Johnny was seen by an abandoned cat washing herself next to the aluminum-can bin of the grocery story.

These humans set off strange phenomena, she thought and made no attachment to the thought. It was what it was, this event, shimmering there between the frozen parking lot of the store and the sky, something unusual and yet quite ordinary.

Like the sun falling fast in the west, this event carried particles of light through the trees.

Some say God is a murderer for letting children and saints slip through his or her hands. Some call God a father of saints or a mother of demons. Lila had seen God and could tell you God was neither male nor female and made of absolutely every-thing of beauty, of wordlessness.

This unnameable thing of beauty is what shapes a flock of birds who know exactly when to turn together in flight in the winds used to make words. Everyone turns together though we may not see each other stacked in the invisible dimensions.

This is what Lila saw, she told Johnny once. The sisters called it blasphemy.

Johnny ran away from boarding school the first winter with his two brothers, who'd run away before. His brothers wrapped Johnny Boy, as they called him, with their bodies to keep him warm. They froze and became part of the stars.

Johnny didn't make it home either. The school officials took him back the next day. To mourn his brothers would be to admit an unspeakable pain, so he became an athlete who ran faster than any record ever made in the history of the school, faster than the tears.

Lila never forgot about Johnny, who left school to join the army, and a few years later as she walked home from her job at Dairy Queen she made a turn in the road.

Call it destiny or coincidence—but the urge to fly was as strong as the need to push when at the precipice of any birth. It was what led her into the story told before she'd grown ears to hear, as she turned from stone to fish to human in her mother's belly.

Once, the stars made their way down stairs of ice to the earth to find mates. Some of the women were angry at their inattentive husbands, bored, or frustrated with the cycle of living and dying. They ran off with the stars, as did a few who saw their chance for travel and enlightenment.

They weren't heard from for years, until one of the women returned. She dared to look back and fell. Fell through centuries, through the beauty of the night sky, made a hole in a rock near the place Lila's mother had been born. She took up where she had left off, with her children from the stars. She was remembered.

This story was Lila's refuge those nights she'd prayed on her knees with the other children in the school dorms. It was too painful to miss her mother.

A year after she'd graduated and worked cleaning house during the day, and evenings at the Dairy Queen, she laughed to think of herself wearing her uniform spotted with sweets and milk, as she left on the arms of one of the stars. Surely she could find love in a place that did not know the disturbance of death.

While Lila lived in the sky she gave birth to three children and they made her happy. Though she had lost conscious memory of the place before, a song climbed up her legs from far away, to the rooms of her heart.

Later she would tell Johnny it was the sound of destiny, which is similar to a prayer reaching out to claim her.

You can't ignore these things, she would tell him, and it led her to the place her husband had warned her was too sacred for women.

She carried the twins in her arms as her daughter grabbed her skirt in her small fists. She looked into the forbidden place and leaped.

She fell and was still falling when Saint Coincidence caught her in his arms in front of the Safeway as he made a turn from borrowing spare change from strangers.

The children crawled safely from their mother. The cat stalked a bit of flying trash set into motion by the wave of falling—

or the converse wave of gathering together.

The Flood

Joy Harjo

It had been years since I'd seen the watermonster, the snake who lived at the bottom of the lake. He had disappeared in the age of reason, as a mystery that never happened.

For in the muggy lake was the girl I could have been at sixteen, wrested from the torment of exaggerated fools, one version anyway, though the story at the surface would say car accident, or drowning while drinking, all of it eventually accidental.

This story is not an accident, nor is the existence of the watersnake in the memory of the people as they carried the burden of the myth from Alabama to Oklahoma. Each reluctant step pounded memory into the broken heart and no one will ever forget it.

When I walk the stairway of water into the abyss, I return as the wife of the water-monster, in a blanket of time decorated with swatches of cloth and feathers from our favorite clothes.

The stories of the battles of the watersnake are forever ongoing, and those stories soaked into my blood since infancy like deer gravy, so how could I resist the water-snake, who appeared as the most handsome man in the tribe, or any band whose visits I'd been witness to since childhood?

This had been going on for centuries: the first time he appeared I carried my baby sister on my back as I went to get water. She laughed at a woodpecker flitting like a small sun above us and before I could deter the symbol we were in it.

My body was already on fire with the explosion of womanhood as if I were flint, hot stone, and when he stepped out of the water he was the first myth I had ever seen uncovered. I had surprised him in a human moment. I looked aside but I could not discount what I had seen.

My baby sister's cry pinched reality, the woodpecker a warning of a disjuncture in the brimming sky, and then a man who was not a man but a myth.

What I had seen there were no words for except in the sacred language of the most holy recounting, so when I ran back to the village, drenched in salt, how could I explain the water jar left empty by the river to my mother who deciphered my burning lips as shame?

My imagination swallowed me like a mica sky, but I had seen the watermonster in the fight of lightning storms, breaking trees, stirring up killing winds, and had lost my favorite brother to a spear of the sacred flame, so certainly I would know my beloved if he were hidden in the blushing skin of the suddenly vulnerable.

I was taken with a fever and nothing cured it until I dreamed my fiery body dipped in the river where it fed into the lake. My father carried me as if I were newborn, as if he were presenting me once more to the world, and when he dipped me I was quenched, pronounced healed.

My parents immediately made plans to marry me to an important man who was years older but would provide me with everything I needed to survive in this world, a world I could no longer perceive, as I had been blinded with a ring of water when I was most in need of a drink by a snake who was not a snake, and how did he know my absolute secrets, those created at the brink of acquired language?

When I disappeared it was in a storm that destroyed the houses of my relatives; my baby sister was found sucking on her hand in the crook of an oak.

And though it may have appeared otherwise, I did not go willingly. That night I had seen my face strung on the shell belt of my ancestors, and I was standing next to a man who could not look me in the eye.

The oldest woman in the tribe wanted to remember me as a symbol in the story of a girl who disobeyed, who gave in to her desires before marriage and was destroyed by the monster disguised as the seductive warrior.

Others saw the car I was driving as it drove into the lake early one morning, the time the carriers of tradition wake up, before the sun or the approach of woodpeckers, and found the emptied six-pack on the sandy shores of the lake.

The power of the victim is a power that will always be reckoned with, one way or the other. When the proverbial sixteen-year-old woman walked down to the lake within her were all sixteen-year-old women who had questioned their power from time immemorial.

Her imagination was larger than the small frame house at the north edge of town, with the broken cars surrounding it like a necklace of futility, larger than the town itself leaning into the lake. Nothing could stop it, just as no one could stop the bearing-down thunderheads as they gathered overhead in the war of opposites.

Years later when she walked out of the lake and headed for town, no one recognized her, or themselves, in the drench of fire and rain. The watersnake was a story no one told anymore. They'd entered a drought that no one recognized as drought, the convenience store a signal of temporary amnesia.

I had gone out to get bread, eggs, and the newspaper before breakfast and hurried the cashier for my change as the crazy woman walked in, for I could not see myself as I had abandoned her some twenty years ago in a blue windbreaker at the edge of the man-made lake as everyone dove naked and drunk off the sheer cliff, as if we had nothing to live for, not then or ever.

It was beginning to rain in Oklahoma, the rain that would flood the world.

Embedded in Muscogee tribal memory is the creature the tie snake, a huge snake of a monster who lives in waterways and will do what he can to take us with him. He represents the power of the underworld.

He is still present today in the lakes and rivers of Oklahoma and Alabama, a force we reckon with despite the proliferation of inventions that keep us from ourselves.

Letter from the End
of the Twentieth Century

Joy Harjo

I shared a half hour of my life this morning with Rammi, an Igbo man from northern Nigeria who drove me in his taxi to the airport. Chicago rose up as a mechanical giant with soft insides buzzing around to keep it going. We were part of the spin.

Rammi told the story of his friend, who one morning around seven—a morning much like this one—was filling his taxi with gas. He was imagining home, a village whose memories had given him sustenance to study through his degree and would keep him going one more year until he had the money to need to return.

As the sun broke through the grey morning he heard his mother tell him, the way she had told him when he was a young boy, how the sun had once been an Igbo and returned every morning to visit relatives.

These memories were the coat that kept him warm on the streets of ice.

He was interrupted by a young man who asked him for money, a young man who was like many he saw on his daily journey onto the street to collect fares. "Oh no, sorry man. I don't have anything I can give you," he said as he patted the pockets of his worn slacks, his thin nylon jacket. He saved every penny because he knew when he returned he'd be taking care of his family, a family several houses large.

He turned back to the attention of filling his gas tank. What a beautiful morning, almost warm. And the same sun, the same Igbo looking down on him in the streets of the labyrinth far far from home.

And just like that he was gone, from a gunshot wound at the back of his head—the hit of a casual murderer.

As we near the concrete plains of O'Hare, I imagine the spirit of Rammi's friend at the door of his mother's house, the bag of dreams in his hands dripping with blood. His mother's tears make a river of red stars to an empty moon.

The whole village mourns with her. The ritual of tears and drums summons the ancestors who carry his spirit into the next world. These he can still hear, the drums of his relatives as they accompany him on his journey. He must settle the story of his murder before joining his ancestors or he will come back a ghost.

The smallest talking drum is an insistent heart, leads his spirit to the killer, a young Jamaican immigrant who was traced to his apartment because his shirt of blood was found by the police, thrown off in the alley with his driver's license in the pocket.

He searches for his murderer in the bowels of Chicago and finds him shivering in a cramped jail cell. He could hang him or knife him—and it would be called suicide. It would be the easiest thing.

But his mother's grief moves his heart. He hears the prayers of the young man's mother. There is always a choice, even after death.

He gives the young man his favorite name and calls him his brother. The young killer is then no longer shamed but filled with remorse and cries all the cries he has stored for a thousand years. He learns to love himself as he never could, because his enemy, who has every reason to destroy him, loves him.

That's the story that follows me everywhere and won't let me sleep: from Tallahassee Grounds to Chicago, to my home near the Rio Grande.

It sustains me through these tough distances.

Anita Endrezze
(1952–)

*"That's not the way it happened.
When you tell a story, you should
get it right. That is, let me tell it."*

Anita Endrezze, "Fish Heads" in
Throwing Fire at the Sun,
Water at the Moon

Grandfather Sun Falls in Love with a Moon-Faced Woman

Anita Endrezze

LONG BEACH, CALIFORNIA, 1937

He was probably drunk, you know, on maize mixed with water. That night, that night, he fell in love for the first time of this life. It was not the first time he drank to forget the long journey, the tramping through alkaline dust white as ground bones, the mud packed on his head like a beehive. It was not the first time he drank to remember the feel of wild horses between his legs and how they would sigh in the morning.

She had a cool, silvery light in her face, the way a woman looks when she bends over still water and studies her face. Or the way water flickers in sea caves, that bending of light and water, sleek as a seal. She was his opposite in many ways: patient when he was hotheaded, quiet when he shouted in anger at life, the cords of his neck strong as bullwhips.

When he approached her, she lifted her chin and stared at him. "You've been watching me," she stated.

"Will you marry me?" he asked. "Will you marry me?" He sat down abruptly, weakened by his boldness.

She laughed. "You're funny."

When he hung his head, shoulders sloping down into his pockets, she laughed harder. "Oh, I like a man who makes me laugh!"

He looked up and grinned. Maybe this was going to turn out all right.

"You men!" she scolded, her face shining in the dark edge of dawn. The strap of her red dress slid down one shoulder. She canted one hip, angling her ankles until the high-heeled shoe slipped off and the small space between heel and earth was like red earth and roses.

He wanted to kiss her heels, let her walk across him, the way he walked across Sonora. Let her step into him, to what he'd become, sitting here on the seawall listening to the Pacific Ocean call her name.

Over and over, he smiled, wanting to make her laugh again. He bared his teeth, pulled his upper lip to cover his nose, let his lips hang loose while he warbled

Mexican love songs. She laughed so hard, she grabbed her middle and bent over into the ocean.

"Okay," she gasped, "I'll marry you . . . on one condition."

He sat up suddenly. "¿Qué?" But she was already gone.

The next night he got there early, said ¡Hola! To the last of the evening's seagulls, who screamed at him.

Well, let them, he thought. He waited for her to stroll down the street again, wearing that dress the color of ripe peaches. He had picked peaches all day, took his money, letting the jingle of coins remind him of spurs. He used to break horses in Arizona, riding the sweat-sleek mustangs until they stopped, quivering, accepting the bit and the hard hawing of his hands on the reins. Now, he was reduced to twisting peaches from their branches, stepping in the rotten flesh, swatting at hornets. Peaches or walnuts, strawberries or lettuce. He'd gone one step lower on the chain of dominance. From animal to vegetable.

I'm a vegetable, he swore to himself, as he tipped back the bottle. He hiccuped. I'm a pickled vegetable. He chuckled softly.

"What's so funny?" she asked. This time she looked a little different, but you know how women can change themselves. It's in their makeup.

But he didn't feel funny after all. He felt sad. Maybe a little bit angry. Okay, a lot angry, if you want to know the truth. He had walked all the way from Mexico in order to end up a vegetable in a country that thought he was scum because he was an Indian.

She sat down beside him. Her skirt was real short and he smelled her, the cornflower smell of her thighs. "Doncha wanna get hitched?" she asked in a low, teasing voice.

He tried to sit up straighter, but vegetables have roots, and his spine was attaching itself to the cement seawall. He was about to become a mineral if he didn't rouse himself.

"Sí." He glanced at her. She made him nervous. She wore a white dress, just like a bride. No veil. No Bible. Did she mean now, like get married *now*?

"Remember?" she asked, staring intently at him.

He was stuck. Remember what? He narrowed his eyes, trying to read the darkness. Somewhere there was an answer. He licked his finger and placed it on an imaginary page, turning it, hoping for answers to fly out at him like pale doves.

"You don't remember, do you?!" She stood up, narrow and suddenly slender, like a sword. "¡Ay, men!" She turned away from him, standing stiffly.

He sweated. Small drops of fermented maize gathered on his brow. I'm sweating vegetables, he thought. He shook his head, flinging off tiny corn plants twisted into the shapes of drunken men.

"Okay, okay," he mumbled, not looking at her. "What did I forget?"

She sighed. It was *that* sigh, the one women make when they think their men have brains like dried calabashes.

"I said I'd marry you." She paused. "On one condition."

"What's that?"

She sat down next to him, the white dress floating like waves around her knees. "You must bring me a gift that will fit me precisely."

He nodded, tried to coax a smile from her by holding his lips inside his mouth until he looked like an old man. But she didn't smile, and he felt foolish. She was too beautiful to be reminded that someday he would be an old man. Maybe he was already.

"At least I have my teeth," he said and was horrified to realize he'd spoken aloud. But when he turned to look at her she was gone, and he thought he saw her thin light glowing on the barnacle-encrusted pier.

The next day he bought only a little corn whiskey. Just enough to loosen his muscles, let the bones straighten out from a day of carrying canvas bags of peaches slung over one shoulder, each bag heavy as a body. One bag over each shoulder, the peaches hard as baby skulls, punching his back. With the other money, the money left over from not buying so much whiskey, he bought her a gift.

All day he had thought about what he should get her, but he couldn't afford any of those things. A peach tree, a garden, a field, a house, a village, the whole city. A city of angels, los angeles, lace mantillas, a gold avocado.

He bought her a belt from Woolworth's. It was white and would go with that white dress. Women liked things that matched, he knew. It might even look good with the red dress. It was a shiny patent leather belt, with a gold-colored buckle and three tiny gold eyelets for the clasp. He wrapped it in the sack the whiskey came in and tied it with a string he'd stolen from the peach bags.

He walked down the pier, whistling. It was an old Yaqui song somebody had taught him long ago. Or maybe didn't teach him, he just remembered it. After his father was killed by the soldiers, no one taught him anything anymore. He was through with learning. All he wanted was to get away. The only thing that was important was that he was alive. Nothing else mattered.

Now, suddenly, when he was a man, love mattered. How it had happened, how he had fallen in love with her, he didn't know. He never knew those kinds of things. He knew how to make music from his mouth and how to calm a horse, lifting its leg in order to clean the hoof. He knew how to eat strawberries without moving his mouth so that the boss wouldn't say he was stealing while he worked. He knew how to sleep under a bench in a park. He knew how to forget where he was. *That* was important. Why did the fathers never teach you things like that?

She sauntered up. This time she was wearing a yellow sarong, like you see in the movie posters, that Hollywood lady. Her breasts were pushed up, two golden moons. He took a deep breath and offered the package to her.

"¡Ay!" she exclaimed. Like a child, she tore at the wrapping, but stopped to look at him. She smiled shyly. Then she continued, unfolding the package. The white belt lay coiled like a ghost snake, a moon snake with gold head and three gold eyes. She put it around her waist.

Even he could see that it was too big. It looked like a barrel hoop. She shook her head as the belt fell to her feet. Her waist was so slender he could see the lean shadows of palm-leaf ribs fluttering through her. She was so thin she was almost transparent.

As she walked away, she looked over her shoulder. "Mañana."

The next day he bought her a bracelet, small enough for a child, made out of a pretty blue plastic. He spat on it, shining it up with the edge of his shirt, then wrapped it in a page of the L.A. *Times.*

He found his spot on the seawall. Took the bottle from his pocket and tipped it until he saw her face glowing in the other end. Quickly, he stopped drinking, wiping his mouth with the back of his hand. He handed her the gift.

She took the bracelet from the sports page and tried to slip it over her hand, but it wouldn't work. The bracelet was too small.

"You got big hands," he said, wondering if that was okay to say to a woman. They didn't like you talking about their big feet or noses. She was looking at him in a strange way. Smiling a bit. But looking as if he wasn't there or she wasn't seeing him. She shook her head, long hair flowing around her, down to her waist.

She looked more substantial today, he decided. A little heavier, maybe. He cocked his head, watching her as she sashayed away, buttocks bouncing like plump peaches. Well, he told himself, don't women get that way. Something to do with the time of the month.

The following day he gave her nothing. It was raining so hard his liquor got diluted, even though he tried to save it by swallowing fast. The next night it was foggy, and he looked for her. She never showed up. Two nights later, the fog blew away and he saw her, strolling down the beach. She looked fat. Just a little, but nice, you know, like you knew you'd find a lot of woman under the ivory-colored caftan. Big round breasts, like melons, and a stomach round as a tomato. A vegetable woman for a vegetable man. He liked that.

But she didn't like his gift. It was a scarf, yellow with white butterflies. It was supposed to fit across her shoulders but was so dwarfed by her greatness that she could have used it as a hankie for her nose. She shook her head and left him.

Bad weather again. No work in the fields, either. No money. No gift. He stood around the alley, sharing a bottle with Rubio and some other mouths.

"Hey, man," sneered one, "ain't this the life?"

"Don't fuck with me," said Rubio. Water dripped off his hair. He looked like a wet chihuahua, shivering in the rain. He took another drink, passed the bottle to another mouth.

"Not fuckin' with you, man. Just talkin', ya know, makin' conversation."

"Well, shuddup."

The rain sounded like drums. Powwow drums. There were drums up in the hills overlooking L.A., singers, too. Mostly displaced Sioux, some of them sent to California to learn how to become civilized, others hoping for a job acting in the movies. He'd gone up once, wanting to be with other Indians who knew they were Indians, as opposed to all those Indians who thought they were Mexicans. He'd gone up to hear the drums and stayed all night, feeling the soft beating coming out of the men's hearts, into their arms, into the drums, then out into the earth, the night air, and into him. When they asked who he was, he said, "I'm Yaqui," and they nodded.

Later they called him Sun because his skin got hot when he drank, sweat sizzling off his cheeks. When the sun came up, he rode back to town with them, six Indians in the back of a pickup, rattling down the switchbacks, tires swaybacked and lame.

He must've fallen in love up there, he thought. That's when it happened. Before he even saw her, he knew he was going to fall in love. It must've been the singing or the drums shaking his dick, rumbling around in his balls until his whole body hummed with wanting.

And he wanted her, waited for the rain to stop, so he could see her again. Drank some more, hoping it was a kind of magic, making a liquid go inside of him so that liquid falling outside would stop. Any dumb thing, to make her come back. Her bright face, round shoulders, fleshy knees.

So when the rain did stop, he wasn't dried out enough to make it over to the seawall. He missed one night. Couldn't remember it going like that. A night that hadn't happened. Sometimes time was that way. But he made it back there the following night and brought her a tablecloth he swiped from someone's backyard on Rio Street. It was a white tablecloth with wine stains on it, but he thought they were pale roses. He had a headache and his eyes hurt.

When she strutted up, he was shocked. She was thin, like a cocktail stirrer. Wore a black dress and spiked heels. Some kind of glassy black rocks for earrings. Her eyes were enormous.

She held up the tablecloth, which he hadn't wrapped at all. A question in her eyes.

"It's a cape," he suggested frantically, "like the rich ladies wear."

She wrapped it around her shoulders. Once, twice, three times she wrapped herself, until she stood like a cocoon and the ancient word for butterfly came fluttering back to him from a past in another land. *Vaeseuoli.*

The tablecloth unwound itself from her thin body. It fell, full of wine and roses and gravy, puddling around her feet. Her ankles were thin as icepicks. She had no hips, just two sharp plates of bone. Her belly was an empty cup. Her breasts were only nipples, two suggestions.

"This isn't going to work," she said sadly. "Nothing fits me precisely."

He stared at his hands. *They* would fit her, mold her, precisely. And his mouth could fit hers. If she'd only give him a chance . . . he'd be a good lover.

"Sorry," she said. Again she made him nervous. And suddenly, he knew why: she had no purse. Other women carried purses, fiddled with them while they flirted, pulled out tubes of red and magenta lipstick, round puffs for powder, little circles of mirrors that gave them his point of view on their lips. Keys, coins, mad money, taxi money, coffee money.

But she had no purse. As if she never needed redder lips or pots of rouge, small bottles of perfume. Or as if she was complete in herself, like a man, not needing a purse to hold in front of her like a shield. Such confidence was unnerving. Real women needed men. He wanted her to need him.

And she didn't. She walked away, narrow as a bone, dark hair braided into one sparse thread. She never looked back.

But he kept looking at her. Every night. He fell.
    He fell in love.
    He fell in love with her.
    He fell.

He drank and fell
    down, looking for her at the bottom of the bottle.
    Those eyes, those lips.

He got married. To an ordinary, beautiful Yaqui woman. One who was smart with money. And who took care of him and the children. A really good woman, with another child born before his. Angelita. A little angel. Not his wife's fault she was raped, but she loved the girl. His wife even loved tramps, gave them food when they knocked on the back door. Tortillas wrapped around stewed chicken. Clear, cold water from the tap. A song from her heart.

Sí, so he was married. But he never stopped mooning for *her*.

When the car came out of the night, he was Sun, hot and feeling the blood pounding in his feet. He danced in the street, watching the headlights give him a stage. He bent over, waiting for the applause, bottle in one hand. It was a magic bottle, like the kind in the stories from Arabia, where a tiny spirit lived inside and gave you whatever you wished. He kept her there and drank until he got what he wanted.

It took a long time to figure out what that was.

So when the car hit him, he thought it was love again. A big punch to the solar plexus.

A real jab to the heart.

He rolled to the side of the street. The car roared away. He laughed when he saw the bottle was unbroken and the moon jangled around inside it, in her white wedding dress. She laughed, too. Good joke.

Knew what he could give her. Should've known then, long ago. What fit, what fit perfectly. Now it was there: in his heart. A package wrapped in blood red. He opened his hand; the bottle fell, clinking.

The gift that fits: one size fits all. *Amor. Love.*

She smiled.

He stirred the stars with his fingers, watched the fragments of light splinter the darkness. Saw her, full and round and womanly. He lay with his head on her lap. He lay with his head on the curb.

Note: The preceding story is a modern version of an old Yaqui myth about the sun and the moon and recounts the waxing and waning of the moon. And love. Or maybe it's about my grandfather Emiterio, who was killed in a hit-and-run accident in 1937.

The Humming of Stars
and Bees and Waves

Anita Endrezze

Long ago, there was a spirit woman and her name was Yomumuli, Enchanted Bee. She made the earth: the rippling grasses swaying in the wind and the scarlet mountains floating on clouds of tiny blue birds. And the day was divided into astonished animal faces, and the night was a fountainhead of stars and the slumber of river turtles.

Since that time, the papery husks of stars have fallen into the seas and mothers have grown older. Rosa is a woman who talks to herself. Although she doesn't remember the first creation, she does, of course, remember the birth of her only child, a son named Natchez.

She made the people and put them in a village. And in the middle of the village was a Talking Tree that hummed like bees.

When Natchez was little, he talked to his shadow, and Rosa talked with the coyotes and ravens and flowers. But now she is old and can't see very well. Once she caught herself talking to a discarded gum wrapper, thinking it was a flower.

   I wonder, she thinks, if my dreams can tell me how to make my eyes better. She knows that her tribe believes in dreams, but since she's half Yaqui, she doesn't always know whether the dreams believe in her. Still, she begs for a dream that would speak healing words. One night she dreams the words "unlined cell differential" and has no idea what they mean. I probably got someone else's dream, she thinks. Another night she dreams about fog, and when she wakes up, her eye is cloudier.

The tree spoke a sacred language. No one could understand it. Not the youngest. Not the oldest. Not the wisest or bravest or strongest. Not even the oldest.

Rosa wakes one morning and remembers a dream that tells her to enter a cave. Grandmother Spider Woman tells her to bring cedar, tobacco, and corn. No walkie-talkie. No flashlight. No strings or bread crumbs to mark the path. Just blind faith.

And so, when the moon is yellow and the mist low under the dark apples... when the fields are gold and dry with rows of stars shining on the tassels... when the horizon is lilac and the mountains to the west are blue-black, Rosa ties the bag with the offerings around her waist and hikes up the trail to the old caves. The caves are usually there, but legends have it that they sometimes disappear. Rosa is not sure what to expect, so she mutters to herself as she walks.

The back of her neck is hot and sticky, even though the air is cooling and rising from the valley. The trail gets steeper and narrows to one foot in front of the other. She puts one hand on her knee in order to propel herself forward on the steepest part and prays that the rest of her will follow.

"Damn stupid thing to do," she mumbles. She's little worried about bears, even though one of her husbands had the spirit of a bear. He loved to sleep and eat. That's how she saw people: this one is a bull, that one a St. Bernard. But in the past few years, she's been feeling too old for the foolishness of love and friendship. After all, she has herself to talk to and she's a good listener who always agrees with her sentiments. Now, at least the talking will keep away the bears, although she knows you should always wear bells around your neck. However, finding the cedar was hard enough. She ended up using the cedar shavings you use to keep away moths.

Finally, she rounds the curve of the mountain. Her heart is beating fast. The cave opens in front of her like a huge toothless mouth. She can feel the cold, musty air push out toward her. The floor of the cave is rough, littered with angular rocks.

She's a small woman with bony knees and one shoulder slightly higher than the other, but her skin is surprisingly smooth for her age and her hair is still thick. She waits until her heart calms down, then notices it's getting dark outside. She might as well go in.

I hope I know what I'm doing, she says. Walking with her hands spread out in front of her, she hears water rushing to her left. A swift underground stream rushing out into the twilight. Don't let me die in here, she prays.

When Yomumuli returned from her creating, she shook off the images of shimmering feathers and jungle greens and small monkey faces, and loosened her fingers from speckled granite and purple-spiked sea urchins, and brushed off the coral sands from her memory, and listened to her children.

They were worried. They had been given something sacred and had not understood it. Some argued that the holy is never understood.

Rosa listens. The stream has a voice and it chants: *earthbowl* and *duskwomb*. The walls have a voice that rumbles: *terra-cotta hands* and *eyes of clay*.

Rosa feels the presence of tiny spider women, sitting with their spindly legs crossed. Minerals drip, drip, into funnels of teethlike spikes, vaginal and wet. The spider women unlid their thousand eyes and reach out, sticky fingerlings, silken threads slivering the cracks of deeper darkness. The threads anchor Rosa, the outworlder. The voices are those from the void: *terra marina, terra noche*. Words from the beginning, when all that was, was not spoken. Land. Sea. Night. In Rosa's ears, she hears the bull-roarer and the raw rushing out of a water drum. It is music as old as the heart.

My own body is full of minerals, she thinks, and thousands of her cells echo the stratification of the earth. She isn't lost.

Yomumuli puts her cheek to the Talking Tree and listens to the humming voice.

Rosa is a stone woman. She is a stone fish swimming through a river of turquoise. A half-blind fish, finny and leaping to the rhythm of a shadowless current. She is aware of the tribes of ghostlike fish and frogs that live in the dark waters, sunless, white creatures that dream only of the moon.

When she was a young woman, she liked men. She still likes men, but none of them will look at her. They don't like old women. When she was young, she needed a cane to walk sometimes. Her sight was good, but not always her insight. She often chose the wrong man. Now, she's got a bad eye and it's life that is lame.

There's more than blood in her veins now. There's experience and wisdom and a deep longing for more life. More stories. More kisses.

She remembers her own grandmother, who lived alone for forty-six years after her husband died, celebrating his birthday with flowers in front of a silver-framed photo and yearly visits to the cemetery. Now Natchez has a baby and Rosa sleeps alone, her husband of thirty years dead for some time. She remembers his nightly whispers to her before they fell asleep. One of his favorite saying was "Life has no guarantees." But, she admits to herself now as she struggles through the cave, she expected life to continue while she was alive!

I've been on the shelf too long, she says, I've gotten dusty.

Yomumuli heard what the tree was saying. She turned to look at her people and spoke, shrugging a cloud from her shoulder: I'll tell you what the Tree says but you must promise to believe me!

Rosa trips and falls to her knee. There's blood and a sharp pain. Shit, she moans. She feels old, old as the clay shards in the lap of the earth, old as the curled fetus shapes in red clay graves, skin wrinkled over thin ribs, and all around, faces of grief. Terra Recepta. Corpus terra. The earth is made of beginnings and endings.

I'm not crazy, she repeats to herself. I'm here for a reason. I know what I need, to see, but not how to do it.

Inching forward, her knee throbbing, she feels the walls narrowing. Then the stream widens into a pool; she can hear the stillness in the center and the rushing out near her feet. The spider women throw a ball of moony webs up into the air, and a soft light fills the cave's inner heart.

So, now what do I do? asks Rosa.

Do you believe in us? click the spider women.

Of course! Of course! And so the people listened; the Tree told the animals how to live...that the deer should eat grass and the puma eat the deer. Then it spoke about the future when men from a far country would come and everything would change. There would be new laws and new deaths, and a great metal snake with smoke plumes would race across the land. When the people heard this, they became afraid.

Being half-Yaqui isn't easy, Rosa thinks. You have to believe that trees and rocks and birds talk, and you have to have faith in glass-walled elevators and voices transmitted from space. Then there's pantyhose that assumes your shape and dreams that struggle to shape your awareness.

Long ago, Rosa got real tired of shape-changing: being Indian with Indians and white with the whites. As she got older, she became less afraid and howled like a coyote in heat whenever she damn well felt like it.

From the ceiling of the cave, tree roots hang down in a gnarled nest. The cave seems to be breathing feathers, eggs, and clouds.

I believe, whispers Rosa.

Some didn't believe Yomumuli. So she left, with her favorite river rolled up under her arm, walking north, her feet like two dark thunderclouds.

Rosa thinks about her white mothers, their names rolling off her tongue like pearls of barley: Jean, Ann, Yohana, Marija, Barbara, Ana, Margareta, Elizabeth, Susie, Giuliana, Anna, Orsola, Felicita. And her Indian mothers, whose names are rich with corn and chilies: Charlotta, Estefana, Empimenia—and others whose names were lost, unwritten, but remembered in a certain flash of eye.

Rosa feels the Grandmother's eyes all around her. She sees with their eyes. She sees the pond, its water clear as spiderwebs.

And some of the people went to live in the sea, their whale songs, tubular and roiling, boom-echo and deep in the interior seas of their throats, longing and sounding all in a moaning song, floating up to the spume moon.

Rosa turns to the cave walls. Clay. She pulls a chunk out and rolls it in her hands, forming a ball. Little clay baby. Cave navel, lodestar, and mother lode. She pinches it into a rough bowl. With her thumbs she shapes it, smooths it.

Quickly, she fills the bowl with pond water. A sip. It tastes like metal and semen and breast milk. It is sour and sweet and musty and white and black and red and yellow.

And some became flying fish, ringing the waves, sparkling, and others became the singers of the sea, with their long hair and rainbow skin. They say that if you're lost at sea, these creatures will help you because they remember the time when we were all one people.

Rosa unties her bag of offerings and puts the tobacco in the bowl. The cedar chips to the right, the corn to the left. Fumbling a bit, she pulls out a book of matches and carefully lights the tobacco. A thin, handlike smoke rises. She has no idea what to do next, or if what she's already done is right.

She thanks her family. She thanks her guardian spirits. She thanks her own strength, which has brought her this far without breaking her neck. She thanks the creator who gives her dreams and daily breath.

The Grandmother's sing: *Ebb and return, web and wheel, smoke and water, the void has wings, we sing and reel. Spinner and spinal songs, spiraling, symphonic, and symbiotic, sightless but full of vision, we Grandmothers, we dreamers.*

The singing stops and Rosa gathers strands of webs into a little ball. She puts it into her weak eye. The tobacco has burnt itself out. She lights the cedar shavings. No fire, but sweet and piercing. She scatters the ground corn on the floor, tipping the rough clay bowl to its side, mingling the yellow with the cedar ash.

Her insight is blooming. It is becoming a way of seeing herself. Her life is not over. She has much to experience yet. She is getting older, but she is not old.

And some of the people were afraid to face the future and descended into the earth and became jointed: jet-black or red. These little ant people who live in the sand will also help you if you are lost.

She took the clay bowl and pressed it back into the cave wall.

For they also remember the time when we were one people.

Rosa stands and feels the darkness fall around her, but it is not from within, for she can see. Her white moon-eye, her shedded-snakeskin eye, her winter-worn-leaf eye: gone the thickening curtain, gone into the thoughts of the spider women. In and spin.

There are cedar trees floating in the air, and the faces of those she has loved waver delicately in front of her. She is seeing with her heart.

She feels the pain burning away. It's the pain of learning to let go. Sierra Rose is the name of the daughter she never had. Let go. Her husband's hands touching her in the morning. Let go. Her little son saying, "I'll always stay with you, Mama." Let go. Herself thinking: I'll never want another friend; they all leave or die and it hurts too much. Let go.

Her eye is clear. There is no division between the worlds of seeing and believing.

Rosa is ready to leave. She knows there is confusion outside and the noise of cars honking in the night. But there are also stars, one thousand billion of them in the Milky Way, and that leaves no room for self-pity. Rosa ties a lace on her Reeboks and turns around.

Those who stayed in the village grew taller as they taught their children how to face the future without fear.

She walks quickly toward the cave entrance, which has a lesser density of darkness. She passes the ancient paintings of red handprints and the pitted engravings of rayed suns. At the entrance itself, there are other human reminders: squashed beer cans, spray-painted initials, and an old McDonald's Coke cup. Golden arches. She sighs, then looks up. The moon is seeping out of the fat wheat heads. It's full and yellow, arching over the litter and the thin-winged twilight.

In the valley, she hears the cottonwoods shaking under the force of their water-filled roots. The bees are sleeping, dreaming of heavy black clouds booming over gold-white fields and sheet-lightning flashing into a hot and crinkly air.

And the ravens are dreaming of circling in a chicory-blue sky. Twirly seeds of yellow star-bursts fall in floating circles to the earth. Rosa feels the circles growing within her, as if she were a tree of immense dawn.

All of her life she's been drawn to the spirit, often equating contemplation with action. It takes energy to think, she'd tell herself. Now she knows why the phone never rang just because she was lonely. She has to get out and find something to do and someone to talk to!

Taking a deep breath, she smiles, thinking of her son and her new granddaughter. She'll give her a nickname: Sierra Rose. I'm not useless, she says firmly, and I'm not alone.

As she brushes the dirt from her clothes, she spares one last look at the cave. Its darkness, its blindness, had terrified her. It was the blindness of death she'd been see-ing with her weak eye, the conception of nothing.

Now she begins the way back. In the distance, the sky is luminous with the lights of the city, and even though it may vaporize into thin air one day, if you are lost, you will know the way home; for home is a remembrance of when we were all one people.

And the people who live there are like enchanted trees, with bones for branches and eyes for leaves. If they listen, they can hear the humming of stars and bees and waves.

These are my ancestors, my future.

Note: While writing this story I developed a temporary eye infection. On a more significant level, writing this story convinced me that I wasn't too old to have another baby. My daughter, Maja Sierra Rose, was born when I was thirty-nine. Both she and my son, Aaron, are my future, but the past lives on in them in the blood and stories they've inherited from our ancestors.

Louise Erdrich
(1954–)

*"In the light of enormous loss,
[Native American writers] must
tell the stories of contemporary
survivors while protecting and
celebrating the cores of cultures left
in the wake of the catastrophe."*

Louise Erdrich, "Where I Ought to
Be: A Writer's Sense of Place"

Le Mooz

Louise Erdrich

Margaret had exhausted three husbands, and Nanapush outlived his six wives. They were old by the time they shacked up out in the deep bush. Besides, as Ojibweg in the last century's first decades, having starved and grieved, having seen prodigious loss and endured theft by agents of the government and *chimookomaanag* farmers, they were tired. You would think, at last, they'd just want simple comfort. Quiet. Companionship and sleep. But times did not go smoothly. Peace eluded them. For Nanapush and Margaret found a surprising heat in their hearts. Fierce and sudden, it sometimes eclipsed both age and anger with tenderness. Then, they made love with an amazed greed and purity that astounded them. At the same time, it was apt to burn out of control.

When this happened, they fought. Stinging flames of words blistered their tongues. Silence was worse. Beneath its slow-burning weight, their black look singed. After a few days their minds shriveled into dead coals. Some speechless nights, they lay together like logs turned completely to ash. They were almost afraid to move, lest they sift into flakes and disintegrate. It was a young love set blazing in bodies aged and overused, and sometimes it cracked them like too much fire in an old tin stove.

To survive in their marriage, they developed many strategies. For instance, they rarely collaborated on any task. Each hunted, trapped, and fished alone. They could not agree on so little a thing as how and where to set a net. The gun, which belonged to Nanapush, was never clean when it was needed. Traps rusted. It was up to Margaret to scour the rifle barrel, smoke the steel jaws. Setting snares together was impossible, for in truth they snared themselves time and again in rude opinions and mockery over where a rabbit might jump or how to set the loop. Their avoidance only hardened them in their individual ways, and so when Margaret beached their leaky old boat one morning and jumped ashore desperate for help, there was no chance of agreement.

Margaret sometimes added little Frenchisms to her *Ojibwemowin*,* just the way the fancy-sounding wives of the French voyageurs added, like a dash of spice, random "*le*"'s and "*la*"'s. So when she banged into the cabin screaming of "le Mooz," Nanapush woke, irritated, with reproof on his lips, as he was always pleased to find some tiny fault with his beloved.

"Le Mooz! Le Mooz!" she shouted into his face. She grabbed him by the shirt so violently that he could hear the flimsy threads part.

"*Booni'ishin!*" He tried to struggle from her grip, but Margaret rapidly explained to him that she had seen a moose swimming across the lake and here were their winter's provisions, easy! With this moose meat dried and stored, they would survive. "Get up, old man!" She grabbed the gun and dragged him to the boat before he'd even mentally prepared himself to hunt moose.

Nanapush pushed off with his paddle, sulking. Besides their natural inclination to disagree, it was always the case that, if one of them was particularly intrigued by some idea, the other was sure to feel the opposite way just to polarize the situation. If Nanapush asked for maple syrup with his meat, Margaret gave him wild onion. If Margaret relished a certain color of cloth, Nanapush declared that he could not look upon that blue or red—it made him mean and dizzy. When it came to sleeping on the fancy spring bed that Margaret had bought with this year's bark money, Nanapush adored the bounce while she was stingy with it, so as not to use it up. Sometimes he sat on the bed and joggled up and down when she was gone, just to spite her. For her part, once he began craftily to ask for wild onion, she figured he'd developed a taste for it and so bargained for a small jar of maple syrup, thus beginning the obvious next stage of their contradictoriness, which was that they each asked for the opposite of what they really wanted and so got what they wanted in the end. It was confusing to their friend Father Damien, but to the two of them it brought serene harmony. So, when Margaret displayed such extreme determination in the matter of the moose that morning, not only was Nanapush feeling especially lazy but he also decided that she really meant the opposite of what she cried out, and so he dawdled with his paddle and tried to tell her a joke or two. She, however, was in dead earnest.

"Paddle! Paddle for all you're worth!" she yelled.

"Break your backs, boys, or break wind!" Nanapush mocked her.

Over the summer, as it hadn't been the proper time for telling the sacred Ojibwe *adisookaanag*, Father Damien had tried to convert Nanapush by telling as many big-fish tales as he could remember, including the ones about the fish that multiplied, the fish that swallowed Jonah. Soon, Father Damien had had to reach beyond the Bible. Nanapush's favorite was the tale of the vast infernal white fish and the maddened chief who gave chase through the upper and lower regions of the earth.

"*Gitimishk!*" Margaret nearly choked in frustration, for the moose had changed direction and they were not closing in quickly enough for her liking.

---

* *Ojibwemowin* translates as the Ojibwe language.

"Aye, aye, *Ahabikwe!*" shouted Nanapush, lighting his pipe as she vented her fury in deep strokes. If the truth be told, he was delighted with her anger, for when she lost control like this during the day she often lost control once the sun went down also, and he was already anticipating their pleasure.

"Use that paddle or my legs are shut to you, lazy fool!" she growled.

At that, he went to work and they quickly drew alongside the moose. Margaret steadied herself, threw a loop of strong rope around its wide, spreading antlers, and then secured the rope tightly to the front of the boat, which was something of an odd canoe, having a flat, tough bottom, a good ricing boat but not all that easy to steer.

"Now," she ordered Nanapush, "now, take up the gun and shoot! Shoot!"

But Nanapush did not. He had killed a moose this way once before in his life, and he had nothing to prove. This time, he wasn't so anxious. What was happening to them was a very old story, one handed down through generations, one that had happened to his namesake, the trickster Nanabozho. He would not kill the moose quite yet. He hefted the gun and made certain that it was loaded, and then enjoyed the free ride they were receiving.

"Let's turn him around, my adorable pigeon," he cried to his lady. "Let him tow us back home. I'll shoot him once he reaches the shallow water just before our cabin."

Margaret could not help but agree that this particular plan arrived at by her lazy husband was a good one, and so, by using more rope and hauling on first one antler and then the other with all their strength, they proceeded to turn the beast and head him in the right direction. Nanapush sat back, smoking his pipe, and relaxed once they were pointed homeward. The sun was out and the air was cool, fresh. All seemed right between the two of them now. Margaret admonished him about the tangle of fishing tackle all around his seat, and there was even affection in her voice.

"You'll poke yourself," she said, "you fool." At that moment, with the meat pulling them right up to their doorstep, she did not really even care. "I'll fry the rump steaks tonight with a little maple syrup over them," she said, her mouth watering. "Old man, you're gonna eat good! Oooh," she almost cried with appreciation, "our moose is so fat!"

"He's a fine moose," Nanapush agreed passionately. "You've got an eye, *Mindi-mooyenh*. He's a juicy one, our moose!"

"I'll roast his ribs, cook the fat with our beans, and keep his brains in a bucket to tan that big hide! Oooh, *ishte*, my husband, the old men are going to envy the *makizinan* that I will sew for you."

"Beautiful wife!" Nanapush was overcome. "Precious sweetheart!"

As they gazed upon each other with great love, holding the rare moment of mutual agreeableness, the hooves of the moose struck the first sandbar near shore, and Margaret cried out for her husband to lift the gun and shoot.

"Not quite yet, my beloved," Nanapush said confidently, "he can drag us nearer yet!"

"Watch out! Shoot now!"

The moose was indeed approaching the shallows, but Nanapush planned in his pride to shoot the animal just as he began to pull them from the water, thereby making their task of dressing and hauling mere child's play. He got the moose in his sights and then waited as it gained purchase. The old man's feet, annoyingly, tangled in the fishing tackle he had been too lazy to put away, and he jigged, attempting to kick it aside.

"Margaret, duck!" he cried. Just as the moose lunged onto hand he let blast, completely missing and totally terrifying the animal, which gave a hopping skip that seemed impossible for a thing so huge, and veered straight up the bank. Margaret, reaching back to tear the gun from her husband's hands, was bucked completely out of the boat and said later that if only her no-good man hadn't insisted on holding on to the gun she could have landed, aimed, and killed them both, as she then wished to do most intensely. Instead, as the moose tore off with the boat still securely tied by three ropes to his antlers, she was left behind screaming for the fool to jump. But he did not, and within moments the rampaging moose, with the boat bounding behind, had disappeared into the woods.

"My man is stubborn," she said, dusting off her skirt, checking to make sure that she was still in one piece, nothing broken or cut. "He will surely kill that moose!" She spoke hopefully, but inside she felt stuffed with a combination of such anxiety and rage that she did not know what to do—to try to rescue Nanapush or to chop him into pieces with the hatchet that she found herself sharpening as she listened for the second report of his gun.

Bloof!

Yes. There it was. Good thing he didn't jump out, she muttered. She began to tramp, with her carrying straps and an extra sharp knife, in the direction of the noise.

In fact, that Nanapush did not jump out of the boat had little to do with his great stubbornness or his bravery. When the moose jolted the boat up the shore, the tackle that had already wound around him flew beneath his rear as he bounced upward and three of his finest fishing hooks stuck deep into his buttocks as he landed, fastening him tight. He screeched in pain, further horrifying the animal, and struggled, driving the hooks in still deeper, until he could only hold on to the edge of the boat with one hand, gasping in agony, as with the other he attempted to raise the gun to his shoulder and kill the moose.

All the time, of course, the moose was running wildly. Pursued by this strange, heavy, screeching, banging, booming thing, it fled in dull terror through bush and slough. It ran and continued to run. Those who saw Nanapush as he passed all up and down the reservation stood a moment in fascinated shock and rubbed their eyes, then went to fetch others, so that soon the predicament of Nanapush was known and reported everywhere. By then, the moose had attained a smooth loping trot, and passed with swift ease through farmsteads and pastures, the boat flying up and then disappearing down behind. Many stopped what they were doing to gape and yell, and others ran for their rifles, but they were all too late to shoot the moose and free poor Nanapush.

One day passed. In his moose-drawn fishing boat, Nanapush toured every part of the reservation that he'd ever hunted and saw everyone that he'd ever known and then went to places that he hadn't visited since childhood. At one point, a family digging cattail roots was stunned to see the boat, the moose towing it across a slough, and a man slumped over, for by now poor Nanapush had given up and surrendered to the pain, which at least, he said later, he shared with the beast, whose rump he'd stung with bullets. The moose was heading now for the most remote parts of the reservation, where poor Nanapush was convinced he surely would die.

"*Niijii*," he cried out to the moose, "my brother, slow down!"

The animal flicked back an ear to catch the sound of the thing's voice, but didn't stop.

"I will kill no more!" declared Nanapush. "I now throw away my gun!" And he cast it aside, after kissing the barrel and noting well his surroundings. But as though it sensed and felt only contempt for the man's hypocrisy, the moose snorted and kept moving.

"I apologize to you," cried Nanapush, "and to all of the moose I have ever killed and to the spirit of the moose and the boss of the moose and to every moose that has lived or will ever live in the future."

As if slightly placated, the moose slowed to a walk, and Nanapush was able, finally, to snatch a few berries from the bushes they passed, to scoop up a mouthful of water from the slough, and to sleep, though by moonlight the moose still browsed and walked toward some goal, thought Nanapush, delirious with exhaustion and pain. Perhaps the next world. Perhaps this moose had been sent by the all-clever Creator to fetch Nanapush along to the spirit life in this novel way. But, just as he was imagining such a thing, the first light showed and by that ever-strengthening radiance he saw that his moose did indeed have a direction and an intention and that that object was a female moose of an uncommonly robust size, just ahead, peering over her shoulder in a way that was apparently bewitching to a male moose, for Nanapush's animal uttered a squeal of bullish intensity that he recognized as pure lust.

Nanapush, now wishing that he had aimed for the huge swinging balls of the moose, wept with exasperation.

"Should I be subjected to this? This, too? In addition to all that I have suffered?" And Nanapush cursed the moose, cursed himself, the fishhooks, and the person who so carefully and sturdily constructed the boat that would not fall apart. He cursed in English, as there are no true swear words in *Ojibwemowin*, and so it was Nanapush and not the Devil whom Josette Bizhieu heard passing by her remote cabin at first light, shouting all manner of unspeakable and innovative imprecations, and it was Nanapush, furthermore, who was heard howling in the deep slough grass, howling, though more dead at this point than alive, at the outrageous acts he was forced to witness there, before his nose, as the boat tipped up and the bull moose in the extremity of his passion loved the female moose with ponderous mountings and thrilling thrusts that swung Nanapush from side to side but did not succeed in dislodging him from the terrible grip of the fishhooks. No, that was not to happen. Nanapush was bound to suffer for one more day before the satisfied moose toppled over to snore and members of the rescue party Margaret had raised crept up and shot the animal stone dead in its sleep.

The moose, Margaret found, for she had brought with her a meat hatchet, had lost a distressing amount of fat and its meat was now stringy from the long flight and sour with a combination of fear and spent sex, so that in butchering it she winced and moaned and traveled far in her raging thoughts, imagining sore revenges she would exact upon her husband.

In the meantime, Father Damien, who had followed his friend as best he could in the parish touring car, was able to assist those who emerged from the bush. He drove Nanapush, raving, to Sister Hildegarde, who was adept at extracting fish-hooks. At the school infirmary, she was not upset to see the bare buttocks of Nana-push sticking straight up in the air. She swabbed the area with iodine and tested the strength of her pliers. With great relief for his friend and a certain amount of pity, Father Damien tried to make him smile: "Don't be ashamed of your display. Even the Virgin Mary had two asses, one to sit upon and the other ass that bore her to Egypt."

Nanapush only nodded gloomily and gritted his teeth as Sister Hildegarde pushed the hook with the pliers until the barbed tip broke through his tough skin, then clipped the barb off and pulled out the rest of the hook.

"Is there any chance," he weakly croaked once the operation was accomplished, "that this will affect my manhood?"

"Unfortunately not," Hildegarde said.

The lovemaking skills of Nanapush, whole or damaged, were to remain untested until after his death. For Margaret took a long time punishing her husband. She ignored him, she browbeat him, and worst of all, she cooked for him.

It was the winter of instructional beans, for every time Margaret boiled up a pot of rock-hard pellets drawn from the fifty-pound sack of beans that were their only sustenance besides the sour strings of meat, she reminded Nanapush of each brainless turning point last fall at which he should have killed the moose but did not.

"And my," she sneered then, "wasn't its meat both tender and sweet before you ran it to rags?"

She never boiled the beans quite soft enough, either, for she could will her own body to process the toughest sinew with no trouble. Nanapush, however, suffered digestive torments of a nature that soon became destructive to his health and ruined their nightly rest entirely, for that is when the great explosive winds would gather in his body. His *boogidiwinan*, which had always been manly, yet meek enough to remain under his control, overwhelmed the power of his *ojiid*, and there was nothing he could do but surrender to their whims and force. At least it was a form of revenge on Margaret, he thought, exhausted, near dawn. But at the same time he worried that she would leave him. Already, she made him sleep on a pile of skins near the door so as not to pollute her flowered mattress.

"My precious one," he sometimes begged, "can you not spare me? Boil the beans a while longer, and the moose, as well. Have pity!"

She only raised her brow, and her glare was a slice of knifelike light. Maybe she was angriest because she'd softened toward him during that moose ride across the lake, and now she was determined to punish him for her uncharacteristic lapse into tenderness. At any rate, one night she boiled the beans only long enough to soften their skins and threw in a chunk of moose that was coated with a green mold she claimed was medicinal, but which tied poor Nanapush's guts in knots.

"Eat up, old man." She banged the plate down before him. He saw that she was implacable, and then he thought back to the way he had got around the impasse of the maple syrup before, and resolved to do exactly the opposite of what he felt. And so, resigned to sacrificing this night to pain, desperate, he proceeded to loudly enjoy the beans.

"They are excellent, *niwiiw*, crunchy and fine! *Minopogwad!*" He wolfed them down, eager as a boy, and tore at the moldy moose as though presented with the finest morsels. "Howah! I've never eaten such a fine dish!" He rubbed his belly and smiled in false satisfaction.

"*Nindebisinii*, my pretty fawn, oh, how well I'll sleep." He rolled up his blankets by the door, then, and waited for the gas pains to tear him apart.

They did come. That night was phenomenal. Margaret was sure that the cans of grease rattled on the windowsill, and she saw a glowing stench rise around her husband, saw with her own eyes but chose to plug her ears with wax and turn to the wall, poking an airhole for herself in the mud between logs, and so she fell asleep not knowing that the symphony of sounds that disarranged papers and blew out the door by morning were her husband's last utterances.

Yes, he was dead. She found when she went to shake him awake the next morning that he was utterly lifeless. She gave a shriek then, of abysmal loss, and began to weep with sudden horror at the depth of her unforgiving nature. She kissed his face all over, patted his hands and hair. He did not look as though death had taken him, no, he looked oddly well. Although it would seem that a death of this sort would shrivel him like a spent sack and leave him wrinkled and limp, he was shut tight and swollen, his mouth a firm line and his eyes squeezed shut as though holding something in. And he was stiff as a horn where she used to love him. There was some mistake! Perhaps, thought Margaret, wild in her grief, he was only deeply asleep and she could love him back awake.

She climbed aboard and commenced to ride him until she herself collapsed, exhausted and weeping, on his still breast. It was no use. His manliness still stood straight up and although she could swear the grim smile had deepened on his face, there were no other signs of life—no breath, not the faintest heartbeat could be detected. Margaret fell beside him, senseless, and was found there disheveled and out cold so that at first Father Damien thought the two had committed a double suicide, as some old people did those hard winters. But Margaret was soon roused. The cabin was aired out. Father Damien, ravaged with the loss, held his old friend Nanapush's hand all day and allowed his own tears to flow, soaking his black gown.

And so it was. The wake and the funeral were conducted in the old way. Margaret prepared his body. She cleaned him, wrapped him in her best quilt. As there was no disguising his bone-tough hard-on, she let it stand there proudly and decided not to be ashamed of her old man's prowess. She laid him on the bed that was her pride, and bitterly regretted how she'd forced him to sleep on the floor in the cold wind by the door.

Everyone showed up that night, bringing food and even a bit of wine, but Margaret wanted nothing of their comfort. Sorrow bit deep into her lungs and the pain radiated out like the shooting rays of a star. She lost her breath. A dizzy veil fell over her. She wanted most of all to express to her husband the terrible depth of the love she felt but had been too proud, too stingy, or, she now saw, too afraid to show him while he lived. She had deprived him of such pleasure: that great horn in his pants, she knew guiltily, was there because she had denied him physical satisfaction ever since the boat ride behind the moose.

"*Nimanendam.* If only he'd come back to me, I'd make him a happy man." She blew her nose on a big white dishcloth and bowed her head. Whom would she scold? Whom would she punish? Who would suffer for Margaret Kashpaw now? What was she to do? She dropped her face into her hands and wept with uncharacteristic abandon. The whole crowd of Nanapush's friends and loved ones, packed into the house, lifted a toast to the old man and made a salute. At last, Father Damien spoke, and his speech was so eloquent that in moments the whole room was bathed in tears and sobs.

It was at that moment, in the depth of their sorrow, just at the hour when they felt the loss of Nanapush most keenly, that a great explosion occurred, a rip of sound. A vicious cloud of stink sent mourners gasping for air. As soon as the fresh winter cold had rolled into the house, however, everyone returned. Nanapush sat straight up, still wrapped in Margaret's best quilt.

"I just couldn't hold it in anymore," he said, embarrassed to find such an assembly of people around him. He proceeded, then, to drink a cup of the mourners' wine. He was unwrapped. He stretched his arms. The wine made him voluble.

"Friends," he said, "how it fills my heart to see you here. I did, indeed, visit the spirit world and there I saw my former wives, now married to other men. Quill was there, and is now making me a pair of *makizinan* beaded on the soles, to wear when I travel there for good. Friends, do not fear. On the other side of life there is plenty of food and no government agents."

Nanapush then rose from the bed and walked among the people tendering greetings and messages from their dead loved ones. At last, however, he came to Margaret, who sat in the corner frozen in shock at her husband's resurrection. "Oh, how I missed my old lady!" he cried and opened his arms to her. But just as she started forward, eager at his forgiveness, he remembered the beans, dropped his arms, and stepped back.

"No matter how I love you," he said then, "I would rather go to the spirit world than stay here and eat your cooking!"

With that, he sank to the floor quite cold and lifeless again. He was carried to the bed and wrapped in the quilt once more, but his body was closely watched for signs of revival. Nobody yet quite believed that he was gone, and it took some time—in fact, they feasted far into the night—before everyone, including poor Margaret, addled now with additional rage and shame, felt certain that he was gone. Of course, just as everyone had accepted the reality of his demise, Nanapush again jerked upright and his eyes flipped open.

"Oh, yai!" exclaimed one of the old ladies. "He lives yet!"

And although everyone well hid their irritation, it was inevitable that there were some who were impatient. "If you're dead, stay dead," someone muttered. Nobody was so heartless as to express this feeling straight out.

There was just a slow but certain drifting away of people from the house and it wasn't long, indeed, before even Father Damien had left. He was thrilled to have his old friend back, but in his tactful way intuited that Margaret and Nanapush had much to mend between them and needed to be alone to do it.

Once everyone was gone, Nanapush went over to the door and put the bar down. Then he turned to his wife and spoke before she could say a word.

"I returned for one reason only, my wife. When I was gone and far away, I felt how you tried to revive me with the heat of your body. I was happy you tried to do that—my heart was full. This time when I left with harsh words on my lips about your cooking, I got a ways down the road leading to the spirit world and I just couldn't go any farther, my dear woman, because I had wronged you. I wanted to make things smooth between us. I came back to love you good."

And, between the confusion, the grief, the exhaustion and bewilderment, Margaret hadn't the wit to do anything but go to her husband and allow all the hidden sweetness of her nature to join the fire he kindled, so that they spent together, in her spring bed, the finest and most elegantly accomplished hours that perhaps lovers ever spent on earth. And when it was over they both fell asleep, and although only Margaret woke up, her heart was at peace.

Margaret would not have Nanapush buried in the ground, but high in a tree, the old way, as Ojibweg did before the priests came. A year later, his bones and the tattered quilt were put into a box and set under a grave house just at the edge of her yard. The grave house was well built, carefully painted in spanking white, and had a small window with a shelf where Margaret always left food. Sometimes she left Nanapush a plate of ill-cooked beans because she missed his complaints, but more often she cooked his favorites, seasoned his meat with maple syrup, pampered and pitied him the way she hadn't dared in life for fear he'd get the better of her, though she wondered why that had ever mattered, now, without him in the simple quiet of her endless life.

Summer 1913/*Miskomini-Geezis*/ Raspberry Sun

Louise Erdrich

PAULINE

The first time she drowned in the cold and glassy waters of Matchimanito, Fleur Pillager was only a child. Two men saw the boat tip, saw her struggle in the waves. They rowed over to the place she went down, and jumped in. When they lifted her over the gunwales, she was cold to the touch and stiff, so they slapped her face, shook her by the heels, worked her arms, and pounded her back until she coughed up lake water. She shivered all over like a dog, then took a breath. But it wasn't long afterward that those two men disappeared. The first wandered off and the other, Jean Hat, got himself run over by his own surveyor's cart.

It went to show, the people said. It figured to them all right. By saving Fleur Pillager, those two had lost themselves.

The next time she fell in the lake, Fleur Pillager was fifteen years old and no one touched her. She washed on shore, her skin a dull dead gray, but when George Many Women bent to look closer, he saw her chest move. Then her eyes spun open, clear black agate, and she looked at him. "You take my place," she hissed. Everybody scattered and left her there, so no one knows how she dragged herself home. Soon after that we noticed Many Women changed, grew afraid, wouldn't leave his house and would not be forced to go near water or guide the mappers back into the bush. For his caution, he lived until the day that his sons brought him a new tin bathtub. Then the first time he used it he slipped, got knocked out, and breathed water while his wife stood in the other room frying breakfast.

Men stayed clear of Fleur Pillager after the second drowning. Even though she was good-looking, nobody dared to court her because it was clear that *Misshepeshu*, the water man, the monster, wanted her for himself. He's a devil, that one, love hungry with desire and maddened for the touch of young girls, the strong and daring especially, the ones like Fleur.

Our mothers warn us that we'll think he's handsome, for he appears with green eyes, copper skin, a mouth tender as a child's. But if you fall into his arms, he sprouts horns, fangs, claws, fins. His feet are joined as one and his skin, brass scales, rings to the touch. You're fascinated, cannot move. He casts a shell necklace at your feet, weeps gleaming chips that harden into mica on your breasts. He holds you under. Then he takes the body of a lion, a fat brown worm, or a familiar man. He's made of gold. He's made of beach moss. He's a thing of dry foam, a thing of death by drowning, the death a Chippewa cannot survive.

Unless you are Fleur Pillager. We all knew she couldn't swim. After the first time, we thought she'd keep to herself, live quiet, stop killing men off by drowning in the lake. We thought she would keep the good ways. But then, after the second return, and after old Nanapush nursed her through the sickness, we knew that we were dealing with something much more serious. Alone out there, she went haywire, out of control. She messed with evil, laughed at the old women's advice, and dressed like a man. She got herself into some half-forgotten medicine, studied ways we shouldn't talk about. Some say she kept the finger of a child in her pocket and a powder of unborn rabbits in a leather thong around her neck. She laid the heart of an owl on her tongue so she could see at night, and went out, hunting, not even in her own body. We know for sure because the next morning, in the snow or dust, we followed the tracks of her bare feet and saw where they changed, where the claws sprang out, the pad broadened and pressed into the dirt. By night we heard her chuffing cough, the bear cough. By day her silence and the wide grin she threw to bring down our guard made us frightened. Some thought that Fleur Pillager should be driven from the reservation, but not a single person who spoke like that had the nerve. And finally, when people were just about to get together and throw her out, she left on her own and didn't come back all summer. That's what I'm telling about.

During those months, when Fleur lived a few miles south in Argus, things happened. She almost destroyed that town.

When she got down to Argus in the year of 1913, it was just a grid of six streets on either side of the railroad depot. There were two elevators, one central, the other a few miles west. Two stores competed for the trade of the three hundred citizens, and three churches quarreled with one another for their souls. There was a frame building for Lutherans, a heavy brick one for Episcopalians, and a long narrow shingle Catholic church. This last had a slender steeple, twice as high as any building or tree.

No doubt, across the low flat wheat, watching from the road as she came near on foot, Fleur saw that steeple rise, a shadow thin as a needle. Maybe in that raw space it drew her the way a lone tree draws lightning. Maybe, in the end, the Catholics are to blame. For if she hadn't seen that sign of pride, that slim prayer, that marker, maybe she would have just kept walking.

But Fleur Pillager turned, and the first place she went once she came into town was to the back door of the priest's residence attached to the landmark church.

She didn't go there for a handout, although she got that, but to ask for work. She got that too, or we got her. It's hard to tell which came out worse, her or the men or the town, although as always Fleur lived.

The men who worked at the butcher's had carved about a thousand carcasses between them, maybe half of that steers and the other half pigs, sheep, and game like deer, elk, and bear. That's not even mentioning the chickens, which were beyond counting. Pete Kozka owned the place, and employed three men: Lily Veddar, Tor Grunewald, and Dutch James.

I got to Argus through Dutch. He was making a mercantile delivery to the reservation when he met my father's sister Regina, a Puyat and then a Kashpaw through her first husband. Dutch didn't change her name right off, that came later. He never did adopt her son, Russell, whose father lived somewhere in Montana now.

During the time I stayed with them, I hardly saw Dutch or Regina look each other in the eye or talk. Perhaps it was because, except for me, the Puyats were known as a quiet family with little to say. We were mixed-bloods, skinners in the clan for which the name was lost. In the spring before the winter that took so many Chippewa, I bothered my father into sending me south, to the white town. I had decided to learn the lace-making trade from nuns.

"You'll fade out there," he said, reminding me that I was lighter than my sisters. "You won't be an Indian once you return."

"Then maybe I won't come back," I told him. I wanted to be like my mother, who showed her half-white. I wanted to be like my grandfather, pure Canadian. That was because even as a child I saw that to hang back was to perish. I saw through the eyes of the world outside of us. I would not speak our language. In English, I told my father we should build an outhouse with a door that swung open and shut.

"We don't have such a thing upon our house." He laughed. But he scorned me when I would not bead, when I refused to prick my fingers with quills, or hid rather than rub brains on the stiff skins of animals.

"I was made for better," I told him. "Send me down to your sister." So he did. But I did not learn to thread and work the bobbins and spools. I swept the floors in a butcher shop, and cared for my cousin Russell.

Every day I took him to the shop and we set to work—sprinkled fresh sawdust, ran a hambone across the street to a customer's beanpot or a package of sausage to the corner. Russell took the greater share of orders, worked the harder. Though young, he was fast, reliable. He never stopped to watch a cloud pass, or a spider secure a fly with the same quick care as Pete wrapped a thick steak for the doctor. Russell and I were different. He never sat to rest, never fell to wishing he owned a pair of shoes like those that passed on the feet of white girls, shoes of hard red leather decorated with cut holes. He never listened to what those girls said about him, or imagined them doubling back to catch him by the hand. In truth, I hardly rinsed through the white girls' thoughts.

That winter, we had no word from my family, although Regina asked. No one knew yet how many were lost, people kept no track. We heard that wood could not be sawed fast enough to build the houses for their graves, and there were so few people strong enough to work, anyway, that by the time they got around to it the brush had grown, obscuring the new-turned soil, the marks of burials. The priests tried to discourage the habit of burying the dead in trees, but the ones they dragged down had no names to them, just scraps of their belongings. Sometimes in my head I had a dream I could not shake. I saw my sisters and my mother swaying in the branches, buried too high to reach, wrapped in lace I never hooked.

I tried to stop myself from remembering what it was like to have companions, to have my mother and sisters around me, but when Fleur came to us that June, I remembered. I made excuses to work next to her, I questioned her, but Fleur refused to talk about the Puyats or about the winter. She shook her head, looked away. She touched my face once, as if by accident, or to quiet me, and said that perhaps my family had moved north to avoid the sickness, as some mixed-bloods did.

I was fifteen, alone, and so poor-looking I was invisible to most customers and to the men in the shop. Until they needed me, I blended into the stained brown walls, a skinny big-nosed girl with staring eyes.

From this, I took what advantage I could find. Because I could fade into a corner or squeeze beneath a shelf I knew everything: how much cash there was in the till, what the men joked about when no one was around, and what they did to Fleur.

Kozka's Meats served farmers for a fifty-mile radius, both to slaughter, for it had a stockpen and chute, and to cure the meat by smoking it or spicing it in sausage. The storage locker was a marvel, made of many thicknesses of brick, earth insulation, and Minnesota timber, lined inside with wood shavings and vast blocks of ice cut from the deepest end of Matchimanito, hauled down from the reservation each winter by horse and sled.

A ramshackle board building, part killing shed, part store, was fixed to the low square of the lockers. That's where Fleur worked. Kozka hired her for her strength. She could lift a haunch or carry a pole of sausages without stumbling, and she soon learned cutting from Fritzie, a string-thin blond who chain-smoked and handled the razor-edged knives with nerveless precision, slicing close to her stained fingers. The two women worked afternoons, wrapping their cuts in paper, and Fleur carried the packages to the lockers. Russell liked to help her. He vanished when I called, took none of my orders, but I soon learned that he could always be found alongside Fleur's hip, one hand gently pinching a fold of her skirt, so delicately that she could pretend not to notice.

Of course, she did. She knew the effect she had on men, even the very youngest of them. She swayed them, sotted them, made them curious about her habits, drew them close with careless ease, and cast them off with the same indifference. She was good to Russell, it is true, even fussed about him like a mother, combed his hair with her fingers, and scolded me for kicking or teasing him.

Fleur poked bits of sugar between Russell's lips when we sat for meals, skimmed the cream from the jar when Fritzie's back was turned and spooned it into his mouth. For work, she gave him small packages to carry when she and Fritzie piled cut meat outside the locker's heavy doors, opened only at five p.m. each afternoon, before the men ate supper.

Sometimes Dutch, Tor, and Lily stayed at the lockers after closing, and when they did Russell and I stayed too, cleaned the floors, restoked the fires in the front smokehouse, while the men sat around the squat, cold cast-iron stove spearing slats of herring onto hardtack bread. They played long games of poker, or cribbage on a board made from the planed end of a salt crate. They talked. We ate our bread and the ends of sausages, watched and listened, although there wasn't much to hear since almost nothing ever happened in Argus. Tor was married, Dutch lived with Regina, and Lily read circulars. They mainly discussed the auctions to come, equipment, or women.

Every so often, Pete Kozka came out front to make a whist, leaving Fritzie to smoke her cigarettes and fry raised donuts in the back room. He sat and played a few rounds but kept his thoughts to himself. Fritzie did not tolerate him talking behind her back, and the one book he read was the New Testament. If he said something, it concerned weather or a surplus of wheat. He had a good-luck talisman, the opal-white lens of a cow's eye. Playing rummy, he rubbed it between his fingers. That soft sound and the slap of cards was about the only conversation.

Fleur finally gave them a subject.

Her cheeks were wide and flat, her hands large, chapped, muscular. Fleur's shoulders were broad and curved as a yoke, her hips fishlike, slippery, narrow. An old green dress clung to her waist, worn thin where she sat. Her glossy braids were like the tails of animals, and swung against her when she moved, deliberately, slowly in her work, held in and half-tamed. But only half. I could tell, but the others never noticed. They never looked into her sly brown eyes or noticed her teeth, strong and sharp and very white. Her legs were bare, and since she padded in beadworked moccasins they never saw that her fifth toes were missing. They never knew she'd drowned. They were blinded, they were stupid, they only saw her in the flesh.

And yet it wasn't just that she was a Chippewa, or even that she was a woman, it wasn't that she was good-looking or even that she was alone that made their brains hum. It was how she played cards.

Women didn't usually play with men, so the evening that Fleur drew a chair to the men's table there was a shock of surprise.

"What's this," said Lily. He was fat, with a snake's pale eyes and precious skin, smooth and lily-white, which is how he got his name. Lily had a dog, a stumpy mean little bull of a thing with a belly drum-tight from eating pork rinds. The dog was as fond of the cards as Lily, and straddled his barrel thighs through games of stud, rum poker, *vingt-un.** The dog snapped at Fleur's arm that first night, but cringed back, its snarl frozen, when she took her place.

"I thought," she said, her voice soft and stroking, "you might deal me in."

There was a space between the lead bin of spiced flour and the wall where Russell and I just fit. He tried to inch toward Fleur's skirt, to fit against her. Who knew but

* Twenty-one in French.

that he might have brought her luck like Lily's dog, except I sensed we'd be driven away if the men noticed us and so I pulled him back by the suspenders. We hunkered down, my arm around his neck. Russell smelled of caraway and pepper, of dust and sour dirt. He watched the game with tense interest for a minute or so, then went limp, leaned against me, and dropped his mouth wide. I kept my eyes open, saw Fleur's black hair swing over the chair, her feet solid on the boards of the floor. I couldn't see on the table where the cards slapped, so after they were deep in their game I pressed Russell down and raised myself in the shadows, crouched on a sill of wood.

I watched Fleur's hands stack and riffle, divide the cards, spill them to each player in a blur, rake and shuffle again. Tor, short and scrappy, shut one eye and squinted the other at Fleur. Dutch screwed his lips around a wet cigar.

"Gotta see a man," he mumbled, getting up to go out back to the privy. The others broke, left their cards, and Fleur sat alone in the lamplight that glowed in a sheen across the push of her breasts. I watched her closely, then she paid me a beam of notice for the first time. She turned, looked straight at me, and grinned the white wolf grin a Pillager turns on its victims, except that she wasn't after me.

"Pauline there," she said. "How much money you got?"

We had all been paid for the week that day. Eight cents was in my pocket.

"Stake me." She held out her long fingers. I put the coins on her palm and then I melted back to nothing, part of the walls and tables, twined close with Russell. It wasn't long before I understood something that I didn't know then. The men would not have seen me no matter what I did, how I moved. For my dress hung loose and my back was already stooped, an old woman's. Work had roughened me, reading made my eyes sore, forgetting my family had hardened my face, and scrubbing down bare boards had given me big, reddened knuckles.

When the men came back and sat around the table, they had drawn together. They shot each other small glances, stuck their tongues in their cheeks, burst out laughing at odd moments, to rattle Fleur. But she never minded. They played their *vingt-un*, staying even as Fleur slowly gained. Those pennies I had given her drew nickels and attracted dimes until there was a small pile in front of her.

Then she hooked them with five card draw, nothing wild. She dealt, discarded, drew, and then she sighed and her cards gave a little shiver. Tor's eye gleamed, and Dutch straightened in his seat.

"I'll pay to see that hand," said Lily Veddar.

Fleur showed, and she had nothing there, nothing at all. Tor's thin smile cracked open, and he threw in his hand too. "Well, we know one thing," he said, leaning back in his chair, "the squaw can't bluff."

With that I lowered myself into a mound of swept sawdust and slept. I woke during the night, but none of them had moved yet so I couldn't either. Still later, the men must have gone out again, or Fritzie come to break the game, because I was lifted, soothed, cradled in a woman's arms and rocked so quiet that I kept my eyes shut while Fleur rolled first me, then Russell, into a closet of grimy ledgers, oiled paper, balls of string, and thick files that fit beneath us like a mattress.

The game went on after work the next evening. Russell slept, I got my eight cents back five times over, and Fleur kept the rest of the dollar she'd won for a stake. This time they didn't play so late, but they played regular, and then kept going at it. They stuck with poker, or variations, for one solid week and each time Fleur won exactly one dollar, no more and no less, too consistent for luck.

By this time, Lily and the other men were so lit with suspense that they got Pete to join the game. They concentrated, the fat dog tense in Lily Veddar's lap, Tor suspicious, Dutch stroking his huge square brow, Pete steady. It wasn't that Fleur won that hooked them in so, because she lost hands too. It was rather that she never had a freak deal or even anything above a straight. She only took on her low cards, which didn't sit right. By chance, Fleur should have gotten a full or a flush by now. The irritating thing was she beat with pairs and never bluffed, because she couldn't, and still she ended each night with exactly one dollar. Lily couldn't believe, first of all, that a woman could be smart enough to play cards, but even if she was, that she would then be stupid enough to cheat for a dollar a night. By day I watched him turn the problem over, his lard-white face dull, small fingers probing at his knuckles, until he finally thought he had Fleur figured as a bit-time player, caution her game. Raising the stakes would throw her.

More than anything now, he wanted Fleur to come away with something but a dollar. Two bits less or ten more, the sum didn't matter just so he broke her streak.

Night after night she played, won her dollar, and left to stay in a place that only Russell and I knew about. Fritzie had done two things of value for Fleur. She had given her a black umbrella with a stout handle and material made to shed water, and also let her board on the premises. Every night, Fleur bathed in the slaughtering tub, then slept in the unused brick smokehouse behind the lockers, a windowless place tarred on the inside with scorched fats. When I brushed against her skin I noticed that she smelled of the walls, rich and woody, slightly burnt. Since that night she put me in the closet, I was no longer jealous or afraid of her, but followed her close as Russell, closer, stayed with her, became her moving shadow that the men never noticed, the shadow that could have saved her.

August, the month that bears fruit, closed around the shop and Pete and Fritzie left for Minnesota to escape the heat. A month running, Fleur had won thirty dollars and only Pete's presence had kept Lily at bay. But Pete was gone now, and one payday, with the heat so bad no one could move but Fleur, the men sat and played and waited while she finished work. The cards sweat, limp in their fingers, the table was slick with grease, and even the walls were warm to the touch. The air was motionless. Fleur was in the next room boiling heads.

Her green dress, drenched, wrapped her like a transparent sheet. A skin of lakeweed. Black snarls of veining clung to her arms. Her braids were loose, half unraveled, tied behind her neck in a thick loop. She stood in steam, turning skulls through a vat with a wooden paddle. When scraps boiled to the surface, she bent with a round tin sieve and scooped them out. She'd filled two dishpans.

"Ain't that enough now?" called Lily. "We're waiting." The stump of a dog trembled in his lap, alive with rage. It never smelled me or noticed me above Fleur's smoky skin. The air was heavy in the corner, and pressed Russell and me down. Fleur sat with the men.

"Now what do you say?" Lily asked the dog. It barked. That was the signal for the real game to start.

"Let's up the ante," said Lily, who had been stalking this night for weeks. He had a roll of money in his pocket. Fleur had five bills in her dress. Each man had saved his full pay that the bank officer had drawn from the Kozkases' account.

"Ante a dollar then," said Fleur, and pitched hers in. She lost, but they let her scrape along, a cent at a time. And then she won some. She played unevenly, as if chance were all she had. She reeled them in. The game went on. The dog was stiff now, poised on Lily's knees, a ball of vicious muscle with its yellow eyes slit in concentration. It gave advice, seemed to sniff the lay of Fleur's cards, twitched and nudged. Fleur was up, then down, saved by a scratch. Tor dealt seven cards, three down. The pot grew, round by round, until it held all the money. Nobody folded. Then it all rode on one last card and they went silent. Fleur picked hers up and drew a long breath. The heat lowered like a bell. Her card shook, but she stayed in.

Lily smiled and took the dog's head tenderly between his palms.

"Say Fatso," he said, crooning the words. "You reckon that girl's bluffing?"

The dog whined and Lily laughed. "Me too," he said. "Let's show." He tossed his bills and coins into the pot and then they turned their cards over.

Lily looked once, looked again, then he squeezed the dog like a fist of dough and slammed it on the table.

Fleur threw out her arms and swept the money close, grinning that same wolf grin that she'd used on me, the grin that had them. She jammed the bills inside her dress, scooped the coins in waxed white paper that she tied with string.

"Another round," said Lily, his voice choked with burrs. But Fleur opened her mouth and yawned, then walked out back to gather slops for the big hog that was waiting in the stockpen to be killed.

The men sat still as rocks, their hands spread on the oiled wood table. Dutch had chewed his cigar to damp shreds, Tor's eye was dull. Lily's gaze was the only one to follow Fleur. Russell and I didn't breathe. I felt them gathering, saw Dutch's veins, the ones in his forehead that stood out in anger. The dog rolled off the table and curled in a knot below the counter, where none of the men could touch him.

Lily rose and stepped to the closet of ledgers where Pete kept his private stock. He brought back a bottle, uncorked and tipped it between his fingers. The lump in his throat moved, then he passed it on. They drank, steeped in the whiskey's fire, and planned with their eyes things they couldn't say aloud.

When they left, I grabbed Russell by the arm, dragged him along. We followed, hid in the clutter of broken boards and chicken crates beside the stockpen, where the men settled. Fleur could not be seen at first, and then the moon broke and showed her, slipping cautiously along the rough board chute with a bucket in her hand.

Her hair fell wild and coarse to her waist, and her dress was a floating patch in the dark. She made a pig-calling sound, rang the tin pail lightly against the wood, paused suspiciously. But too late. In the sound of the ring Lily moved, fat and nimble, stepped right behind Fleur and put out his creamy hands. Russell strained forward and I stopped his mouth with both fists before he yelled. At Lily's first touch, Fleur whirled and doused him with the bucket of sour slops. He pushed her against the big fence and the package of coins split, went clinking and jumping, winked against the wood. Fleur rolled over once and vanished into the yard.

The moon fell behind a curtain of ragged clouds, and Lily followed into the dark muck. But he tripped, pitched over the huge flank of the pig, who lay mired to the snout, heavily snoring. Russell and I sprang from the weeds and climbed the boards of the pen, stuck like glue. We saw the sow rise to her neat, knobby knees, gain her balance and sway, curious, as Lily stumbled forward. Fleur had backed into the angle of splintered wood just beyond and when Lily tried to jostle past, the sow raised her powerful neck and suddenly struck, quick and hard as a snake. She plunged at Lily's thick waist and snatched a mouthful of shirt. She lunged again, caught him lower so that he grunted in pained surprise. He seemed to ponder, breathing deep. Then he launched his huge bulk in a swimmer's dive.

The sow screamed as his body smacked over hers. She rolled, striking out with her knife-sharp hooves and Lily gathered himself upon her, took her foot-long face by the ears, and scraped her snout and cheeks against the trestles of the pen. He hurled the sow's tight skull against an iron post, but instead of knocking her dead, he woke her from her dream.

She reared, shrieked, and then he squeezed her so hard that they leaned into each other and posed in a standing embrace. They bowed jerkily, as if to begin. Then his arms swung and flailed. She sank her black fangs into his shoulder, clasping him, dancing him forward and backward through the pen. Their steps picked up pace, went wild. The two dipped as one, box-stepped, tripped one another. She ran her split foot through his hair. He grabbed her kinked tail. They went down and came up, the same shape and then the same color until the men couldn't tell one from the other in that light and Fleur was able to vault the gates, swing down, hit gravel.

The men saw, yelled, and chased her at a dead run to the smokehouse. And Lily too, once the sow gave up in disgust and freed him. That is when I should have gone to Fleur, saved her, thrown myself on Dutch the way Russell did once he unlocked my arms. He stuck to his stepfather's leg as if he'd been flung there. Dutch dragged him for a few steps, his leg a branch, then cuffed Russell off and left him shouting and bawling in the sticky weeds. I closed my eyes and put my hands on my ears, so there is nothing more to describe but what I couldn't block out: those yells from Russell, Fleur's hoarse breath, so loud it filled me, her cry in the old language and our names repeated over and over among the words.

The heat was still dense the next morning when I entered slowly through the side door of the shop. Fleur was gone and Russell slunk along the woodwork like a beaten dog. The men were slack-faced, hungover. Lily was paler and softer than ever, as if his flesh had steamed on his bones. They smoked, took pulls off a bottle. It wasn't yet noon. Russell disappeared outside to sit by the stock gate, to hold his own knees and rock back and forth. I worked awhile, waiting shop and sharpening steel. But I was sick, I was smothered, I was sweating so hard that my hands slipped on the knives and I wiped my fingers clean of the greasy touch of the customers' coins. Lily opened his mouth and roared once, not in anger. There was no meaning to the sound. His terrier dog, sprawled limp beside his foot, never lifted its head. Nor did the other men.

They didn't notice when I stepped outdoors to call Russell. And then I forgot the men because I realized that we were all balanced, ready to tip, to fly, to be crushed as soon as the weather broke. The sky was so low that I felt the weight of it like a door. Clouds hung down, witch teats, a tornado's green-brown cones, and as I watched, one flicked out and became a delicate probing thumb. Even as Russell ran to me, the wind blew suddenly, cold, and then came blinding rain.

Inside, the men had vanished and the whole place was trembling as if a huge hand was pinched at the rafters, shaking it. We ran straight through, screaming for Dutch or for any of them. Russell's fingers were clenched in my skirt. I shook him off once, but he darted after and held me close in terror when we stopped. He called for Regina, called for Fleur. The heavy doors of the lockers, where the men had surely taken shelter without us, stood shut. Russell howled. They must have heard him, even above the driving wind, because the two of us could hear, from inside, the barking of that dog. A moment, and everything went still. We didn't dare move in that strange hush of suspension. I listened, Russell too. Then we heard a cry building in the wind, faint at first, a whistle and then a shrill scream that tore through the walls and gathered around the two of us, and at last spoke plain.

It was Russell, I am sure, who first put his arms on the bar, thick iron that was made to slide along the wall and fall across the hasp and lock. He strained and shoved, too slight to move it into place, but he did not look to me for help. Sometimes, thinking back, I see my arms lift, my hands grasp, see myself dropping the beam into the metal grip. At other times, that moment is erased. But always I see Russell's face the moment after, as he turned, as he ran for the door—a peaceful look of complicit satisfaction.

Then the wind plucked him. He flew as though by wires in the seat of his trousers, with me right after, toward the side wall of the shop that rose grand as a curtain, spilling us forward as the building toppled.

Outside, the wind was stronger, a hand held against us. We struggled forward. The bushes tossed, rain battered, the awning flapped off a storefront, the rails of porches rattled. The odd cloud became a fat snout that nosed along the earth and sniffled, jabbed, picked at things, sucked them up, blew them apart, rooted around as if it was following a certain scent, then stopped behind us at the butcher shop and bored down like a drill.

I pitched head over heels along the dirt drive, kept moving and tumbling in such amazement that I felt no fear, past Russell, who was lodged against a small pine.

The sky was cluttered. A herd of cattle flew through the air like giant birds, dropping dung, their mouths opened in stunned bellows. A candle, still lighted, blew past, and tables, napkins, garden tools, a whole school of drifting eyeglasses, jackets on hangers, hams, a checkerboard, a lampshade, and at last the sow from behind the lockers, on the run, her hooves a blur, set free, swooping, diving, screaming as everything in Argus fell apart and got turned upside down, smashed, and thoroughly wrecked.

Days passed before the town went looking for the men. Lily was a bachelor, after all, and Tor's wife had suffered a blow to the head that made her forgetful. Understandable. But what about Regina? That would always remain a question in people's minds. For she said nothing about her husband's absence to anyone. The whole town was occupied with digging out, in high relief because even though the Catholic steeple had been ripped off like a peaked cap and sent across five fields, those huddled in the cellar were unhurt. Walls had fallen, windows were demolished, but the stores were intact and so were the bankers and shop owners who had taken refuge in their safes or beneath their cash registers. It was a fair-minded disaster, no one could be said to have suffered much more than the next, except for Kozka's Meats.

When Pete and Fritzie came home, they found that the boards of the front building had been split to kindling, piled in a huge pyramid, and the shop equipment was blasted far and wide. Pete paced off the distance the iron bathtub had been flung, a hundred feet. The glass candy case went fifty, and landed without so much as a cracked pane. There were other surprises as well, for the back rooms where Fritzie and Pete lived were undisturbed. Fritzie said the dust still coated her china figures, and upon her kitchen table, in the ashtray, perched the last cigarette she'd put out in haste. She lit and finished it, looking through the window. From there, she could see that the old smokehouse Fleur had slept in was crushed to a reddish sand and the stockpens were completely torn apart, the rails stacked helter-skelter. Fritzie asked for Fleur. People shrugged. Then she asked about the others, and suddenly, the town understood that three men were missing.

There was a rally of help, a gathering of shovels and volunteers. We passed boards from hand to hand, stacked them, uncovered what lay beneath the pile of jagged two-by-fours. The lockers, full of meat that was Pete and Fritzie's investment, slowly came into sight, still intact. When enough room was made for a man to stand on the roof, there were calls, a general urge to hack through and see what lay below. But Fritzie shouted that she wouldn't allow it because the meat would spoil. And so the work continued, board by board, until at last the solid doors of the freezer were revealed and people pressed to the entry. It was locked from the outside, someone shouted, wedged down, a tornado's freak whim. Regina stood in the crowd, clutching Russell's collar, trying to hold him against her short, tough body. Everyone wanted to be the first to enter, but only Russell and I were quick enough to slip through beside Pete and Fritzie as they shoved into the sudden icy air.

Pete scraped a match on his boot, lit the lamp Fritzie held, and then the four of us stood in its circle. Light glared off the skinned and hanging carcasses, the crates of wrapped sausages, the bright and cloudy blocks of lake ice, pure as winter. The cold bit into us, pleasant at first, then numbing. We stood there for a moment before we saw the men, or more rightly, the humps of fur, the iced and shaggy hides they wore, the bearskins they had taken down and wrapped about themselves. We stepped closer and Fritzie tilted the lantern beneath the flaps of fur into their faces. The dog was there, perched among them, heavy as a doorstop. The three had hunched around a barrel where the game was still laid out, and a dead lantern and an empty bottle too. But they had thrown down their last hands and hunkered tight, clutching one another, knuckles raw from beating at the door they had also attacked with hooks. Frost stars gleamed off their eyelashes and the stubble of their beards. Their faces were set in concentration, mouths open as if to speak some careful thought, some agreement they'd come to in each other's arms.

Only after they were taken out and laid in the sun to thaw did someone think to determine whether they were all entirely dead, frozen solid. That is when Dutch James's faint heartbeat was discovered.

Power travels in the bloodlines, handed out before birth. It comes down through the hands, which in the Pillagers are strong and knotted, big, spidery and rough, with sensitive fingertips good at dealing cards. It comes through the eyes, too, belligerent, darkest brown, the eyes of those in the bear clan, impolite as they gaze directly at a person.

In my dreams, I look straight back at Fleur, at the men. I am no longer the watcher on the dark sill, the skinny girl.

The blood draws us back, as if it runs through a vein of earth. I left Argus, left Russell and Regina back there with Dutch. I came home and, except for talking to my cousins, live a quiet life. Fleur lives quiet too, down on Matchimanito with her boat. Some say she married the water man, *Misshepeshu*, or that she lives in shame with white men or windigos,* or that she's killed them all. I am about the only one here who ever goes to visit her. That spring, I went to help out in her cabin when she bore the child, whose green eyes and skin the color of an old penny have made more talk, as no one can decide if the child is mixed blood or what, fathered in a smokehouse, or by a man with brass scales, or by the lake. The girl is bold, smiling in her sleep, as if she knows what people wonder, as if she hears the old men talk, turning the story over.

It comes up different every time, and has no ending, no beginning. They get the middle wrong too. They only know they don't know anything.

---

* A windigo is an evil spirit who turns humans into ice.

Almost Soup

Louise Erdrich

WINDIGO DOG

You will end up puppy soup if you're born a pure white dog on the reservation, unless you're one who is extra clever, like me. I survived into my old age through dog magic. That's right. You see me, you see the result of dog wit. Dog skill. Medicine ways I learned from my elders, and want to pass on now to my relatives. You. So listen up, *animoshug*. You're only going to get this knowledge from the real dog's mouth once.

There is a little of a coyote in me, just a touch here in my paws, bigger than a dog's paws. My jaw, too, strong to snap rabbit bones. Prairie-dog bones as well. That's right. Prairie. I don't mind saying to you that I'm not a full-blood Ojibwa reservation dog. I'm part Dakota, born out in *Bwaanakeeng*, transported here. I still remember all that sky, all that pure space, all that blowing dirt of land where I got my name, which has since become legendary.

Here's how it happened.

I was underneath the house one hot slow day panting in the dirt. I was a young thing. Just chubby, too, and like I said white all over. That worried my mother. Every morning she scratched dirt on me, threw me in the mud, rolled me in garbage to disguise my purity. Her words to me were this. My son, you won't survive if you lick your paws. Don't be respectable. Us Indian dogs have got to look as unappetizing as we can! Slink a little, won't you? Stick your ears out. Grow ticks. Fleas. Bite your fur here and there. Strive for a disreputable appearance, my boy. Above all, don't be clean!

Like I say, born pure white you usually don't stand a chance, but me, I took my mama's advice. After all, I was the son of a blend of dogs stretching back to the beginning of time on this continent. We sprang up here. We had no need to cross on any land bridge. We know who we are. Us, we are descended of Original Dog.

I think about her lots, and also about my ancestor, from way way back, the dog named Sorrow who drank a human's milk. I think about her because I know it was the first dog's mercy and the hand-me-down wit of the second that saved my life that time they were boiling the soup.

I hear these words—Get under the house, Melvin, fetch that white puppy now. Bam! My mama throws me in the farthest house corner and sits down on me. I cover up with her but once Melvin is in play distance I can't help it. I've got that curious streak of all the Indian dogs. I peek right around my mother's tail and whoops, he's got me. He drags me out and gives me to a grandma, who stuffs me in a gunnysack and slings me down beside the fire.

I fight the bag there for a while but it's warm and cozy and I go to sleep. I don't think much of it. Just another human habit I'll get used to, this stuffing dogs in sacks. Then I hear them talking.

Sharpen up the knife. Grandma's voice.

That's a nice fat white puppy. Someone else.

He'll make a good soup, but do you think enough to go around? Should we kill another one?

Then, right above me, they start arguing about whether or not I'll feed twenty. Me, just a little chunk of a guy, *owah*! No! I bark. No! No! I'm not enough for even five of your big strong warrior sons. Not me. What am I saying? I'm not enough for any of you! Anybody! No! I'm sour meat. I don't want to be eaten! In response, I get this tap from a grandma shoe, just a tap, but all us dogs know feet language. Be quiet or you'll get a solid one, it means. I shut up. Once I stop barking all I can do is think and I think fast. I think furious. I think desperate puppy thoughts until I know what I'll do the moment they let me out.

A puppy has just one weapon, and there really is no word for it but puppyness. Stuck in that bag, I muster all my puppyness. I call my tail wags and love licks up from deep way back, from the dogs going back to dogs unto the beginning of our association with these strange exasperating things called humans. I hear them stroking the steel on steel. I hear them tapping the boiling water pot. I hear them deciding I'll be enough, just barely. Then daylight. The bag loosens and a grandma draws me forth and just quick, because I'm smart, desperate, and connected with my ancestors, I look for the nearest girl child in the bunch around me. I spot her. I pick her out.

She's a visitor, sitting right there with a cousin, playing, not noting me at all. I give a friendly little whine, a yap, and then, as the grandma hauls me toward the table, a sharp loud bark of fear. That starts out of me. I can't help it. But good thing, because the girl hears it and responds.

"Grandma," she says, "what you going to do with the puppy?"

"Where'smyogleyzigzichaogleyzigzicha," mumbles Grandma, the way they do when trying to hide their actions.

"What?" That gets her little-girl curiosity up, a trait us dogs and children share in equal parts, what makes us love each other so.

"Don't you know, you dummy," shouts that boy cousin in boy knowledge, "Grandma's going to boil it up, make it into soup!"

"Aaay," my girl says, shy and laughing. "Grandma wouldn't do that." And she holds out her hands for me. Which is when I use my age-old Original Dog puppy-ness. I throw puppy love right at her in loopy yo-yos, puppy drool, joy, and big-pawed puppy clabber, ear perks, eye contact, most of all the potent weapon of all puppies, the head cock and puppy grin.

"Gimme him, gimme!"

"Nooo," says Grandma, holding me tight and pursing her lips in that terrible way of grandmas, when they cannot be swayed. But she's dealing with her own descen-dant in its purest form—pure girl. Puppy-loving girl.

"*Grandmagrandmagrandma!*" she shrieks.

"Eeeeh!"

"GIMMEDAPUPPY! GIMMEDAPUPPY!"

Now it's time for me to wiggle, all over, to give the high-quotient adorability wiggle all puppies know. This is life or death. I do it double time, triple time, full of puppy determination, desperate to live.

"Ooooh," says another grandma, sharp-eyed, "quick, throw him in the pot!"

"Noooh," says yet another, "she wants that puppy bad, her."

"Give her that little dog," says a grandpa now, his grandpa heart swelling up. "She wants that dog. So give her that little dog."

My girl's doll-playing fingers are brushing my fur. She's jumping for me. Spinning like a sweet maple seed. Straining up toward her grandma, who at this point can't hold on to me without looking almost supernaturally mean. And so it is, I feel those ancient dog-cooking fingers giving me up before her disappointed voice does.

"Here."

And just like that I'm in the most heavenly of places. Soft, strong girl arms. I'm carried off to be petted and played with, fed scraps, dragged around in a baby car-riage made of an old shoe box, dressed in clothing of tiny brothers and sisters. Yes, I'll do anything. Anything. This is when my naming happens. As we go off I hear the grandpa calling from behind us in amusement, asking the name of the puppy. Me. And my girl calls back, without hesitation, the name I will bear from then on into my age, the name that has given so many of our breedless breed hope, the name that will live on in dogness down through the generations. You've heard it. You know it. Almost Soup.

Now, my brothers and sisters, shortly after I received my name I was transported up north to this reservation. Here on the ground where we now sprawl and scratch, I have lived out my years of strength, fertility, and purpose. As you see, I have survived into my tranquil old age. It is said of course by Ojibwas that those Indians who live on the plains eat dogs while they, the woods Indians, eat rabbits. However, it is my dog experience that this is not entirely true. I tell you now, relatives and friends, it is best to beware. Even in Ojibwa country, we are not out of danger.

There are, of course, the slick and deadly wheels of reservation cars. Poisons, occasionally, set out for our weaker cousins the mice and rats. Not to speak of the coyotes, the paw-snapping jaws of clever Ojibwa trapper steel. And we may happen into the snares set as well for our enemies. Lynx. Marten. Feral cats. Bears whom of course we worship. I learned early. Eat anything you can at any time. Fast. Bolt it down. Stay cute, but stay elusive. Don't let them think twice when they've got the hatchet out. I see cold steel, I'm gone. Believe it. And there are of course all sorts of illnesses we dread. Avoid the bite of the fox. It is madness. Avoid all bats. Avoid all black-and-white-striped moving objects. And slow things with spiny quills. Avoid all humans when they get into a feasting mood. Get near the tables fast, though, once the food is cooked. Stay close to their feet. Stay ready.

But don't steal from their plates.

Avoid medicine men. Snakes. Boys with BB guns. Anything ropelike or easily used to hang or tie. Avoid outhouse holes. Cats that live indoors. Do not sleep under cars. Or with horses. Do not eat anything attached to a skinny, burning string. Do not eat lard from the table. Do not go into the house at all unless no one is watching. Do not, unless you are absolutely certain you can blame it on a cat, eat any of their chickens. Do not eat pies. Do not eat decks of cards, plastic jugs, dry beans, dish sponges. If you must eat a shoe, eat both of the pair, every scrap, untraceable. Sit quietly when they talk of powwows. Slink into the woods when they pack the vans. You could get left behind in *Bwaanakeeng*. Dog soup, remember? Dog muffins. Dog hot-dish. Don't even think of hitching along.

Always, when in doubt, the rule is you are better off underneath the steps. Don't chase cars driven by young teenage boys. Don't chase cars driven by old ladies. Don't bark or growl at men cradling rifles. Don't get wet in winter, and don't let yourself dry out when the hot winds of August blow. We're not equipped to sweat. Keep your mouth open. Visit the lake. Pee often. Take messages from tree stumps and the corners of buildings. Don't forget to leave in return a polite and respectful hello. You never know when it will come in handy, your contact, your friend. You never know whom you will need to rely upon.

Which is how I come to my next story of survival.

Within the deep lakes of the Ojibwa there is supposed to live a kind of man-monster-cat thing that tips boats over in the cold of spring and plucks down into his arms the sexiest women. Keeping this cranky old thing happy is the job of local Indian humans and they're always throwing their tobacco in the water, talking to the waves. But when the monster takes a person in whatever way—usually by drowning—there is some deeper, older, hungrier urge that must be satisfied by a stronger item than tobacco. You guessed it. Lay low, *animoshug*. I tell you, when a man goes out drunk in his motorboat, hide. Say he's just good-timing, lapping beer, driving his boat in circles, and hits his own wake coming at him. Pops out of the boat. Goes down.

Humans call that fate. We dogs call that stupidity. Whatever you name it, there's always a good chance they'll come looking for a dog. A white dog. One to tie with red ribbons. Brush nice. Truss in a rope. Feed a steak or two. Pray over. Pet soft. Not worth it. Stones around the neck. Then, splash. Dog offering!

My friends and relatives, we have walked down the prayer road clearing the way for humans since before time started. We have gone ahead of them to present their good points to the gatekeeper at that soft pasture where they eat all day and gamble the night away. Don't forget, though, in heaven we still just get the bones they toss. We have kept our humans company in darkest hours. Saved them from starvation—you know how. We have talked to their gods on their behalf and thrown ourselves in front of their wheels to save them from idiotic journeys, to the bootlegger's, say. We're glad to do these things. As an old race, we know our purpose. Original Dog walked alongside *Wenabojo*, their tricky creator. The dog is bound to the human. Raised alongside the human. With the human. Still, half the time we know better than the human.

We have lain next to our personal human shrouded in red calico. We have let our picked-clean ceremonial dog bones be reverently buried in bark houses. We have warned off bad spirits from their babies, and talked to the irritating ghosts of their suicide uncles and aunts. We have always given of ourselves. We have always thought of humans first. And yet, for me, when Fatty Simon went down I did not hesitate. I took to the woods. I had puppies, after all, to provide for. I had a life. Next time, there was a guardrail accident way up on the bridge and Agnes Anderson met her end that way. Again, not me. Not me tied like a five-cent bundle and tossed overboard. Not when the lake took Alberta Meyer or the Speigelrein girls, not when old Kagewah fell through that spring sitting in his icehouse or even when our track star Morris Shawano disappeared and his dad's boat washed up to the north. Not me. Not Almost Soup. *Bungeenaboop.* In the Ojibwa language, that is my name and I refuse to give it up for human mistakes or human triumphs.

I refused, that is, until my girl weakened and got sick.

Cally was her name. The girl who saved my life. She loved me best of any other dog, put me up there with her human loves. As I told you she saved my life, but also saved me from worse—you know. (And now I specifically address my brothers, the snip-snip. The big C. the little n. The words we all know and watch for in their plans and conversations.) My little Cally hid me whenever her Mama tried to drag me to the vet. Thus, she saved my male doghood and allowed me full dogness. I have had, as a result of her courage, the honor of carrying our dogline down the generations. For this, alone, how could I ever thank her enough? And then she got sick, as I say.

One foul night in a blizzard far off in the bush, she got sick with a fever and a cough and it worsened, worsened, until the truth is, I sensed the presence of the black dog. We all know the great black dog. That is, death. He smells like iron cold. Sparks fly from his fur. He is the one who drags the creaking cart made of sticks. We have all heard the wheels groan as they turned, and hoped they kept on past our house. But on that cold late winter night, up north, he stopped. I heard his hound breath, felt the heat of his lungs of steam and fire.

Lazy Stitch

ALMOST SOUP

Curled underneath the beading table with the unshoed feet of women, you hear things you'd never want to know. Or things you do. Maybe it's the needles, Poney Number Twelve, so straight and fine they slip right through the toughest hide. Maybe it is my own big ears that catch everything, and more. Maybe it's the colors of the seed beads that work up in stitches so intimate and small—collect, collect—until you have a pattern to the anguish.

We dogs know what the women are really doing when they are beading. They are sewing us all into a pattern, into life beneath their hands. We are the beads on the waxed string, pricked up by their sharp needles. We are the tiny pieces of the huge design that they are making—the soul of the world.

See here, Rozin says, holding out her work with a trembling hand. We dogs know already what happened down in Gakahbekong and why she left for her mothers' house. Her twin mothers. Well, she doesn't know which one of them is actually her blood mother. They won't tell her. But she also was a twin, at first anyway, and so she is not confused that her mother comes as a set.

She left the city because her own child breathed poison and was spirited off to the other side of the world. Deanna passed through the western door. Her father didn't. He slept off his whiskey head and went out to the garage the next morning. The truck had shut down. Had to use the gas can he kept for the lawn mower. Mad at himself, he drove to town for aspirin or maybe the hair of the dog. Decided against that last remedy. Bought groceries. Loading the pickup, he dragged the coats off his little girl. At first, he thought she was sleeping.

Rozin. She swam in the grief, she cooked with it, she bagged it up and froze it. She made a stew, burned it out in the backyard, dug a hole and threw it in, sacked it for garbage, put it up on a shelf, brought it to the trees she loved, and set it free out in the leaves. She worshiped it, curled around it like a sweet dog, smoothed the hair of her remaining daughter underneath her hand, and decided to have nothing to do with men. Rozin left her husband and her lover both behind. Took her daughter Cally and came north to live with Zosie, Mary, and me, Almost Soup, once again.

Let me tell you about this flower, she rambles to her mothers now, this leaf, this heart-in-a-heart, this wild rose, this child of mine.

She knows everything about me.
What things, for instance?
Ridiculous things!

Rozin lowers her velvet and the old twins' eyes glide over at the swimming vines, the maple leaf in three blends of green beads, the powerful twist of the grape tendril, and her four roses of hearts that she's finishing in a burst of dangerous pinks. Rozin is shrinking into the wall of grief, becoming tiny and bird-boned. She has developed a drooping eye. You could think this eye was giving you the curse. Or you could think it was giving you the come-on.

So how, ridiculous?

Just listen!

My girl Cally, she and I get confused about each other. It happens with mothers and daughters, you know it does. Deanna. Why didn't she come inside, change her body with mine? Why didn't we switch minds? Why didn't she use my body for a while to rest so that she could understand this thing.

Eyah, n'dawnis.

They look at each other briefly, under their eyelashes. Rozin is talking fast, to either outrun the big stash of antidepressants she is on or beat the pain they won't solve. Either way, both Zosie and Mary nod her onward and listen.

She was only eleven years old! That's too young, Rozin says a million, two million times. Plus around that age we're so close with our daughters. Closer than when they are stuffed inside the same body. She'd look deep into my eyes, completely seeing her mama, but I would never get to the bottom of hers. She would hold me, and she was just the right height for holding, too, her grass-smelling hair.

Rozin jabs her finger with the needle, then jabs it on purpose, again.

There, she says, sometimes I have to stop these sad thoughts.

Next month it will be a year since that late March snow. One year. The temperature sinks bitterly that night in the moon of crusted snow. All day, Cally does exactly what the trees do in that fickle seesaw month of warm and cold snaps. Days, the sun shines so hot on the bark it fools the tree and brings the sap up, only to freeze. The sap expands, the veins crack, the trees pop and fall ill if they're young. That's what Cally does. I play along with it. She stomps massive clearings out on her snowshoes and throws her jacket off, her hat, for me to run with and toss. We see a mink flash by. She loses her mittens for me to find. Then she loses her *indis*, her bead-wrapped *indis*, where I can't retrieve it, ever. She tears into the house, face dark with joy, cheeks blazing, the raw cold and sweat of icy breezes swirling in her hair.

Rozin is confused with the sorrow over her one twin into lack of care for her other one. That's what her mothers see. She lets Cally run wild and shrugs when they tell her, saying, What good did all my worry do for Deanna? Just cut into her good-time fun, her pleasure in life. Now Cally, she can have all the fun she wants. No, Rozin isn't always careful with her only daughter. But then, Rozin was the only daughter, too, used to being taken care of by two mothers. Rozin paints her fingernails a golden satin pink while Cally burns her mouth on hot bread behind her back.

Cally...!

Ow, Grandma!

But Cally is laughing, fanning off the tip end of her tongue, taking the next piece of dough her grandma fries with more care. Instead of eating once it cools, however, my girl suddenly sets down the golden crust, unfinished. She coughs hard, not hard enough to stop herself, and then she is tired. She curls up by Zosie, who keeps a stack of old newspapers by her easy chair. I sneak under the edge of the couch cover fringe. They usually don't let me in the house—only when Cally sneaks me.

Zosie reads all of the summer news through long winter nights. She calls out to Mary occasionally, exclaiming over a visit from the Pope, another shooting, the practices of cults and movie stars. Now she shades Cally from lamplight as she curls into a knitted afghan. It is only later when my girl wakes, flushed in her first misery, that anyone except me even knows she is sick.

Her fever shoots up abruptly. Rozin takes the steel bowl and washcloth. She wrings the cloth reluctantly, sloppily, and bathes down the fever, wiping slow across her daughter's arms and throat. Faster, faster! I think desperately, whining. She touches the girl's stomach and Cally weeps. Her face wrenches suddenly.

"Mama!"

Rozin bundles off the knitted blankets, brings fresh sheets and remakes the couch. All that night they are up, then down. I am constant. Under the couch, I keep faith and keep watch. Rozin falls asleep on the roll-away in the next room and Mary sleeps beside Cally's couch in the recliner, covered up with an old hunting jacket and a giveaway quilt. Every hour, Cally cries out and is sick with nothing in her stomach, her whole body straining, her face fiery with heat again.

There is almost six inches of new snow on the ground next morning, and Rozin wakes to a still and contained brightness in the tiny bitterly cold closet where she slept as a child. She curls for a moment into the sleeping bag, deeper, then rolls wearily over when Cally whimpers for help. She closes her eyes, aching for the warmth again, waiting for Zosie or Mary to respond. Cally continues to cry softly. Rozin rips the covers down with an almost angry gesture and hops out, stretching. Shit, she mumbles, walking into the next room. Her hand, though, touches down gently on her daughter's forehead and cheeks as she strokes. She refills the basin, then sponges her daughter's blazing gold forehead, throat. She lifts her head and puts the cloth against the back of her neck and again rubs her daughter's chest, again waits out the dry heaving.

An hour passes, and then she pours a little ginger ale into a cup and sits down, careful not to jostle Cally. She feeds her daughter teaspoon by teaspoon, waiting for each spoonful to settle. Cally's lips are dry. Rozin puts a bit of Vaseline on her finger, rubs their deep and punished color. Cally lies back in the pillows, impossibly still.

When Mary comes in the door, Rozin turns.

It's no good, Mary's look says. The phones were unreliable anyway, now cut off.

Then Cally can't keep down even those precious teaspoons of ginger ale and the whole miserable process begins again. She'll get dehydrated, Rozin says as her mother comes in from outdoors, from her lean-to where she's been searching through rolls and bags of bark for the best slippery elm, the strongest sage to boil to make a healing steam. Zosie goes back out and all morning they hear the regular fall of her ax as she builds up the woodpile. I go out to encourage and guard her. Slip back in, dart under the couch. Hardly eat. By the end of the afternoon, Mary's eyes narrow, her lips crease with worry. The smell of cooking upsets Cally. More snow falls and all day they take turns sleeping and eat cold food.

Cally is shrinking, thinning, hardening on her bones, coughing in explosive spasms that shake the springs just over my head. Weeping tiredly. Cranky. Then she loses the energy to fight and grows too meek. I lick the hand that hangs over the edge of the couch until Mary calls out, *Gego*! I curl up, retreat, call upon my ancestors and their old ones for help. That night, she seems even worse. She stares blankly at Rozin, who takes the sleeping bag and sleeps in the chair and sends Zosie to sleep. Rozin coaxes her daughter back to sense after that odd stare, and falling instantly into my own sleep, I dream of hissing cats.

Bad omen! Bad things! I wake at Cally's cry and Rozin jumps to her. Cally thrashes her arms and legs, but then silently and rhythmically. The regular movement of the seizure stiffens us to a calm horror and Rozin holds Cally as best she can until the climbing movements of her arms and legs cease. She sags, unknowing, her face at her mother's breast, eyes staring out of the whited mask of her features.

Cally.

Rozin's voice is deep, from a place in her body I have never heard. Cally. She calls her daughter back from a far-off tunnel path. Cally's mouth opens and she vomits blood into Rozin's hands, her shirt she holds beneath her daughter's mouth. She calls until her daughter stops looking through her mother and brings her troubled gaze to bear. She regards her mother from a distance, then, with eyes that soften in a grown woman's pity.

Rozin wipes her daughter's mouth, her forehead, her twig wrists, the calves, so fine, burning, dry. The soles of her feet. She wipes and wrings and wipes again until Cally stops looking at the ceiling. Rozin keeps on stroking with the cloth, finds herself humming. Slowly singing, she wipes up and down the pole arms. The forehead, her daughter's beating throat. She wipes until Cally says, I'm thirsty, I'm so thirsty, in a normal voice.

You have to wait. Just wait a little bit. Rozin's voice shakes.

Cally falls back. Her eyes shut. Her lips have darkened, cracked in fine, bloody lines, and her skin dries the wet cloth. Rozin keeps on wiping the fever away. I know she feels it underneath her hands, swirling, disappearing, but always coming back. After a while, I can see the fever itself, a viral red-yellow translucence creeping behind the blue of the wiping cloth. She puts the fire out, all night she puts the fire out, wiping until the sweet blue trembles in her daughter and she herself is light, lighter, rising to her feet to get the teaspoon again, shucking off the bloody shirt, fetching the ginger ale, the cup. She adds more water to the boiling kettle on the stove, more bark. The air is steaming, the windows a solid black with frost, a heart-rent blue, a dim gray, then white when Mary rises to take her place.

Rozin sleeps, but her nerves are shot through with adrenaline. She lasts one hour and then rises strong with fear. She washes her face—the water icy from the tap—brushes her teeth. Her eyes in the mirror are staring, young and round. She slicks her hair back into a tail and chews a nail impatiently.

Go to bed.

Mary sends her back, fierce, almost slapping at her. And so a day passes. Another evening. Another night in which Rozin and Cally do as before, the same routine, no change, except that Cally is weaker, Rozin stronger in her exhaustion.

You get too tired, you'll get sick too.

The twins send Rozin to bed with hard words, but their eyes are warm and still with a mixture of worry, sympathy, and something Rozin has not seen in their faces before. Drifting away she wonders at it, but then the dark well opens and she drops into an unconsciousness so profound she does not hear the four-wheel-drive winter ambulance groan and whine down the road that Zosie is killing her heart to shovel.

The ride down to IHS* is complicated by new drifts and whiteouts. I jump in the back and hide just as they swerve off. No way that I'll get left behind, though there are only a couple of gunnysacks to crouch on for warmth. The dark comes on quickly as we drive along, silent. In the back Rozin holds our girl in the sleeping bag. Snowlight flicks through the branches as the wheels grind and tear and the ambulance swings patiently along. Rozin stares into her daughter's face and whispers. Cally's skin goes white as wax, her dark eyes bore into her mother's face, intent and strange. Her skin is rough as velvet when cool, then slides up to the skid of wax again when hot. They finally get there, carry her into the emergency room, into the hands of the nurses and doctor.

One look at her blood pressure and the doctor orders an I.V. Cally has surprising strength. I watch through the hospital window. Hear her yells and shouts. See her tug away, or try to, but Rozin holds her close in a fixed and tender grip saying calm words, calm though wrenched inside out at her daughter's feeble terror. They put a cot up right beside her in the hospital room and then, with Zosie downstairs on the phone, signing papers and arranging things, with Cally on the I.V. suddenly unhollowed, full of color, strengthening and falling into sleep, Rozin lies still, breathing calmly.

It is then, in the hospital room, halfway asleep, that Rozin feels me put her daughter's life inside of her again. Unknown to her, I have taken it with me to keep it safe. Waiting for her daughter to return, Rozin feels some confusion, a fall of silver, a branch loaded with snow, the snow crashing through her arms, and then Cally is back in her own bed and they are separate, drifting off under different

* Indian Health Services.

cotton blankets, in sterilized sheets, into deeper and deeper twilight, entering new ravines.

Rozin is sewing the roses onto a shawl of black velvet, a border of madder pink and fuchsia flowers, twining stems, fancy leaves that never grew on any tree except in her mind. She has an odd thought—Cover the whole world with lazy stitch! Then Cally walks in the door and says, There's nothing lazy about it! Rozin rubs the corner of her one drooping eye, but she says nothing. It's a small thing, this mind reading that Cally does on her these days, and it's harmless except that sometimes her daughter gets big feelings that she's not ready for yet. The old, dead, angry love between her and Richard, unfinished sadness so big and devouring that she can't understand it herself. The worry at what he has become. The lonely wish to walk small between her mother, her aunt again, their arms curving over her like tree branches, making a smooth dim path for her to travel.

She takes agonizing stitches. Uses harrowing orange. They almost shoot fire in the dark room, these pinks. The word for beads in the old language is *manidominenz*, little spirit seed. Though I live the dog's life and take on human sins, I am connected in the beadwork. I live in the beadwork too. The flowers are growing, the powerful vines. The pattern of her daughter's wild soul is emerging. With each bead she plants in the swirl, Rozin adds one tiny grain.

Kimberly M. Blaeser
(1955–)

*"The pocket of my grandma's apron
must have held stories, for she
would often pause, her hand in the
bottom of that pocket as if fingering
something, and then exhale a laugh
and begin the account of someone's
foolishness while out hanging
clothes or picking berries or gone
visiting."*

Kimberly M. Blaeser, "Rituals
of Memory" in *Here First*:
*Autobiographical Essays by Native
American Writers*

Like Some Old Story

Kimberly M. Blaeser

I

"We got that deer way up by Strawberry Mountain, skinned it, butchered it, and packed it out, all the way back to Twin Lakes. I remember thinking how much warmer I felt wrapped in that deer meat. But it weren't vury long 'fore it began to feel awfully heavy. Jeezus we was sure happy to get home that night. All youse little kids woke up and wanted to eat right then."

We sit at the old man's table. I trace the knife cuts in the oil cloth as he talks. His hands remember that journey in the air. His chin, his lips, know the directions. I see the dance in his cloudy eyes and hear him laugh at the memory of that feast. "How-wah, we sure took the wrinkle out of our bellies that night!"

We hunt this way together often now. We clean and oil the guns, sharpen the knives. He brings a new box of shells out of the kitchen cabinet. (Good thing about being a bachelor he always said—you can keep your bullets handy.) We make us a lunch. He shuffles around the trailer, breathing pretty hard as he gets dressed. I pretend not to notice the way he has to lift his bad leg with his hand to get it into the boot. We sit down to a cup of coffee before going out. It's still dark and too early anyway.

"Wonder if you could show me how to make snares."

He answers in that way that he has. Gesturing with his neck and chin, his head bopping slightly, a throaty series of ahhs, and then a long drawn out "Well, sure I kin show you. You know what pitcher wire is?" I bring him things from here and there about the trailer. He shows me each of his tools, remembers just what he used to use and how he came to get the ones he has now. By the time I get the hang of the cutting, the tying, the sun's been up a while.

"Well lookit that. Them deer musta wondered what heppened to us. Spose they're out there looking at their clocks saying, 'Where is that ole hunter?' Jeez, what kind of hunter you gonna make, if you forget all about going out? I spose you gonna hunt just like my girls—out of my freezer. Well we mighd's well eat these sandwiches. Heppened to Dad and me like this one time we was camping where that ole McDougall used to have his sugarbush. I remember it was raining jest hard..."

II

The boys came in looking kind of funny. Awfully quiet, too. No teasing. Just set themselves to cleaning up. Boiling water to wash, emptying their pockets of spare shells and the match sticks they always carried. Soon your dad went to get some tobacco and a kind of a mumbled argument was going on in the back room. Tried to keep it secret they did, but Mum and Dad wouldn't have it. Sent for one of the uncles. Sent us little kids upstairs to the loft. Then they got the story out.

It was that man-deer spirit that's said to come out when them graves have been disturbed. Happens every forty years or so. Someone forgets. Gets too cocky. Pretty soon it's there on the edge of the clearing, antlers catching the early evening light. It looks straight at you when you take aim. Some reason you pause. Get a chill, a funny feeling. Talk yourself out of it. And, just as you set your finger to the trigger, the thing stands up on its man legs. And then is gone. Don't seem it was really there. But you're shaking.

III

The short squat little man comes out from behind a tree, walks furtively across the little field to position himself on the edge of some small wetlands. He's wearing the classic camouflage clothes in browns and tans, and waders that are fastened now just below his knees. Perhaps it's the duck-hunting hat or the way that he wears it with the ear flaps down, but something seems a little comical in his appearance, reminiscent somehow of a cartoon character.

He doesn't wait long before two mallards fly over. Perhaps he hasn't gotten settled yet, because his aim is off and he misses—twice. The gunfire must be muffled somewhat by the morning dampness because the birds seem strangely unruffled as the shots ring out and they fly on easily out of sight. His next shot brings down a honker, but the fourth, at a low-flying goose, hits a tree and ricochets, cartoon fashion. Soon the hunter seems to have found his rhythm and he brings down four more of the birds, which arrive miraculously in swift succession.

Suddenly the action stops. But the little man seems satisfied. He walks about picking up the birds from where they have fallen, putting the ducks in the large pockets of his hunting jacket. Like a magician he produces a small square cloth which, with a single flourish, turns into a shoulder pack. Into this he deposits the geese. Then, his weapon pointed down like he was taught in gun safety class, he walks off in the opposite direction from which he had come. The wetland scene seems hardly disturbed by the episode.

Then the tempo of the music picks up and a clone of the first man emerges again from the right edge of the screen.

IV

It was when the women were cooking together that I'd hear the other side of those stories. Like the one about the year the two deer were stolen from that tree down in the hollow. You know who always got blamed for that, don't you? I wondered at first why Aunt Maggie let those boys take the blame. But then I thought, well it was true often enough and could just as well have been true this time, too. "Good enough for them," Maggie would have said. But I never did let on or ask her about it. Later I realized how it *was* good for them—you know, to realize what a reputation they had earned. So I never told.

You remember how it happened? The men were all at Gram's having the big dinner the women had cooked in between their card games that day. Those pies were on the cook stove, looking jest juicy and waiting to be cut into. I saw when that blue pickup went by 'cuz I was sitting on the steps outside the screen door, you know, just far enough away so they would forget I was around but close enough to hear the stories. Anyway, pretty soon someone was walking up the path from where Ron's house used to be. It was June Bug's uncle, I forget his real name, but us kids used to jest call him Antler 'cuz he had that funny bump on the side of his head and it was covered with pale soft hairs so it looked to us like an antler jest beginning to pop out in velvet.

He never said *boozhoo** or nothing. "Somethin's after yer deer." Thems the only words I remember him saying as he stood outside on the steps looking in on those happy hunters. His nose was against the screen door when he spoke, but he jumped back pretty quick 'cuz the chairs started scraping inside and six guys came out in a real hurry. Not mad, yet, 'cuz they thought dogs or maybe a bear.

I was just about to run after them when my aunt showed up, coming from the other side of the house, wiping her hands on a rag. "Your ole man sure can tie 'em up tight. Thought sure I was going to get caught there. Then what would we have said?"

"You manage?" It was my mom asked that.

"Ayah. Got that Brown boy to haul 'em. Said he could have a hind quarter."

Plenty of kids would have tole, you know, right that night. But I was patient, even then. I knew if you wanted to find things out you had to wait. Turns out I didn't have to wait long. Next day the women couldn't tell it enough, how they tricked their husbands into hunting for that halfblood woman Sarah Goes Lightening. She was a Sioux, you know, and had those five kids. Used to live out on the Snyder Lake road, way back. I guess the men had it in for Sarah 'cuz they thought she done wrong

* In Objiwe, *boozhoo* means "hello."

by one of their own, LeRoy Beaulieu. But the women thought differently. I'm still hunting that story, but it'll come along some day. I know how to wait for stories.

V

The old man is standing there just where he said we should pick him up. He has his gun and a stick about a yard long which he holds up when he sees us approach. "Looks like he got him one," Auntie says in the back.

"Wonder how long he's been waiting," my mom says. "Wish he wouldn't go out like that alone."

"You could go with." We all laugh at that. "This one ain't my hunter," Grandpa used to say about my mom. "Sure about that?" Grandma would ask. "That girl is gonna surprise you with what she brings home some day." I guess she did, too. Brought home my dad. But I don't think that's what Grandpa meant, although it might be what Grandma had in mind. Never could tell about that woman either.

He holds up his stick when we get out and lifts his head toward what's hanging on it—a deer heart pierced through. "Had to fight a great big animal to save this heart for youse girls." It takes him a long time to say this because his words are always surrounded by gestures and because certain sounds he draws out, moving them up and down in his throat. He laughs then at what he's said, but doesn't tell us the story until later, until we've managed between the four of us to drag a small buck out of the woods where he left it, until we've heaved it into my trunk onto the gunny sacks I've laid out to catch the blood drippings, until we've driven back into the little village and sit inside drinking coffee and getting ready to butcher.

"It was a little weasel. Come out and tried to steal that heart right off the stick. You know how them little buggers are. Tough. Sure was mad at me, and didn't want to give up his supper. So I cut him a little piece." He looks over at me. "Shoulda said, 'Do your own hunting.'" He knows I'll take the part of the weasel. We both pretend I have to convince him.

I dream about the weasel that night. He's a least weasel in my dream and he's old. He sits on a log in the sun watching the birds, thinking of the time he was quick enough to snatch a bird before it could launch itself out of his reach. Dreams always come that way from life and life from dreams, don't they? I saw a least weasel snatch its dinner just that way once, a bird twice its size, too. That time becomes this time when I sleep, but it's only the weasel's dream. He's too old now. He needs some help, too, just like any old hunter.

I wake up to deer meat frying and come out to find him cleaning his gun again at the table. "Thought you were gonna sleep all day." I look outside. It's still dark, maybe five a.m. I smile when he cranes his neck toward the stove. I take the cups from the counter where he's laid them, pour in some canned milk, take the hot pad, letting myself sniff its stale flour smell, before I reach for the coffee pot.

"Spose we could be out and back before them ladies even wake up," I say pretty casual-like when I put the cups and plates on the table, like this is part of something old we've always done.

He nods, pretending with me again. "There's some boots you kin wear behind that wood stove there. You gut gloves?"

We both begin to eat fast and hearty, as if we hadn't just stuffed ourselves last night. "Howah, pretty good stuff." We're laughing too loud and wake up my mom.

"What are you two doing?" she drawls between yawns.

"Going hunting," I say, dropping my voice like it's the last line in some old story—like someone is going to answer, "*Aho.*"

Growing Things

Kimberly M. Blaeser

"You have to go deep to do any good," Spanish heard him say. He went on gesturing and explaining to her about fertilization. She found it hard to meet his eyes, so she turned small rocks over with her toes, half alert for a fossil. Every so often she would look up at the old oak—seventy-five to a hundred years old he had told her.

Now he was writing things down: formulas, brand names, equipment she would need. She wanted to laugh every time she looked at him. It's the way she felt ever since he came down the drive in that sporty Mazda. Like his shirt, it was some kind of blue she couldn't name—one of the designer colors invented in some laboratory, custom made for yuppies. For this yuppie tree doctor.

She stood squinting trying to superimpose some distinctive character over his smooth, round, dimpled cheeks. She tied a bandanna pirate-style over his head. No, that didn't work. She rolled it into a headband, but that looked silly on his close-cropped hair, made his little bald spot more prominent. Well, maybe a hat . . . an Aussie hat . . . or a scar across his cheekbone . . .

"Well, that should do it. Got it? I'd bring the mulch out to here if you don't mind the looks of it. Miss?"

"Hmmm? Oh, I think so. Mulch, fertilizer injections, pruning . . ."

"In the dead of winter."

"Right. But you say you can't promise it will do any good."

"Know in three to five years—if you're still here. I'll leave you my card if you think of something you forgot to ask."

And then he was bending over his notebook again. Suddenly she wanted to touch the little hollow on his chin, fill it with her finger. Feel the smooth curve of it. A tree doctor after all. Some ancient blood, some spirit must have left its mark, somewhere palpable. Her hand moved to caress the cold smooth dip of the brown spirit stone in her pocket.

He himself he had hardly touched anything. The bark for no more than a few seconds. A branch pulled down for a hasty look at the leaves. *"Boozhoo,** my friend

---

* In Ojibwe, *boozhoo* means "hello."

Oak," her grandpa would say as he grasped a bare low branch in a handshake. "This here is my little Spanish." He would lift her giggling to the handshake, to the solemn introductions he used to make. "Good day, Mrs. Birch. What fine dress you wear." "Grandpa, her dress is torn," she would whisper, knowing he must pretend to correct her manners.

Because of her grandpa, the world of Spanish's childhood was furry, prickly, sticky with life. A place of rocks, cold and wet, their colors made vibrant by the waves breaking over them, rocks to be turned and admired in the hand, to be felt and heard with the hands. The world she knew was a place of sharp thorns, coarse or sleek animal fur, slippery bodies of fish. It was mossy forest floors upon which they lay, bodies cushioned, remembering a nest of crisp fall leaves, imagining the soft bed of clouds.

To know the world by touch is to know it by heart. That, thought Spanish, was the single lesson her grandpa taught. Did he realize the many troubles she would encounter because she learned it so well?

Touch was of the devil—the lesson the nuns taught. Keep your hands folded on your desk in the classroom, in your lap when you sit, in front of you when you walk. Wear white gloves to church like nice young ladies do. Keep your hands clean. Don't play in the mud, don't put your fingers in the food, don't play with your hair, and don't touch boys—ever.

And yet, Spanish remembered how all the miracles in the Bible stories came about because of touch. Jesus touched the blind man's eyes, the dead, the lame, the sick. He blessed the loaves and the fishes. He broke the bread with his hands. The Bible knew the power of touch.

Was this power that the nuns feared? The reason Spanish spent so many afternoons writing one declaration or another five-hundred times, saying in words what she wouldn't say with her heart, that she wouldn't hold hands behind the silo, wouldn't swing on birches, wouldn't touch the Host with her fingers. Wouldn't trail her fingers along the tree doctor's palm during their parting handshake until he looked up startled and laughed uneasily.

"Well, goodbye then. Call me if you want... another checkup. If you have questions. If you..." He closed the car door on his own half-expectant mumbling. Spanish held up her left hand in farewell, her right hand again fingering the stone in her pocket. She stood squinting into the sun, watching the yuppie tree doctor drive off and wondering what she had expected.

Spanish had prepared for his arrival as if he were deserving of ritual honor, as if she had summoned him with a gift of tobacco—like a sucking doctor called to heal the sick. She had not completely settled in, so her preparation required she search the still-packed boxes for the odd group of items she thought appropriate. On the built-in side table she placed special teas and a tumbler of whiskey. She filled a kettle for the stove, set out a turtle-shaped bowl, matches and cedar. She dressed carefully, slipping a heavy silver bracelet onto her wrist, wearing the dream catcher earrings given her by cousin Julia, and pulling her hair back in a beaded barrette with a thunderbird pattern she had designed herself. Dragon, her mixedblood spaniel, she closed in the loft. "Sometimes them doctors need it real quiet." Her grandma's voice, consoling Spanish when she must tie her old reservation dogs away from the house before a medicine man was due to come.

Old habits. She laughed as now she sat on the steps, her fingers buried deep in the hair around Dragon's neck, her caresses a peace offering for his recent banishment. The tree doctor—*Shelby Mathews, Arborist*, his card said—had not come into Spanish's new log home, had not tasted tea or whiskey, had not made any offering, told any story, done any healing. Spanish told herself she was being unfair. She knew where she was coming when she moved here. The lake country of Southern Wisconsin: rural, but still middle America. Maybe her romps in the surrounding woods had tricked her, brought back memories, built her expectations. But Shelby Mathews was an arborist, not really a tree doctor as she had thought of him, certainly not a *jiisakiiwinini** or conjurer.

"Still he has potential, eh, Dragon?" Spanish said, thinking of his hard-muscled legs and the quiet feel of his spirit. But then she laughed when she recalled his notebook and yuppie earnestness. "Should have asked him in for tea anyway. Maybe I could teach him what I know about the healing touch. Well let's get about this mulch thing. Wanna ride in the wheelbarrow, Dragon?"

In the weeks that followed, Spanish would gaze intently at the oak, trying to see signs that her care was working. She felt what she knew was an inordinate amount of guilt for its threatened health. Even though she had fenced an eight-foot-wide circle off limits for the heavy equipment during building, the oak's root system must have suffered.

Proximity, such a tricky business. Seven cousins layered together in the back of that old rusty pickup, their three moms crowded into the cab. Kids bouncing along singing to hear their voices jar and crack with the bumps. Going to town, going fishing, going visiting, just going along. Spanish thought about the close kin system of her childhood. Three generations sharing beds, clothes, chores, food, and fun, living together in tight quarters. What made it work? Living in Texas with cowboy Dale, the whole ranch hadn't been big enough for the two of them. She had fumbled through several relationships—the watercolor artist in Colorado, the school teacher in Illinois—always one or the other party began to feel threatened by the closeness. Claustrophobia. Not the classic panic in small spaces, but some fear of personal closeness. A need for freedom, for personal space—my space.

Last time, with Jim Snow, Spanish was the one who ran. She ran here. Built a cabin. Did freelance editing on her PC. Fished. Roamed the countryside. Looking for that space. Constantly reminded of the problems of proximity by this damn oak tree.

The arborist came back in late January—the dead of winter. Spanish had called him about the pruning. Small preparations this time and Dragon at her side, where she kept her nervous hands busy in his winter coat.

_____

* *Jiisakiiwinini* means "shaking tent doctor" or "seer" in Ojibwe.

"How you liking it out here?" he asked while setting up. "Pretty quiet in the winter, isn't it?"

"I keep myself busy. I like quiet." Dumb answer, Spanish, dumb. She watched him find the rhythm of his pruning routine. Lotsa science in this guy, she thought, but some music too, maybe a little bit of magic he doesn't acknowledge yet.

It hurt her to watch the cutting, so she turned away, performing small duties about the grounds as she listened to his movements. Pruning wasn't in her blood. Not like it must be in the blood of the bonsai masters, and maybe in the blood of Shelby Mathews. She remembered the hollow feeling that came the first time she saw a woodchipper at work. Branches gobbled up by the shrieking machine, spit out as bits and sawdust. That was true modern magic, she supposed, but not for her. But this, this pruning for health was a different kind of cutting, maybe an art. *Shelby Mathews, Tree Doctor, Artist.* Spanish smiled as she conjured the business card in her mind.

He was done. It didn't look like art, not yet anyway. Poor stump branches, she thought. Together Spanish and Shelby carried the fallen pieces to her woodpile. "Come in for coffee or hot chocolate while I write you a check?" she offered.

"Sure, thanks."

He was fingering her chess set when she returned with the serving tray. He had removed his gloves and held an onyx knight in his hand, following its lines.

"Pretty set."

"Thanks. You play?"

"A little, sometimes."

"Want to?"

"What? Oh, play? Now?"

"Or... sometime."

They both laughed then at the awkwardness. "I'm sorry," Spanish began. "Out here, conversation, well, isn't my strong suit these days."

"No, I'm sure it's me. Pruning puts me in a bit of a trance, I guess."

A trance. It was a perfect answer. An arborist yes, but a tree doctor maybe a little, too.

They didn't play chess. Just talked a little about the area, his business, her house, and about Dragon when he demanded attention. Shelby didn't stay long, but he admired a lot of things in her house: the wood finishes, fish decoys, black ash baskets, books. Maybe one of them would bring him back, she thought when he left. Maybe she would.

Maybe if she knew about love medicines. Sympathetic magic was what the anthropologists called it when dolls were tied together to conjure a bond. Did those dolls break their leather ties when one of the lovers fled in search of personal space? What kind of love was it that created such a largeness in a relationship that no one became afraid? What kind of love had eluded her? Would this tree doctor who knew about root systems know about that magic?

As a child she had watched her old cat Mrs. Tom give birth and lick each newborn kitten dry. "Why does she do that, Grandpa? Doesn't she get tired?"

"She's waking up their blood, Spanish, the way you wake yours up each morning when you stretch. She's gettin' that blood to move around in their bodies... bringing them life."

Science would later tell her that the mother cat was stimulating her offsprings' circulation, but Spanish would always think about it as waking up their kitten blood. And when later she would lie with a lover whose hands gently petted and caressed her, who ran kisses down her neck and arms, she knew he was waking up her kitten blood, too, and filling the life vessels of her body. What stopped that magic?

The tree doctor came back a week later, pulled into the yard in a brown four-wheel drive Bronco. "Mazda's kind of impractical in this weather," he told her when she asked.

"I had a job down the road a ways, saw you in the yard..."

"I'm glad you came. I was just studying this tree."

"You won't know for awhile, I thought I explained."

"You did, but I can't help searching for a sign." Spanish traced the bark pattern lightly with her fingers. "I try to encourage it, it's too grand to be destroyed by humans crowding in."

"I saw the tobacco."

"Huh?"

"The first day I came. You had some kind of ceremony."

"Made an offering. Appeasement, I guess."

"I wondered. And me? Hedging your bets?"

Spanish glanced up at his face and his raised eyebrows. But before she could respond, he laughed. "It's okay. I'm as used to skepticism as, well as you are I guess. After you've explained to forty people about some invisible fungus invading through the root system or tried to counter the story of some TV fertilizer wizard, you just accept it: some people are going to think you inhaled too much nitrogen or something."

She could have told him then, but he didn't seem in any hurry. If anyone did, he knew about waiting. Three years healing for the tree if she helped it along. "Oh, I believe in science," she could have said, "just not by itself."

Someday she might show him the tamarack stands, the jackpines, the maple sugar grounds of her childhood. He might burn with fury when he saw the scars of clear-cutting in her homeland. Or they might sit together watching the waves of heat, wiping their foreheads with a folded red bandanna, and singing for rain to feed the rows and rows of saplings set before them. "Feel these furrows, Child. They are the same on the great oak, on the marked land, and now on the forehead of your *mishoomis*."* "Grandpa, are you turning to bark?" They laughed then. As Spanish did now with this smooth-faced tree doctor. She could almost see him turning to bark, too. And waited.

* In Ojibwe, *mishoomis* means "grandfather."

Misha Nogha
(1955–)

"Well here he is, his black eyes like
expectant words, waiting to be read
on the whites of his pages she's
smiling at him, a shattered chain
of words scattering from her hands,
we've stopped believing in grief in
straw words in iron crosses on fields
of snow you're putting your ashes
and sand under the dripping ink, his
needles holding back his edge
of tears...."

Misha Nogha, "Red Spider" in
Red Spider, White Web

Memekwesiw

Misha Nogha

> *The drum in a dream*
> *pounds loud to the dreamer.*
>
> —Carl Sandburg

The moon is a fire drum polishing the anthracite sky in silent booms. She stands before a steel cage that holds this week's exhibit. A white bear with muzzle of frost. Cold blue light crackles around its spirit pelt. The sheer bulk of the bear punches through her chest and leaves a cavelike hole that sucks her through herself into the bowels of the earth. Still, she watches her hand, the silver key strobing in the starlight, as it stretches forward and unlocks the door. There is a long moment of dead silence after the solitary click. She turns to run and is frozen by the sheer volume of bear roars. The bellow whirls her around to face the bear just as it strikes out and slaps the top of her skull off. It's a skull juggler. Her scalp flaps away into the night. Before the woman can fall, the bear sinks its massive jaws deep into her chest and begins to chew her; smacking and crunching, it rips the flesh from her bones. A bear hungry as fire licking her bone dry and white under the taut moon drum. She is screaming and screaming, horribly conscious of all the pain, the black blood and grayish fat flying in moonlight, as the bear rends her alive. The bear stands full height and roars, its muzzle frozen with crystallized gore. A small ivory chip of a bone seed spins slowly on the black ice. It reverses direction, spins faster, and explodes once again into a woman clothed in flesh.

She bolts upright with a sharp intake of breath. Slaps her palms against her chest. Sheets of moonlight fall through the window on the cream-colored Pendleton blanket. Her husband stirs beside her. "What is it?"

"Horrible," she gasps, feeling her flesh, brown hands covering her naked self, feeling light-headed, newborn.

"Dreaming of bears again?" He turns, ever the therapist, even with his own wife, especially with his own wife.

"I felt it. It hurts. I was eaten alive by a bear, and I felt every bite, every slice of claw." She was breathing in great heavy gasps. "It was real."

He leans up on the pillow. His voice is calm, dry, his Mongol eyes gleaming silver in the moonlight. "You're going to have to face it."

"What?" she gasps, still feeling the prickly fur in her mouth, the musky smell of bear pelt in her eyes and ears, all of her trembling.

"Your Native self," he says, rolling back into the blanket, his Slavic/Mongol form, itself bearlike, falling back into snores of ursine contentment.

She crawls off the floor mat onto the bare particleboard floor. Reaches for a light, a wisp of smoke. The moon lights up the drum above her bed; she makes out the ghostly form of her dun draft horses outside the window. "My drum is my horse," she says to the horses out the window; they nicker back to her.

In the morning a young grizzly cub sits by the refrigerator licking milk from its nimble paws. The kids are yelling, "Can we keep him?" But she grabs the cub by the ruff and drags it, bawling, across the floor and throws it out the door. It's crying like a child outside the door and she feels sorry and pours it another bowl of creamy milk. That night, the bear grows huge and rips the shack door right off its hinges. She is trying to hold the door back, but the bear is too strong.

"Why don't you do something about your Native side?" Her husband steps around the bear, shakes his head "No, no" at it, sits at the table with his paper, ignoring its huge bulk, its savage odor of blood and dung.

As soon as she sees the black bear, she knows it is coming for her. Its sleek hide galloping as fast as her horse can run. She takes the kerosene lantern from the hook above the lintel, swings it at the bear, but it only circles her warily, keeps coming back. Not to maim or kill, but to embrace her. Her husband stands silently watching, the red glow of a cigarette dangling from his lips. "You can't fight truth with illumination," he says coolly. She stops swinging the lantern and the bear snuffles her palm with his wet black nose.

Later that week, paddling away from the steep sloped sides of the Minam, she looks up at the slate rock cliffs and sees the mother grizzly. Two red cubs are smacking their lips and standing on their hind legs. They swim out to the green canoe. The mother is as long as the boat. She slides noiselessly into the Minam, her amber pelt cutting the cream of the rapids into her own dark whirlpool. The woman tries to hold off the bear with the paddle, but, lightning fast, the bear knocks it away with a single swipe. The woman watches the paddle skimming through the air like a slender wooden bird. The bear heaves her bulk into the canoe, capsizing it. The woman wakes up on the stone bank in the arms of the bear and cubs. "There, there, it's not so bad," the woman says to the griz, "it's not so bad."

The husband scratches the bear under the muzzle and she faintly purrs. He understands things ursine, black and hairy under layers of human flesh.

Her Oglala friend takes her to a sweat.* "You'll understand your bear dreams," she promises the woman who keeps dreaming of bears. But at the lodge there are protesters. Only enrolled tribe members, the signs say. Go away wannabes.† The woman is stricken with horror. No papers for the daughter of a Métis,‡ no papers from a white man guaranteeing her Indian blood. She turns under the scorn of racial purism preferring the fury of bears to the contempt of picketers. Her tribe is scattered bone seeds. Each one springing up into a new chimeric monster, scorned by both red and white people, welcomed only by the animals.

The bears dig roots in the moonlight. By day she claws the earth loose from those roots and hangs them to dry over the woodstove. The house is filled with the odors of sage, sweetgrass, and drying herbs. At night she hears the bears padding softly around the house. They scratch at the door, but she only pulls the covers around her ears refusing to answer.

She becomes ill, her body paralyzed and her face twisted into a false face mask.** The white doctor shakes his head. Says he doesn't know what causes it, what is a cure. After three weeks of agony she goes to a white bear, he hands her a piece of topaz, gold and sticky, puts the sweet comb to her mouth, and she becomes well.

Pieces of bears come in the mail. A claw from her cousin, a scrap of fur from a sister, a jet bear with a red arrow from a Zuni friend. From Arizona her brother brings her a bear carved of onyx. All these things she puts on the shelf, ashamed of dreams that keep pouring into her daily life.

The first strike of her drum calls the bears from the four corners of the earth. Lightning shaped into a bear paw claws down five of her neighbor's cows. She says nothing but thinks of it often. The dream books tell her that dreaming of bears means someone unbearable is in her life. But the only thing she dreads is the savage sounds of bears. Bear grunts and snorts, steamy bear breath, bear wallows, bear claws prying up rocks, sliding across the tin door, heavy bear paws groaning across the porch and clasping her to woolly breasts.

At night she is afraid to sleep, so she walks to the top of the hill on the farm. Her drum horses watch her go with questioning eyes. These ponies are not Native ponies, but ponies from the land of berserkers, also her white ancestors. Everywhere she goes she sees the bears. At the top of the hill she climbs a big pine tree; halfway up she sees that it is painted with vermillion horizontal stripes. She keeps climbing past little streamers in the colors of the four directions. As she nears the top of

---

* A sweatlodge ceremony is a purifying ritual, often part of a larger set of ceremonial practices.

† A "wannabe" is a derogatory term for white persons who pretend to be or "wanna be" Indian.

‡ Métis is the French Canadian term for mixedblood.

** "False Faces" are wooden masks used in healing ceremonies by the False Face Society, a medicine society of the Iroquois in the Northeastern United States.

the tree, she finds a bear skull. It is painted with Cree chin stripes like those of her ancestors. At the top of the tree the wind is blowing from the west, and she turns and faces the skull direction, east. She takes a buckknife from her pocket and slices it deep into the skin of her forearm. She expects to find mixed blood, pink and thick as Pepto-Bismol, raises her arm toward the raw red sun. But the blood is crimson, streams from her uplifted arm, and covers her in a blanket of scarlet. Memekwesiw speaks to her from the black earth below.

He says, "Now you have found your dream."

Sakura

Misha Nogha

She is hot from dancing, a beautiful orchid in ballet pink, her frills gray with grime, droplets of dew run down her face, the missing track lights leave her elegant dance for lonely shadows, a draft wisps across the dusty wood floor, the mirrors are pitted and cracked, the wash of her pink figure sailing back and forth between them, the dance of a tropical fish, the sounds of creaking planks, her jumps and thumping of boards, her shallow and deep breathing, her rhythm under the breath counting, the leather toe shoes shushing on the gritty floor, the pink fire licks the mirrors, the door swings in a gust of breeze, a window latch is undone, she never notices you standing there, shadow with teeth shining in the darkness, your eyes magnetized to her movement, we watch with anticipation, never a creature so lovely, the sailing of parachutes, leaping of gazelles of pink butterflies and cake trimmings you move forward, a line of drool slipping down your chin, it glistens in the half-light, you are clapping for her and your naked smile covers her face, you are her flesh-eating audience, she pushes harder, faster, for you alone she pirouettes, she doesn't know you, but she needs you, you are reaching your hands to her, she is swaying in exhaustion, the dying swan, you reach out, I hold her hand, her sweating body, in a fever of dance, she is spent, it's so easy to help her, I am helping her lay down, her thin sweaty legs in my hands, her frosting lips parting, gasping for breath, her constricting tights, I remove them, I do, I alone can help her quiet, calm, her sad little dance beaten back at every step, I free her from the encumbrance of flesh, I am wrapping her white neck with the throat of the dying swan, and she is still, waiting to dance, to dance again as I am lifting her, her leap of silence into clouds from years of molting feathers from a broken lawn flamingo once again a silent pink swan.

Beth H. Piatote
(1966–)

"A good story gets under your skin, and I don't mean this in the metaphorical sense. Stories have a material, cellular presence when they take residence in the body, and thus, over time, can release into our systems their endless power, wisdom, and beauty."

Beth H. Piatote

Beading Lesson

Beth H. Piatote

The first thing you do is, lay down all your hanks, like this, so the colors go from light to dark, like a rainbow. I'll start you out with something real easy, like I do with those kids over at the school, over at Cay-Uma-Wa.

How about—you want to make some earrings for your mama? Yeah, I think she would like that.

Hey niece, you remind me of those kids. That's good! That's good to be thinking of your mama.

You go ahead and pick some colors you think she would like. Maybe three or four is all, and you need to pick some of these bugle beads.

Yeah, that's good, except you got too many dark colors.

You like dark colors. Every time I see you you're wearin' something dark. Not me. I like to wear red and yellow, so people know I'm around and don't try talkin' about me behind my back, aay?

The thing is, you got to use some light colors, because you're makin' these for your mama, right, and she has dark hair, and you want 'em to stand out, and if they're all dark colors you can't see the pattern.

I got some thread for you, and this beeswax. You cut the thread about this long, a little longer than your arm, but you don't want it too long or it will tangle up or get real weak. You run it through the beeswax, like this, until it's just about straight. It makes it strong and that way it don't tangle so much.

You keep all this in your box now. I got this for you to take home with you, back to college, so you can keep doin' your beadwork.

How do you like it over there at the university? You know your cousin Rae is just about gettin' her degree. She just has her practicum, then she'll be done. I think her boyfriend don't like her being in school though, and that's slowing her down. It's probably a good thing you don't have a boyfriend right now. They can really make a lot of trouble for you, and slow you down on things you got to do.

Now you gotta watch this part. This is how you make the knot. You make a circle like this, then you wrap the thread around the needle three times, see? You see how my hands are? If you forget later you just remember how my hands are, just like this, and remember you have to make a circle, OK? Then you pull the needle through all the way to the end—good—and clip off the little tail.

I'll show you these real easy earrings, the same thing I always start those men at the jail with. You know I go over there and give them beading lessons. You should see how artistic some of them are. They work real hard, and some of them are good at beadwork.

I guess they got a lot of time to do it, but it's hard, it's hard to do real good beadwork.

You got to go slow and pay attention.

I know this one man, William, he would be an artist if he wasn't in jail. I'll show you, he gave me a drawing he did of an eagle. It could be a photograph, except you can tell it's just pencil. But it's good, you would like it. There's a couple other Indian prisoners—I guess we're supposed to call them inmates, but I always call them prisoners—and sometimes I make designs for them for their beadwork from what they draw. The thing is, they don't get very many colors to work with.

They like the beadwork, though. They always got something to give their girl-friends when they come visit, or their mothers and aunties.

You have to hide the knot in the bead, see, like this, and that's why you got to be careful not to make the knot too big.

Maybe next time you come they will be having a powwow at the prison and you can meet my students over there, and they can show you their beadwork. I think they always have a powwow around November, around Veteran's Day. Your cousin Carlisle and his family come over from Montana last time, and the only thing is, you got to go real early because it takes a long time to get all your things through security. They have to check all your regalia and last time they almost wouldn't let Carlisle take his staff in because they said it was too dangerous or something.

What's that? Oh, that's all right. Just make it the same way on the other one and everyone will think you did it that way on purpose.

Your mama is really going to like these earrings. I think sometimes she wishes she learnt to bead, but she didn't want to when she was little. She was the young-est so I think she was a little spoiled, but don't tell her I said that. She didn't have to do things she didn't want to, she didn't even have to go to boarding school. I think she would have liked it. It wasn't bad for me at that school. Those nuns were good to me; they doted on me. I was their pet. I think your mama missed out on something, not going to St. Andrews, because that's when you get real close with other Indians.

I like that blue. I think I'm goin' to make you a wing dress that color.

I think you'll look real good when you're ready to dance. Once you get going on your beadwork I'll get you started on your moccasins, and you know your cousin Woody is making you a belt and I know this lady who can make you a cornhusk bag. You're goin' to look just like your mama did when she was young, except I think she was younger than you the last time she put on beadwork.

I used to wonder if you would look like your dad, but now that you're grown you sure took after her. I look at you and I think my sister, she must have some strong blood.

Hey, you're doin' real good there, niece. I think you got "the gift"—good eyesight! You know, you always got to be workin' on something, because people are always needing things for weddin's and memorials and going out the first time, got to get their outfits together. Most everything I make I give away, but people pay me to make special things. And they are always askin' for my work at the gift shop. My beadwork has got me through some hard times, some years of livin' skinny.

You got to watch out for some people, though. Most people aren't like this; most people are real big-hearted. But some people, when they buy your beadwork, they think it should last forever. Somebody's car breaks down, he knows he got to take it to the shop, pay someone to get it goin' again. But not with beadwork—not with something an Indian made. No, they bring it back ten years later and they want you to fix it for free! They think because an Indian makes it, it's got to last forever. Just think if the Indians did that with all the things the government made for us. Hey, you got to fix it for free!

You done with that already? Let me show you how you finish. You pull the thread through this line, see, then clip it, then the bead covers it up. That's nice.

That's good. I'm proud of you, niece. You got a good heart. Just like your mama and dad.

I think your mama is really goin' to like these earrings, and maybe she'll come and ask you to teach her how you do it. You think she'll ever want to learn beadwork? Maybe she'll come and ask me, aay?

What do you think of that? You think your mama would ever want to learn something from her big sister? I got a lot of students. There's a lady who just called me the other day, she works at the health clinic, and she's a lot older than you and she wants to learn how. I said sure I'll teach her. It's never too late. I teach anyone who wants to learn; that's our way to keep it goin'. I just keep thinkin' if I stay around long enough, everyone's goin' to come back and want to learn beadwork, even your mama.

Life-Size Indian

Beth H. Piatote

Nathaniel T. Redmoon looked as though he'd been discharged from the Army last week, but it had been nine months already. There were certain things he did to maintain his just-discharged look, including a strict exercise regimen (which he did every morning, hangover or not) and a biweekly visit to the barber to get his head shaved. On this particular Saturday night in mid-February, Nate was fiddling with the top button of his shirt. Button. Unbutton. He wasn't sure. In the Army, he would perfect the slightest fold of his collar that would make him different from the troops around him. Now, cashing in his college money, he could do as he pleased. Button. Unbutton. Finally bored with it, he unbuttoned the top button, smoothed his hand over his dark head, and reached for his jacket. On the way out he checked himself in the mirror one more time.

Nate stepped out from his basement apartment into a world that seemed still and almost warm. Soon it would begin to snow. He climbed in the driver's side of the tan 1978 El Camino that was once his uncle's and eased the door shut, hearing the familiar click as it latched. The auto body guy had never got the doors right. Nate had wanted to take it back, but his mom said it would be more good money after bad, so Nate learned to be gentle. The car had belonged to his uncle, who had moved irrigation pipe the entire summer of 1987 to buy it from a Pendleton wheat farmer. Then last spring his uncle died. It hadn't been a year yet, so still no one would say his name. Sometimes Nate would just mouth the word, "Uncle," with no sound coming out. He hoped that he could be forgiven for this.

He had been his uncle, but he had only been two years older than Nate, which maybe would seem that he should have been more like a cousin or a half-brother. But lots of people had uncles and aunts younger than them. Nate's cousin Modesta had an uncle five years younger than her, and she used to call him Baby Uncle. Even at his wedding she called him that. Nate had grown up with his uncle, playing summer league baseball, smoking pot under the bleachers of the rodeo grounds, riding in together at the Happy Canyon Pageant during the Round-Up. When a girl broke his heart in ninth grade, it had been Nate who found his uncle crying on the porch and sat beside him, saying nothing. That's how close they were: not brothers or cousins, but always uncle and nephew.

Nate glanced around the cab and noticed a gum wrapper on the floor, which he wadded up and stuffed in the ashtray. Then he let out a long breath and stretched out his right arm, placing his hand on the dash. It was an old gesture. He wanted something, but he couldn't say what. He rested his hand on the dash. He didn't know how long he sat like that, but he suddenly became aware of the cold. He moved his hand to the ignition, and the El Camino roared to life.

When he arrived at Charlie Bean's slate blue apartment complex, Nate saw that Bean was dressed in jeans and a western shirt with pearly grey snaps down the front. He had his light brown hair pulled back in a tight, sleek ponytail. Bean had been discharged from the Army right after the war. They called him Choctaw Charlie in the Army, or sometimes just "Chief." Nate and Bean hadn't known each other in the service, but had met this year at the Native American student union and bonded over their Persian Gulf experience.

Not that they ever actually talked about it.

Bean liked going out with Nate because he was so handsome that he drew all of the attention, which gave Bean the opportunity to ogle women with impunity. It was as good as being invisible, except girls would eventually talk to him, even if it was only for the chance to flutter around the bronze glow of Nathaniel Redmoon. Nate had a broad face with a deep dimple in his left cheek, and the kind of long, straight eyelashes that women both covet and desire. Bean, on the other hand, had his own allure; despite being thin and physically graceless, he nonetheless exuded a type of brotherly sweetness that caused girls to alternately dote on him when happy and confide in him when miserable. Bean actually cultivated his nice-guy image while drafting off of Nate's aura of inaccessibility. Girls were crazy about guys they couldn't have, and Bean was there to provide comfort and relief. They were a team: Nate broke hearts and Bean taped them back together. While this often translated into no more than a few hours of long, artistic kissing (Bean's stealth talent) to repair some girl's fractured self-image, in general he felt it was enough to get by.

This night, the two friends were of distinctly different opinions regarding their destination. Standing in the kitchen, slipping his arm into the welcoming sleeve of his jacket, Bean resumed the argument they had started earlier that day in the student union.

"So. What do you think about Mel's party?"

Nate narrowed his eyes slightly and tipped his head at a thoughtful angle. He seemed to be studying the fold of the room where the wall met the ceiling. He held this pose for a moment, then leveled his gaze back at Bean.

"Let's not," he said.

"Dude, you weren't even thinking about it. It's so obvious you just don't like her. What is your deal? Why don't you like her?"

"She's fake."

"Fake what?"

"Fake Indin."

"You think she's a fake Indian."

"No, that's not what I said. I said she's a fake Indin. There's a difference."

Bean pulled a wooden chair with peeling red paint from its place at his grey formica table and sat down. He couldn't think of anything to say, so he just sat there, caressing the sleek nub of his brown ponytail in his right hand. Nate quietly drew out the other chair and sat down beside him. Bean knew that he would regret what he was about to say, but he said it anyway.

"Isn't she from Umatilla?"

"She's not *from* there."

"Yeah, but isn't her family from there? I mean, it's not her fault if her..."

"Look, you don't know. It's not like Oklahoma, OK?"

Bean stood up and went to the fridge. He opened the door to reveal a twelve-pack of Pepsi, three cans of Miller Genuine Draft, a carton of eggs, an unfinished plastic container of macaroni salad, a half-gallon of milk, a jar of salsa, and a tiny bottle of Tabasco sauce. He withdrew two cans of MGD and cracked one open, then took the longest, loudest draw off the top that he could. Without looking at him, he extended the second can to Nate. Bean circled around Nate to the cupboard and methodically extracted a bag of tortilla chips, which he tore open and poured into a bowl. Then he went back to the fridge, stiffly reached inside and drew out the salsa. He set each of these items before Nate, who quietly accepted the small offerings.

They communed like that for some time.

"She's too close to you: that's why you hate her."

"What? She's not close to me at all."

"She is. She's like..." And here Bean had to pause and rifle through his collection of metaphorical references. "Like dolphins and porpoises. Dolphins *hate* porpoises because they are so much like them. That's what she is like to you."

"Like a porpoise."

"Yes." And it is true that Bean, while advancing his marine life allegory, was actually pursuing a somewhat different line of thought. He wasn't looking for explanations from Nate as much as he wanted assurances. He wanted to be certain that Nate did not care for Melanie at all.

Nate considered the dolphin-porpoise paradigm for a moment. He had heard that dolphins were actually vicious bastards, contrary to their portrayals as talkative aquatic friends of man, loyal and trustworthy. "OK, fine," Nate said. "Maybe we could go to the Relief Pitcher for a bit. Shoot some pool. Then, you know, stop by Melanie's party."

"Yeah, we could do that." Bean leaned back in his chair, balancing on the back two legs. He studied his friend. "Who's at the Relief Pitcher?"

"No one," Nate said. "Jen."

Bean's chair thumped down hard. "Jen? That girl from econ? The redhead? Dude, she is so out of your league. She's like... rich girl from L.A. You can't—don't even think about it."

Nate knew this wasn't true. No girl was out of his league. He knew that he was handsome, and he had learned over years of practice how to channel his natural shyness into something like mystique. "Yes I can," he replied. "Because I'm an Amer-I-can!" They both laughed at the stupid joke. Nate tipped his chin then, to gesture at the clock. "Let's go," he said, picking up the keys.

The first flakes of snow were spiraling down from the sky as Nate and Bean arrived at the Relief Pitcher, a divey sports bar famous for its copious taps, deep-fried okra, and recreation-oriented electronic arcade games. Nate scanned the room for Jennifer, and spotted her on a barstool at the bar next to two women who he assumed were her friends. Her gaze was fixed on the basketball game on the television monitor above, while the two women chatted indifferently beside her. Nate admired the angle of her neck, the thick fiery curls of hair that framed her beautiful face, the look of devotion in her eyes, fixed solidly on the monitor. She hadn't noticed him come in. He bought a pitcher of MGD and filled a glass for himself and Bean, but as they were making their way to a table, Jen's glance caught Bean's eye.

"What's the score?" Bean yelled.

"Seventeen twenty-one," she replied. "Clippers."

She caught Nate's eye and smiled. He tipped his chin at her and smiled back, then settled in for a beer with Bean, who told Nate he got points for picking a girl who liked sports. At halftime, Jen glided over to their table and invited them to join her. Bean, taking his cue, excused himself to try the video arcade bowling.

Nate followed Jen to her barstool. "You a Clippers fan?" he asked, taking the stool beside her. It turned out that she was. Nate raised one eyebrow in surprise. "I figured you for a Lakers girl."

She wrinkled her nose in distaste. "I hate the Lakers," she said. "And even if I didn't, I'd still root for the underdog." Nate took in this information with some pleasure. He attempted to calculate how this detail might impact his overall chances of later getting laid. Could go either way, he decided. Sitting side-by-side, watching the game, talking about very little besides free throw averages and conference standings, Nate felt something he hadn't known in some time. It was an intoxicating sort of intimacy, as though they had known each other for a long time already, as though they were children about to nap, or lovers waking up. Her arm would touch his, just barely, and he would feel the sensation ripple through his body. In uneven slices of conversation, they shared their respective high school basketball careers. She had been a forward. He had been a guard. They were made for each other.

Just as the Clippers finished the Blazers (final score: 92–83) a booth opened up. Sitting across from her, Nate suddenly felt awkward, like he had to start the whole thing over again. He felt almost claustrophobic in the big wooden box of the booth. His gaze passed quickly across her face and landed on her clavicle bone.

She fingered her necklace, a slim gold chain with a tear-shaped diamond suspended from it. She seemed unaware of how she ran the pendant up and down the chain, her fingers fanning away from it like a bird's wing.

"That's nice," Nate said. "Diamond."

"Thanks. My dad gave it to me for my sixteenth birthday. My parents divorced when I was little, so I hardly ever see him. My dad's a lawyer in Phoenix. My mom sells real estate, and she just works all of the time. She's married to my stepfather, and he's a pretty nice guy."

Nate nodded. They sat in silence.

"What do your parents do? Are they divorced?" she asked.

"No, they're married." The words sounded strange. "My dad works for the tribe in economic development. My mom takes care of my sister's kids. She actually takes care of lots of people around there."

Jen started to ask him more questions about his family, but the more he tried to describe his life in Pilot Rock the more he imagined her receding from him. It was partly the way she was sitting, with the back of her head resting against the flat wooden surface of the booth seat, her chin forward; it was the way she languorously gazed at him, smiling a half-smile when he talked about his grandma. She had beautiful teeth. And a strong neck. He tried to change the subject, to talk about his service in the war. He had been around the world; he had played in the swimming pools of Iraqi princes. He knew about death and fear and patriotism, military discipline that could crush a weaker soul. But somehow he wasn't able to parlay these details into the conversation, because all she wanted to talk about was his family. Question after question: how long had it been since his grandma came to live with them? What was it like to have so many siblings? Did he share his room with anybody? What were their family reunions like?

"We don't really have family reunions," he said. "Well, except this one time." He smiled to himself.

"Tell me," she said.

He cleared his throat. "OK, I was in high school, and I got into trouble with my friend Marvin, because we were skipping school. It wasn't any big deal. But we got caught, and we're sitting in the principal's office, and he's going to suspend us from track—but then he says, 'If you're willing to do some volunteer work, you can do that instead.' So we say OK, and we get signed up for this thing at my school called 'Spirit Corps,' where you volunteer to do stuff in the community. We show up at the school on Saturday morning and it's this really nice spring day. Pretty soon three of my cousins show up, not because they'd done anything wrong, but because they actually *had* school spirit and volunteered. We looked around and we were like, 'Hey, it's a family reunion!'

"So they told us to go out to this rich guy's place. He was a big-time farmer and on the school board, plus he had this crop dusting business and he was kind of a hot shot. Well, he had donated a big section of his yard to be used for the new elementary school playground, and we were supposed to move it for him. So they show us how to use this sod cutter, and to roll up these little sections of grass, load it on a truck, and take it back to the school and roll it back out.

"We get to the guy's place and he's not there—he's off flying his plane because, you know, it was such a perfect day and all. We're standing in the driveway, and it's pretty clear that we're supposed to take the grass from this big field right there, but it's all seeded in that crested wheatgrass stuff that's all tough and prickly. Then we look at the lawn in front of his house, and it's all green and cushy and thick, like nice carpet. So Marvin says, 'Let's just take that.'

"So we went at it. We had that guy's lawn chopped up in like, two hours. And the funny thing is, he's up there flying in his plane and decides to wing by, and he looks down and all he sees is this big brown patch in front of his house and a bunch of Indians rolling up his lawn. He damn near drove the plane out of the sky."

Jen laughed.

"Yeah, so every once in a while we're together and we say, 'Remember that family reunion?' And that gets everyone going." "I wish I had a story like that," she said.

"I'm sure you do."

"No, really. I don't."

"You saying you never got into trouble?"

"No, I'm not saying that. Just not with anyone else." She paused. "With my friends, sure, we got into trouble for drinking at the pool and stuff like that. But I don't have stories like that with my family." She went on to explain that her family reunions are actual family reunions, where her two cousins and aunt come out from Florida, and her grandparents from Beverly Hills, and they all go to a resort in Carmel or take a cruise. She said that she always has the best time, especially with her cousin Lisa, who was only six months older. "She feels like my best friend for five days," Jen said. "Then she leaves, and I don't see her again for another two years."

He thought that he detected a certain wistfulness to her voice, perhaps a sense of longing. And then it occurred to him that he could love her, or perhaps he already did. Here she was, a rich girl from L.A., but no brothers and sisters to play and fight with, and hardly any cousins to speak of. And her dad probably never came to her basketball games, and her mom was always on the phone and making deals and probably getting work done on her body. Yes, and her mother, far from being nurturing, was probably *competitive* with her, and probably said all kinds of horrible things to destroy Jen's self-image. Nate projected all of these things into the slight details that Jen had offered, and he began to imagine the world that he could give her: dozens of cousins and aunties and grandmas and refrigerators overflowing with potato salad and hot dogs and berry pie. Houses that smelled of brain-tanned leather, beeswax, fried chicken and sweat because they were never empty. Uncles who played practical jokes and drank too much and cried when they heard certain songs. He would fill her up with these things, fill her up with himself. Fill her, fill her, fill her.

He decided to pursue this line.

"Tell me about your dad," he said.

She looked surprised. Then she yielded. "Well, there's not much to say. He hasn't been around much. Of course, my mom can't stand him. He loves Phoenix. He's like, really into Native Americans."

"What do you mean?"

"Well, you know. . . . " Jen glanced away, shifted in her seat. "I don't know. I shouldn't have brought it up. It's just the whole Phoenix thing: he's got the adobe office, the zig-zaggy rugs, the little Zuni pots in a glass display case." She took a long sip of beer while Nate studied her. Then she let out an awkward little laugh. She leaned forward, conspiratorially. "I probably shouldn't tell you this. But in his office, he has a life-size Indian made out of leather. It's covered with beadwork—it's really amazing."

Nate stared at her without blinking.

"What do you mean? He has a big leather Indian?"

"Yeah. He bought it from some guy on a reservation. I don't even remember where. South Dakota, I think. It has all this beadwork on it and feathers. I know it sounds weird but it's really beautiful. But he loves to talk about all of the people who have tried to buy it from him, and he just won't sell. He's been offered thousands of dollars, but he won't sell it. He always says, 'Sentimental value!'" Jen leaned back and took another sip of beer, and it seemed to Nate that the glass in her hand came down hard on the table, like a gavel. She laughed a little again, and shook her curly red head.

"He's such a jerk," she said.

Then she sighed. "Let's talk about something else."

Nate couldn't imagine what something else would be. He gave a hard, silent stare at the base of her glass with her fingers curved around it.

Then he made an exaggerated gesture of looking at his watch. "Whoa. It's twenty-three hundred hours already. I told my buddy we'd head over to a friend's party, so I guess I'd better get going."

She had a look of anticipation in her eyes, an openness to her expression. He knew that she wanted him to invite her. "I'd like you to come," he said. "But I really couldn't bring you. It's kind of an Indian thing."

She showed no emotion, but he knew that he had hurt her. She smiled (bravely, he thought). "That's cool," she said. "Maybe another time."

"Yeah," he said, making more of a show than he should have in extracting his wallet and peeling off a few ones for the barmaid. He dropped them on the table in front of Jen. "Thanks," he said. "I had a good time."

Making their way across the parking lot, Bean bragged that he had attained six of the top ten arcade bowling scores. His mood was light, knowing that they were headed to Melanie's house. The snow marched in steady procession, and another couple of inches had piled up on the car. Bean and Nate wiped the windows clean with wide strokes of their arms. Then Nate turned the keys in the ignition and nothing happened. He tried again. Nothing. Not even a spark.

"Something's wrong," Bean said.

Nate nodded.

"It's dead."

Nate put his hand on the dash and breathed deeply. Bean shifted in his seat. Nate tried the engine again. Nothing.

"You know," Bean said, trying to sound casual. "We could walk to Melanie's from here. She could give us a jump."

Nate stared intensely at the horizon line of the hood.

"Or we could call her," Bean offered.

Nate said nothing.

"I'm going in to call her," Bean said, reaching for the door handle.

"NO!" Nate yelled. He slammed his fist into the dash. He swore. Then he said, "It's dead, dead, dead." And swore again.

"Hey, man, relax. It's just the battery. I'll call Mel and she can help us. It's no big deal." As he spoke, he eased the door open and slipped out. His face reappeared in the passenger-side window. "I'll be right back."

Bean returned, but didn't get in. Nate eventually got out, locked the doors, and leaned against the car. Bean blew warm air into his cupped hands and did jumping jacks to stay warm. Soon they heard the steady rattle of Melanie's car engine, a blue two-door 1984 Dodge Charger, and the deliberate crunch of snow under the wheels. Melanie slowly rolled the window down on the passenger's side. "Hey, I don't have cables," she said. "But I can get you home." She pushed open the door. The two men looked at each other, uncertain who would move first.

"What about your party?" Nate asked.

"Oh, it was quiet. It's over. Everyone left early," she said. "People wanted to drink." She looked from Bean to Nate, as if measuring them.

"Nate, get in back," she ordered.

"I think I'll walk," he answered, and immediately turned and headed the other direction.

Melanie watched him go. Bean climbed gingerly into the car, and she turned the car around. In short order she had pulled up next to Nate. "C'mon, man," Bean said. "Get in."

Nate stopped walking and stood still. Melanie braked. Nate stared at the cast of light from the headlights on the snowy street. It reminded him of a feeling he couldn't quite reach. A memory from some other time. Just the cast of lights on the snow, the warm car idling in the darkness. Maybe it was a memory of Marvin, his friend from high school. Or maybe it was Auntie JoAnn's car when she brought them a big pot of elk stew one winter. Maybe it was . . . he couldn't say. Just some other time. Bean opened the door and got out so Nate could get into the back seat.

Nate climbed in the back without comment. He rode silently while Bean and Melanie swapped stories, mostly about car trouble and getting caught in snowstorms. She dropped Bean off at his place first, giving him an affectionate wave as he headed up the staircase to his apartment.

The ride to Nate's house was quiet except for the occasional rubbery scrape of the wipers clearing the windshield and the constant blast of the heater. Melanie pulled up in front of Nate's apartment and put the car in neutral. She looked at him through the rear view mirror.

"Your ears are red," she said. Nate tipped his head ever so slightly. "Here," she said, pulling off her knit cap with one hand. "Put this on. Then when you go inside, it won't hurt so bad when you start warming up." She handed it back to him. The cap was hand-knit from lumpy brown wool yarn and had a big round pom-pom on top.

His nose was cold but he could barely detect the scent of her hair when she pulled the cap off. Sort of a vanilla smell. He pulled the cap on over his ears as Melanie watched in the mirror.

"Looks good on you," she said. He was watching the top layer of Melanie's long, dark hair float around her head, awakened by static electricity.

She locked with his eyes in the mirror.

"You thinking about growing your hair back?" she asked. Nate shrugged and looked away. Melanie kept her brown eyes fixed on the rear view mirror. His eyes returned.

"How are you doin'?" she asked.

"Good." Nate's eyes narrowed slightly, but his expression didn't change. Melanie looked away from the mirror, down at her mittened hands.

"You could thank me."

Nate nodded. "Thanks for the ride," he said.

After a moment, she leaned across the front seat to open the door on the passenger's side. Nate pushed the seat forward and crawled out.

"You be safe getting home?" he asked.

Melanie laughed. "I think I'll make it."

Nate nodded and carefully closed the car door. Melanie sat in the idling car until Nate let himself in. Then she carefully backed out of the lot and turned home. Inside of his apartment, Nate stood in the dark at the door, watching the lights turn, watching her leave through the small pane of glass that formed the window, thinking of home, and light, and cold.

Reid Gómez
(1968–)

"I live in language. My Grandfather would come in from the yard and tell us, 'Look at what my stories grew.' Connection, beauty and responsibility to the People and the land, with these I stand upright. Without community there is no art, and without art there is no community."

Artist's Statement, http://www .neshkinukat.org/artists/gomez.html

electric gods

Reid Gómez

*In cases of physiologically conditioned
depression, in which the religious
responses are often involved, modern
medicine with great success applies the
electric shock treatment, passing an
electric current through leads placed in
contact with the patient's temples. These
are often people who in their state of
depression also despaired of their spiritual
salvation, who were prey in other words
to what has been called in theological
literature 'certainty of damnation.' And
lo and behold! What the minister of
religion had tried in vain to achieve with
comforting exhortations and encouraging
words from the Bible and the Catechism
has now been accomplished by the
electric current!*

—Karl Heim, *Christian Faith and Natural Science*

Sylvia doesn't keep much in pockets. Inside they are warm envelopes. She likes them empty, hides her hands there, and doesn't like to run into things, like earth out of sorts or feeble attempts at order. Money is so dirty, and overlaid with finger oil and handprints. Her flesh like those black light lamps at the gates of amusement parks. They pick up the traces of everything. There on the surface, glowing yellow and phosphorescent. A crime scene in the movies, fluid stains everywhere. People leave their whirls and lines all over. They bother her and she finds herself caught on them, the impressions, like so many rusty nails.

She walks to work, she walks home, all with her hands in her pockets. Her money in a silver clip in her upper left chest pocket. She lifted the clip off a woman she called the sky hoe for her blue sheets. She spent several nights with her when she was eighteen and still hadn't quite managed a satisfactory means of interaction; that was 2,380 mornings before this one. The fog here thick, the air cool; everything begins to move in and out, in so many cycles. She likes today because it is beautiful. She breathes the air, her face crisp and almost freezing, her finger tips small heaters. Things re-happen now and she walks right through. Rehappenings occur here at great frequency no matter how many washings or shaking outs of skin cells.

Somewhere in the evening she asked a series of questions. Yellow lights glow in the air, calmness coming down like an answer for everything. She rolled over beneath blankets that remember, and Alecia becomes a resident of a faraway space beside her. Just before dreaming, a pattern emerges. She becomes part of it, sitting in the center, a world takes shape around her. In the distance there are men. Their voices go on all night. A fire glows red like the sky outside her eyelids. She enters the moment; it is beautiful.

On the ridge of the mountain the trees look like neurons. In her mind she sees them, inside a microscopic sphere, a glass surface spread over with dye: neurons in the red sky. A wind rushes through. The trees, though, are quiet.

Her feet are bare and naked; their temperature is inviting. Sitting there her breasts descend like small circles molded in another lifetime. She is a woman, in the dreaming. The mountain is a moment still inside her. She exists in a small circle of earth, a round dwelling with a small opening to breathe through. It is still inside and she stretches within that silence. The space outside in perfect proportion to the space inside. Pressure is released. Oxygen flows in, carbon dioxide flows out; she senses the molecular structure. There is no fear to frighten her. She hears the words to the old woman's singing. She understands them. Runs swiftly and without anxiety on new foot pads. Outside there are shadows outside the dreaming; and she understands that they continue on without her. For one evening she lives there.

The mattress is white and clean. She saved for seven months with the single intention of buying a new, never-used Ortho from Sears over on Masonic and Geary. They delivered it on a Sunday. She had to pay extra. The world became more tranquil. She sleeps atop the whiteness and something wondrous is set in motion. No other body has been on top of this surface. It's the cleanest thing she owns. Memory's blankets do not damage it. She burned the old one outside, got the police called, but manages to talk her way out of a citation or incarceration.

The field of white molded her voice, lovely, different than she ever imagined it could be, more lovely than anything. City light outside the window is a constant companion. Stillness—motion slowed to a manageable unit—began to hold things together like so many cells making up connective tissue. Colors rise from steam heat and soil from places she had never been to, or run from.

She rested, and for the last thirty years the night became a place of great potential. Sometime, not too long ago, she began arriving at a door, just beside her sternum. No one had touched her there, ever, in that place where bone ascends and provides a framework for breathing. The door has a rounded top and is hand molded, and painted over with cheap paint from the hardware store. It is the color of the sky hoe's sheets. She stands in front, for what seems like one month or four. Tonight began by entering. Touch me here. Foot pads quietly make movement over ground. Inside the dream in progress. She sits down, directly in its center. There is no waking, only a reemerging.

The building is a short box, a rectangle maze pressed flat against the pavement. All windows are waist high and covered with chicken wire glass and iron cross bars. There is an illusion of open space and ventilation.

The floors are all one color, and carpet in the dayroom. The walls, the ceiling, it makes no difference which way you spend your life looking. They're all the same and all significantly different—hospitals and halfway homes—blue rugs and matching tiles, white floors with colored tape for following directions, another one with browns and oranges someone donated to facilitate the contractors' low bidding. This structure smells like a mixture of feces and cleaning fluid. Geriatrics and children's wards reek of a foulness worse than all the others. It's the plainest expression they could imagine. No decoration, just plaster, paint, and wires. She shared a room with no one. They let some girls go two to a space, but not her, and she is grateful. She desires more than she can manage. How the fuck did she end up here? In the range of incarceration it's a low-to-moderate security facility. Most of the people shuffle around, too sick to pick up their feet. They scrape by, they scrape the floor, they scrape themselves out of their bodies.

The double doors out are blue and shiny. They can only be pushed open when they are buzzing. On this side of them, there is a small room of vending machines and soda, and the huge day room with the tables, TV and carpet. It's only got three sides to it, the fourth wall a non-existent structure into the hallway. Face the blue doors. Never turn your back on them, they might believe you've resigned yourself to staying. Face the blue doors. To your left, the hall of patient rooms; to your right, various means of therapeutic intervention: individual, group, occupational therapy, and finally the hall of showers.

She's an adult and knows that she is lucky. Psychosis smells better than behavior disorders and dementia. Her age group is still threatening, so there are more attempts to pay attention. She sees this only from the inside. Doesn't remember coming, doesn't remember going. She does not remember the means of transportation. Once they strap you in, there is nothing you can do to stop them. The small rubber ring keeps them safe from bloody tongues and broken tooth enamel. They believe in a method beyond the madness, a way of releasing what they think is behind this. Eyes, hands, the idea that they are helping. Can they really believe the things they read? Various manuals in three-ring binders. In the northeast corner, one orange, two navy blue, a fourth binder, white with nothing in it but a set of five dividers. She commits every detail to a skin cell. They never clean the floor. Dust bunnies hop around the corners. There's one too many chairs and a coffee stain in the shape of Idaho.

On the ceiling the small dots of soundproof interlocking covers. They added the squares recently to the previous construction. It lowered everything four and one-quarter inches. They look used, but they're just old and water-damaged. It fades to a pitch of green every time they do her.

Unilateral interventions, described neatly in the doctor's orders. She pushed his face and name out, every time he tried to enter. Too many questions, too much advice, he did nothing but try to get inside her. Buzz, buzz, the telephone was buzzing. Phil Spector's wall of sound surrounds her. The ceiling sprinklers shoot iodine, the ward is covered and recolored. It will fade slowly by tomorrow morning. She comes back so soon it scares them. A giant vacuum sucked her in, it would spit her out once she recovered from the physical shock of torture. Flash. Flash. Flash. She hated this Flashing, almost more than the initial buzz and buzzing. It came later, at intermittent moments. Her back hurt. Her butt hurt. Her neck felt like she just exited a twelve-round match of boxing.

She was more tired than she was angry. Tomorrow the feelings would return, only at ten volumes higher. *Go away little girl. Go away little girl, before I beg you to stay.* Donny Osmond's voice was everywhere. She slept because she had to. The body capable of no other means of responding. Experimental manipulations, white walls, white floors, white blankets binding.

In the group room they'd show *Wild Kingdom.* They were only allowed to change the station once per hour and the energy required for that level of decision making and cooperation was often too much for most of them. Sylvia, on the other hand, had ample energy and desire. They'd labeled her "impulsive" on several hospital documents, but it was their limited appreciation for the way she saw things: immediately with passion.

She liked *Wild Kingdom,* so there it was: Jim Perkins and Mutual of Omaha, in live-action blood and gore. The run captivated her. The way they stalked each other, one feigning ignorance and then surprise. It was, above anything, an intricately orchestrated exchange of power. The flesh and blood only beginning the bond forged between them during that moment of flight and capture. Deer were particularly beautiful in the moment of death. Their bodies heavy and somewhat awkward for those inexperienced with carrying them. The mountain lions too, their teeth reaching in and carrying. The big animals like elephants and hippos were of less interest to her, but she sat there watching like a sponge absorbing.

The group room annoyed her, but she tolerated it in order to view the hunting. In this structure, so dramatically removed from living, she needed that show. She could disappear herself in a moment, somehow dissolving into it. She'd learnt various tricks to call herself out, or prevent total dissolution. They worked for the most part, with two important exceptions: during sex and while watching run and capture. In a moment of attentiveness she would fall there, into the screen with its small dots and electrical frequencies, and into the women, their legs open, mouths smiling.

The attendants sat there watching. She was calm, surrounded by the other crazies. They thought Sylvia her most peaceful then and for that single hour, five o'clock on Sunday evenings, they let themselves forget to fear her. She'd sit there open-legged and with both hands on her knees. Her feet flatly planted on the floor, her eyes reactive and slightly extending from their sockets. Her breath slow and constant. She sat there for the entire hour without flinching, ticking, or uttering a sound. Even her breathing was below their hearing.

She was, in their minds, one of the most tightly strung and potentially violent patients. So they valued these moments like a junkie values his dope. They were stupid with their cravings and this made them unable to see what was right before them. Sound image and the television console, a large box warm with humming, three feet and seven inches directly in front of her. Every Sunday Sylvia sat there gathering power.

There was a mix-up in the schedule. A permanent and careless moment when they relinquished control and anything could happen. They grew complacent with their position. Small plastic name tags convinced them they were special. They kept themselves at arm's distance, believed they were somehow above this. The crazies were damaged and incapable of calculating an intelligent response to their intolerable situation. They gave the crazies what they wanted, cigarette breaks and candy. No sharp objects and no long and twisted fabrics. Convinced that death was the only option, suicide was the only thing they watched for.

Sylvia kept her abilities under cover, behind the look and the eyebrow's movement, like wings upon her forehead. She kept everything immediately available. Her treatments only caused her momentary incapacitation and a permanent influx of arousal. There were twelve minutes they could not account for. She loved details more than ever. Twelve minutes was entirely more than she could ask for, eight minutes and forty-eight seconds would have been sufficient. Twelve was like a gift from every god she'd ever heard of.

She only needed to exploit the opportunity they provided. See it. Shape it. Make it into something that could help her. In the dark it would be perfect. She could be invisible just like her Uncle Isaac. Once out, there would be no way to trace her, no prints, no ripples on the surface. She knew how to step in front of things and fade immediately inside them. How to sing his songs and walk straight out the door and past them. They were so arrogant it was easy. She even took her blanket in case she'd need it when she stopped to sleep, some time later. She had no idea where she'd be going, but different voices guided her: don't get too ahead of the present situation. Occupy a stance and occupy the movement through it. Twelve minutes, step outside the room, walk close to the wall, and do not hide yourself, sing it inside strongly, and do not let it leak outside you, believe all earth, all earth *nizhó 'ní 'go.** A step through the blue door he leaves so carefully cracked right open. Four minutes to exit in the main hall, out glass doors; the night air is a wash of ice cold water. There is a color with no name: it's a liquid jet you must experience. She is inside of the next detail she is inside of. Twelve minutes becoming. It began an aspect of eternity. And they never knew what happened.

Summer provided another moment altogether. Outside watercolors paint themselves into shapes that flow and mix, wet on wet, wet on dry. Red, orange, yellow, green, blue, indigo, and violet. Nothing remained the same to her, the beauty was before her, new and unequaled difficulty directly across her body. She was so happy to be free and unaware of how to handle it. A new responsibility coincided, a new challenge in the change of membranes. She had a lot of buzzing still in half-lives running through her. They did something she'd have to manage a repair for. Too many questions, like birds flying overhead; she sat and looked up and found them indescribable.

New clothes, stolen at a laundry mat. New shoes were harder, but she was tender footed and had been warned, inside, against walking without protection. She found a woman she could trade with, cigarettes and Keds from the supermarket for a promise and an afternoon of listening. She walked as much as she could, just to make a larger spread of space between them. The wind was on the inside. Green leaves, and colored light reflecting small bodies, small mirrors, glistening, shining, polishing the surface space outside her.

She never imagined it could be so different. In some ways still slightly before the center. On the other side of things she understood there'd be a difference. Right now it was amazing she was still breathing. Her wrists hurt like they always would. Once broken, the bones remember. Still she was in a large flatland of disorientation. She needed an incline, a table, a better place to see from. It took her twelve days to arrive in Reno, one for every minute. Days are a single brush of white across the landscape, thick paint in need of thinning. Water, water. She was inconceivably dry and thirsty.

Olivia came to them several months after the "crazy bitch" broke out. Sylvia had become a bit of local attendant history. No one had ever got out, not out and stayed out. She grew in their stories to her entire five feet and three inches, 152 pounds. They had given her the nickname—"crazy bitch"—'cause that was what she called them, each and every one.

Sylvia's voice was an anomalous circumstance in every hospital she had been in. But that one phrase she had perfected. In the last place, they viewed her as violent and angry so they shocked and restrained her. It was their means of managing. She screamed back at them with her most delicate and intricate of vocalizations. It rose

* In Diné Bizaad (that is, in the Diné language), *nizhó 'ní* translates as "it is pretty." With the addition of "go," an adverbial element, the phrase may be translated as "pretty, set in motion."

low, a single note from wind, a reed resonating down the halls, through ear canals and in that space there is no name for.

No one who heard her ever forgot her, least of all Olivia. Tall and thick like most good women from her side of creation, she stood there as a living specimen. She was from a place not one hospital employee had memory of. No one really knew how this one got there or why they kept her. They read her file, but the words dropped out before they could ascertain their meaning. Because of its total unintelligibility they made a habit of reading her file out loud, as if it was their favorite book from childhood. It was a strange habit even among these men who were, for the most part, strange.

The doctors and nurses kept up with the task of writing down orders, observations, and continually evolving diagnoses. Her file was thick and stained with food from all the hands scratching marks and attempted readings. With all this attention they had only learned four things: Olivia Red Sky, Northern Cheyenne, no children, refuses all attempts at communication.

They should have called home. Olivia knew a law existed somewhere requiring them to do so. She remembered hearing it somewhere on the street a long time ago. She remembered it and knew she could think about it on occasions such as this. But their language didn't compel them so they busied themselves reading pages and pages of words that, in the end, told them nothing. She spoke in Cheyenne just to frustrate them, saying nothing about the environment: the orange shag carpet; the plastic tables with the brown tops attempting to look like wood; GE fans they turned on for themselves in the heat of summer; and the floor with its growing collection of scuff marks and scratches.

The locks she never spoke about, not that anyone understood her anyway. She was careful and intelligent about what she let them observe about her thinking. Access to the keys didn't seem likely. Besides she didn't want any more physical contact than necessary. They spoke often about the "crazy bitch" and, with the fifth mention of her, Olivia knew something was coming undone.

Early in 1985 Olivia killed a white man in the bathroom of a bus station. She'd gone inside to wash up, tie her hair back and collect herself before the scheduled departure. It was an ordinary hour of an ordinary day. The sun came up with a particular brilliance and she said words to it as she had done every morning since she could remember. She was thick, but people often mistook her for being quite delicate and easily persuadable. She stood there, her body bent over the long porcelain sink. A man came up behind her and in an instant two things happened. She lived. He died. There is nothing left to say.

Outside is a reality some people no longer have access to. It is a privilege denied, or handed out like cheap cigarettes for good behavior. The old women, no one can find them; the old men are encouraged to sing; the boys and girls are given prizes for Bingo; and the people in the middle, they make crafts. There is a subtle cruelty in the making of tiled mosaic hot plates. There is no cooking allowed, no daily preparation of meals for sustenance and grounding. And more importantly, there is no fire, not even for smoking. Attendants light cigarettes and the ends are guarded with serious attention.

Olivia does not participate in their grotesque displays of ignorance and is mostly offended by the way they treat her. She remembers being five and being given tasks of great importance. She remembers beading small squares of hide into intricate patterns more thought out and significant than these kits of four uncomplementary colors. They intended her to fashion them onto a bed of Popsicle sticks with glue and little room for true expression.

She thinks there in the corner of her own kitchen, making sense of something coming over. The occupational therapist comes by and puts her hand on Olivia's shoulder. At that moment, she knows she is leaving soon. She looks up at the lady, smiles, because something before her is becoming clearer. The woman smiles back, believing she has touched her and somehow healed her, if only minutely. The hour is over. They all rise and leave. Eleven brown-and-orange hot plates and one pile of squares sitting still on the table in the middle of the room.

Olivia is tired and believes in resting. This is usually noted down as a sign of depression and she collects marks in a column they construct indicating the need for treatment. They've found that depressed women seem to respond well to shock therapy. She is a woman. In diagnostic hindsight, that crazy bitch Sylvia bordered on schizophrenia and gender identity disorder. They used the ECT on her because she was unruly. She was small, though they remember her increasingly as a little mannish and therefore bigger.

This woman, Red Sky, was a little larger and when they thought of her, they couldn't help themselves or their imaginings. The doctors were far beyond these sorts of concepts. They simply read the files and made the decisions, making as little contact with the patient as necessary. Her assigned doctor had yet to find an adequate schedule to maintain a satisfactory relationship with her, so he relied on the nurses' notes and the attendants' gossip floating upwards, informing his clinical observations. He scheduled the first of what was estimated to be a short series of ECT treatments.

Thirty-four letters set in motion Olivia's introduction to Sylvia. Neither of them knew what they were getting into. Inside that particular configuration of frequency and amplitude, they connected forever. Electrodes, like man-made synaptic clefts, transferred from one head to another. Lubricant easing communication and facilitating the exchange of energy. Olivia was to understand almost everything about Sylvia in that single moment of therapeutic intervention.

Exactly what they shared is hard to describe. Sylvia was someone outside. Direction extended all around her and she had stepped out into it, stronger than she had ever been. Soon Olivia would be outside, too. It was something they both would have to get used to: an entirely new means of experiencing, another pattern emerging— elusive and pervasive. It was a fire in Electriclady land that passed between them, and Olivia would hold it in her changing skin till she grew older and it passed out of her like so much living.

Touch. Touch. Touching.

Reid Gómez

There is beauty at the surface. It is there in an eye, on the edge of skin, in a touch once made, unending. If she fell it would be an endless pool of liquid. Smooth and warm and each sensation at the right frequency for the exact duration. Touch. Touch. Touching. The air is so wonderfully all around her. She runs, she runs, she wakes up running. Sleep another story waiting for the right moment, the right time of the day, a year changes shape in a pattern she is learning to follow the flow of. Nothing is a puzzle. She is uninterested in solving it. She walks and walks and there are wires overhead; they crisscross from pole to building and back again. She looks up. It's a Kandinsky.* She looks up. It is moving. Silence. Song. Just air, wind, color, motion, and nothing stands in for anything. It is. It is. It is something she is a part of. Standing underneath a blue, a red, an orange sky just southeast of Boulder. She has no memory she has the standing.

Leaves hang like hummingbirds from the trees. It is so windy, and every one is dancing. She is every age she's ever been before. Riding ponies just like her Auntie. She knows nothing beyond the narrow strips of story. Piece work and resourcefulness. She was never good at threading things. Spinning was an art form. Dick Buttons said so, he said it once if he said it a hundred times. Round and round, so many things made to move in revolutions. Centrifuge. Centripede. There was a moment when the muscles felt like they would burst and go spilling out of their casings. Chorizo† in a cast iron, the intestinal walls were so transparent and thin, they were strong enough, but not impenetrable. Chitlins was a delicacy she had never heard of. You had to trust that person, if you were to eat from them.

There are tons of old folk, she never noticed their lives before. Never noticed anything because the overwhelming volume was so forceful. The eyes were simulta-

---

* Wassily Kandinsky was a Russian-born modern abstract painter, well known for his conceptualizations of the relationship between color and sound.
† Chorizo is a spicy Mexican pork sausage.

neously inverted and hyper extending. No muscle control. No focus. No means of collecting herself long enough to stand upright and in her skin stretched in a perfect fit exactly over. She knows things before they happen. Does things without explanation or visible instruction. Shush. Shush. Shushing on the inside. No more candy cigarettes and no more burning. It's so beautiful inside the fire. Sometimes there is nothing but air feeding, blowing, shaping skin and sound and the small bits of wood gathered carefully like it's always been.

The carpet is still a piece of fabric laying over. Small synthetic fibers glued and rolled on giant tubes of cardboard. The insides of paper towels are thin and flimsy, good for nothing but small cylinders for storage. They play cards, they play slots, she sits there on the chair and it's some aspect of the sitting. People rarely bring their families. The children are left outside or in the room watching Home Box Office or Showtime. They pull down, insert another quarter, pull down, every once in a while a ching ching and some old person gets excited they are winning. Three more quarters in the slot. Pull. Pull. Pull down and no more chinging. The sitting here, inside, is for herself. After an hour, she understands that. She'll only stay the weekend. It may be the last time she comes back out of this one need and confusing hunger. Her body changed and she knows now, this is a part of the attempt to insert a violent means of breaking.

Their diagnosis defined her. First cause, second cause, they had a whole list of things she should do different. Too much random fucking, too many ancestors, too much time seeing things she had no business seeing. She thought too much, got caught in details and moments that were long gone and beyond her ability to control. Half of this shit didn't even happen directly to her. She was wrong for feeling everything was connected. It was the pieces they wanted her to quickly turn away from. Too many pieces, too many relations. She had a list of things they thought it was best for her to get over.

Steamrolled asphalt, each piece of gravel some small part of the picture, she sat directly in the center. Railroads. The Colorado Plateau. Mountain Bell and Pacific Gas and Electric. Iron Spikes in the soil. Small electrodes at her temples. Open the land. Open the brain. Move whatever you want over quickly, and into any space you find available. Move over, I'm trying to sit here. Stop touching yourself. Stop touching me. Voices from the bar, down one row, across from a small train of wagons. They follow passes drawn on paper and sold to travelers. What I saw in California. There were travelers traveling everywhere. They sold belief. How did they get here? She was lost at the store, in downtown Denver. The basement at Woolworth has the best sales. Where was her Auntie Cora?

Her people hid the names thinking they could somehow escape the torture. Disappear. Disappear. Isn't that what they were supposed to do with each other. Indians in slavery. Blacks a part of the relocation. They married themselves off and off and off in silence. Dates matter to white folks, slips of paper and maps with longitude and latitude. Push down, twist and open. They were pagan babies on sale at church in milk cartons, a load of change could buy any one of them. Someone was the first to believe their stories. They were too afraid not to. That's a lie. It goes further back than that. One individual cannot exist in isolation. The highway, past La Veta, down toward the Colorado, the San Juans, in an arroyo, beyond the river. They stand with their feet half cracked in the red earth they used to understand the words of. Mexico came, shortly after another state, and another country. The United States attempted to define them. They went outside, and stood proud beneath the cotton-woods, then faded because they forgot the words, the songs, the ancestors they were born for. It was so scary they gave their heads over.

She sits in Harrah's* for herself. This much she is clear of. Another set of hours pass, like parts of sky right over. The first day was something she understood and prepared for. A coming to terms with all the images she had no words for. No narrative means of spinning, hanging, slipping string through for the larger picture. It was still a mountain of details, each leaf, each drop of water, each grain being what it was and that was everything she knew. She'd explode if she saw it all, at the same time, together right then, right there. It could happen. It had happened before. She got up, went outside and stood beside the door. There were so many bodies all snipping and trimming the loose strings that hung from their ears and from their shoes like overcooked spaghetti. It wasn't a hallucination. Even though that's what they always called it. It was horror. She saw their thoughts. She saw their fears. She saw everything they convinced themselves they were hiding.

She touches the pole and it shocks her. It hurt, up to the elbows. She felt it linger, the current, for a while after. Numb and hard, she didn't like it but she knew it was important. Shocks came in waves, three or four days at a time, sometimes all seven, then two weeks of calm before the next series of contacts. It was something uncomfortable but not painful like the people. Sharp rocks like the words she spit out at the hospital. The last place she ever let them do her. A line had to be drawn and she drew it. It was a decision. She was aware of. For the first time ever, right then, right there, with her left hand rubbing her elbow, it was still numb and sore from the last shocking pole at the corner.

Olivia.

You have to open your eyes to see her. The words are not able to convey the sensory stimulation. They are pressed flat and the eye is not like the ear when it comes to reading. There are a thousand moments where she is available, standing over, and wandering in the way she does because she has to. It has come to this, an unrest resulting from the initial shock and her decision to step through the hole, on her own account, and somehow pass on the information. It was important to her to attempt a passing on of the information. The permanent dislocation something she decided she was willing to learn to live with. There were things, given to her from gods she had not met before. The great spirit was not alone. They made love in their shared

---

* Harrah's is a famous resort hotel and casino.

connection. Sylvia. Olivia. Two woman wards of the same court and surviving the same attempt at a spiritual conversion. Suicide offended.

Conversion factors are listed neatly on the inside flaps of Peechee's. They have a system for saying one thing is now another. They claim they made the world because they redefined it. The Mormons kept their records. The American Psychiatric Association kept theirs. They were reported and relocated, names, lands, and bodies, from the Department of War to the Department of the Interior.* Christian Science government. They act like biological diversification and natural preservation are equally applied to people and to landscapes. They subtract one from the other and delegate their care and classification to different bodies and different structures. Architecture, water rights and subsurface drilling. They claim they are attempting to relieve the pressure, too many demands from gods and plants they are afraid of. Wild woods. Wild earth. Wild women.

There was a collection of things that brought them close together, moments, or specific surfaces they shared or passed through: mines, iron, railroads and relocation. The movements they made now stand in some relation. There were at least five different organs of sight. Five places, five languages, five sets of gods and understandings. Each one is responsible for their own means of bringing things together. No one can step away from their mind and corresponding responsibility. The red. The black. Each describe something different. People. People. There was so much beauty to be made from them. Yoruba. Navajo. Congolese and Cheyenne.

Some people say they cannot understand them. *Shaiyena* is reported to mean those that speak a language that is unintelligible. The red sticks. The black sticks. Their language is a special means of understanding the structure they live inside of. Olivia is not interested in their various limitations. She's energy, strength and action. She is force and knowledge. There is no external means available to control her. No measurement. No gauge. No small slot to put your quarter in. Do not attempt to see how long you can hold the handle. She comes. She comes and when she comes there is no resisting her.

It's still early, Saturday night. Sylvia stands outside. It is a poem.

She stands in the river.

She stands on the mountain.

She stands on a hill.

She stands in the ocean.

There are women.

They are standing.

---

* The Bureau of Indian Affairs was founded in 1824 by the Secretary of War; the Indian Commissioner's responsibilities were transferred to the Department of the Interior in 1849.

Author Biographies and Bibliographies

Paula Gunn Allen (Laguna Pueblo and Sioux)

Laguna, Sioux, and Lebanese, Paula Gunn Allen, a well-known poet, fiction writer, scholar, editor, and feminist, grew up on the Laguna Pueblo in New Mexico. In 1966, she received a B.A. degree from the University of Oregon, followed by an M.F.A. in 1968. She completed a Ph.D. at the University of New Mexico in 1976.

Her anthology, *Spider Woman's Granddaughters: Traditional Tales and Contemporary Writing by Native American Women* (1989), received the Susan Koppelman Award from the Popular and American Culture Associations, the Native American Prize for Literature, and the American Book Award from the Before Columbus Foundation. In 2001, Allen was awarded the Lifetime Achievement Award from the Native Writers' Circle of the Americas. Allen received a Lannon Literary Fellowship in 2007.

After a long career teaching at Fort Lewis College; Durango Community College; University of New Mexico, Albuquerque; and University of California, Berkeley, and directing the Native American Studies Program at San Francisco State University, she retired from the English Department at the University of California, Los Angeles, in 1999. She now lives in northern California.

As Long as the Rivers Flow: The Stories of Nine Native Americans. New York: Scholastic, 1996.

Blind Lion: Poems. Berkeley, Calif.: Thorp Springs Press, 1974.

A Cannon between My Knees (Poems). New York: Strawberry Press, 1981.

Coyote's Daylight Trip. Albuquerque, N.M.: La Confluencia, 1978.

Grandmothers of the Light: A Medicine Woman's Sourcebook. Boston: Beacon Press, 1991.

Hózhó, Walking in Beauty: Short Stories by American Indian Writers. Los Angeles: Lowell House, 2001.

Life Is a Fatal Disease: Collected Poems 1962–1995. Albuquerque, N.M.: West End Press, 1997.

Off the Reservation: Reflections on Boundary-Busting Border-Crossing Loose Canons. Boston: Beacon Press, 1998.

The Sacred Hoop: Recovering the Feminine in American Indian Traditions. Boston: Beacon Press, 1986.

Shadow Country. Los Angeles: American Indian Studies Center, UCLA, 1982.

Skins and Bones: Poems 1979–1987. Albuquerque, N.M.: West End Press, 1988.

Song of the Turtle: American Indian Literature, 1974–1994. New York: Ballantine Books, 1996.

Spider Woman's Granddaughters: Traditional Tales and Contemporary Writing by Native American Women. Boston: Beacon Press, 1989.

Star Child. New York: Blue Cloud Quarterly Press, n.d.

Studies in American Indian Literature: Critical Essays and Course Designs. New York: Modern Language Association of America, 1983.

Voice of the Turtle: American Indian Literature 1900–1970. New York: Ballantine, 1994.

The Woman Who Owned the Shadows. San Francisco: Spinsters Ink, 1983.

Kimberly M. Blaeser (Anishinaabe)

Kimberly Blaeser is an Associate Professor of English at the University of Wisconsin–Milwaukee, where she teaches courses in Native American literature, creative writing, and American nature writing. An enrolled member of the Minnesota Chippewa Tribe, she grew up on the White Earth Reservation. Blaeser's publications include a collection of poetry, *Trailing You,* which won the 1993 First Book Award from the Native Writers' Circle of the Americas, and a critical study, *Gerald Vizenor: Writing in the Oral Tradition.* Her poetry, short fiction, personal essays, introductions, and scholarly articles have been published in more than twenty-five journals and anthologized in more than thirty-five Canadian and American collections, including *Earth Song, Sky Spirit, Reinventing the Enemy's Language, Narrative Chance, Women on Hunting, The Colour of Resistance, This Giving Birth, Dreaming History, As We Are Now, Returning the Gift, Talking on the Page, Other Sisterhoods, Unsettling America, Blue Dawn, Red Earth,* and *Nothing but the Truth.* One of Blaeser's poems was selected for installation as a sculptured doorway in the Midwest Express Building in Milwaukee. She has lectured or read from her work in more than a hundred locations in the United States, Canada, and Europe; had one of her talks chosen by Writers' Conferences and Festivals for inclusion in the organization's anthology of the best lectures given in 1992; was chosen to inaugurate the Western Canada Lecture Series in 1995; and was a recipient of a lecture award from Wordcraft Circle of Native Writers in 1999. In 2001, she received a Wisconsin Arts Board Fellowship in Poetry. In 2002, she was given a double award by the Wordcraft Circle of Native Writers and Storytellers: Wordcrafter of the Year and the Wordcraft Circle Writer of the Year Award for Creative Prose/Personal Essay. Blaeser is also the editor of a collection of Anishinaabe prose, *Stories Migrating Home.* Currently, she lives on six and a half acres of woods and wetlands in rural Lyons Township, Wisconsin, with her husband, son, and daughter.

Absentee Indians and Other Poems. East Lansing: Michigan State University Press, 2002.

Gerald Vizenor: Writing in the Oral Tradition. Norman: University of Oklahoma Press, 1996.

Stories Migrating Home: A Collection of Anishinaabe Prose (Editor). Greenfield Center, N.Y.: Greenfield Review Press, 1998.

Trailing You: Poems. Greenfield Center, N.Y.: Greenfield Review Press, 1994.

Beth E. Brant (Mohawk/Degonwadonti)

Born in Melvindale, Michigan, in 1941, Beth Brant is known for works in which she delineates her identity as a Mohawk and a lesbian. Her belief that her work is charged with a political and nationalist consciousness and that the power and beauty of language will heal and open hearts and minds is evident in all her writings. A writer and part-time teacher of creative writing and Native women's writing, she has been a lecturer at the University of British Columbia and at the University of Toronto. She was awarded the Creative Writing Award by Michigan Council for the Arts in both 1984 and 1986, the National Endowment for the Arts in 1991, and the Canada Council Award in Creative Writing in 1992.

Food and Spirits: Stories. Ithaca, N.Y.: Firebrand Books, 1991.
A Gathering of Spirit: A Collection by North American Indian Women. Ithaca, N.Y.: Firebrand Books, 1988.
I'll Sing 'Til the Day I Die: Conversations with Tyendinaga Elders. Toronto, Ontario: McGilligan Books, 1995.
Mohawk Trail. Ithaca, N.Y.: Firebrand Books, 1985.
Sweet Grass Grows All around Her (Editors Beth Brant and Sandra Laronde). Toronto, Ontario: Native Women in the Arts, 1996.
Writing as Witness: Essay and Talk. Toronto, Ontario: Women's Press, 1994.

Anita Endrezze (Yaqui)

Anita Endrezze was born in Long Beach, California, in 1952. Her father is Yaqui; her mother is of Italian, Slovenian, and German-Romanian descent. Endrezze earned her M.A. from Eastern Washington University and continues to reside in Spokane, where she is a mother, teacher, poet, short story writer, storyteller, and artist. Anita Endrezze's creative work draws on influences from her Native American heritage, as well as from the South Pacific, Australia, Africa, Asia, and European sources. Her watercolor paintings and illustrations have been exhibited in the United States, Great Britain, Finland, and Denmark. She also creates fiber works and hand-made books. She received the Weyerhauser/Bumbershoot Award in 1992 and the 1993 Washington Governor's Writers Award for her book of poetry, *At the Helm of Twilight.*

At the Helm of Twilight. Seattle: Broken Moon Press, 1992.
The Humming of Stars and Bees and Waves: Poems and Short Stories. Guildford, England: Making Waves, 1998.
The North People. Marvin, S.D.: Blue Cloud Quarterly Press, 1983.
Throwing Fire at the Sun, Water at the Moon. Tucson: University of Arizona Press, 2000.

Louise Erdrich (Ojibwe)

Louise Erdrich was born in Little Falls, Minnesota, and raised in Wahpeton, North Dakota. A member of the Turtle Mountain Chippewa, she and her family regularly visited the reservation. In 1972, Erdrich went to Dartmouth College as one of the first group of women to be admitted and as part of an early group of Native Americans to be recruited. She graduated with a B.A. in English and Creative Writing from Dartmouth College in 1976 and for two years taught in the Poetry in the Schools Program sponsored by the North Dakota State Arts Council. After earning a Master of Arts degree from the Writing Program at Johns Hopkins University in 1979, she settled into the life a full-time writer.

One of the most acclaimed American Indian writers, Erdrich's poetry, fiction, and essays have been published internationally and translated into numerous languages. Her books of poems include *Jacklight* (1984) and *Baptism of Desire* (1989). The novel/short story cycle for which she is best known is *Love Medicine* (1984, new and expanded edition 1993), which was awarded the National Book Critics Circle Award for the best work of fiction, the Sue Kaufman Prize for best first fiction from the American Academy and Institute of Arts and Letters, the Virginia McCormick Scully Award for the best book of 1984 dealing with Western Indians, the *Los Angeles Times* Award for Fiction, the American Book Award from the Before Columbus Foundation, and the Great Lakes Colleges Association Award for best work of fiction. *Love Medicine*, part of an extended story cycle, was followed by *The Beet Queen* (1986), *Tracks* (1988), and *The Bingo Palace* (1994), which together tell the story of Anishinaabe, mixed-blood, and European families living on and around a fictional reservation in North Dakota. *Tales of Burning Love* (1996), *The Antelope Wife* (1998), *The Last Report on the Miracles at Little No Horse* (2001), and *Four Souls* (2004) continue the family saga. With Michael Dorris, she published a travel narrative, *Route 2*, and a novel, *The Crown of Columbus* (1991). In addition to an autobiographical account, *The Blue Jay's Dance: A Birth Year* (1995), Erdrich has written several children's books, one of which—*The Birchbark House* (1999)—received the Wordcraft Circle Writer of the Year award in 2000. She lives in Minnesota with her daughters and owns Birchbark Books, a small, independent bookstore.

The Antelope Wife. New York: HarperFlamingo, 1998.

Baptism of Desire: Poems. New York: Harper & Row, 1989.

The Beet Queen. New York: Holt, 1986.

The Best American Short Stories 1993: Selected for US and Canadian Magazines (Editor, with Katrina Kenison). Boston: Houghton Mifflin, 1993.

The Bingo Palace. New York: HarperCollins, 1994.

The Birchbark House. New York: Hyperion Books for Children, 1999.

The Blue Jay's Dance: A Birth Year. New York: HarperCollins, 1995.

Books and Islands in Ojibwe Country (Editor, with Symmie Newhouse). Washington, D.C.: National Geographic, 2003.

Conversations with Louise Erdrich and Michael Dorris (Edited by Allan Chavkin and Nancy Feyl Chavkin). Jackson: University Press of Mississippi, 1994.

The Crown of Columbus (With Michael Dorris). New York: HarperCollins, 1991.

Four Souls. New York: Harper Perennial, 2004.

The Game of Silence. New York: HarperCollins, 2005.

Grandmother's Pigeon. New York: Hyperion Books for Children, 1996.

Jacklight. New York: Henry Holt, 1984.

The Last Report on the Miracles at Little No Horse. New York: HarperCollins, 2001.

Love Medicine (New and Expanded Edition). New York: Harper Perennial, 1993.

The Master Butchers Singing Club. New York: HarperCollins, 2003.

The Painted Drum. New York: HarperCollins, 2005.

The Range Eternal. New York: Hyperion Books for Children, 2002.

Route 2 (With Michael Dorris). Northridge, Calif.: Lord John Press, 1990.

Tales of Burning Love. New York: HarperCollins, 1996.

Tracks. New York: Henry Holt, 1988.

Diane Glancy (Cherokee)

Diane Glancy was born in 1941, in Kansas City, Missouri. She obtained a B.A. degree from the University of Missouri in 1964, an M.A. degree from Central State University in 1983, and an M.F.A from the University of Iowa in 1988. Realistic language and vivid imagery in presenting spirituality, family relations, and her identity as a person of mixed descent are her trademarks. A poet, short story writer, playwright, and essayist, she is a professor of English at Macalester College in St. Paul, Minnesota. She was awarded the Pegasus Award from the Oklahoma Federation of Writers in 1984 and the Wordcraft Circle Writer of the Year (Theatre-Playwriting/Scriptwriting) Award in 1997. She was awarded the Writer of the Year (for Screenplays) for 2003–2004 by the Wordcraft Circle of Native Writers and Storytellers and a 2003 National Endowment for the Arts Fellowship for poetry.

(Ado)ration. Tucson, Ariz.: Chax Press, 1999.

American Gypsy: Six Native American Plays. Norman: University of Oklahoma Press, 2002.

Asylum in the Grasslands. Wakefield, R.I.: Moyer Bell, 1999.

Boom Town. Goodhue, Minn.: Black Hat Press, 1995.

Claiming Breath. Lincoln: University of Nebraska Press, 1992.

The Closets of Heaven. Tucson, Ariz.: Chax Press, 1999.

The Cold-and-Hunger Dance. Lincoln: University of Nebraska Press, 1998.

Coyote's Quodlibet. Tucson, Ariz.: Chax Press, 1995.

Designs of the Night Sky. Lincoln, University of Nebraska Press, 2002.

Drystalks of the Moon. Tulsa, Okla.: Hadassah Press, 1981.

Firesticks: A Collection of Stories. Norman: University of Oklahoma Press, 1993.

Flutie: A Novel. Wakefield, R.I.: Moyer Bell, 1998.

Fuller Man: A Novel. Wakefield, R.I.: Moyer Bell, 1999.

In-between Places: Essays. Tucson: University of Arizona Press, 2005.

Iron Woman. Minneapolis: New Rivers Press, 1990.

Lone Dog's Winter Count. Albuquerque, N.M.: West End Press, 1991.

The Man Who Heard the Land. Minneapolis: Minnesota Historical Society, 2001.

The Mask Maker. Norman: University of Oklahoma Press, 2002.

Monkey Secret. Evanston, Ill.: TriQuarterly Books, 1995.

Offering: Poetry and Prose. Duluth, Minn.: Holy Cow! Press, 1988.

One Age in a Dream: Poems. Minneapolis: Milkweed Editions, 1986.

The Only Piece of Furniture in the House: A Novel. Wakefield, R.I.: Moyer Bell, 1996.

Primer of the Obsolete. Amherst: University of Massachusetts Press, 2003.

Pushing the Bear: A Novel of the Trail of Tears. New York: Harcourt Brace, 1996.

The Relief of America. Chicago: Tia Chucha Press, 2000.

Rooms. Cambridge, England: Salt Publishing, 2005.

The Shadow's Horse. Tucson: University of Arizona Press, 2003.

Stone Heart: A Novel of Sacajawea. New York: Overlook Press, 2003.

The Stones for a Pillow. Rochester, Mich.: National Federation of State Poetry Societies Press, 2001.

Trigger Dance. Boulder, Colo.: Fiction Collective Two, 1990.

Two Worlds Walking: Short Stories, Essays, and Poetry by Writers with Mixed Heritages. New York: New Rivers Press, 1994.

Visit Teepee Town (Editor, with Mark Nowak). New York: Consortium Books, 1999.

The Voice That Was in Travel: Stories. Norman: University of Oklahoma Press, 1999.

War Cries. Duluth, Minn.: Holy Cow! Press, 1997.

The West Pole. Minneapolis: University of Minnesota Press, 1997.

Reid Gómez (Navajo)

Reid Gómez is an urban-raised Navajo from the Rock formerly known as Potrero Hill. Her love for San Francisco, the land and its Black and Indian inhabitants, informs every word she places, like poetry within the madness. From the chaos that is alcohol and garbage, she examines the ways we are more beautiful than broken. Audacious and esoteric, she descends twelve feet deep inside women's bodies and the connections that exist between ancestors and landscapes. Her work is a refusal to go quietly into the madness of neglect and isolation. She gives readings regularly throughout the San Francisco Bay Area.

Janet Campbell Hale (Coeur d'Alene)

Janet Hale was born in 1947, in Riverside, California. As a child, she lived on the Coeur d'Alene and Yakima reservations. After receiving her B.A. in Rhetoric from the University of California, Berkeley, she completed an M.A. in English from the University of California, Davis, in 1984. She has taught at several colleges and universities: Iowa State University in Ames, College of Illinois in Springfield, and University of California, Santa Cruz. Her awards and honors include the 1964 New York Poetry Day Award, a 1985 Pulitzer Prize nomination for *The Jailing of Cecelia Capture*, the 1994 American Book Award for *Bloodlines: Odyssey of a Native Daughter*, a 1995 Creative Writing Grant from the National Endowment for the Arts, and the 1998 Fellowship in Creative Writing from the Idaho Commission on the Arts.

Bloodlines: Odyssey of a Native Daughter. New York: Random House, 1993.

Custer Lives in Humboldt County. New York: Greenfield Review Press, n.d.

The Jailing of Cecelia Capture. Albuquerque: University of New Mexico Press, 1987.

The Owl's Song. Garden City, N.Y.: Doubleday, 1974.

Women on the Run. Moscow: University of Idaho Press, 1999.

Joy Harjo (Muscogee)

Born in Tulsa, Oklahoma, Joy Harjo is a well-known poet, musician, writer, and performer. She earned an M.F.A. in Creative Writing from the University of Iowa. She has published several books, including *She Had Some Horses, In Mad Love and War, The Woman Who Fell from the Sky, A Map to the Next World,* and *How We Became Human, New and Selected Poems,* from W. W. Norton. Her first children's book, *The Good Luck Cat,* was published by Harcourt. She has also coedited an anthology of Native women's writing, *Reinventing the Enemy's Language: Native Women's Writing of North America,* and a book of poetic prose with photographs by Stephen Strom, *Secrets from the Center of the World.* She has received several awards for her writing, including the 2002 Beyond Margins Award from PEN, 2001 American Indian Festival of Words Author Award from the Tulsa City County Library, the 2000 Western Literature Association Distinguished Achievement Award, the Lila Wallace-*Reader's Digest* Writers Award, 1997 New Mexico Governor's Award for Excellence in the Arts, and the Lifetime Achievement Award from the Native Writers' Circle of the Americas. She is a member of the National Council on the Arts.

In addition to her writing, Harjo performs nationally and internationally as a tenor saxophonist, both solo and with a band, Poetic Justice, for which she writes music. Her first CD, *Letter from the End of the Twentieth Century,* was released by Silverwave Records in 1997. In 1998, the CD was honored by the First Americans in the Arts with the award for Outstanding Musical Achievement. In addition, she was awarded the 2003–2004 Writer of the Year (Poetry) and the 2003–2004 Storyteller of the Year award by Word-craft Circle of Native Writers and Storytellers. That same year, she was given the Lifetime Achievement Award from Native Writers' Circle of the Americas. In 2005, she was presented the Writer of the Year Award (Film Script) by Native Writers' Circle of the Americas. Currently, she is teaching at the University of California, Los Angeles. When she is not teaching and traveling, she lives in Honolulu.

The Good Luck Cat. San Diego: Harcourt Brace, 2000.
How We Became Human: New and Selected Poems. New York: W. W. Norton, 2002.
In Mad Love and War. Middletown, Conn.: Wesleyan University Press, 1990.
The Last Song. Las Cruces, N.M.: Puerto del Sol Press, 1975.
A Map to the Next World: Poetry and Tales. New York: W. W. Norton, 2000.
Reinventing the Enemy's Language (Coedited with Gloria Bird). New York: W. W. Norton, 1997.
Secrets from the Center of the World (Photographs by Stephen Strom). Tucson: University of Arizona Press, 1989.
She Had Some Horses. New York: Thunder's Mouth Press, 1983.
The Spiral of Memory: Interviews (Edited by Laura Coltelli). Ann Arbor: University of Michigan Press, 1996.
What Moon Drove Me to This? Berkeley, Calif.: Reed and Cannon, 1979.
The Woman Who Fell from the Sky. New York: W. W. Norton, 1994.

Linda Hogan (Chickasaw)

Linda Hogan was born in Denver, Colorado, and grew up in Oklahoma. A poet, short story writer, novelist, playwright, essayist, and autobiographer, Hogan obtained an M.A. degree from University of Colorado at Boulder in 1978. Hogan has played an important role in the development of contemporary Native American poetry and fiction, addressing specifically environmental and women's issues. She taught at the University of Minnesota and the University of Colorado, Boulder. In 1984, she received the Five Civilized Tribes Playwriting

Award and in 1997 the Wordcraft Circle Writer of the Year (Prose-Fiction) award for *Mean Spirit*. She was presented a Lifetime Achievement Award from the Native Writers' Circle of the Americas in 1998. In 2002, she received the Wordcraft Circle Writer of the Year (Creative Prose: Memoir) for *The Woman Who Watches over the World: A Native Memoir*.

The Book of Medicines. Minneapolis: Coffee House Press, 1993.
Dwellings: A Spiritual History of the Living World. New York: W. W. Norton, 1995.
Eclipse. Los Angeles: American Indian Studies Center, UCLA, 1983.
Face to Face (Editor, with Brenda Peterson). New York: North Point Press, 2003.
From Women's Experience to Feminist Theology. Sheffield, England: Sheffield Academic Press, 1995.
Intimate Nation: The Bond between Women and Animals (Editor, with Deena Metzger and Brenda Peterson). New York: Fawcett Books, 1999.
Mean Spirit. New York: Atheneum, 1990.
Power. New York: W. W. Norton, 1998.
Red Clay. Greenfield Center, N.Y.: Greenfield Review Press, 1991.
Savings. Minneapolis: Coffee House Press, 1988.
Seeing through the Sun. Amherst: University of Massachusetts Press, 1985.
Solar Storms. New York: Scribner, 1995.
The Sweet Breathing of Plants: Women Writing on the Green World (Editor, with Brenda Peterson). New York: North Point Press, 2001.
The Woman Who Watches over the World: A Native Memoir. New York: W. W. Norton, 2001.

Misha Nogha (Métis)

Of Métis and Norwegian descent, Misha Nogha is a writer and musician who produces poetry, short stories, and novels. Born in St. Paul, Minnesota, she studied English Literature and Secondary Language at Eastern Washington University, Portland State University, and Eastern Oregon University. Her first novel, *Red Spider, White Web*, what one reviewer referred to as a "masterpiece of cyberpunk," won the Readercon Small Press Award in 1990 and was a finalist for the Arthur C. Clarke Award. Formerly editor of *New Pathways* magazine, she is working on a new novel, *Yellowjacket*, and planning a sequel to *Red Spider White Web*. A small book of poetry, *Magpies and Tigers*, and several short stories are just out. She has almost completed the libretto for the chamber orchestra of Amsterdam. She lives with her husband on a farm in Cove, Oregon, where she plays the flute and saxophone and raises Norwegian draft horses.

Dr. Ihoka's Cure. n.p.: Pelzmantel Publications, 1993.
Ke-Qua-Hawk-As. La Grande: Wordcraft of Oregon, 1994.
Prayers of Steel. Le Grande: Wordcraft of Oregon, 1988.
Red Spider, White Web. Lancaster, England: Morrigan, 1990.

Beth H. Piatote (Nez Perce)

Beth H. Piatote is a scholar and writer. She earned a Ph.D. in Modern Thought and Literature from Stanford University in 2007. She is currently an assistant professor of

Native American Studies at the University of California, Berkeley. Her research interests include Native American literature, law, and culture; Native American and American cultural studies; Native American/First Nations literature and federal Indian law in the United States and Canada; indigenous feminisms, and Ni:mi:pu: (Nez Perce) language and literature. Her dissertation, "Home/Ward Bound: The Making of Domestic Relations in Native American Literature and Law, 1886–1936," investigates the ways in which indigenous legal concepts and metaphors are expressed in literary texts to variously articulate, refigure, and subvert political relations with colonial forces in the United States and Canada. She is currently working on a theory of indigenous diasporic imagination along the U.S.-Canadian border. In addition to her scholarly publications, she has published widely in the field of journalism. The stories in this collection are her first published works of fiction. She lives in the San Francisco Bay Area with her husband and two children.

"Bodies of Memory and Forgetting: 'Putting on Weight' in Leslie Marmon Silko's *Almanac of the Dead*." *Paradoxa: Studies in World Literary Genres* 15 (2001).
"By Hand through Memory: The High Desert Museum and the Haunting of the Plateau." Forthcoming in *Annals of Scholarship*.

Patricia Riley (Cherokee)

Patricia Riley is a storyteller, teacher, and educator. Of Cherokee and Irish descent, she earned her Ph.D. in Ethnic Studies at the University of California, Berkeley, in 1994. Her dissertation, "Opposing the Ideology of the Split: Mythological Synergy as Resistance Discourse in the Novels of Louise Erdrich," contributes to scholarly considerations of how indigenous myth is translated and used by contemporary Native writers. For several years, she taught in the English Department at the University of Idaho.

Growing Up Native American: An Anthology. New York: Morrow, 1993.

Leslie Marmon Silko (Laguna Pueblo)

Leslie Marmon Silko was born in Albuquerque, New Mexico, and grew up on the Laguna Pueblo Reservation. Silko received her B.A. from the University of New Mexico in 1969. Not long after beginning law school, she quit to become a writer. She published stories as early as 1969 and her first collection of poetry, *Laguna Woman*, in 1974, but her most famous novel, *Ceremony*, was published in 1977 and ensured her position as a preeminent Native author. Since that time, she has published work in a variety of genres: *Storyteller* (1981), a multigenre autobiographical collection; *The Delicacy and Strength of Lace* (1986), letters; *Almanac of the Dead* (1991) and *Gardens in the Dunes* (1999), novels; and *Yellow Woman and a Beauty of the Spirit*, essays. She has taught at the University of New Mexico, Albuquerque; Navajo Community College in Tsaile, Arizona; and the University of Arizona, Tucson. Among the best-known Native writers, Silko has received many awards. Among the most prestigious is the MacArthur Foundation "Genius" Fellowship she was awarded in 1981.

After a Summer Rain in the Upper Sonoran. Madison, Wisc.: Black Mesa Press for Woodland
    Pattern, 1984.
Almanac of the Dead. New York: Penguin Books, 1992.
Ceremony. New York: Penguin Books, 1977.
A Circle of Nations: Voices and Visions of American Indians. Hillsboro, Okla.: Beyond Words
    Publishing Company, 1993.
Conversations with Leslie Marmon Silko (Edited by Ellen L. Arnold). Jackson: University
    Press of Mississippi, 2000.
The Delicacy and Strength of Lace: Letters between Leslie Marmon Silko and James Wright
    (Edited by Anne Wright). St. Paul, Minn.: Graywolf Press, 1986.
Gardens in the Dunes. New York: Simon & Schuster, 1999.
Laguna Woman. Tucson, Ariz.: Flood Plain Press, 1994.
Leslie Silko. Trumansburg, N.Y.: Crossing Press, 1974.
Sacred Water: Narratives and Pictures. Tucson, Ariz.: Flood Plain Press, 1993.
Storyteller. New York: Seaver Books, 1981.
Yellow Woman (Edited by Melody Graulich). New Brunswick, N.J.: Rutgers University
    Press, 1993.
Yellow Woman and a Beauty of the Spirit: Essays on Native American Life Today. New York:
    Simon & Schuster, 1996.

Anna Lee Walters (Pawnee and Otoe)

Anna Lee Walters was born in Pawnee, Oklahoma, and was influenced by both her
Pawnee mother and Otoe-Missouria father. Walters earned her B.A. and an M.F.A.
in Creative Writing from Goddard College in Vermont. She has worked as a library
technician at the Institute of American Indian Arts in Santa Fe, a technical writer for the
Dineh Corporation, and a curriculum developer for Navajo Community College. She
has served as Director of Public Information and Relations and Director of the Navajo
Community College Press. She received the American Book Award in 1986.

Ghost Singer. Flagstaff, Ariz.: Northland, 1988.
Neon Pow-Wow: Native American Voices of the Southwest (Editor). Flagstaff, Ariz.: Northland,
    1993.
The Otoe-Missouria Tribe: Centennial Memoirs. 1881–1981. Red Rock, Okla.: Otoe-Missouria
    Tribe, 1981.
The Pawnee Nation. Mankato, Minn.: Bridgestone Books, 2000.
The Sacred Ways of Knowledge, Sources of Life (Coauthored with Peggy V. Beck). Tsaile,
    Ariz.: Navajo Community College Press, 1977.
The Spirit of Native America: Beauty and Mysticism in American Indian Art. San Francisco:
    Chronicle Books, 1989.
The Sun Is Not Merciful. Ithaca, N.Y.: Firebrand Books, 1985.
Talking Indian: Reflections on Survival and Writing. Ithaca, N.Y.: Firebrand Books, 1992.
The Two-Legged Creature: An Otoe Story. Flagstaff, Ariz.: Northland, 1993.

Anthologies of Native American Literatures

(LISTED BY DATE OF PUBLICATION, THEN
ALPHABETICALLY BY AUTHOR'S LAST NAME)

Cronyn, George W., ed. *The Path on the Rainbow: An Anthology Songs and Chants from the Indians of North America.* Intro. Mary Austin. New York: Boni and Liveright, 1918.

Austin, Mary, ed. *The American Rhythm.* New York: Harcourt, 1923.

Astrov, Margot, ed. *The Winged Serpent: American Indian Prose and Poetry.* Boston: Beacon Press, 1946.

Day, A. Grove, ed. *The Sky Clears: Poetry of the American Indians.* New York: Macmillan, 1951.

Milton, John R., ed. *The American Indian Speaks.* Vermillion: University of South Dakota, 1969.

Milton, John R., ed. *American Indian II.* Vermillion: University of South Dakota, 1971.

Momaday, Natachee Scott, ed. *American Indian Authors.* Boston: Houghton Mifflin, 1972.

Witt, Shirley Hill, and Stan Steiner, eds. *The Way: An Anthology of American Indian Literature.* New York: Knopf, 1972.

Sanders, Thomas Edward, and Walter W. Peek, eds. *Literature of the American Indian.* New York: Glencoe Press, 1973.

Levitas, Gloria, Frank Robert Vivelo, and Jacqueline J. Vivelo, eds. *American Indian Prose and Poetry: We Wait in the Darkness.* New York: G. P. Putnam's Sons, 1974.

Rosen, Kenneth, ed. *The Man to Send Rain Clouds: Contemporary Stories by American Indians.* New York: Viking, 1974.

Turner III, Frederick W., ed. *The Portable North American Indian Reader.* New York: Viking, 1974.

Ramsey, Jarold, ed.. *Coyote Was Going There: Indian Literature of the Oregon Country.* Seattle: University of Washington Press, 1977.

Nabokov, Peter, ed. *Native American Testimony: An Anthology of Indian and White Relations, First Encounter to Dispossession.* New York: Crowell, 1978.

Velie, Alan R., ed. *American Indian Literature: An Anthology.* Norman: University of Oklahoma Press, 1979.

Hobson, Geary, ed. *The Remembered Earth: An Anthology of Contemporary Native American Literature.* Albuquerque: University of New Mexico Press, 1981.

Ortiz, Simon J., ed. *Earth Power Coming: Short Fiction in Native American Literature.* Tsaile, Ariz.: Navajo Community College Press, 1983.

Brant, Beth, ed. *A Gathering of Spirit: A Collection of North American Indian Women.* Rockland, Maine: Sinister Wisdom, 1984.

Cochran, Jo, ed. *Bearing Witness/Sobreviviendo. An Anthology of Native American/Latina Art and Literature.* Corvallis, Ore.: Calyx Press, 1984.

Green, Rayna, ed. *That's What She Said: Contemporary Poetry and Fiction by Native American Women.* Bloomington: Indiana University Press, 1984.

Hogan, Linda, Carol Bruchac, and Judith McDaniel, eds. *The Stories We Hold Secret: Tales of Women's Spiritual Development.* Greenfield, N.Y.: Greenfield Review Press, 1986.

Roscoe, Will, coord. ed. *Living the Spirit: A Gay American Indian Anthology.* New York: St. Martin's Press, 1988.

Allen, Paula Gunn, ed. *Spider Woman's Granddaughters: Traditional Tales and Contemporary Writing by Native American Women.* New York: Fawcett Columbine, 1989.

Lerner, Andrea, ed. *Dancing on the Rim of the World: An Anthology of Contemporary Northwest Native American Writing.* Tucson: Sun Tracks and the University of Arizona Press, 1990.

Sands, Kathleen Mullen, ed. *Circle of Motion: Arizona Anthology of Contemporary American Indian Literature.* Tempe: Arizona Historical Foundation, 1990.

Allen, Paula Gunn, ed. *Grandmothers of the Light: A Medicine Woman's Sourcebook.* Boston: Beacon Press, 1991.

Bruchac, Joseph, ed. *Raven Tells Stories: An Anthology of Native Alaskan Native Writing.* Greenfield Center, N.Y.: Greenfield Review Press, 1991.

Lesley, Craig, ed. *Talking Leaves: Contemporary Native American Short Stories.* New York: Laurel, 1991.

Trafzer, Clifford E., ed. *Looking Glass.* San Diego, Calif.: San Diego State University, 1991.

Velie, Alan R., ed. *American Indian Literature: An Anthology,* rev. ed. Norman: University of Oklahoma Press, 1991.

Velie, Alan R., ed. *The Lightning Within: An Anthology of Contemporary American Indian Fiction.* Lincoln: University of Nebraska Press, 1991.

Astrov, Margot, ed. *The Winged Serpent: American Indian Prose and Poetry,* reprint. Boston: Beacon Press, 1992.

Hirschfelder, Arlene B., and Beverly R. Singer, eds. *Rising Voices: Writing of Young Americans.* New York: Charles Scribner's Sons, 1992.

Nabokov, Peter, ed. *Native American Testimony: A Chronicle of Indian–White Relations from Prophecy to the Present, 1492–2000.* Foreword by Vine Deloria Jr. New York: Viking, 1999.

Erdrich, Louise, ed. *The Best American Short Stories 1993.* New York: Houghton Mifflin, 1993.

Fife, Connie, ed. *The Colour of Resistance: A Contemporary Collection of Writing by Aboriginal Women.* Toronto, Ontario: Sister Vision, 1993.

Kenny, Maurice, ed. *New Voices from the Longhouse: An Anthology of Contemporary Iroquois Writing.* Greenfield, N.Y.: Greenfield Review Press, 1993.

Riley, Patricia, ed. *Growing Up Native American: An Anthology.* New York: Morrow, 1993.

Trafzer, Clifford E., ed. *Earth Song, Sky Spirit: Short Stories of the Contemporary Native American Experience.* New York: Doubleday, 1993.

Walters, Anna Lee, ed. *Neon Pow-wow: New Native American Voices of the Southwest.* Flagstaff, Ariz.: Northland Publishing, 1993.

Allen, Paula Gunn, ed. *Voice of the Turtle: American Indian Literature, 1900–1970.* New York: Ballantine, 1994.

Bruchac, Joseph, ed. *Returning the Gift: Poetry and Prose from the First North American Native Writers' Festival.* Tucson: University of Arizona Press, 1994.

Glancy, Diane, and C. W. Truesdale, eds. *Two Worlds Walking: Short Stories, Essays, and Poetry by Writers with Mixed Heritages.* New York: New Rivers Press, 1994.

Roman, Trish Fox, ed. *Voices under the Sky: Contemporary Native Literature.* Freedom, Calif.: Crossing Press, 1994.

Sarris, Greg, ed. *The Sounds of Rattles and Clappers: A Collection of New California Indian Writing.* Vol. 26, Sun Tracks, an American Indian Literary Series. Tucson: University of Arizona Press, 1994.

Swann, Brian, ed. *Coming to Light: Contemporary Translations of Native Literatures of North America.* New York: Random House, 1994.

Bruchac, Joseph, ed. *Aniyunwiya/Real Human Beings: An Anthology of Contemporary Cherokee Prose.* Greenfield Center, N.Y.: Greenfield Review Press, 1995.

Evers, Larry, and Ofelia Zepeda, eds. *Home Places: Contemporary Native American Writing from Sun Tracks.* Tucson: University of Arizona Press, 1995.

Littlefield, Daniel F., and James W. Parins, eds. *Native American Writing in the Southeast: An Anthology, 1875–1935.* Jackson: University Press of Mississippi, 1995.

Vizenor, Gerald, ed. *Native American Literature: A Brief Introduction and Anthology.* New York: HarperCollins, 1995.

Witalec, Janet, ed., with Sharon Malinowski. *Smoke Rising: The Native North American Literary Companion.* Detroit: Visible Ink Press, 1995.

Allen, Paula Gunn, ed. *Song of the Turtle: American Indian Literature 1974–1994.* New York: One World, Ballantine Books, 1996.

Francis, Lee, and James Bruchac, eds. *Reclaiming the Vision: Past, Present and Future: Native Voices for the Eighth Generation.* Greenfield Center, N.Y.: Greenfield Review Press, 1996.

Trafzer, Clifford E., ed. *Blue Dawn, Red Earth: New Native American Storytellers.* New York: Anchor Books, 1996.

Harjo, Joy, and Gloria Bird, eds. *Reinventing the Enemy's Language: Contemporary Native Women's Writings of North America.* New York: W. W. Norton, 1997.

Blaeser, Kimberly, ed. *Stories Migrating Home: A Collection of Anishnaabe Prose.* Bemidji, Minn.: Loonfeather Press, 1998.

Bloom, Harold, ed. *Native Women Writers* (an electronic book). Philadelphia: Chelsea House, 1998.

Hogan, Linda, Deen Metzger, and Brenda Peterson, eds. *Intimate Nature: The Bond between Women and Animals.* New York: Fawcett Columbine. 1998.

Trout, Lawana, ed. *Native American Literature: An Anthology.* Lincolnwood, Ill.: NTC/Contemporary Publishing, 1998.

Dunn, Carolyn, and Carol Comfort, eds. *Through the Eye of the Deer: An Anthology of Native American Women Writers.* San Francisco: Aunt Lute Books, 1999.

Glancy, Diane, and Mark Nowak, eds. *Visit Teepee Town: Native Writings after the Detours.* Minneapolis: Coffee House Press, 1999.

Nabokov, Peter, ed. *Native American Testimony: An Anthology of Indian and White Relations from Prophecy to the Present, 1492–2000,* 2nd rev. ed. New York: Penguin Books, 1999.

Kenny, Maurice, ed. *Stories for a Winter's Night: Short Fiction by Native Americans.* Buffalo, N.Y.: White Pine Press, 2000.

Kilcup, Karen L., ed. *Native American Women's Writing, c. 1800–1924: An Anthology.* Malden, Mass.: Blackwell, 2000.

Allen, Paula Gunn, and Carolyn Dunn Anderson, eds. *Hózhó, Walking in Beauty: Native American Stories of Inspiration, Humor, and Life.* Chicago: Contemporary Books, 2001.

Benson, Robert, ed. *Children of the Dragonfly: Native American Voices on Child Custody and Education.* Tucson: University of Arizona Press, 2001.

Hogan, Linda, and Brenda Peterson, eds. *The Sweet Breathing of Plants: Women Writing on the Green World.* New York: North Point Press, 2001.

Purdy, John, and James Ruppert, eds. *Nothing but the Truth: An Anthology of Native American Literature.* Upper Saddle River, N.J.: Prentice Hall, 2001.

Erdrich, Heid E., and Laura Tohe, eds. *Sister Nations: Native American Women Writers on Community.* St. Paul: Minnesota Historical Society Press, 2002.

Ochoa, Annette Pina, Betsy Franco, and Traci L. Gourdine, eds. *Night Is Gone, Day Is Still Coming: Stories and Poems by American Indian Teens and Young Adults.* Introduction by Simon Ortiz. Cambridge, Mass.: Candlewick Press, 2003.

McMaster, Gerald, and Clifford E. Trafzer, eds. *Native Universe: Voices of Indian America.* Washington, D.C.: National Museum of the American Indian, Smithsonian Institution (in association with National Geographic), 2004.

Swann, Brian, ed. *Voices from Four Directions: Contemporary Translations of the Native Literatures of North America.* Lincoln: University of Nebraska Press, 2004.

Regier, Willis, ed. *Masterpieces of American Indian Literature.* Lincoln: University of Nebraska Press, 2005.

Tigerman, Kathleen, ed. *Wisconsin Indian Literature: Anthology of Native Voices.* Madison: University of Wisconsin Press, 2006.

Index

CPSIA information can be obtained
at www.ICGtesting.com
Printed in the USA
JSHW041352241020
8937JS00006B/1

9 780195 109252